GREEK ISLANDS

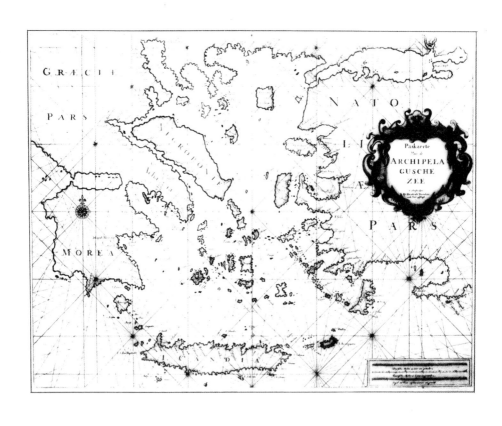

THE
Webb & Bower
DUMONT GUIDE
GREEK ISLANDS

edited by
Evi Melas

translated by
Russell Stockman

EXETER, ENGLAND

FRONT COVER:
Thira (© Laenderpress, Düsseldorf)
BACK COVER:
Church bells, Thira (© James Rudnick)
BACK FLAP:
Windmill, Mykonos (© Ted H. Funk/The Image Bank)

British Library Cataloguing in Publication Data
Greek Islands.—(DuMont guide)
1.   Islands of the Aegean—Description and
travel—Guide-books   2.   Ionian Islands
(Greece)—Description and travel—
Guide-books
I.   Melas, Evi   II.   Die Griechischen Inseln.
English   III.   Series
914.95'0476   DF895
ISBN 0-86350-040-4

Copyright © 1985 by DuMont Buchverlag GmbH & Co.

First published in Great Britain in 1985 by Webb & Bower (Publishers) Limited.
9 Colleton Crescent, Exeter, Devon EX2 4BY

English language edition first published by
Stewart, Tabori & Chang, Publishers, Inc., New York, New York,
under exclusive world-wide English language license
from DuMont Buchverlag GmbH & Co.
All rights for all countries are held by DuMont
Buchverlag GmbH & Co., Limited, Cologne, West Germany.
The title of the original German edition was
Die griechischen Inseln, edited by Evi Melas.

The Practical Travel Suggestions were prepared by Elisa Turner.

First Printing, 1985

Printed in Spain

C O N T E N T S

PIRAEUS AND THE ISLANDS IN THE SARONIC GULF

THE CYCLADES

THE DODECANESE

ISLANDS OF THE EASTERN AND NORTHERN AEGEAN

THE SPORADES

THE GREAT ISLAND, EUBOEA

THE IONIAN ISLANDS

THE GREEK ISLANDS
AT A GLANCE

T I M E L I N E

Height of Minoan civilization	2	0	0	0	B.C.
Cnossos destroyed					
Height of Mycenaean civilization					
Fall of Troy					
Dorian invasion					
Greeks begin colonizing Ionia	1	0	0		
Homer					
First Olympic Games	7	0	0		
Archilochus of Paros					
Sappho and Alcaeus of Lesbos	6	0	0		
First Pythian Games					
Polycrates of Samos					
Themistocles					
Aeschylus	5	0	0		
Persian Wars					
Sophocles					
Herodotus					
Euripides					
Delian League is founded					
Pausanias					
Thucydides					
Socrates					

Pericles in Athens

Peloponnesian War

Plato founds academy   *4   0   0*

Aristotle

Philip of Macedon conquers Greece

Demetrious Poliorcetes

Alexander the Great

The Diadochi (Wars of the Successors)

Colossus of Rhodes completed   *3   0   0*

Roman Empire founded   *2   0   0*

Greece becomes a province of Rome

B.C.

0

A.D.

Christianity becomes state religion   *3   0   0* A.D.

First Council of Nicaea

Constantinople founded

Olympic Games end

Roman Empire is divided

Fall of Rome   *4   0   0*

Sassanid Empire conquers Syria and Egypt   *6   0   0*

Cyprus and Rhodes fall to the Arabs

Iconoclastic controversy begins   *7   0   0*

Second Council of Nicaea

Second period of Iconoclasm   *8   0   0*

Great Schism   *1   0   0   0*

Seljucks conquer most of Asia Minor

Venice granted commercial privileges

Crusades begin

Constantinople is sacked

Fall of Constantinople

Suleiman the Magnificent conquers Rhodes

Great Britain annexes Ionian Islands

Greek War of Independence

Greek nation founded

Otto I, first king of Greece

Great Britain returns Ionian Islands

Italy takes Rhodes

Greece joins Allies

War between Greece and Turkey

Corfu bombed by Mussolini

Germans occupy Greece

Liberation

Greece annexes Rhodes

Civil War

1 2 0 0
1 4 0 0
1 5 0 0
1 7 0 0
1 8 2 0
1 8 3 0
1 8 6 0
1 9 1 0
1 9 2 0
1 9 4 0

PIRAEUS AND THE ISLANDS IN THE SARONIC GULF

PIRAEUS

THE PROMONTORY ON WHICH GREECE'S LARGEST port, Piraeus, now stands was originally an island that probably rose from the sea in the Tertiary period. Then, through the millennia, a marshy causeway developed between the island and the mainland. Thus from a geological point of view, Piraeus can justly be included in a book dealing with the islands of the Aegean. More important, it is from Piraeus that nearly all of the shipping lines serving these islands depart.

Until the sixth century B.C., the Athenians generally favored the harbors on the east coast of Attica, such as Prasiae and Thoricus. Another common anchorage was in the Bay of Phaleron on the west coast, whence ships sailed for Troy and Crete. It was from this bay that the legendary Attic hero Theseus set sail with the tribute of seven youths and seven maidens regularly demanded of Athens by the Cretan king Minos. During this expedition, Theseus slew the Minotaur, the monster with the head of a bull that would devour these young people, and Athens was henceforth spared this

gruesome sacrifice. Theseus had promised his father, Aegeus, that if he returned from Crete alive he would see that his ship's black sail was exchanged for a red one, but in his excitement over his conquest he forgot his vow. When Aegeus saw the ship returning under a black sail, he plunged into the sea in despair. In memory of the tragic death of this king, this sea has ever since borne his name: the Aegean.

Only after Athens had expanded its sway over Salamis and the Saronic Gulf, early in the fifth century B.C., did Piraeus begin to hold interest for them as a harbor. In 492 B.C., Themistocles convinced the Athenians to fortify Piraeus and fitted out a fleet in preparation for the impending war against the Persians. The Delphic oracle had advised him to "take to the planks" at the Persians' approach, and, thus encouraged, Themistocles set about preparing for a naval battle. The subsequent Greek victory at Salamis was crucial to the later history of the world. Piraeus was continually expanded through the remainder of the fifth cen-

View of Mikrolimano. Athens is in the background.

Map of Piraeus.

1. *Larissa train station*
2. *Station of the Peloponnesus Line*
3. *Cantharus harbor*
4. *Archeological Museum*
5. *Hellenistic theater of Zea*
6. *Pasalimani harbor*
7. *Naval Museum*
8. *Mikrolimano harbor*
9. *Munichia hill*

tury B.C.; its defenses were improved, and it was connected to Athens by the so-called Long Walls (see map, p. 18).

In great haste, a circular wall just under 4 miles long was erected around the promontory in 479–478 B.C. Its base was constructed of stone and its upper sections of clay bricks. All available materials were incorporated into it, even gravestones. This massive defense wall was finally completed by Cimon ten years later, when it was supplemented by the North Wall and the Phaleron Wall. The city and its harbor then formed a single fortified complex. In 445 B.C., these defenses were further strengthened by Pericles, who added a third barrier, known as the South Wall. In time of war, the entire population of Attica could take shelter behind the Long Walls.

Pericles also commissioned Hippodamus, an architect from Miletus in Ionia, to rebuild Piraeus and give it a regular network of streets. This was done not so much for sheer love of order or reasons of aesthetics but rather to capitalize on the hygienic advantages of having the prevailing sea winds cleanse the air of the harbor's narrow streets.

Hippodamus impressed the Athenians with his knowledge of meteorology and mathematics, but they criticized him severely for his Ionic love of elegance and his extravagance. Nevertheless, thanks to him, Piraeus acquired the facilities that would make it the major trading center for the entire Greek world. His construction projects, which included expansion and improvement of the quays, went far beyond mere military necessity; he therefore drew much criticism from the generals. In the agora at Piraeus, Hippodamus built the first example of a strictly Ionic market hall with columned porticos on the Greek mainland. The structure came to be known as the Agora of Hippodamus. And, at the same time, temples were erected in honor of Zeus Soter (the Savior) and Athena Soteira (the Savior), to Aphrodite, Artemis Munichia, Hestia, and various other deities. Piraeus rapidly became a showplace of altars dedicated to heroes, impressive communal buildings, and freestanding monuments. The largest of its three harbors was called Cantharus, for its shape resembled that of the two-handled drinking vessel of that name. It was reserved primarily for commercial shipping. Nearby lay the Emporion, an enclosed area, nearly 3,000 feet long and 825 feet wide, that consisted of five large halls—one of which served as the stock exchange—a major grain warehouse, numerous wharves, and ninety-four ship-sheds for the fleet. To the east of Cantharus, next to the Agora of Hippodamus, was the political center of the city. This district contained the buildings occupied by the people's assembly and the supervisors of trade.

The other two harbors of Piraeus held warships. Like Cantharus, these were fitted out with ship-sheds and their entrances could be blocked off with chains. One of these was Zea, today Pasalimani, which contained 196 of these covered moorings; the other, the Munichia, provided another 82. This latter is today the Mikrolimano yacht basin. Near the Zea, the architect Philo erected the great Skeuotheke (tool-and-machine shed), a long, three-aisle building with Ionic columns. At Phreatto, also nearby, sat the court where murderers were tried.

Between April and October, when the prevailing winds blew from the east, freighters would arrive in Piraeus from the Hellespont, Egypt, Cyprus, and Lebanon, heavily laden with grain, cypress wood, cedar, fruits and spices, papyrus bast, and

View of Piraeus from William Henry Davenport Adams's The Mediterranean Illustrated, *1877.*

ivory. The cultural life of the city was enhanced by splendid religious ceremonies, popular festivals, regattas, and performances of tragedies and comedies.

This heyday of Piraeus came to an end with the Peloponnesian War, a twenty-seven-year conflict between Athens and Sparta that ended with the Athenians' defeat. In 404 B.C., Athens was forced to relinquish its role as a major sea power, and Sparta demanded that the Long Walls and the other defenses of Piraeus be torn down. Xenophon related how the Spartan general Lysander sailed into the harbor with his fleet and noted that supporters of Sparta, who had been banished during the war, returned to the city. The walls were then razed to the accompaniment of flute music—the flute being the instrument associated with peace.

The hill of Munichia played an important role in 404–403 B.C., during the rule of the Thirty Tyrants, when it served as a stronghold for the democrats under Thrasybulus. He and a small band of Athenians who had been banished or had emigrated fought from here to liberate Athens from that reign of terror. Despite support from the Spartans, the tyrannical regime finally collapsed in 403, and Thrasybulus returned to Athens in triumph. Tensions between Athens and Sparta continued, however, for the

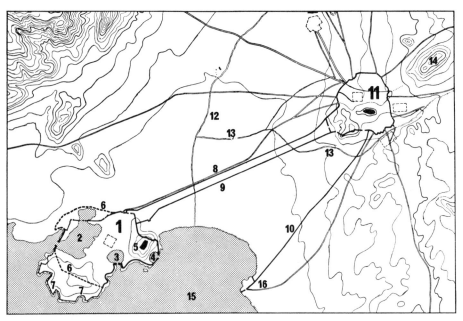

Athens and Piraeus, with its harbors and the Long Walls in the fifth century B.C. (after a drawing by John Travlos, Athens). (1) Piraeus; (2) Cantharus harbor; (3) Zea harbor; (4) Munichia harbor; (5) acropolis of Munichia; (6) wall of Themistocles; (7) wall of Conon; (8) north Long Wall; (9) south Long Wall; (10) Phaleron Wall; (11) Athens; (12) Cephisus river; (13) Ilissus river; (14) Lycabettus hill; (15) Saronic Gulf; (16) Phaleron.

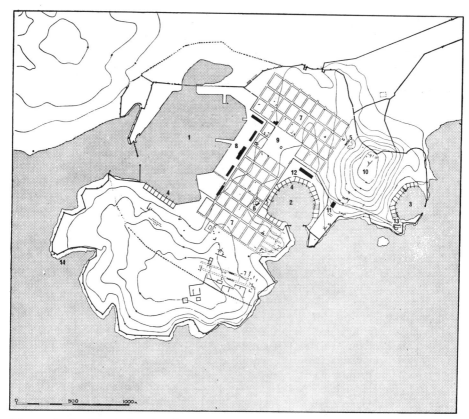

Piraeus in the Classical period (after a drawing by John Travlos, Athens). Upper right: beginning of the Long Walls. (1) Cantharus harbor; (2) military harbor of Zea; (3) military harbor of Munichia; (4) neosoikoi *(ship-sheds); (5) Classical theater; (6) Hellenistic theater; (7) reconstruction of the checkerboard city plan of Hippodamus; (8) Emporion; (9) agora of Hippodamus; (10) acropolis of Munichia (today named for the prophet Elijah); (11) Asclepieion; (12) Skeuotheke of Philon; (13) shrine of Artemis Munichia (today the yacht club); (14) grave of Themistocles.*

Athenians now hated the Spartans even more than they did their traditional enemies, the Persians.

At the beginning of August 394 B.C., the Athenian general Conon and the Persian satrap Pharnabazus won a decisive victory over the Spartans near Cnidus, bringing an end to Sparta's ten-year sway over the Aegean and the coastline of Asia Minor. Conon returned to Athens in the following year. With gold provided by his Persian allies he rebuilt the ring wall of Piraeus and the Long Walls, strengthening the city to the point that it could again keep Sparta in check.

Sections of these walls can still be seen

today, chiefly along the Peiraiki peninsula, on the west coast of Piraeus. It is well worth taking a drive along this panoramic shoreline, which includes a number of small bays dotted with fishermen's taverns and captains' houses. There are always countless vessels of all sizes approaching or leaving the port. Tradition holds that Themistocles was buried here on the Peiraiki, near an ancient lighthouse (see map, p. 19).

The subsequent history of Piraeus consists of the comings and goings of Macedonians, Romans, Byzantines, Goths, Crusaders, Venetians, Turks—and pirates of all nationalities. By the time of the birth of Christ, the port had become only an insignificant settlement dominated by the temple of Zeus the Savior at its center.

In September 1687, when the area was under Turkish control, the Venetian doge Morosini and his fleet arrived in Piraeus, landed some 10,000 men, and laid siege to the Acropolis in Athens. During this siege, portions of the Parthenon were destroyed: the Turks were using it as a powder magazine and it was exploded by the Venetians. When Morosini sailed away, in the following spring, he took with him a marble lion that had stood in the harbor of Piraeus, one that had caused the port to be known as Porto Leone throughout the Middle Ages. It is one of the Greek lions now standing in front of the Arsenal in Venice, currently the Naval Museum.

Once Piraeus was liberated from the Turks, on January 25, 1827, travelers from western Europe began to arrive. They found only a few customs officials, who lived with their families in the most primitive of dwellings, some modest coffee houses, and an assortment of seamen, fishermen, and mule drivers. Visitors generally rode to Athens on mules, donkeys, or

horses, while their supplies were carried on the backs of camels.

One such pilgrim was the Vicomte de Marcellus, a French ambassador. He foolishly declined to ride, preferring to make his way on foot. At that time, the Acropolis rose up dramatically above the plain, for there were no tall buildings to hide it from view as there are today. The viscount was so entranced by the classical ruins and the vast olive groves leading up to them that he soon found himself mired in a swamp. This marshy area, which extended as far as Phaleron, was a breeding ground for malaria-carrying mosquitoes. From antiquity until the very recent past, it posed immense difficulties for city planners, generals, travelers, and commercial traffic. Only in this century was it finally drained.

Once the Bavarian dynasty had firmly established itself in Greece under King Otto in the mid-nineteenth century, German architects leapt with enthusiasm on Athens and Piraeus. Schaubert and his Greek friend Cleanthes, the famous Leo von Klenze, and Ernst Ziller all designed plans for the port city. Unfortunately the more imaginative and radical of them were never realized. The checkerboard pattern in the central area was restored; customs halls, warehouses, and the city hall were the first new public buildings. A number of the private houses that were added later still stand; they frequently present a strange mixture of styles from classical to neo-Gothic and Baroque. These survivors from the nineteenth century, once scorned as deliberately tasteless, are again coming into vogue. Compared to the boring modern apartment buildings, they seem beautiful indeed.

Most people then lived in one- or two-story houses surrounded by gardens. Families would take their goats and sheep to graze along the cliffs. There, among rose-

Map of Piraeus from J. B. LeChevalier's Voyage de la Troade, *1802.*

mary, lavender, oleander, and wildflowers, they would gather wild vegetables for their soup kettles. Fishermen could count on abundant catches; fish of all kinds and sizes were plentiful. Mussels, oysters, and crabs could be gathered on the beaches and rocks.

Considerably less idyllic was the widespread use of hashish in special dens, a practice that peaked in about 1920. Ad-

dicts and gangsters completely controlled the Drapetsona and Keratsini quarters. Once, owing to a misunderstanding between an officer and a hashish dealer, the Naval School was surrounded and fired on by the gangsters. The police have by now largely suppressed the smuggling of narcotics after decades of effort, once again making Piraeus a rather harmless port town. However, one can only lament other developments: the sea is polluted, swimming is unhealthy, and the cliffs are now barren.

Piraeus, nonetheless, continues to fascinate both natives and tourists. They love to ride to the top of Munichia to enjoy its view of the city and the sea or to spend the evening in one of the seafood restaurants of Munichia harbor (Mikrolimano), watching countless boats and sailing vessels rock on the waves. This small, shell-shaped bay, with the snow-white clubhouse of the Greek Yachting Club perched on the promontory, was a base for Athenian galleys in antiquity. During the Middle Ages, it was used only by poor fishermen. Now it shelters the yachts and sailboats of the rich.

Public beach swings with bright-colored awnings have recently been introduced along the waterfront, the main streets are lined with flowerpots and flower stands of white-painted wrought iron, and illuminated fountains play in the squares— Riviera-like touches that may seem a bit out of place in the midst of this busy industrial port.

One old tradition lives on in Piraeus. Every year, on January 6 (the Epiphany), the priests bless the sea and the ships. They throw a cross into the water, and some swimmer, impervious to the cold, fishes it out again.

VISITORS TO PIRAEUS WHO ARE INTERESTED IN antiquity have to rely more on imagination and knowledge than on powers of observation. Virtually no ancient monuments survive here except for fragments of the wall and the small theater from the second century B.C., next to the museum. In the small museum, worth a visit for a number of masterpieces, you can see statues, marble reliefs, and funeral steles. If you are lucky, other treasures may be on temporary display. For example, bronze statues of Apollo, Athena, and Artemis were shown here before being transferred to the National Museum in Athens. These statues, which the Roman general Sulla intended to ship to Rome in 86 B.C., were so well packed that they were unharmed when a fire swept through the ship-sheds.

During the 1930s, the temple of Artemis was excavated on the Munichian Peninsula. But its relatively well-preserved ruins unfortunately disappeared beneath the modern yacht-club buildings. The theater on the western slope of the hill of Munichia met a similar fate; scarcely had it been excavated when a house was built on top of it.

John Travlos, an architect, archeologist, and longtime associate of the American Archeological Institute, has spent much of his life working on important digs here. Examples of his drawings may be seen on pages 18 and 19 of this book.

TODAY, THE NOMOS (GOVERNMENTAL DISTRICT) of Piraeus includes the islands of Salamis, Aegina, Hydra, and Spetsai. The region contained 200,000 inhabitants in 1981.

To get to the islands, you go to one of the countless shipping agencies that line the quays of Piraeus. In the harbor, you can see passenger ships and cargo vessels, from the smallest motorboats to luxury liners, flying the colors of all nations.

An unexpected adventure awaits everyone at the beginning of a trip to the islands. All who board ship at Piraeus must be prepared for the fact that schedules are treated like state secrets. Domestic shipping is not always adequate for the large influx of tourists during the summer months. Occasionally the same cabin is sold to three different parties, and a frightful crowding on deck is the rule. Moreover, despite years of complaints, nothing has yet been done about the fact that all shipping lanes radiate from Piraeus and that there are few direct connections between the Aegean Islands and Crete. Thus, in order to reach Patmos or Lesbos from Siphnos or Paros, for example, it is necessary to return to Piraeus first and then take another ship. As soon as one has landed on the Aegean Islands, however, the traveler is richly compensated for any inconvenience he or she has suffered.

SALAMIS

SALAMIS, AEGINA, AND POROS ARE THE THREE largest islands in the Saronic Gulf, which was named by the ancients after the mythical king Saron. Salamis, Salamina in modern Greek, lies off the shoreline of Eleusis and Attica, less than a mile from Cape Cynosura.

Until World War II, many Athenians spent their summer holidays on this peaceful island, swimming from its beaches lined with pine trees, strolling through vineyards and olive groves, and dining on freshly caught fish. But the island now houses a military port on its northeast coast and the headquarters of the Greek navy; thus the tranquility of the island has been disrupted and its waters have been polluted. Former fishermen now work in the factories and shipyards that have disfigured the coastline between Athens and Eleusis.

Mythology relates that Salamina and Aegina were daughters of the Peloponnesian river god Asopus. From this family was descended the hero Ajax (Aias), who, according to Homer's *Iliad*, sailed to Troy with twelve ships in order to take part in the Trojan War. He was king of Salamis, then a populous island. The density of that population is attested to by excavations that have uncovered countless Mycenaean set-tlements; archeologists are still searching for the royal palace. The inhabitants supposedly built a temple to Ajax, consecrated an ebony statue to him, and celebrated athletic contests in his honor. As Pausanias and Ovid tell us, a purple flower sprang from the blood of Ajax, spilled when he committed suicide before the gates of Troy. On its petals one could make out the letters "AI-AI," representing the first letters

The Bay of Eleusis above Salamis,
from J. C. Grimmell's
Biblische Lander in Sonnenschein, *1897.*

of the hero's name and the traditional mourning cry of the ancients. The inhabitants of Salamis believed that this wild plant, a member of the iris family, and its swordlike blossoms first appeared on their island when Ajax took his own life with his sword. Botanists have identified the plant as *Gladiolus communis L.* It still grows on Salamis and in stony soil elsewhere in Greece. Sophocles wrote a tragedy with Ajax as the protagonist, and the National Museum in Athens features a large number of vases painted with scenes from the hero's life.

In ancient times, Salamis was fought over by neighboring Megara and Athens. In the sixth century B.C., Athens annexed Salamis, which did not free itself from Attic rule until the fourth century B.C., when Macedonia was flourishing and Salamis attached itself to that state.

Salamis went down in world history in 480 B.C. In that year, the naval battle between the Persians and the Greeks in the waters off the island ended in the Persians' defeat. After the Battle of Thermopylae, the Persian army had plundered Attica, conquered Athens, and burned down the Acropolis. The Persian fleet was approaching the Phalerian coast from Euboea. The Athenian general Themistocles succeeded in tricking the Persians, whose fleet was congregated in the strait near Salamis. He was thus able to put the Persians to flight with his considerably smaller fleet. In their rush to flee, the enemy ships got in each other's way. The Persian king, Xerxes, sat on a golden throne on Mount Aegaleus, across from the island, and helplessly watched the destruction of his grand fleet. The poet Aeschylus described the battle and the tragedy of Xerxes quite vividly in his *Persians*; remarkably, Aeschylus managed to portray Xerxes without any Greek chauvinism.

Anyone interested in history should make a one-day outing to Salamis from Athens. From Perama, the ferry landing between Piraeus and Eleusis, boats leave constantly for Salamis, and there are also larger ferries that accommodate cars. You come ashore south of the modern military

The island of Salamis.

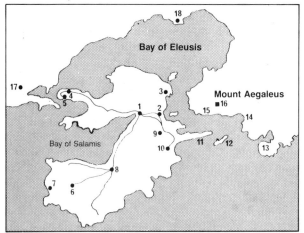

1. *Salamina (Kouluri)*
2. *Paloukia*
3. *Skiradi*
4. *Phaneromeni*
5. *Voudoro peninsula*
6. *Aghios Nikolaos*
7. *Kanakia*
8. *Moulki*
9. *Ambelakia*
10. *Selinia*
11. *Cynosura peninsula*
12. *Psytaleia*
13. *Piraeus*
14. *Keratsini*
15. *Perama*
16. *Throne of Xerxes*
17. *Megara*
18. *Eleusis*

The Gulf of Salamis, from The Mediterranean Illustrated, *1877.*

port, near the village of Paloukia. At the beginning of the great battle, the Greek ships (triremes) lay between this spot and Cape Cynosura.

From here you proceed to the villages of Kamatero and Ambelakia, which were respectively the capital and harbor of the island in Classical and Hellenistic times. The acropolis, of which wall fragments are still preserved, rose up on the heights near Kamatero. Beneath the concrete harbor pier, you can see huge stone blocks taken from ancient buildings. On the northeast point of the island, archeologists have discovered the remnants of a temple to Athena.

On the way from Ambelakia to Selinia, the small Aghios Ioannis church stands to the left of the road. Here, Byzantine frescos have been uncovered that had been repeatedly painted over at later dates. Selinia is a summer vacation center with modest hotels and restaurants. It offers a view of Psytaleia, across the water, whence the Persians launched their attack on the Greeks in 480 B.C. To the left, one sees Cape Cynosura. Here, the ancients erected a tomb for the people who died at Salamis, adorning it in memory of their victory with portions of Persian ships and even an entire trireme.

Another road leads from Ambelakia to the island's present-day capital, Salamina, or Koulouri, as it is known by the residents. Here, as throughout the island, ugly concrete buildings have taken the place of the colorfully painted old houses of the fishermen and peasants.

Mycenaean vases, tomb reliefs from the Classical period, and steles bearing inscriptions are exhibited in the local museum. One of the churches in Koulouri is worth a visit: the Panaghia tou-Katharou, with lovely icons on its choir wall and frescos on its crypt.

Taking the local road to the south, you come upon the village of Aiantio, or Moulki. Its churches attest to the town's flowering during the Byzantine period. The

Koimisis church on the village square and the Metamorphosis tou-Sotiros church at the edge of town are cruciform churches with cupolas dating from the twelfth or thirteenth century.

From Moulki you can take a sidetrip to the eighteenth-century monastery Aghios-Nikolaos-tis-Lemonias, which stands on top of a wooded elevation. In the outside walls of the monastery church, a basilica, there are plates from the island of Rhodes and marble sculptures from an older (twelfth or thirteenth century) church. Nearby, among the olive trees, is hidden the fifteenth-century Aghios-Ioannis-Kalyvitis church, with a few surviving frescos. From here, there is a road leading down to the picturesque harbor of Kanakia.

Driving about 3½ miles westward out of Koulouri, you reach the monastery Phaneromeni. The nuns' cells make up the rectangular courtyard, and a basilica with cupola stands in the center. Its façade is ornamented with relief slabs from the thirteenth and fourteenth centuries and multicolored pottery plates from Asia Minor. Ghiorghios

Markos and his pupils painted the interior walls in 1735. Icons by the same artists, who were among the best of their time, are also on view here. In the wall paintings at Phaneromeni, you can discern the influence of Western art on the severe Greek religious tradition. An inscription next to the entrance doorway preserves the date of 1661, when the church was consecrated. At the beginning of the war of liberation against the Turks, in 1821, a number of precious objects from Attic churches and monasteries were hidden at Phaneromeni because it was felt that the monastery was invulnerable—and, in fact, it did withstand all Turkish attacks.

Behind the cloister, you can still see the remains of a system of defenses, the Poudoro, built by the Athenians in the sixth century B.C. in order to ward off the Megarans from Salamis and Attica. At the foot of the hill on which Phaneromeni stands, visitors can board a ferry back to the mainland and get the freeway to Athens.

AEGINA

AEGINA IS A PRIVILEGED ISLAND, RICH IN NATURAL beauty and prized for its healthful climate and clear air. The island, 33 square miles in area, is not far from Piraeus. Ships sail here from Piraeus, especially in spring and summer, up to several times a day.

Aegina can reflect on an eventful history. An important and uncommonly rich body of myth, whose heroes were famed throughout all of Greece, is associated with the island. Pindar, the poet of the ancient Panhellenic games, referred to some of these myths when he celebrated in eleven odes the eleven "children" of Aegina at the Isthmian, Nemean, Pythian, and Olympic games.

Pausanias, the author of *A Description of Greece* (*Periegesis*) in the second century

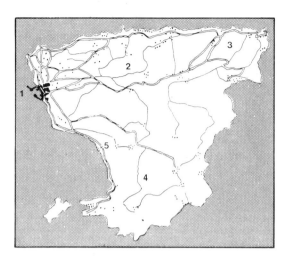

The island of Aegina.

1. Modern town of Aegina and ancient ruins
2. Palaiochora
3. Aphaea temple above Aghia Marina
4. Oros, the highest mountain on the island, with the sanctuary of Zeus Hellenios
5. Marathon

(Based on a drawing by Athina Kalogheropoulou.)

A.D., placed great importance on the cults of the various Greek cities and he cited the major myths of Aegina. According to the legends that he recounted, there were originally no people on the island. Zeus brought his lover Aegina, the beautiful daughter of the river god Asopus, and sister of Salamina, to the desolate island in the Saronic Gulf, which was then known as Oenone. But Aeacus, the son of Zeus and Aegina, changed its name in honor of his mother. Aeacus is one of the great figures in Greek mythology. For his sake, his father, the king of the gods, changed the ants (*myrmekes*) of the uninhabited island into people so that he might have subjects. These islanders were known in antiquity as Myrmidones. The son of Aeacus was Peleus; his son, in turn, was Achilles. Ajax and his brother Teucer also descended from the island goddess Aegina. These Homeric heroes were venerated in all of Greece.

THREE ARCHEOLOGICAL SITES ON THE ISLAND ARE especially noteworthy. These are Kolona, on the west coast, on the outskirts of the modern city of Aegina; the Cape of Aghia Marina, on the north coast, with its famous temple of Aphaea—dedicated to the local goddess of ancient Aegina—rising above the picturesque bay; and finally Aegina's highest mountain, Mount Oros, roughly 1,755 feet high, in the south of the island. This peak, on which Zeus Hellenios (or Panhellenios) was worshipped, has preserved its antique name along with a newer one, Prophitis Elias (Prophet Elijah). According to Theophrastus, people looked to the clouds around the summit of Mount Oros for signs of impending rain.

Excavations on Mount Oros in 1829–1830 uncovered a fortified farming settlement from the thirteenth century B.C. Dryopes, Myrmidones, or some other Thessalian group had established themselves there and remained until the close of the Mycenaean epoch. At that time, it appears, the island was attacked—we do not know how or why—and the inhabitants of this settlement and others in Aegina were either deported or killed. The island then remained abandoned, or virtually so, until

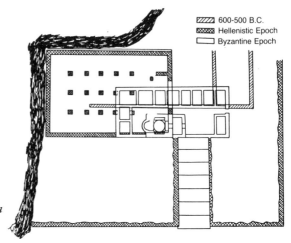

Aegina: steps leading to the sanctuary of Zeus Hellenios.

600-500 B.C.
Hellenistic Epoch
Byzantine Epoch

(Based on a drawing by Athina Kalogheropoulou.)

shortly before 1000 B.C., when Dorians from the Peloponnesus (possibly from Argolis) invaded it under their leader Deiphontes. It was they who brought the worship of Zeus Hellenios to Aegina.

There is a magnificent view from Mount Oros. The visitor reaches the mountain by way of the road that leads from Pharos to Marathon. You climb up toward Pachiarachi-Sphyrichtres; from there, a steep path leads up to the summit. From the top of the mountain, you can look down on all of Aegina. In clear weather, it is possible to see Cape Sounion and the coast of Attica to the east. To the north, you can discern Salamis, Megara, and the Isthmus; to the south, Poros, Hydra, the mountains of Argolis, and Epidaurus.

In Pausanias's time the only significant structure on Mount Oros was the temple of Zeus; the mountain was called Panhellenion because it was a sanctuary of this god's cult: Zeus, the king of the gods, was here venerated as a bringer of rain. Pausanias related the legend: Once Greece was afflicted by a great drought. There was no rain either in the Peloponnesus or beyond the Isthmus. Messengers were sent to Delphi to consult the oracle to discover the cause of the drought and learn how to end it. The oracle replied that Zeus should be appeased, and she stipulated that only an appeal from Aeacus, the just and honorable king of Aegina, would be heard. Aeacus thus made sacrifice to Zeus Panhellenios, his father, on the island's highest mountain and begged him to send rain to Greece. Zeus heard his prayers and released the country from the drought that had plagued it for so many years. In gratitude, Aeacus built the temple in honor of Zeus Hellenios near the summit of Mount Oros. The inscription "To Zeus Hellenios" has survived on fragments of copper vessels from the beginning of the fifth century B.C.

You climb Mount Oros along its western slope. A stairway lined with votive images once led to a terrace where the ancient Taxiarchon church stands today. The ground there had been leveled and trans-

Aegina: east pediment of the temple of Aphaea. (Reconstruction after Adolf Furtwängler.)

formed into a rectangular terrace whose front overlooked the plain. To the left, at the top of a flight of steps 23 feet wide, stood a large building whose roof was supported by three rows of columns; their foundations are still visible. This may have been a hostel for pilgrims visiting the temple. Somewhat higher up, there are the foundations of a small portico and, beneath it, two cisterns.

In Byzantine times, a monastery was built on the ancient ruins of the terrace; in the center is the Taxiarchon church, with the monks' cells surrounding it.

A VISIT TO THE TEMPLE OF APHAEA, ABOVE THE Cape of Aghia Marina, is unforgettable. The temple stands at the top of a hill in a pine grove and offers a broad panorama of the sea. Nearby, construction from the late Neolithic period (circa 3000 B.C.) has been discovered. Together with recent finds in Kolona, it is among the oldest on the island. These finds resemble fragments from Argolis and Arcadia, leading to the assumption that the inhabitants of Aegina were connected in some way to those of the eastern Peloponnesus at that time.

According to myth, a daughter, Britomartis, was born to Zeus and Carme. Britomartis delighted in hunting and was much loved by the goddess Artemis. In order to escape from King Minos, who lusted after her, Britomartis threw herself into the sea. Unfortunately, though, she became entangled in the fishermen's nets and thus came into their hands. One of the fishermen also fell in love with her, so she plunged into the sea again. This time, she landed in Aegina, where she disappeared into a grove and, thanks to Artemis, became invisible (*aphanes* in Greek, hence her new name, Aphaea). Pausanias mentioned that the Aeginetans called Britomartis by the name Aphaea, while the Cretans knew her as Dictynna.

According to legend, Aphaea hid in a cave at the northeast corner of the wall surrounding her ancient sanctuary. There, in 1901, many clay images of gods and other objects from the Mycenaean period were discovered, revealing that a goddess had been venerated there since prehistoric times.

Near the spot where this cult was based in prehistoric times, three successive tem-

Aegina: reconstruction of the temple of Aphaea.

The temple of Aphaea, as painted by Otto Magnus von Stackelberg.

ples were built in the historical period. Each was larger than the one before, and all three occupied the same site.

Only a small foundation survives from the first of these. The second had an altar on its east side. The third, a Doric temple built of soft limestone, is the one we see today. On its east side, there is a huge altar. The visitor enters the sanctuary through a large *propylon* (vestibule). To the east of it, the remains of baths and the priests' dwellings have been preserved; farther to the south is a smaller *propylon* (see ground plan, p. 33).

Battle scenes are portrayed on both pediments of the temple. The dominating, central figure is Athena. The temple we see today was built in about 485 B.C. After the Persian Wars, a portion of the eastern pediment was destroyed, possibly by a lightning bolt. The surviving figures were then set up inside the sanctuary, and, in accor-dance with ancient custom, the demol-ished ones were buried. In place of the old figures, one of the famous sculptors of Ae-gina created new pediment sculptures; again these portrayed a battle scene and highlighted the goddess Athena in the cen-ter. Thus a slight but obvious difference in date arose between the sculptures of the two pediments. The pediment sculptures were discovered in 1811 during excava-tions by Baron von Hallerstein and C. R. Cockerell, an architect. Under their direc-tion, the sculptures were removed to Za-kinthos, then under British control, thence to Italy. Ultimately they were auctioned, and in 1813 they were acquired by the Grecophile king of Bavaria, Ludwig I, the father of Otto. At Ludwig's behest, the sculptures were restored in Rome and then placed in the Munich Glypthothek.

Adolf Furtwängler, a German archeolo-gist, systematically researched this sanctu-

"View in the Interior of Aegina," from Christopher Wordsworth's
Greece: Pictorial, Descriptive and Historical, *1844.*

ary in 1901. Until then, it had been thought to be a temple in honor of Athena, for it was her likeness that dominated the two pediments. However, Furtwängler found an archaic inscription with the name of the local goddess, Aphaea. This proved that the sanctuary was constructed not in honor of Athena but of Aphaea. Scholars interpret the fact that Athena and not Aphaea occupies the central position in both pediments as an attempt on the part of the Aeginetans to bring about official recognition of Aphaea as an Olympian divinity; such efforts were made on behalf of local deities in other Greek cities as well. The first temple to Aphaea dates back to the early sixth century B.C. The third appears to have been built in around 500 B.C.

The pediment sculptures, depicting battles for Troy, were executed with extraordinary care in 490–480 B.C. Antiquity knew two campaigns against Troy. In the first, Heracles, with Iolaus, Telamon, and a host of Tiryntians, fought against the Trojan king Laomedon. In the second, the Trojan War recounted in Homer's *Iliad,* the Greeks, under the leadership of Agamemnon, besieged the city in order to retrieve Helen, who had run away from her husband, Menelaus, with Paris, one of the sons of King Priam of Troy. The eastern pediment refers to the first of these wars; the western one, to the second. Both assaults were associated with mythical heroes from Aegina: Aeacus's son Telamon had taken part in the first one and Telamon's sons Aias (Ajax) and Teukros (Teucer) in the second. Both scenes illustrate the heroic deeds of the Aeginetans' great ancestors. Indirectly, the inhabitants of Aegina were also alluding to the fact that they had been of crucial importance in the victory at Salamis and could claim precedence even over the Athenians. Furtwängler's excavations uncovered portions of the demolished east pediment, which are now in the National Archeological Museum in Athens. Huge marble flowers flanked by *korai* served as

Ground plan of the Aphaea sanctuary.

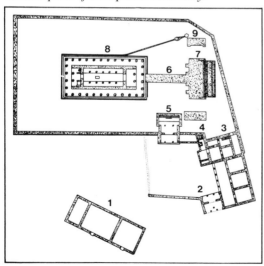

1. *External building*
2. *Small propylon*
3. *Dwelling of the priests*
4. *Bath*
5. *Large propylon*
6. *Processional walk*
7. *Altar*
8. *Temple*
9. *Cisterns*

(Based on a drawing by Athina Kalogheropoulou.)

acroteria (gable ornaments). The corners were decorated with griffins or sphinxes.

THE MEMORY OF THE EARLIEST TIMES ON AEgina, preserved in the ancient myths, is constantly associated with the name of Aeacus. This venerable person is related to the archeological site at Kolona. Aeacus was an unfortunate father. His two famous sons, Peleus and Telamon, hated their half-brother, Phocus, who was born of a different marriage. In the pentathlon, when it was Peleus's turn to throw the discus, he purposely struck Phocus with it—or so Pausanias tells us. Phocus died, and Peleus and Telamon fled the island. Peleus went to Thessaly and never returned. Telamon first went to Salamis, but he was homesick for Aegina. He sent a messenger to tell his father that he had not sought the death of Phocus. One evening he put ashore on the coast of Aegina near Kolona and erected a funeral monument to his murdered broth-

er. The next morning he built a dike in the Kryptos Limen, a coastal harbor. He did not dare to set foot on the island itself for fear of his father's curse. From his dike, Telamon tried to justify himself to Aeacus, but he was unable to convince his father of his innocence. He was not permitted to return to Aegina and had to bear the guilt of his brother's death. He went back to Salamis.

Because of the willpower he had demonstrated in upholding justice above his paternal feelings—and also because of his piety—Aeacus was famous far and wide. It was even said that after he died the gods named him a judge of the underworld along with Rhadamanthys and Minos.

The city of Aegina, on the island's west coast, is typical of small Greek cities a century ago. A number of classical mansions stand at the edge of town. Several buildings constructed after the liberation of Greece in 1828, from the time of the island's first governor, Ioannis Kapodistrias (1776–

Map of the city of Aegina in the fifth century B.C.

1. *Commercial harbor*
2. *Military harbor (Kryptos Limen, or "hidden harbor")*
3. *Temple of Poseidon*
4. *Aeaceion (shrine of Aeacus)*
5. *Bouleuterion (city hall)*
6. *Two temples to unknown deities*
7. *Tomb of Phocus*
8. *Attaleion, built by Attalus of Pergamum*
9. *Theater*
10. *Stadium*

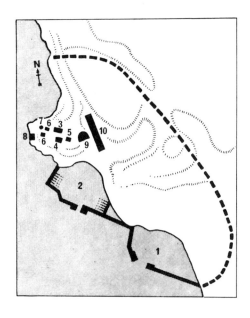

(After a drawing by Athina Kalogheropoulou.)

1831), are also preserved. The museum in the center of town displays many most interesting artifacts from the island's history. The modern harbor was the city's commercial wharf in antiquity; small additions were built in the Roman period and under Venetian rule. The military harbor, Kryptos Limen, lies near the village of Karantina; remnants of ancient moorings are still preserved there. The city and its two harbors must have been fortified during Aegina's heyday, just before the Persian Wars. It is estimated that the docks could accommodate as many as sixty triremes.

The hill of Kolona seems to have been the most famous one in ancient Aegina. Even Pausanias described its monuments. Most impressive are the traces of the island's pre-Greek and mid-Helladic settlements with their strong fortifications. The pre-Greek fortifications lie somewhat below the ancient temple of Apollo (circa 520 B.C.), of which only a single column

(*kolona* in Greek) still stands; this column gave the area its name. The temple was formerly thought to be dedicated to Aphrodite, but today it is believed that the temple of Aphrodite—the protectress of navigation and sailors, venerated nearby as Aphrodite Pontia (seafarers' or harbor goddess)—must have stood near the commercial port, or beneath the present-day city. Settlement of the hill of Kolona, as the various finds and structures attest, goes back to the very earliest times. Cult worship at the site began in the last phase of the Mycenaean period.

Surviving from the Doric temple of Apollo are the one column from the *opisthodomos* (back room) and the foundation. Among these are the remnants of a prehistoric settlement, above which the temple foundations were laid precisely. The temple of Apollo was a *peripteros*, a cella surrounded by six columns at either end and twelve along each side. During German ex-

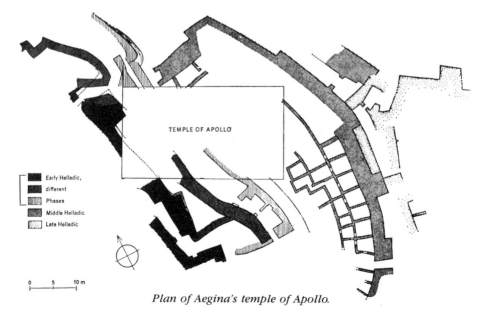

TEMPLE OF APOLLO

Early Helladic,
different
Phases
Middle Helladic
Late Helladic

0   5   10 m

Plan of Aegina's temple of Apollo.

The temple of Aphaea: drawing by Copley Fielding, c. 1844.

cavations, portions of the pediment sculptures, dating from about the sixth century B.C., were unearthed. And in front of the temple, there was an older temple. Various fragments of this earlier structure were found, including a clay *acroterion* 5½ feet in diameter and with a scale pattern of ornamentation.

To the west of the temple of Apollo, you can discern the foundations of two smaller temples, probably to Artemis and Dionysus. And to the south of the temple of Apollo are the remains of the rectangular Aeaceion. According to Pausanias, an olive grove and a low altar were here consecrated to Aeacus. On the altar, he wrote, the Aeginetans were depicted swimming about Aeacus, begging him to intercede with his father, Zeus, to bring rain.

In fact, some portions of a marble relief, dating from roughly 490 B.C., were discovered during excavations. These are in the city museum. Fugitives were granted asylum in the Aeaceion, among them the Athenian orator Hyperides. When the Macedonians under Antipater took him away

from it by force, they were killed for thus having violated the right of asylum. Farther to the north lay the Bouleuterion, Aegina's city hall.

Near the Aeaceion, the grave of Phocus has also been discovered. It is a round structure covered with earth and without side walls. It must have been built near the end of the sixth century B.C. Not far from the Kryptos Limen, the military harbor, there was a theater. This structure, from the Classical period, was seen by Pausanias and doubtless survived until the third century A.D. At that time, its stone bleachers—and those of the adjacent stadium—were used to help fortify the city; today there are no signs of either the theater or the stadium. According to Pausanias, the theater was similar in size and design to the one that was recently discovered at Epidaurus. On the western slope of the hill are the remains of the Attaleion, a building from the Hellenistic period.

A FAMOUS ASCLEPIEION, MENTIONED IN ARIStophanes' *The Wasps* (first performed in

422 B.C.), stood on Aegina, and great numbers of patients flocked to it from near and far. Veneration of Asclepius, the god of healing, may have spread to Aegina from Epidaurus. On the basis of Pausanias's descriptions, it has been presumed that the Asclepieion was located near the temple of Aphaea. Mental illnesses were also treated there, as is clear from *The Wasps*. Some archeologists believe that there was also a shrine to Hecate in the area of the ancient Oies (modern Palaiochora). Huge festivals were celebrated on Aegina in honor of Hecate, and even a number of Athenians used to participate in them.

Two further spots are of interest on Aegina: the Palaiochora, where for centuries the islanders sought refuge from sudden attacks by pirates; and the famous small church of St. Theodore (Aghioi Theodoroi), known as Beautiful Church (Omorphi Ekklisia). The walls of this single-nave basilica are constructed of massive limestone slabs that probably came from an ancient temple. According to the dedicatory inscription, the church was built in 1289. It is known for its splendid frescos that depict fifteen episodes from the life of Christ; the Crucifixion on the west wall and the Resurrection above the altar arch are especially powerful. In the lower wall area, there are full-figure portrayals of church fathers and saints.

The Palaiochora lies northeast of the modern city, above the monastery of the Holy Trinity (Aghia Trias), atop a steep cliff on which there are both chapels and ruins. The first structure was built in 896 after an attack by Saracen pirates. It was continuously inhabited until 1800 and therefore exhibits architectural elements from nearly all of the historical epochs connected with the island's occupation by various enemies. On the southwestern slope, there are some small, squarish medieval houses stacked above one another like the bleachers of an amphitheater. Narrow, cobbled streets end in stairways or steeply climbing alleys. The people who lived in the Palaiochora were traders and seafarers; they used the harbor at Surala and the bays along the north coast. Today, the spot, with its dilapidated buildings and roughly twenty churches adorned with frescos, radiates peace and calm. The frescos date from the thirteenth to the eighteenth centuries.

POROS AND TROEZEN

THE TWO PARTS OF THE ISLAND OF POROS ARE connected by a small isthmus. The island's interior can be reached not only by ship but also by car—a drive of only three and a half hours along the coast road, via the Isthmus and Epidaurus. Although a number of hotels have been built here and prominent Athenians have owned vacation houses here for decades, the island has never been fashionable like Hydra or Spetsai. The little sand and gravel beaches that are inaccessible by land are well worth exploring with a sailboat or motorboat.

On the southwest coast are the remains of the old military harbor that the Russians laid out, with the sultan's blessing, in the

Painting of Poros by Otto Magnus von Stackelberg.

eighteenth century. The famous Greek warship *Averof*, which played a major role in 1912, during the Balkan War, is docked in front of the Poros Naval School as a museum piece. The Naval School dates back to the days of King Otto. Even older is the house of Admiral Tombasis, next to the narrow causeway on the outskirts of the town of Poros. The Koryzis family home at the opposite end of town, next to the quay facing the Peloponnesus, is soon to be made a local museum.

From the harbor, you can take a bus for the 2½-mile ride to the monastery of Panaghia Zoodochos Pighi ("Holy Virgin as Life-Giving Fount"), an eighteenth-century structure with two tall cypresses in its courtyard. Only a few monks still live there today. Noteworthy is a wooden, gold-painted iconostasis, dating from the eighteenth century and adorned with late Byzantine illustrations from the New Testament. It was presumably brought to Poros from Asia Minor. To the left of the back wall of the choir hangs a painting donated to the monastery by an Italian painter in 1849 as a memorial to his eighteen-year-old daughter, who died of tuberculosis and lies buried in the cloister cemetery alongside freedom fighters. The painter gave the face of the Virgin his daughter's features. A small icon of the Virgin, covered with sil-

ver, was found in a spring on this spot—
supposedly the reason that the cloister was
built here.

Fresh spring water is very scarce on
Poros, and it has to be piped to the island
from the nearby mainland. Fortunately it is
only a short distance across to the Peloponnesus; the narrow strait (*poros* in Greek)
gave the island its name in relatively recent
times. In antiquity, the major part of the island was known as Calauria. In the travel
descriptions of Pausanias and Strabo, we
read that Calauria had a circumference of
roughly 30 stadia (3½ miles) and belonged
to a religious association of seven towns
that included Athens as well. They all par-

ticipated in sacrificial festivals held in hon-
or of Poseidon, the sea god, on Calauria.
Poseidon had a famous sanctuary here. Until quite recently, you would have had to
climb roughly an hour on foot to get to the
ruins of the sanctuary of Poseidon, but you
can now easily drive from the coast right
up to the foundations of the temple, the island's only ruin dating from the sixth century B.C., which was excavated in the
nineteenth century. From up here you can
look across to Salamis, Aegina, and Meth-
ana, with Argolis in the background.

This sanctuary served as an asylum for
shipwrecked sailors, pirates, and political
refugees. The Athenian orator Demosthe-

nes, Macedon's enemy, took his own life here in 322 B.C., when the new Macedonian rulers of Athens, to whom he was an arch-enemy, were pursuing him.

The sanctuary lies in lovely surroundings, luxuriant with green shrubs. The cracks between the gray stone blocks are filled with countless specimens of the true sea onion, which loves rocky and sandy soil. Shiny, lance-shaped leaves appear in the fall and do not wither until the summer of the following year, when stalks appear bearing great numbers of white, green-veined blossoms from August through October. The plant contains a poison that can be fatal in large doses; the ancients were aware of it, and the modern Greeks use it as a pesticide.

ALL WHO VISIT POROS SHOULD MAKE A SIDE TRIP to Troezen, on the Peloponnesus. To reach it, you can take a ferry from the harbor of Poros to the village of Galatas, directly opposite. The ferry runs between Poros and Galatas throughout the day. Lemon and orange groves climb up the slopes of the Peloponnesus. The Lemonodhasos ("the lemon grove") has been frequently visited by Greek and foreign writers during blossom time and celebrated in their books. For example, in his *Colossus of Maroussi*, which appeared just before World War II, Henry Miller wrote:

Coming into Poros gives the illusion of the deep dream, suddenly the land converges on all sides and the boat is squeezed into a narrow strait from which there seems to be no egress.... The island revolves in cubistic planes, one of walls and windows, one of rocks and goats, one of stiff-blown trees....Yonder, where the mainland curves like a whip, lie the lemon groves and there in Spring young and old go mad from the fragrance of sap and blossom.

Leaving Galatas, along the coast road toward Epidaurus, you will see a church on the edge of town. Next to it, a cypress tree and a pine tree have grown together. These trees, according to a fairly recent Greek legend, represent a pair of lovers who were unable to be together in life and were transformed into trees after they died. A few miles farther on, a road leads off to the left toward the town of Troezen. From here, you have to hike for about half an hour to reach the ruins of the ancient city of the same name.

You first pass greenhouses in which carnations, gladioli, and early vegetables are grown. A landmark along this path is a tower built during the Hellenistic period. A short detour leads to the old Diavolo-ghephyri, or Devil's Bridge, which supposedly collapsed whenever a notorious liar attempted to cross it.

THE ANCIENT IONIAN COLONY OF TROEZEN IS AN attraction primarily for scholars and lovers of Greek mythology and the Attic tragic cycles. It is impressive more for its role in these tales than for ancient architecture and works of art. Theseus was raised here by his grandfather Pittheus, one of the Seven Sages of Greece, and the Phaedra tragedy took place here.

Hippolytus, Theseus's son by his mar-

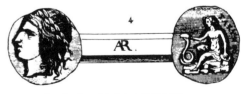

Ancient coin from Troezen.

riage to an Amazon, was a timid young man who hated women and sacrificed only to the virginal Artemis, totally ignoring Aphrodite, the goddess of love. The offended Aphrodite avenged herself by making her devoted priestess Phaedra, who happened to be Hippolytus's stepmother, fall passionately in love with the young man. Phaedra went to Troezen just as regularly as her stepson did, and she spied on him from behind a myrtle tree as he practiced alone with his horses on the racetrack. Phaedra was unable to arouse love in the youth, and she eventually hanged herself from the myrtle tree. Euripides transformed the story from mythology into a tragedy in which Phaedra's unrequited love turns into hate. She leaves a letter for Theseus in Athens in which she accuses Hippolytus of being a seducer. Theseus lays a curse on his son and brings about his death as a result.

Troezen contains a few remnants of the sanctuary of Hippolytus, with temples, guesthouses, and traces of the racetrack. In his time, as is the case everywhere in Greece, Pausanias saw much more. When he wrote, there was still a sanctuary to the Muses here, for example, and he reported that people made sacrifices on its altar to the Muses and to Hypnos (sleep), who was held to be the Muses' favorite deity. Moreover, he saw:

a very impressive sanctuary with a temple and an ancient cult statue dedicated to Hippolytus.... All virgins cut off a lock of their hair before their weddings and donated it to the temple.... The Troezeneans do not wish to admit that Hippolytus died, and they do not show his grave, though they know where it is.

HYDRA

NAKED AND GRAY, EVEN GRIM, HYDRA SEEMS AN outsider among the green islands that surround it. But suddenly and surprisingly the small and welcoming harbor town appears from behind the monolithic cliffs that shelter it. All around the protected bay, houses climb the slope, and each of the town's quarters differs from the others. To the right and left of the natural harbor stand the *archontika*, or houses of the gentry; behind them, like a wreath around the hill of Kiapha, come those of the bourgeoisie. Along the quay are the colorful shops of the marketplace, with the marble tower of

the Holy Virgin Cloister in the center.

Amid the white, cubic houses of the town, the massive gray *archontika* stand out. They date from the heyday of Hydra, at the beginning of the nineteenth century, when the *kapetanaioi* (shipping magnates) plied the seas and brought home gold coins in such quantity that they were sometimes used for ballast for their ships. Many are still inhabited by descendants of their original owners. However, of the roughly twenty *archontika*, many are in ruins.

Well-preserved and open to visitors are

Western section of the town of Hydra.

the beautiful, imposing houses of Lazaros and Georghios Koundouriotis, the two brothers who were heroes in the war of liberation, and that of Demetrios Vulgaris, who was prime minister of Greece from 1855 to 1857. Others include the huge mansion of Admiral Iakovos Tombasis, today the Academy of Fine Arts, and the houses of the two Tsamados brothers, who served bravely in nearly all of the sea battles against the Turks. The Merchant Marine Academy is housed today in one of these. The severe, gray stone façades of the *archontika* belie their interiors: old, richly carved furnishings; Venetian candelabra and gilt-frame mirrors; carved chests; porcelain from England and Murano; ancient sculptures and inscriptions collected in the nearby Peloponnesus.

Narrow alleys and steep staircases lead from one quarter to the next. The monotony of white walls is broken again and again by a century-old doorway with doors of cypress wood, a blue window frame, scarlet steps, or an ochre or dark green garden wall; the Hydriots are not afraid of bright colors. It is as though one were standing on a stage set for a play about bold nineteenth-century seafarers. However, ruins and abandoned mills remind us that Hydra is no longer the favored island of Greece's richest shippers.

Changing times have left their mark here quite clearly. For centuries, Hydra was un- known and only thinly settled because of its rocky soil, its lack of water, its inhospita- ble coastline. But these same factors con- spire to make it a uniquely colorful and picturesque landscape, so in the past fif- teen or twenty years, Hydra has become the cosmopolitan Mediterranean island *par excellence*. The combination of its raw nat- ural beauty and the wonderful harbor town has been irresistible; writers and painters have come from all parts of the world to es- tablish a permanent colony. Blond children from the northern lands now sit side by side with their Hydriot contemporaries in school, and foreign families participate en- thusiastically in the traditional local festi- vals and holidays.

And Hydra has gradually become a sum- mer hideaway for increasing numbers of people. On weekends the harbor is filled with luxury yachts as well as the modest lo- cal vessels. Dignified receptions in the *ar- chontika* take place alongside unrestrained feasts in the tavernas, boat rides, and out- ings to the monasteries on the backs of donkeys or mules. The local character is still pervasive. It draws not only on ancient times, the "heroic" past, but on the more recent shipbuilding and sponge-diving tra- ditions of the islanders—a legacy that we also encounter on islands such as Andros, Chios, Karpathos, and Syme.

A number of strange customs have been preserved on the island up to the present day. One example is the Good Friday ob- servance at St. John's in Kamini (meaning "kilns"—potters have long made their homes here), where the *epitaphios* (a wooden coffin that symbolizes Christ's tomb) is borne into the sea until the four young men supporting it on their shoul- ders can barely stand. They are surrounded by the faithful, who carry the dark candles of this day of mourning. On Good Friday, the Hydriots honor all those who have died at sea.

Each spot on Hydra is rich in legend and tradition; each of its 143 churches has a unique story of its own origins. The church of St. Cyprian, to the west of Palamidas, was built using wine as an ingredient of the mortar, for on the saint's name day a caïque full of wine was fished out of the water. In Klimaki, there once lived a giant serpent, so the legend goes, that hid in the dense forest and devoured the sheep. Some shep- herds surprised the monster in its sleep and burned it, along with the forest. This story may only be an alibi invented by those who cut down the precious trees of Hydra in order to build ships.

TRADITION HAS IT THAT THE HYDRIOTS BECAME shipbuilders by sheer coincidence during the Turkish occupation. When the Turkish fleet dropped anchor off Hydra in 1645, there was much plundering on the island. Two well-respected men, Dedes Kriesis and Ghiorgis Ghionis, went to the Turkish

A carpenter in ancient times.

admiral, begging that the monastery of Panaghia and its miraculous icon of the Holy Virgin be spared. Both men were taken captive and sent as slaves to Crete, where they studied and worked in a shipyard. When they returned home, they taught the Hydriots their new skill. In 1657, a rudimentary ship was built with only a saw, an axe, and an auger; the ship's planks were held together by wooden pegs. But with primitive vessels such as this, the Hydriots began to trade with the Peloponnesus.

IT APPEARS THAT HYDRA HAS BEEN CONTINUOUSly inhabited since the Mycenaean epoch. Shards of vases from the late Mycenaean period through Roman times have been found on the hill of Chorisa, roughly 1¼ miles southwest of the harbor and opposite the islet of Ioannis Theologos with its tall fig trees. The first scholarly work about archeological finds on Hydra was published in 1911 by August Frickenhaus and Walter Muller, who described the ancient acropolis on Chorisa. This structure dominated the small harbor of Vlychos, or Glyphos, named for the brackish taste (*glyphiso* in Greek) of its spring water. Later teams excavated the walls of the acropolis, especially its retaining walls. Unearthed shards, the

Women pounding meal.

head of a Mycenaean idol, spearheads, and loom weights all found their way into Hydra's Naval Museum. There can thus be no doubt that the area around the Bay of Vlychos was settled at least as early as the hill of Chorisa. Its first residents were probably fishermen, seafarers, and soldiers who guarded the strait between Hydra and the Peloponnesus.

The ancient remains of Chorisa lie on the northwestern and western slopes of the hill, opposite Hermione on the Peloponnesus. Herodotus mentioned that Hydra was a colony of Hermione in about 525 B.C. Hermione later abandoned Hydra to the Samians, who, in turn, sold it to Troezen, which lies somewhat farther north along the coast of the Peloponnesus. The only native of Hydra known to us from the Classical period is the comedian Evages. The facts that Hydra changed ownership so easily, without war, and that it was scarcely mentioned in ancient writings lead us to conclude that, given its forbidding terrain and lack of water, it was no more than a refuge for sailors, a fishing settlement, or a grazing area for the goats of its wealthy neighbors on the Peloponnesus.

Hydra also passed unnoticed through the Roman period. Visitors have found Byzantine gold and copper coins in Episkopi and near St. Andreas's Church in Vlychos. During those long, silent centuries, life was presumably concentrated there, at the foot of the hill of Chorisa.

Such was Hydra's history until the seventeenth century. Then, it appears in travel descriptions as a hideout for refugees from the Peloponnesus; it was an island that was rarely visited and offered safety from the cruelties of the Turks. At some uncertain date, the first Albanians settled here. They intermarried with the Greeks who came to live on Hydra after the war between Turkey and Russia in 1770. These new inhabitants revitalized the island and constructed the town around the harbor in the form in which it is seen today.

Like all the islands, Hydra was privileged under Turkish rule; its ships were permitted to sail everywhere and trade with friend and foe alike. Hydriot navigators proved themselves during Nelson's blockade of Europe during the Napoleonic Wars; they were the first to break the blockade in the Mediterranean. Gold coins began to fill the island's coffers. But foreign gold did not dampen the islanders' love for their homeland at all: in 1821, the Hydriots assumed the entire cost of the sea war against the Turks and outfitted a hundred ships themselves. Along with the neighboring island of Spetsai and the island of Psara, Hydra became famous for the heroic deeds of its freedom-fighting captains and crews.

THE FIRST HYDRIOT WE KNOW OF AFTER THE ANcient poet Evages is a fisherman who became a confidant of the immensely wealthy pirate Mustaphas Reis in 1610 and called himself Nicephorus Jusuph Ras Bei. Another emigré from Hydra became the captain of a Turkish ship; his own mother pushed this renegade off a cliff in Kiapha. Toward the end of the eighteenth century, many Hydriots became known in connection with the island's independent government: the battles against the Turks immortalized the names of Miaoulis and his fireships, of the Koundouriotis brothers, of Sachtouris, and the Tombasis. Another native son was Kovotos, the first naval minister of free Greece.

The fame and wealth that Hydra attained more than 150 years ago caused the development of a brilliant social life here. Its receptions and balls became famous; full orchestras would play at the Loggia, the Vulgaris family mansion. However, only a few generations enjoyed the heyday of Hydra; following the war of liberation, the island fell into decline again. The Hydriots increasingly had to emigrate and seek a new life elsewhere.

Today, great numbers of people come to Hydra. P.J. Launay, a French novelist who wrote a guide to the Greek islands, echoed the sentiments of many when he wrote: "We came here for a few hours and stayed four days; would that I could say we had never left again."

Spetsai

SPETSAI IS NEITHER THE MOST BEAUTIFUL NOR THE most picturesque island in the Saronic Gulf. But it radiates a gentle grace, a particular magic that is immediately apparent to even the short-term visitor. Its attraction probably derives from the fact that it appears to be timeless and unchanged. There are some new, ugly hotels, hideous modern plastic chairs in the old *kapheneia*, and noisy motorcycles and transistor radios that disturb the noonday silence. But essentially, life proceeds calmly, marked by the changing seasons. In winter, the men go to sea and the women take care of their families and fields. In summer, when the population doubles, the stern, black costumes of the peasant women give way to all kinds of fantastic tourist clothes. The islanders welcome this invasion, since tourism represents their most important source of income. For their part, the summer guests count on finding the same atmosphere year after year: the familiar old ship and the same boatman, the sweet black coffee, the same small tavernas, the heady aroma of jasmine and orange blossoms, the crystal blue sea, the whitewashed hilltop monasteries surrounded by slender cypresses, and the gardens with their blue-painted tin cans in which fragrant basil thrives. And in the background, as far as the eye can see, stretch the mountains of the Peloponnesian mainland—an endless curtain that is constantly changing its shade of blue.

IN CLASSICAL TIMES, SPETSAI WAS CALLED PItioussa, which means "the one overgrown with pines." And in fact, Aleppo pines still grow all over the island today; some of

A woman spinning.

them stand with their roots in the water. Their bundles of needles change color according to the season, yellow, gold, or dark green, blending with the silver foliage of the olive trees.

Unfortunately, only the pine trees have survived from antiquity. Recent excavations near Aghia Marina have brought a few prehistoric settlements to light, but these are of interest only to the expert archeologist. Only with the greatest effort can the tourist distinguish whether he or she is looking at a shard thousands of years old or a piece of a clay jar that was thrown into the ocean last year.

Spetsai did not play an important role in ancient history. However, Spetsiot captains and their ships fought alongside those of the neighboring island of Hydra and the island of Psara against the Ottoman Empire during the rebellion of 1821, when Greece was finally able to free itself from hundreds of years of Turkish occupation. Bouboulina, Greece's national heroine, was a Spetsiot woman who took command of her husband's ship after he had been slain. She fought at least as bravely as the other captains. Grandmothers tell their rapt grandchildren about Bouboulina's beauty, strength, and love affairs.

According to another story, the Turkish fleet appeared off the coast of Spetsai one day when all of the men happened to be away. The women didn't lose their nerve for a moment. They collected all of the red fezzes they could find (all of the peoples subject to the Turks had to wear these hats) and placed them on the asphodel plants that grew in masses along the shore. From a distance, the fezzes swaying in the wind looked like warlike hordes, and the enemy fled at the sight of them. This "victory" is commemorated annually on the island. A mock battle is staged, a Turkish flagship made of cardboard is burned in the middle of the harbor, and there are splendid fireworks. Of course, everybody dances, too.

Spetsai had actually been ravaged fifty years before the war of liberation began because it had taken part in the so-called Orloff Rebellion of 1760. As usual, the Russians had their eyes on the Mediterranean. Under the pretext of coming to the aid of their Orthodox coreligionists in Greece, Catherine the Great dispatched her favorite, Orloff, to organize a rebellion there. Presumably her real aim was to conquer Constantinople for Russia. The Spetsiots rose up in unison against the Turkish oppressors and followed Orloff in his expedition, which ended in total defeat. In revenge for its role in this uprising, the Turks destroyed the island, killed half its inhabitants, and sent the rest into exile on Cythera. Only one or two buildings from before 1760 survived this catastrophe. The museum, where mementos of Bouboulina and the war of liberation are preserved, is today housed in one of these. This building, with its narrow windows, high steps, and slender vaulting, looks rather melancholy, and a few years ago there was even a little piece of paper tacked to its entrance that read: "The Museum is closed every day."

The architecture we see today on Spetsai dates primarily from the early nineteenth century. During the Napoleonic Wars—especially during the British blockade of the Continent, which severely limited western European shipping—the Greeks took advantage of the opportunity of excelling in sea trade and made huge fortunes virtually overnight. Now well-to-do, they returned to their native islands and built spacious, comfortable houses, nearly all of them designed according to the same simple scheme: they are two stories high, with roof terraces and balconies; they have gardens and, if possible, space for boats and tackle. Especially important to every house is the cistern in which rain water is collected—the sole source of fresh water on this rocky island. These large stone cisterns look like vaulted chambers that lie below the roof terrace. The more imposing houses on the shore generally stand on top of concave retaining walls 100 to 130 feet high. These walls protected the buildings not only from Turks and pirates but also from the pounding of the waves.

All construction came to a sudden halt when the eagerly awaited war of liberation against the Turks became a reality. Now captains and merchants no longer spent their money self-indulgently but carefully hid it in order to finance the coming rebellion. Children still firmly believe that there is gold lying at the bottom of the cisterns, hoarded there by their ancestors, anxious for freedom.

Spetsai developed into a vacation island in the first decade of the twentieth century. This was primarily the work of a man called

A soldier in armor.

Anargyros. This typical Greek adventurer left Spetsai as a boy without even a penny in his pocket (his name, appropriately, means "without silver"), and through his intelligence and hard work he amassed a great fortune in America. He returned home, and his only dream was to help his island and his friends. He had an electric plant built and gave Spetsai a grotesque but splendid hotel of the kind one sees in the south of France, with terraces, little towers, gardens, and the many palm trees then in such favor. The waiters wore tails, and there was chamber music every evening. Athenians who could afford it would spend their summer holidays here. Wives and children would arrive, accompanied by English or French governesses; every Friday, they would eagerly await the boat bringing the exhausted husbands and fathers to the island for the weekend.

During World War II, Spetsai suffered indescribably under the occupation forces. The islanders went hungry and lost everything. But once the war was over, the island recovered rapidly, and its untroubled, happy summer life began anew. Today, fast, modern boats arrive daily from Piraeus, and it is now even possible to fly to Spetsai. A fine, broad highway runs along the beautiful Peloponnesian coast, so it is possible to drive in four hours from Athens to a small harbor where a boat awaits to take visitors to this island paradise. On Spetsai, the days pass uneventfully. Yet no one day is precisely like the next. The most urgent questions here are: Where shall we swim? What shall we take along to eat? How long should we nap? and Which taverna shall we have supper in tonight? All of the nights seem to be lit by the full moon, and the mild air always seems to be perfumed with exotic aromas. As soon as you land in Spetsai's harbor, you leave all problems behind, eager to spend a month, a week, or even a single day peacefully, relaxed and happy, between the sky and the sea, surrounded by hospitality.

Page 49: Church in Oia, Thira. (© David L. Winston/H. Armstrong Roberts)

Pages 50–51: Paros. (© Susan Shapiro)

Page 52: The coast of Thira. (© Susan Shapiro)

Page 53, top: Monastery, Corfu. (© John Lewis Stage/The Image Bank)

Page 53, bottom: Lindus Acropolis, Rhodes. (© Isabel Brit/The Image Bank)

Pages 54–55: Chora, Patmos. (© Michael Pasdzior/The Image Bank)

Page 56, top: Nets drying on Mykonos. (© John Lewis Stage/The Image Bank)

Page 56, bottom: Church bells, Thira. (© James Rudnick)

Page 57: Narrow street, Mykonos. (© Adam Woolfitt/Woodfin Camp and Associates)

Pages 58–59: Windmill on Mykonos. (© Ted H. Funk/The Image Bank)

Pages 60–61: Main harbor at Mykonos. (© Stephen Green-Armytage/The Image Bank)

Pages 62–63: Temple on Delos. (© Stephen Green-Armytage/The Image Bank)

Page 64: Harbor, Rhodes. (© Joseph F. Viesti)

THE CYCLADES

KEOS (TZIA)

FROM LAURIUM, ON THE NORTHEAST COAST OF Attica, a small steamer sails to a Cycladic island that its inhabitants call Tzia; the ancients called it Ceos; its official name is Keos (Kea). This journey would take little more than an hour if one did not have to go around Makronisos.

Makronisos ("long island") is less than a mile wide. It resembles a sheet of ice, and the feet of its bare cliffs of gray-black granite clutch at the sea like claws. Makronisos has few inhabitants or harbors, and it is not very hospitable. This island has been largely ignored by both nature and modern history. It was the site of a concentration camp for the defeated Turks after the First Balkan War (1912) and for the defeated Greek Communists after the civil war in 1949. The ancients, however, named it after the lovely Helen of Troy, for Helen was said to have made a stopover here on her journey home from Troy to Sparta. So Pausanias tells us. Traces of prehistoric habitation, obsidian and pottery shards, have been found on Makronisos. There are also remains of ancient buildings.

ONCE THE STEAMER HAS CURVED AROUND MAKronisos, one glimpses Keos. Its mountains seem to be one single massif, and no harbor is visible. But high up on the mountain named for the prophet Elijah one can see the white buildings of Chora. As on many other Greek islands, the site for this main settlement of Keos was chosen to be far enough from the sea that it would be protected from attack by pirates.

There is a strait between a cliff crowned by the church of Aghios Nikolaos, the patron saint of seafarers, and Cape Corisia, opening to a spacious bay. This is the famous harbor of Aghios Nikolaos, where pirates had a base between the thirteenth and sixteenth centuries. And the fleet of the Greek liberation hero Lambros Katsonis used it as a hiding place during the Battle of Andros against the Turks in 1790. In Corisia—Livadi in the vernacular—the steamer drops anchor. The harbor now comes to life only during the summer months.

Today, Keos, with roughly 2,000 inhabitants, seems like a dying island. But in antiquity, it was one of the most flourishing islands of the Cyclades. Its four Ionic cities—Corisia, Iulis, Carthaea, and Poiessa —were autonomous city-states, each with its own currency. Ruins of these cities, in-

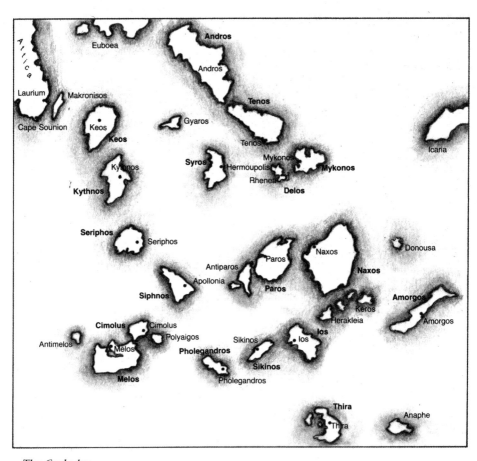

The Cyclades.

scriptions, and works of art, along with the ancient writers, testify to their wealth and the high level of their social and intellectual life. They owed their wealth primarily to trade in acorns and minerals. In the Trypospilies (caves) near the harbor of Otsia, ancient mining tunnels in the cliffs have survived. We know that ancient Athens long monopolized the purchase of enamels from Keos.

Keos was the first island to send its triremes to assist Athens when that city-state was attacked by the Persians (490–470 B.C.). For this reason, its name appears before those of all the other islands on the base of the statue of Zeus at Olympia and on the tripod of the Apollo of Delphi.

Plato called the laws of the city-states of Keos the best in Greece, and Aristotle devoted an essay, which has unfortunately been lost, to their form of government. Tradition held that the inhabitants of Keos were pessimists. A number of ancient writers mentioned an extraordinary custom that developed here, one unique in Greece, the *keion nomimon*: the citizens of Keos who were over seventy and could no longer work committed suicide by drinking hemlock. This practice was supposed to have originated during a siege, when the elders volunteered to die so that the fighters would have enough food, and it persisted well into the Roman era. The general Pompey was an eyewitness to one such suicide: a woman of ninety refused to be dissuaded by Pompey, gave final instructions to her children and grandchildren, took up the beaker filled with hemlock, and emptied it calmly and with dignity.

Keos was the home of countless notables of the ancient world. Two important poets were born in the city of Iulis: Simonides (560 B.C.) and his nephew Bacchylides (518 B.C.). Simonides began his career on

Keos and then moved to Athens, where he was surrounded by admirers of his dithyrambs in praise of the victories in the Persian Wars, at the same time that Aeschylus was gathering laurels in the theater. Bacchylides was famous throughout Greece by the time he was twenty, and he competed in poetic contests with his contemporary, the great Pindar. Bacchylides never forgot his homeland; he twice returned to Keos, and his odes celebrated those of his fellow islanders who had been victorious in the athletic contests at Olympia, Delphi, Nemea, and Isthmia. An inscription found in Iulis (No. 11,563 in the inscription collection of the National Museum in Athens) describes the people of Keos as especially good sprinters and boxers.

Iulis was also the birthplace of the sophist Prodicus, who was, as he himself said, a mixture of philosopher and politician. He taught in Athens at the same time as Socrates. Prodicus's writings have been lost. However, Plato (in his *Protagoras*, for example) gives us much information about Prodicus's precepts. With his pupils he discussed the behavior of Heracles, who when faced with a choice decided for virtue. To Prodicus, the tasks of man were not the pleasures of the easy life but rather struggle and conquest. Other natives of Keos were the philosopher Ariston, who directed the Peripatetic School in Athens in the third century B.C., and the important physician Erasistratus (late fourth or early third century B.C.).

Excavations on Keos have brought to light the oldest Neolithic settlement in the Cyclades. It lay in the northwestern corner of the island, near Cape Cephalas, and dates from 4000–2800 B.C. And traces of a settlement from 1580–1100 B.C. have been discovered on the hill of Troullos, which dominates the Bay of Tris Ammoudhies

("three sand beaches"), south of Cape Cephalas. To the north of the Aghios Nikolaos
harbor, near the church of Aghia Irini, the
American School of Classical Studies, under the direction of J. L. Caskey, has excavated a small but significant settlement
from the Late Neolithic period that flourished between 2800 and 1500 B.C. This
well-constructed city, which was surrounded by a massive wall and towers,
contained large temples and two-story
buildings. An earthquake destroyed it in
about 1500 B.C. The excavations revealed
portions of the walls, staircases, plumbing,
entrances, carefully paved streets, and the
ruins of an imposing temple. The most important finds were large sacrificial clay objects that were found in the temple. There
are indications that the Linear A script was
used here, and countless vases—imported
from Crete and the Cyclades, from Troy
and the Greek mainland—attest to active
trade with all the important cities of the
Aegean.

From the little neighboring fishing village of Vourkari, an unpaved road leads for
less than 2 miles to the peaceful harbor of
Otsia, where Athenian trading vessels took
on the raw materials from which enamel
was made. The road then runs steeply upward toward the largest and most important monastery on the island, the Panaghia
Kastriani (Holy Virgin of the Castle). This
eighteenth-century clifftop structure appears to float between the sea and the sky.

NOTHING REMAINS OF THE ANCIENT CITY OF
Corisia except for portions of the city walls
on the surrounding hills and the few sparse

*Map of Keos from Olfert
Dapper's* Naukeurige Beschryving
der Eilanden, in de Archipel der
Middelantsche Zee, *1688.*

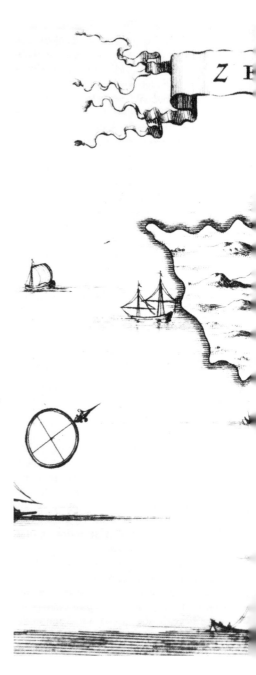

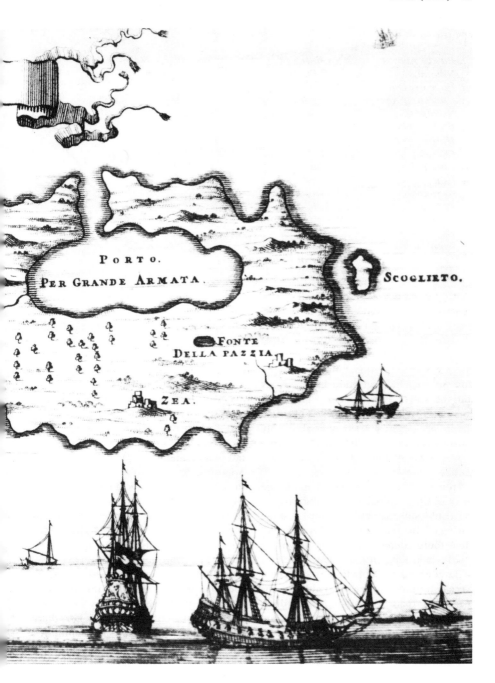

PORTO.
PER GRANDE ARMATA.

SCOGLIETO.

FONTE
DELLA PAZZIA.

ZEA.

The island of Keos.

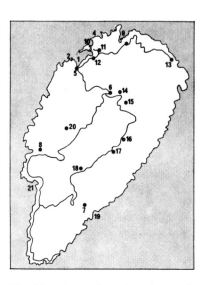

1. Bay of Aghios
   Nikolaos
2. Cape Corisia
3. Church of Aghios
   Nikolaos
4. Cape Cephalas
5. Harbor town of
   Corisia
6. Chora, formerly
   Iulis
7. Carthaea
8. Poiessa
9. Harbor of Otsia
10. Bay of Tris
    Ammoudhies

11. Church of
    Aghia Irini
12. Vourkari
13. Monastery of
    Panaghia Kastriani
14. Monastery of
    Aghia Anna
15. Monastery of
    Episkopi
16. Astra
17. Ellinika
18. Kato Meria
19. Bay of Poles
20. Church of
    Aghia Marina
21. Bay of Koundouros

ruins of a temple to Apollo Smintheus. In 1930 a worker found a statue of a young man standing upright in the ground near Corisia. Today one finds this so-called Kouros of Keos, from 530 B.C., as Inventory No. 3686 in the National Museum in Athens. An ancient inscription has been set into the wall of a modern house in Corisia. It reads: "I am the old Corisia. At some time the Romans came and conquered me. My citizens are eagerly rebuilding me. From now on I will no longer be an unimportant harbor in the Aegean."

From Corisia, a paved road climbs to the town of Chora. Nineteenth-century travelers could still marvel at the artful stone paving of this road, which follows the ancient route connecting the two towns. In 1840, when King Otto and Queen Amalia of Bavaria rode to Chora from Corisia, they were determined to see the builder of this marvelous road. A peasant in gala dress stepped in front of the royal pair. "Are you the architect?" asked Otto. The peasant was silent; he had indeed engineered the road, but he had no idea what an architect

was. The king wanted to see the tools used to build such a road. The peasant brought a hammer, a piece of string, and a lead weight. He would accept the payment that the king offered only when it was explained to him that it would be an insult to the king to refuse.

Chora, which maintained itself as the major town on the island even under Venetian and Turkish rule, was built on top of ancient Iulis. The acropolis stood on the summit of the hill, the temple of Apollo and of Aphrodite Ktesylla were in the center of the city. A few portions of the city wall are still visible near the tourist hotels. Other surviving relics are fragments of ancient statuary that have been set into façades or displayed in the local museum. A little more than a mile northeast of Chora, along a road lined with olive trees, you reach a rock that was chiseled into the form of a huge lion in the sixth century B.C. Larger than life, the king of beasts lies there with an archaic, untroubled smile that recalls the old saga: nymphs once lived happily and peacefully on Keos until a lion turned up one day. They fled by leaping into the sea and swimming to Karystos, on Euboea.

Those who wish to view the scant ruins of the third of the great ancient cities, Carthaea, on the south coast, must hike along the dusty road that begins in Chora and follows the traces of the ancient route from Iulis. The eastern part of Keos is desolate; two small monasteries, three modest churches, and a few farmhouses lie in the deep stillness of the landscape. You first see the monastery of Aghia Anna high atop a mountain. To reach it, you must climb for about half an hour. The monastery church, originally built in the sixteenth century, has a nave and side aisles, a vestibule topped by a cupola, and a typical island bell tower, all completely restored. To the left of the main road lies the ruined Episkopi monastery, from the seventeenth century. All that survives is its small church, with an inscription over the door that gives 1651 as the year of its construction. Descending the slope of Ai-Elia, you pass through oak and almond groves. The road then leads through three tiny villages: Astra, with the little church of Aghios Ioannis Prodromos; Ellinika, with the church of Aghios Nikolaos and its eighteenth-century wall frescos; and Kato Meria, whose cruciform cupola church of Aghioi Apostoloi contains faded wall paintings from the thirteenth century. From here, it is only a short walk to Carthaea.

The first excavations in Carthaea, on a rocky hill above the Bay of Poles, were undertaken in 1811 by the Danish scholar Bronsted. Sparse ruins of the massive wall and the entrance have survived. A temple to the goddess Athena stood to the right of the entry gate. It was built in the fifth century B.C. and had Doric columns in a 6:11 ratio. All that can be seen today is one love-ly capital and assorted fragments of archaic statues from the fifth century B.C. This city's temple of Apollo stood on a cliff, but the cliff collapsed, taking a portion of the temple with it to the bottom of the sea. A larger-than-life statue of the god was discovered in front of the temple and taken to Copenhagen in 1811.

The ancients held an annual festival here in honor of Apollo, and on one such occasion the poet Simonides first presented his hymns. The young maidens of Carthaea danced and sang about the altar. At one time, the lovely Ktesylla was one of these dancers. A young Athenian, Hermochares, fell passionately in love with her. They married, and Ktesylla followed Hermochares to Athens. Their happiness was brief, however, for Ktesylla died while giving birth to her first child. When the people of Keos learned of the death of their beautiful countrywoman, they elevated Ktesylla into the goddess of love, worshiping her as Aphrodite Ktesylla.

In the plain, near the Vathypotamos River, the ruins of a Doric temple have been identified. Nearby, one can see the remains of an ancient theater. Ruins from antiquity lie strewn about the entire area.

A sacrifice to Apollo: detail from a Greek vase painting.

Anyone interested in the island's flora and unafraid of some strenuous hiking can follow another path from Chora to the southwest of Keos. The bare hills and steep slopes along it are adorned with unusual wildflowers in spring. In a green valley at the foot of the mountain, one comes upon an odd architectural complex: a tall yellowish tower rises next to the small white church of Aghia Marina. The tower dates from the fourth century B.C. and is constructed of carefully fitted stones that rest on a stone foundation. As late as 1840, when King Otto and Queen Amalia of Bavaria visited Keos, this tower was still completely preserved as an impressive example of a square tower from antiquity. But lightning later struck its east wall, and year by year the tower collapses a bit further. Its north and west sides are still in good condition, however, as are the strong inner wall that bisects the tower and the marble window frames.

The road continues on to the fourth ancient city, Poiessa, of which virtually nothing remains. In this area is the only truly green valley on the island—a small oasis with vegetable gardens, fruit trees, and cypresses that stretches down to the broad, sandy beach beside a crystalline sea. Some-what farther along, on the Bay of Koundouros, a tasteful bungalow hotel provides its guests with all the modern comforts and an idyllic peace.

Native skill and inborn good taste are evident in even the poorest peasant huts, stalls, fireplaces, retaining walls, and sheds. There are no real villages on Keos. The farmers live in Chora, and during sowing and harvesting seasons, they stay in huts of the sort designated as monuments of Greek folk art by the Folk Art Archives in Athens. These huts are quite small, but their construction is Cyclopean—meaning that they are built of fitted stone blocks as high as ten feet tall. The roofs rest on stone pillars. Joints between the individual stone blocks are weatherproofed with moist clay. In summer, figs are spread out on the roofs to dry.

The ancient people of Keos, as we have seen, scorned a joyless old age and preferred passing over into Hades. For as the comedian Menander wrote in the fourth century B.C.: "He who cannot live well should at least avoid a miserable life." The present-day inhabitants preserve the ancient custom in a modified form appropriate to our own times: they emigrate, searching for a better life in foreign lands.

ANDROS

ANDROS, THE NORTHERNMOST AND SECOND LARGEST (after Naxos) island in the Cyclades, is dominated by massive mountains. There is no room here for open plains. The imposing Mount Kouvara falls steeply into the sea in the south and west. The northeast coast, however, is richly varied; its countless little bays are lined with beaches of sand or gravel and framed by gray marble and dense shrubbery. Through the millennia, various harbors and anchorages have been developed: on the west coast, Gavrion, Batsi, and

The island of Andros.

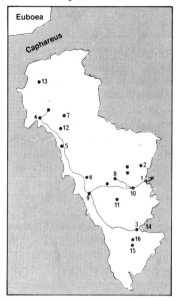

dros. This crossing takes about three hours.

From the ruins surrounding it, one can see that Gavrion was an important harbor in antiquity; and the marble quarry near Pelekiti and Kato Fellos was used by the ancients. A half-hour's walk inland, there is a monumental tower, near the village of Aghios Petros, dating from the Hellenistic period. Its base, constructed of stone blocks, is 69 feet in circumference. The shaft of the cylindrical tower still rises to a height of 65 feet. Local tradition claims that dragons worked these stones, and the inhabitants still show visitors the marks supposedly made by their claws.

The road that connects all of the towns on Andros begins in Gavrion. This rather narrow asphalt ribbon first runs along the sea to the broad bay where Batsi, a favorite holiday resort, is located. Batsi resembles a large amphitheater, with steep, white alleyways. Flowerpots adorn its old patrician houses, and there are fountains at their corners.

The third harbor on the west coast belongs to the village of Palaiopolis. Nearby lies the ancient city of Andros, the former capital of the island. One reaches it by climbing down a hundred steps from the asphalt road toward the sea. Amid lush vegetation, you can see the remains of a city wall and a gate, inscriptions on marble fragments, and broken pottery. Reliefs and

Palaiopolis; on the east, Andros (Chora), Stenies, and Korthion. We do not know where the first settlers landed. Legend has it that a brother of King Minos of Crete, Rhadamanthys, a man famous for his sense of justice and the ruler of the Cyclades, sent the hero Andros to the island. Andros, of divine descent, is said to have given the island its name and served as its first king. In antiquity, Andros was an important stopover between Attica, Euboea, and Asia Minor.

Crossing the 6 nautical miles that separate the northern tip of Andros from Euboea is no pleasure, even for experienced mariners. The Strait of Caphareus—euphemistically named the Cavo d'Oro by the Venetians—sees scarcely a day without strong winds and crashing waves. For this reason, steamers and ferries sail from Rafina along the north coast of Attica, avoiding the Cavo d'Oro, to Gavrion on the west coast of An-

coins from Palaiokastro can be seen in the museum in Chora, the present-day capital. In 1832, a farmer came upon a larger-than-life statue in his field, a stunning female figure known as the "great female Heracles," and a male statue of the god Hermes Psychopompos (the guide of souls into the underworld). The Hermes is a copy from the first century B.C. of the famous original by Praxiteles. These finds created such enthusiasm that the young King Otto and his father, Ludwig I of Bavaria, journeyed to Andros, bought the two statues, and donated them to the National Museum in Athens. They were recently returned to Andros and are now housed in the new Archeological Museum in Chora.

The ancient fortification walls of Palaiopolis are largely preserved. From the tower, you can follow their western section all the way down to the sea. Excavations in 1956 located the agora of the Hellenistic period and uncovered the bases of votive sculptures in front of a columned portico. It is known that the ancient inhabitants were skillful seafarers who grew rich from the trade and sale of minerals, enabling them to mint silver coins in the seventh century B.C. and establish colonies on the Macedonian coast and on the Chalcidice Peninsula. One of these was Stageira, the home of Aristotle. Andros came to be viewed as a desirable ally and a feared opponent by the Greek city-states. Beautiful mosaic floors in ruined Early Christian basilicas near Palaiopolis attest that the ancient capital was still a major city in the fifth century A.D.

The people of Andros worshiped Dionysus, to whom the island owed its vineyards and its exceptional wine. During the festival known as the Dionysia, the god is said to have caused wine to flow from the springs near his temple as a sign of his favor. Pausanias and Pliny the Elder both described this event:

The stream of wine was as divine as it was abundant, forming a river and flowing into the sea. Men wearing wreaths of ivy and greenbriar danced along the shore extolling liquid that neither horses nor cattle might wade in. The wine of Dionysus was reserved solely for man, and it was drunk unmixed. It brought men strength, courage, and intelligence. At the mouth of the stream of wine there were tritons catching the drink in shells and welcoming the god, who came to the festival in Andros on a sailing ship. In his train were satyrs, maenads, and sileni.

The natives point out the Spring of Dionysus in the village of Menites. Beneath the church of the Panaghia springs flow from an extremely ancient well.

AFTER PALAIOPOLIS, NEAR STAVROPEDA, THE ASphalt road crosses another route. At this intersection, you leave the west coast behind, traversing the green Messaria Valley on the way to the east coast and the present-day capital of Chora. (*Chora* means "main city" and is the name of the capital of many of the Aegean islands.) The Messaria was the center of the island during the Byzantine period, when Andros enjoyed a second economic and intellectual flowering. It then owed its wealth to the silk trade. Mulberry trees were planted everywhere; their leaves served as food for silkworms. Silk fabrics were spun from the cocoons. In the Middle Ages, silks from Andros were exported to western Europe. European merchants visited the Cyclades, and Jewish traders settled here and formed a colony.

In the ninth century, a young man came

A sacrifice to Dionysus.

to Andros from Constantinople and took instruction in rhetoric, philosophy, and mathematics from a local scholar. He then withdrew to the rich libraries of the quiet monasteries and acquired the knowledge that earned him the nickname "the wise" when he reigned as the Byzantine emperor Leo VI in Constantinople from 886 to 912.

More than ten monasteries with important libraries were built at about this time. The largest, whose influence extended far beyond the island, was Panaghia Panachrantos. Endowed by the Byzantine emperor Nicephorus Phocas (963–969), these buildings were erected on the steep slope of Mount Kataphyghio. Today, a few monks still occupy them. This fortresslike complex of Byzantine cloisters is well worth seeing, as are the Byzantine cruciform cupola church and various later, smaller churches that were incorporated into the layout. One of these is the Aghios Ioannis church, from the fifteenth century, where treatment of the mentally ill was attempted by tying the afflicted to the lone marble column for forty days; during this period, a preacher would read them daily sermons,

lasting for hours, from the evangelists. The marble iconostasis is a lovely example of primitive religious art. It features engraved coats of arms borne by angels and beasts. The Aghios Panteleimon church, from the eighteenth century, is a basilica with a flat roof. Inside are a remarkable choir wall of carved wood, marble slabs with reliefs of plants, and marble candelabra.

At the convent of Aghia Moni, an hour's climb from Batsi, valuable manuscripts and codices are preserved. Most of the churches here were built in the eleventh and twelfth centuries as cruciform structures with cupolas. Only few traces of wall frescos survive in their interiors. The outside walls are built of gray stone framed by narrow bands of red brick. Today, of course, most of them have been whitewashed, including their slate roofs.

The following churches in the Messaria Valley are also worth a visit: (1) Taxiarchis, near Melida, from the eleventh century; (2) Taxiarchis, near the village of Ypsilos, from the eleventh century; (3) Koimisi ("the Death of the Virgin"), in the village of Mesathouri, from the twelfth century; and (4) Taxiarchis, in the village of Messaria. This last church, consecrated to the archangel Michael as the leader of the heavenly hosts *(taxiarchis)*, is the only one that has not been whitewashed. We can thus still see the marble window frames and columns and all of its decoration. The eighteenth-century Aghios Nikolaos church, also in Messaria, has become something of a Byzantine museum, for marble reliefs from old churches in the area have been set into its walls.

Remains of towers and fortresses in the interior of the island date back to the Middle Ages. At that time, fear of attacks by pirates drove the few inhabitants away from the coasts. In the fifteenth century, some

Hermes Psychopompos:
relief from an ancient tomb.

2,000 people lived on Andros. On the north of the island stands the half-ruined Venetian tower of Makrotantalos. Until only a few decades ago it was still well preserved, but then a British warship chose it as a target during maneuvers. Above the Bay of Korthi, the ruins of a medieval town remain on the summit of a 2,000-foot hill: dwellings, churches, cisterns, walls more than 6 feet thick, and towers.

Chora became the capital in the Middle Ages. Its fortification wall has been destroyed; however, a number of its buildings have preserved their fortresslike character. They turn their backs on the sea, and their façades, huddled together and with high-placed windows, face the interior. At the tip of the peninsula, at the top of a steep cliff, stands another half-fallen Venetian tower. It was once part of the fortress built by the Venetian Marino Dandolo, nephew of the famous doge and general Enrico Dandolo, when he captured Andros in 1207. The arched stone bridge connecting the rock on which this tower stands and

the town has withstood the sea salts.

The Archeological Museum, which was endowed by the Goulandris family and opened in Chora in 1981, contains on the ground floor a number of marble statues from the ancient capital of Palaiopolis as well as the "great female Heracles" and Hermes, which were returned to Andros from the National Museum in Athens after much hue and cry. In addition, one can see mosaic floors from Early Christian basilicas. The geometric pottery on the second floor, only recently discovered on the west coast of Andros, is particularly interesting. Those interested in modern Greek art will also find in Chora a collection of sculptures and paintings from the nineteenth and twentieth centuries: the Andros Museum of Modern Art is also a foundation of Basil and Elise Goulandris.

IN THE SEVENTEENTH AND EIGHTEENTH CENTURIES, Andros, like various other islands of the Cyclades, was granted privileges by the Sublime Porte, the Ottoman court. As a result, a kind of local feudal government developed. The Kotsambasides, descendants of great Byzantine and Crusader families, became the administrative representatives of the Turks and were responsible for keeping order. Trade and travel were under their control, thus enhancing their wealth. On their estates, they built patrician houses with three stories, high iron doors, embrasures, cellars, and places where the women could be hidden securely during enemy attacks. Unfortunately only a few of these private fortresses still stand, and these are half-ruined. A great breach separated the ruling class from the peasants, one that was not overcome until very recently and that developed on almost no other island. For example, a peasant never approached his lord's estate on the back of his donkey.

When he saw the tower from afar, he dismounted and continued humbly on foot; if he caught sight of any of his masters, he doffed his cap. When the nobles then lost their wealth, they held on to their pride, especially when dealing with the *nouveaux riches* shippers who became the monied class after the liberation from Turkish rule in the nineteenth century. For the old rich, marriage with the new rich continued to be forbidden.

The first trading vessels were built in Chora and the neighboring harbor of Stenies. Then the Andriots began to buy larger ships from the nearby island of Syros. Most of the young men of the island became sailors or captains. Andros grew rich from shipping, and the first successful shippers loaned money to the needy at low interest. In the more remote villages, you can still see signs of this eighteenth- and nineteenth-century flowering. It is rewarding to seek out some of the dwellings, with their lovely courtyards and charming dovecotes, hidden among cypress, olive, and lemon trees. A number of shipping magnates who now live in Paris, London, or New York return to the island in the summer and donate generously to its institutions.

Before leaving Andros, you should also visit the valley of Korthi. At the intersection near Stavropeda, the road branches off to the south, first running through barren hills; the visitor is impressed here by the walls built of loose stones *(xerolithies)* that the peasants have built around their small tracts of land. The valley of Korthi then rewards those who delight in lush vegetation. In Ano Korthi, you should see the abandoned patrician houses and the twelfth-century church; in Kato Korthi, the sandy beach that seems to continue endlessly.

KYTHNOS

YOU HAVE JUST ARRIVED ON KYTHNOS, AT MERIcha, either by steamship from Piraeus or, in summer, by ferry from Rafina, on the north coast of Attica. You may have suffered from the ceaseless wind of the Aegean or be disappointed by the treeless, barren landscape, but you should not decide that your voyage has been a mistake. Kythnos makes a deceptive first impression, and the hasty visitor can scarcely discover this island's unique beauty. You need time for long, contemplative walks and encounters with the inhabitants. The people here are enmeshed in their traditions, and it is well worth getting to know them in their everyday lives, especially when they are celebrating—if possible, at a marvelous Kythnian wedding. The Kythnians are excellent musicians and untiring dancers.

However, everyday life on Kythnos revolves around work. The island, some 33 square miles in area, lying south of Keos and north of Seriphos, produces legumes, barley, wine, figs, excellent honey, and the

The island of Kythnos.

1. *Mericha*
2. *Chora (Kythnos, Messaria)*
3. *Loutra*
4. *Sylakkas (Dryopis)*
5. *Kanala*

Kythnian cheese famous since antiquity *(kythneios tyros)*. The island's iron mines have not been worked since World War II. But fishing has grown more profitable. The sandy bays—especially the one at Aghia Irini—are truly fishermen's paradises.

AT SOME POINT IN THE DIM PAST THE LEGEND-ary hero Kythnos is supposed to have land-ed here with his Dryopes from Euboea. Since then, the island has borne his name. Later the Ionians came and settled here. The Kythnians first chose to be neutral dur-ing the Persian Wars, but later two of their ships fought in the battles of Salamis and Cape Artemisium. Also, between 431 and 404 B.C., the Kythnians were allies of the Athenians against the Spartans in the Pelo-ponnesian Wars. Aristotle praised the con-stitution of Kythnos in his *Kythnion Politeia.*

In 338 B.C., the Macedonians ruled the is-land, later the Egyptian Ptolemids, the suc-cessors of Alexander the Great, and then once more the Macedonians, who estab-lished such a powerful garrison on Kythnos in 202 B.C. that the Romans were repulsed on more than one occasion, finally con-quering the island in 146 B.C. But the Ro-mans were no more permanent than their predecessors. In 68 B.C., a dangerous pirate of the Aegean named Pseudo-Nero at-tacked Kythnos with his band and made the island his base. But Calpurnius Aperna-tus, the Roman governor of Galatia and Pamphylia, put him to death. The Romans then made Kythnos a place of exile. Even in our century, the Greek dictator Metaxas (1936–1940) exiled Panaiotis Kanellopou-los, later prime minister, to this island.

In antiquity, Kythnos was not only an in-ternational battleground but also a haven of the arts. The painter Timanthes (416–376 B.C.) was, as Pliny the Elder related, a master of suggestion: the less he depicted, the more one was able to imagine in his works. And therefore he emerged victori-ous over his no less famous competitor Parrhasius. *The Sacrifice of Iphigenia* was Timanthes's most widely known work. An-other famous painter, Cydias, born on Kythnos in 320 B.C., painted in the manner of Egyptian mummy portraits—with colors mixed with wax, or in encaustic. Centuries later, the Roman collector Ortensio pur-chased Cydias's *Argonauts* for 164 talents and presented the painting to his wife.

The island's stormy history—which stands in sharp contrast to its present-day tranquility—continued into more modern times. The Venetians ruled here for a time, and after the Turks gained control, one of the Venetian families, the Gosadinos, was permitted to govern until 1617, when they were finally driven out. When the liber-ation from Ottoman rule was won—Kyth-nos had been one of the first islands to take part in the uprising of March 25, 1821—ju-bilation knew no bounds, even though the Turks had not been as oppressive here as elsewhere.

FROM THE SMALL HARBOR OF MERICHA, WHERE you landed, an asphalt road runs to Chora, the capital of the island, which is reminis-cent of countless towns in the Cyclades; it has tightly packed, whitewashed buildings, alleys paved with dark slates, and a few windmills and churches from the sixteenth and seventeenth centuries. Worth seeing are the sanctuary screens and icons in the churches of Aghia Triada, Aghios Savvas, Soteira, and Theologos. In this vicinity, too, some ancient graves and some remains from the Roman period have been found.

It is well worth taking an hour's hike up from Chora, also known as Messaria, across a narrow spit of land to the Kastro, a fortress built atop a rock that thrusts 1,650 feet out of the sea. We do not know when the Kastro was constructed; within its defense walls only some ruined buildings and churches are left. The Kastro was destroyed in 1537 by pirate Chaireddin Barbarossa. Legend has it that the ruler of the island, the *archon*, barely managed to escape on his horse, which collapsed beneath him on the site of the present-day Chora, which was thus founded as an extension of the old Kastro.

In Chora, one can visit the church of Aghia Triada (Holy Trinity), but unfortunately its seventeenth-century frescos have been destroyed. The other churches in Chora are Aghios Savvas, from 1613, Soteira (Holy Virgin Salvatorix), and Aghios Nikolaos, the patron saint of sailors, which boasts icons by Antonis Skordilis (circa 1700). His icon of the Holy Virgin in the church of Panaghia Kanala—also well worth a visit for its surroundings—is believed by the inhabitants to work miracles. The Skordilises were a family of painters from Crete who, like many other Cretans, fled to Kythnos after the Turks conquered their own island. Their icons, also found in other churches in Chora, derive from the Cretan-Venetian school. In the church of Aghios Ioannis Theologos, we can admire, among others, the remarkable icon of the Panaghia Athenia (Athenian Holy Virgin), which is said to have swum to Kythnos

after the Turks captured Athens.

From Chora, you can drive to the small harbor and spa of Loutra in ten minutes. The natural healing waters of Loutra are highly prized. The spring water of Aghioi Anarghyroi is 38.6° C (97.6° F); that of the Kakaros spring is 52.3° C (116.1° F). They are widely recommended for rheumatism and arthritis. Queen Amalia of Bavaria had a hotel built here in 1858 so that the baths' facilities would be more widely accessible. Since then, of course, both the hotel (now called the Xenia) and the baths have been modernized. For some time after the twelfth century, Kythnos was called Thermia because of its hot springs; in the Venetian dialect Thermia became Fermena. Oddly enough, the ancients made no mention of the Kythnos springs, though those of Ypati or Aidipsos on Euboea were frequently praised by writers of that time. Is this because Mount Soros, a now extinct volcano, only brought forth healing waters after a later eruption? The shepherds have an interesting belief that if one throws an animal into the great crater of Mount Soros, it will reappear unharmed in Loutra by way of an underground passageway.

The picturesque village of Sylakkas (Dryopis) is divided into two parts by a cascading stream. Nearby is the Sanctuary Cave, with stalactites and mysterious chambers.

The ancient town on Kythnos is Vryokastro. The hiker first encounters a magical view of a green gate and lemon trees, then a tower. Legend has it that a king built this tower to shelter the townswomen in case of an attack by pirates.

Vryokastro lies on a spit of land between two bays of remarkable beauty. You can still see remains of carefully hewn stone blocks from the fortifications, of temple foundations, altars, and water mains. The island just offshore, once a part of Kythnos, is also called Vryokastro and boasts the traces of an agora. Countless graves have been discovered around the bays outside the ancient ring wall. They contained coins, clay vessels, and gold jewelry. In this area a great number of tomb reliefs have also been found. During the final centuries of antiquity, Vryokastro was held to be an impregnable fortress.

SYROS

SHIPS APPROACHING THE HARBOR OF HERMOUpolis, the capital of Syros, on the east side of the island, are greeted by two distant hills crowned by churches. The Greek Orthodox church of Aghios Nikolaos stands on the right-hand one; the ancient Catholic church of St. George, on the left—two different worlds, but harmonious nonetheless.

These hills are strewn with buildings. There is an air of nostalgia in the narrow alleys upon which the venerable buildings of the town press in with their terraces. From the lower town, a broad flight of steps leads up the left-hand hill to Upper Syros, the medieval Ano Syros, which seems to have nearly died out beginning in the early nineteenth century. At about the same time Hermoupolis, which climbs up the right-hand hill, developed into an economically and culturally important center of neo-Hellenism.

The story of Syros goes back a long way, though it does not appear to have been prominent in antiquity. Homer mentioned the island in the *Odyssey,* calling it Syrie and describing it as being rich in cattle, sheep, wine, and grain. But even then Syros was underpopulated, though there is mention of two powerful city-states. Homer also spoke of attacks and plundering by the Phoenicians. Archeological digs have located prehistoric settlements, near the modern villages of Chalandriani and Kastrio, and unearthed countless finds.

In historic times, the small harbor of Grammata, on the northwest coast, has offered a welcome refuge to mariners during storms. On the surrounding cliffs are found testimonials: hundreds of inscriptions, prayers, expressions of gratitude from Roman and Byzantine days.

In the thirteenth century, Venetian rule began on the Cyclades, including Syros. Galleys brought Duke Marco Sanudo, who chose the island of Naxos as his main residence, and penniless Italian peasants came to share the island with the poor Syriots. In the fifteenth century, the traveler Buondelmondi related that the people of Syros lived on goat's meat and carob beans. He further reported that they had tried to fortify their hilltop settlements with deep trenches and strong walls out of fear of attacks by pirates. This is the origin of the medieval town of Ano Syros.

Gradually, the Byzantine Empire collapsed, and the pope began to dispatch Catholic priests to the Aegean Islands. The dukes of Naxos supported him. The Greek Orthodox clergy was no match in terms of education for their Roman Catholic counterparts, especially on Syros. In the Middle Ages, Syros was called "the Pope's Island." In the eighteenth century, there were 6,000 Greek Catholics living here and only 12 Greek Orthodox families. The rest of Greece did not regard the Syriots with any prejudice; converts to Catholicism were still considered true Greeks who preserved their heritage and traditions.

The Roman Catholic clergy maintained its influence on Syros even after the Venetian flag of St. Mark gave way to the Ottoman crescent in 1537. In the sixteenth century, the Sublime Porte concluded a treaty that enabled France to assume protection of the Catholics in Greece and the Middle East. French Capuchin monks founded a monastery on Syros in 1633, and they took over the administration of the courts, the schools, and the care of the sick. Jesuits constructed a monastery in Ano Syros in 1747. It is still standing, as is the Catholic school of the Ursulines, who settled here in 1751.

European ships frequently dropped anchor in the harbor of Syros because their crews were ceremonially received by the consuls of France, Venice, Russia, and England and served delicious bread, excellent wine, and figs.

The Greek war of liberation from Turkish rule that began in 1821 marked a change in the life of Syros, though the island did not itself participate in the uprising. Instead, it remained neutral for three years, unobtrusively protected by the French. Thousands of Greek refugees from the Peloponnesus, Chios, Crete, Macedonia, Psara, and Hydra—people who had lost all their possessions and had barely managed to escape death or enslavement—sought refuge on the peaceful island during that time. The harbor, previously so calm, presented a colorful picture of the most varied regional costumes: the wide trousers of the Hydriots, Cretan headscarves, the elegant clothing of Smyrna. All kinds of dialects were jumbled together in a miniature chaos of people and ethnic groups. And yet a characteristic of all Greeks came to the fore: the ability to work with little, using improvisation, adaptability, and imagination, and to take care of oneself successfully. First the newcomers built barracks; then they cultivated the barren fields, knocked some boats together, constructed some primitive docks, and began to conduct foreign trade. In this way, a new harbor town arose. They named it in honor of the ancient god of trade, Hermes, calling it Hermoupolis. Within three years, the island was able to supply the Greek freedom fighters with food and supplies. The wounded were cared for in the Elpis ("hope") Hospital, built in 1826.

Hermoupolis rapidly became the center for the New Greeks. It was a progressive, flourishing town whose citizens were open to the ideas of the Enlightenment and the French Revolution. Syriot contact with these European movements was enhanced by the fact that the island gradually became a major stopover in the eastern Aegean. On the one hand, large numbers of foreigners docked here. On the other, Syriot merchants returned home after extensive journeys through the capitals of western Europe, imbued with the desires to give their children a solid education, to adorn their houses, and generally to raise their standard of living.

A grammar school was opened here in 1823; a girls' preparatory school followed

Drawing of Syros from Annie Brassey's Sunshine and Storm in the East, *1890.*

in 1828, then a naval school, and, in 1833, a literary society. Writers attended literary salons like those in Paris and made names for themselves in the new Greek world of letters. A distinguished printing house has operated here since 1828, publishing literary and scientific works. Journalism flourished; some 200 newspapers were founded on Syros during the nineteenth century. In 1831, there was even a bilingual one, in Greek and French. The Volunteer Theater began staging its productions in a coffeehouse in 1826, and since 1840, Italian troupes frequently visited the island; their operas enjoyed special popularity here. The people of Hermoupolis built a cenotaph to honor those who had fallen in the war of liberation—the first use of a form of memorial that was imitated internationally after World War I.

consigned grain in Russia, iron and cotton in England, wool in Asia Minor, fabrics in Germany, mastic on Chios, wine on Samos. They transported foodstuffs from western European harbors to Turkey, and they exported Syriot products. For on the island itself, mills ground its grain, factories spun its cotton and silk, and there were glass blowers, olive presses, hat factories, and famous potteries. Today, the ships' figureheads produced here are highly sought after, and blacksmithing, an old, traditional craft of the island, is especially popular. Artfully crafted iron gratings, still to be seen on many of the old buildings, are leftovers from Syros's "Golden Century."

As you can read in countless travel descriptions from the nineteenth century, Hermoupolis resembled western European cities in its appearance and quality of life more than any other city in the eastern Mediterranean. Broad, paved streets led into spacious squares. The French architect Chabeau came to Syros especially to construct the Community Club in 1861 and, a year later, the theater, a charming copy of La Scala in Milan. The German architect Ernst Ziller built the monumental City Hall in 1876. More and more private houses were built in the neo-Classical style. Rich merchant and shipping families would spend the summer months at their huge villas, some of which were constructed in imitation of western European castles— odd sights under the Aegean sun. Many of them can still be seen, though in desolate condition, in the favorite holiday resort of Della Grazia. Months before Carnival, the highlight of the year, the celebrants would fervently study the latest fashion magazines from Paris and Vienna. The balls would begin with a polonaise and end with hot chocolate, something totally new to Greece at that time.

Economic prosperity on the new Syros kept pace with the island's cultural flowering. Once the first shipyards were established, they soon instituted mass-production techniques. Agencies of foreign corporations and the first Greek shipping and insurance societies opened. Foreign ships were constantly dropping anchor to take on supplies and learn the new trading prices, which were fixed here. Syriot ships

In his travelogue, the French writer Théophile Gautier related that he enjoyed the best lemon ice he had ever tasted in Hermoupolis. The cosmopolitan character, the industry, the women dressed in Paris fashions and walking along the shore on their husbands' arms—all made an indelible impression on him. Gautier spent one evening on a platform out on the sea, on which a Hungarian orchestra played a potpourri of Italian opera.

The politics of the citizens of Hermoupolis were by no means conservative, as one might suspect of such a well-to-do bourgeoisie. They were consistently on the side of the opposition, first against the first governor of the new Greek state, Kapodistrias, in 1830; later, in 1862, they supported rebels against Otto, the Bavarian prince who had been made the king of Greece.

Throughout this golden age, the peasants and workers remained unaffected by foreign movements, influences, and fashions. They continued living with their Greek traditions, some harboring memories as well of their lost homeland in Asia Minor. The dance called the *syrtaki* that has become well known abroad thanks to the film *Zorba the Greek* is a variation of the Syriot *zeimbekiko*. The mournful folksongs and dances of Syros are frequently performed in the quarters of Piraeus by Syriots who have emigrated to the mainland. (The poor Syriots leave for Piraeus, while the rich leave for Athens or western Europe.)

Once-flourishing Hermoupolis became an unimportant provincial town once the Corinth Canal was opened in 1893. This canal made the great revival of Piraeus possible when wars cut off trade with the cities on the Black Sea and in Asia Minor.

TENOS

TENOS LIES SOUTHWEST OF ANDROS, NORTHEAST of Syros, and quite close to the famous Mykonos. Though boats from Piraeus and Rafina go to Tenos at least twice a day, the island is hardly visited by foreigners. For the Greeks, however, it is the best-known island in the Aegean. Thousands of pious Greeks come here throughout the year, but especially on March 25 and August 15, to visit the church that houses the miracle-working icon of the Holy Virgin (Panaghia Megalochari). During the entire month of August, Chora—the harbor town, capital of the island, and home of this church—swarms with Orthodox pilgrims from all parts of Greece and beyond. Often, these pilgrims—young and old, healthy and infirm, mothers and children—come for only a few hours to make a wish, fulfill a promise, find consolation, all hoping for direct assistance from the Holy Virgin. If one is not averse to such mobs, then one really ought to visit Tenos once, on August 15, and experience the now-rare phenomenon of living faith, indeed religious ecstasy.

The church of Panaghia Evangelistria was built between 1828 and 1830 on the spot where, legend has it, the miraculous

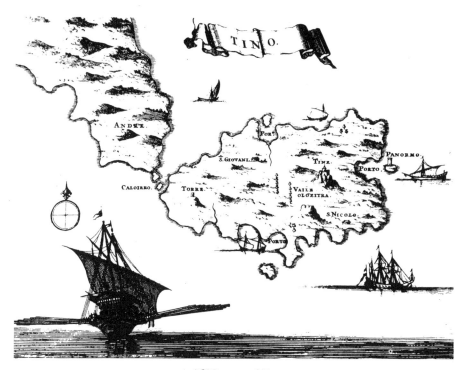

A 1688 map of Tenos.

discovery of the Panaghia Icon was made. It is said that the Holy Virgin appeared in a dream to Hosia Pelaghia, a nun in the Byzantine Maria cloister, not far from Chora, and told her where the icon painted by the evangelist Luke might be found. The Teniots, who are experienced workers in marble, proved both their skill and their piety in the construction of this church. In creat-

ing its monumental decorations, they used marble from the quarries lying on the north side of the island and from the ancient temple to Poseidon; marble was even brought from Paros and from the ancient ruins on the nearby island of Delos. This classical building, with its apparently Baroque staircase and tall bell tower, is one of the most beautiful examples of nineteenth-

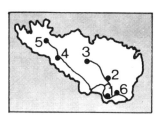

The island of Tenos.

1. *Chora*
2. *Dio Choria*
3. *Kalloni*
4. *Isternia*
5. *Panormos*
6. *Site of ancient Tenos*

Chora, Tenos: drawing by J. B. Hilair, c. 1782.

century Greek architecture. The small, three-aisle interior of the main church is filled with countless votive offerings: hundreds of silver and gold hanging oil lamps, bronze and gold candelabra, thousands of small, usually tin, representations of parts of the body (eyes, hands, feet, whole human figures, and so on), and luxurious jewels. They all represent thanks from sick people or sailors faced with death who vowed to bring a gift here in remembrance of their hour of need. Other people donate money, olive oil for the lamps, or the huge beeswax candles, often as tall as a man, that burn in the church all year round. The icon itself, depicting the Annunciation, is hardly visible any longer, having been obscured by layer upon layer of precious votive offerings.

This "little Lourdes" of Greece is not only of interest to the Orthodox faithful, however. Belonging to the structural complex of the church of the Panaghia are 120 smaller whitewashed spaces, the *kellia*, or cells, arrayed about an arcaded inner courtyard paved with marble. This complex, called the Panhellenic Foundation Evangelistria, is a public institution that contains, among other collections, the Museum of Tenos Artists. Here you can see works from the nineteenth and twentieth centuries, either originals or plaster copies of works by sculptors including Chalepas, Sóchos, Philippotis, Tompros, all of whom were born in Pyrghos, the marble district on the island's north coast. This museum of Tenos also houses various works by Nicephorus Lytras (1832–1904) and the landscape painters Nikolaos and Periklis Lytras.

Next door is a spacious hall recently transformed into a museum of post-Byzantine art: carved wooden iconostases (sanctuary screens) brought here from remote village churches, candelabra, vestments, ecclesiastical objects, but primarily small icons make up the bulk of this small museum and document the religious life and artistry of the medieval Teniots.

Since so little is known about the history of the island during the Byzantine period, this small collection and the churches of the island enable one to sense something of the living tradition of the Byzantine culture, how it has been preserved for centuries in religious life and art. From the Late Byzantine and especially from the post-Byzantine periods, however, written documents, monuments, and works of art are plentiful.

Following the Crusaders' conquest of Constantinople in 1204, the Venetians occupied the Aegean Islands. From 1207 to 1390, Tenos was ruled by the well-known Ghisi family. And it remained under Venetian rule until it was the last of the Cyclades to fall to the Turks. Very few monuments have survived to attest to the Venetian occupation of the island, and scarcely any Venetian influences on art and native crafts are evident. Even Italian painting has left only a few stylistic traces on icon painting, as one can see in the collection of the Panaghia Megalochori.

In the inner courtyard of the church of the Panaghia, another art gallery recently opened. Copies of famous Renaissance paintings are exhibited here, along with original works by modern Greek painters such as Iakobides, Volanakis, Parthenis, and Bouzianis.

A narrow paved street leads directly from the monumental portal of the Panaghia church complex to the harbor. It is one of the few streets in Chora, and its small merchants' stands preserve something of the picturesqueness of the town.

In contrast to this street, the new, broad, asphalt boulevard, running parallel to it, is an example of the modern civilization that

Xomburgo: a 1688 Dutch drawing.

has sadly distorted the character of the town. On this street, quite near the church of the Panaghia, stands the Archeological Museum, whose exhibits illustrate the history of the island in antiquity.

It appears that Tenos has been settled since the third millennium B.C. But because only isolated finds of shards and obsidian have been made, mainly near Vrekastro (a twenty-minute hike east of Chora), little about this very early period is known for certain. We do know, however, that the island was inhabited since the eleventh century B.C., the Geometric period, and had its own ceramic workshops. Tombs containing Geometric vases have been found in Kardiani and Ktikados. The most important finds revealing the life, art, and religion of these ancient people were made by Kontoleon at Xomburgo, some 8 miles from Chora. These discoveries are important to understanding not only the history of the island but also the Greek art of vase making in general, and they are on display in the museum. They include gigantic clay vessels, known as *pithoi*, ornamented with reliefs made separately and later added to them. The decoration of these vases incorporates figural representations from Greek myths and sagas. The *pithoi* were produced locally, are dated to the late eighth and seventh centuries B.C., and bear witness to the flowering of art in the Cyclades.

Smaller vases and marble fragments reveal the skill of the Teniots in the sixth century B.C. One finely modeled marble grave stele with the figure of a young man in a severe style dates from the early fifth century B.C. The fourth century is represented by a stele fragment depicting a hunter, which is dated to circa 350 B.C. Sculptures from the Hellenistic period, the third and second centuries B.C., are also exhibited in the museum and its small inner courtyard. Dolphins, Nereids, and fragments of various sea creatures come from the nearby temple to Poseidon. Statues, Roman busts, and various sculptural fragments and mosaics transport the visitor into the Roman period. The inscriptions on view are of particular interest to the specialist. Finally, there is a wonderful sundial, the best-preserved one we have from antiquity.

Not far from the Archeological Museum, behind the church of the Panaghia, you can see the remains of the ancient town wall. This harbor town, called Asty in the surviving inscriptions, was probably founded in the fifth century B.C., while the major city,

the *polis,* lay in the island's interior, near Xomburgo, and was already in existence in the Geometric period. Near the church of the Panaghia, there are also the remains of ancient aqueducts.

OUTSIDE CHORA, NEAR STAVROS (A TWENTY-MINute walk), the remains of the ancient harbor are still visible. Nor far from this lovely bay, only ten minutes, the shrines to Poseidon and Amphitrite stand on the Kionia Plain. Surviving from this famous sanctuary, founded in the third century B.C., are a few remains, basically only foundations. In some spots, the wall surrounding the temenos is still easily recognizable. The temple sculptures are now in the museum at Chora. Right next to the temple are the altar and a Doric portico that served as a dining hall for the countless pilgrims to the shrine. The exedra, where statues of the gods presumably stood, still impresses the visitor with its size.

The present-day condition of the sanctuary only hints at its ancient splendor. Ancient writings, inscriptions, and the few surviving votive offerings and coins permit

Poseidon's contest with Athena: from an ancient vase painting.

The wedding of Poseidon and Amphitrite: detail from an ancient marble.

us to form a better understanding of the history of the shrine and its influence throughout the Greek world. We learn, for example, that the cult of Poseidon on Tenos was very old, for according to legend the god once freed the island from a plague of serpents. Poseidon was first revered here as a god of healing. Later, possibly in the third century B.C., his wife Amphitrite, the protectress of seafarers, also found a place within the sanctuary. The inscriptions surviving speak of statues dedicated to the two deities by persons who had been healed or otherwise favored. A major annual festival, the Posideia, was held here.

This festival can be compared to the modern *paneghyri* (celebration) of the Panaghia, for it brought Greeks from the most remote parts of the country to Tenos. Coins that have been found in the sanctuary—from Sicyon, Thessalonike, Sipylon in Magnesia (Asia Minor), Tarentum, Croton, Rhegium, and elsewhere—suggest the far-flung origins of its pilgrims. The marble steles erected within the precinct also attest to visitors from all sections of Greece. The ancient authors tell of the huge crowds that the shrine attracted from the third century B.C. until late antiquity. The Tenos shrine, unlike the temple to Apollo on Delos, even enjoyed a second flowering

during the Roman Empire, as is shown by a number of inscriptions, fragments of statues, and bases of statues. A verse written in the time of Augustus commented: "... who would have thought to see Delos abandoned and Tenos continuing to thrive?"

A WALK OR A SHORT DRIVE OUT OF CHORA INTO the vicinity of the church of Aghia Trias (Holy Trinity) brings the visitor back into the modern age. This whitewashed church, built in the early eighteenth century, houses an interesting collection of folk art. Among the loveliest examples are the stone or marble slabs called *pheggites* (*phego* means "shine"), which ornamented the upper parts of doors and windows. These *pheggites* are worked either in the form of flat reliefs or with popular motifs that derived from the Byzantine or Venetian decorative tradition: cypresses, birds, the double eagle with the insignia of the Byzantine emperors, the sun, trees, ships, and crosses are most frequent. One encounters these *pheggites* everywhere on the island—on churches, chapels, private houses, even on dovecotes and cemetery gateways. Most are the work of anonymous stonecutters; the dates of their creation are seldom given. The oldest examples known to us bear the date 1778.

If you drive into the interior of Tenos,

you can appreciate the true character of the island and its almost unknown side: many mountains with springs and caves on their slopes, green valleys, and plains. A high promontory, Mount Tsiknias (2,250 feet), dominates the island. According to legend, Aeolus, the god of the winds, had his seat on this mountain. The basis of this myth is easy to understand, for Tenos is still exposed to fierce north winds. For this reason, and doubtless even more for fear of the pirates who terrorized the Aegean for centuries, the Teniots built their villages, except for Panormos, in the interior. In centuries of patient effort, the inhabitants have transformed the mountain slopes into fertile terraces that give the landscape a picturesque quality.

In nearly every field, on nearly every cliff, and throughout the valleys, white-washed churches and chapels appear. There are 800 of them on Tenos. Yet these churches are outdone in both number and elegance by another characteristic feature of the island—its nearly 1,300 white and richly decorated dovecotes. These can be seen everywhere, but they are most numerous near the village of Tarambados. Nearly every field on Tenos has a family chapel or a dovecote, often both.

Today, there are forty-eight inhabited villages—easily reached by bus—but there were sixty-seven in the eighteenth century. The villages of Tenos are virtually untouched by modern civilization, but they are gradually being abandoned by their inhabitants, who leave for Chora and often Athens in search of a more promising future. A square paved with marble or slate generally forms the heart of the Teniot village; here, there will be one or more *kapheneia* and *pantopoleia*, the small shops that sell all the goods the villagers need. Narrow alleyways paved with slates or

Servants of Tenos: drawing by J. B. Hilair, c. 1782.

cobblestones often lead through arched passageways, *kamares*, built of dry stone walls and roofed with stone slabs and wooden beams. These *kamares* presumably originated under Venetian influence or out of fear of pirates; protection from the north wind was doubtless another factor in their development.

Quite close to the harbor, on Mount Kechrovouni, lies the Mary Cloister, which is thought to have been founded in the twelfth century. The cloister comprises a small but interesting church with an elegant bell tower, thirty-eight cells for its ninety nuns, and narrow, paved, whitewashed alleyways. The villages Triantaros, Dio Choria, and Arnados, which lie near the cloister, offer a broad panorama of the island and its capital.

North of the cloisters, there are twenty tiny white villages, collectively called *Pano Meria* ("upper part"). In the village of Steni, you can visit the church of Aghios Antonios, with its very beautiful seventeenth-century iconostasis. For those interested in the geology of the island, a hike to Phalatados and Volax is highly recommended.

The visitor to Tenos ought to see the area around Xomburgo, for since antiquity this tall rock (2,100 feet) has been the symbol of the island. Xomburgo lies near the lovely village of Tripotamos, eight miles from Chora. On the summit of the mountain you can see the remains of the Venetian fortifications; this fortress and the Venetian capital were completely ruined and abandoned in 1715, when the Turks conquered the island. South and east of the mountain are the foundations of the ancient city, the *polis* of Tenos. Here too was the shrine to Demeter in which the relief *pithoi* now in the museum were discovered.

From Xomburgo, you proceed through the island's Catholic villages, a living reminder of the Venetian occupation. Among them are Kampos and Xinara, the seat of the Catholic bishopric of all of the Cyclades. The large village of Loutra has almost-bourgeois houses, fountains, and an Ursuline convent. Not far away is the beautiful Kolymbithra Bay. The lands around the villages of Komi and Kalloni comprise the green and fertile "gardens" of the island. Northwest of Xomburgo, you come across the villages in the Tarambados region, where the loveliest and most numerous dovecotes are found.

After a long drive, the large village of Kardiani looms before the traveler. It is built like an amphitheater and boasts the church of Aghios Antonios. Isternia, not far from Kardiani, is one of the largest and most beautiful towns on the island. Among its highlights are spacious paved squares

Citizens of Tenos:
drawing by J. B. Hilair, c. 1782.

with plane trees, narrow, white alleyways, the church of Aghios Athanasios, from 1453, and the Katapoliani church, built in 1786.

Just before coming to the most distant village on Tenos, you pass the church of Hosia Xeni. A number of legends and miracles associated with it make it especially beloved by the islanders.

Pyrghos (Pirgos) is the village farthest from Chora. Its inhabitants have demonstrated their artistic gifts on every wall in this village. It is no coincidence that the most important Greek artists in the nineteenth and twentieth centuries were born here. The nearby marble quarries also played a part in this. The small museum of the sculptor Chalepas, the art school, the entrances to the houses, the vaulted passageways, and especially the cemetery reveal the artistic taste and skill of the people of Pyrghos. Less than 2 miles away is the only village built on the shore; this is Panormos, facing Andros.

To name only some of these villages is to do an injustice to the rest, for all of them together make up the unique character of Tenos. And similarly, though it is impossible to name them all, every church and chapel on the island is worth seeing. Each of them, even the small one-room chapels, is interesting and likely to be decorated inside with primitive frescos. Wooden or marble iconostases (sanctuary screens) complete the picture of these churches and attest to the coexisting Byzantine and Venetian traditions on Tenos.

To experience the true character of the people of the island, you definitely ought to stay somewhere else than Chora. The large hotels next to the harbor are not particularly inviting, and the constant stream of pilgrims there has given rise to a devotional industry that some find off putting. However, in the small villages, you can find that openness, radiant friendliness, and hospitality that characterize the inhabitants of all of the Aegean Islands.

MYKONOS

MYKONOS POSSESSES THE INCOMPARABLE BEAUTY that is characteristic of all the Cyclades. But whereas the landscape of nearby Paros, which boasts the famous white, nearly transparent marble of the antique masterpieces, gives an impression of being somehow "blonde," the granite of Mykonos appears much darker and somewhat harsh, with a touch of severity. Because of the Mykoniots' critical manner, both natives and strangers have given them a number of nicknames that are the source of much good humor here.

The highest mountain peaks on Mykonos rise little more than 1,150 feet above sea level. Yet they are covered with massive rocks that may have given rise to the old myth that the Titans defeated by Heracles lie buried here.

AN ENGLISHMAN WROTE A TRAVEL BOOK ON Mykonos in 1675. He reported that he had been unable to find any traces of antiquity on the island, while the other islands—Naxos, Melos, Thira (Santorin)—were famous for their ancient treasures. Nearby, however, is Delos, sometimes called the Greek Pompeii and, like Mykonos, granite-colored, dark, and harsh. Twice a day, a boat leaves for Delos. One can also rent a large motorboat to cross the strait separating the two islands, if one is prepared to brave the turbulent seas whipped by the north wind.

But even on Mykonos there are finds and remains from all the ages of the past. From Byzantine times there are finely worked wooden sanctuary screens and beautiful icons in many of the churches. From the days of the Venetians (1200–1537) there are gilt mirrors, chests, and tables everywhere. Following the Venetians came the

Turks, who conquered Mykonos in 1537 and ruled it, except for one brief Russian occupation (1770–1774), for nearly three centuries. But they did not leave behind any of the monuments, such as wells and fountains encased in stone or marble, that they did in most of the places they controlled. This could be because Mykonos has always had a shortage of water (even today, its houses have flat roofs from which rain water is channeled into cisterns that supply drinking water). On the other hand, there are few springs on any of the Cyclades.

Only in the harbor town on the western shore of the island are there three fountains on a small square, the Tria Pigadia. Here the buildings are pressed tightly together, and the labyrinthine streets were constructed deliberately for reasons of defense; pirates used to plague Mykonos. The confusing network of streets also provides protection from the north wind, catching and breaking its force. The wind is known as the "chair wind" *(kareklatos)*, for it is often so strong that it sweeps the chairs from the outdoor coffeehouses into the harbor. Since it often rings the churchbells, it is also called the "bell wind" *(kambanatos)*.

The houses of Mykonos, without exception, are white. So are the churches, the windmills, the dovecotes—everything, in fact, that human beings have built. The visitor may well imagine that he or she is in North Africa rather than Greece. For Greek architecture and sculpture have generally striven for color since time immemorial, not for mere white. Throughout the mainland and on the islands, everywhere one still runs across the brick red and ochre that were favored by the painter Polygnotus in antiquity. The great sculptor Auguste Rodin once remarked that the Greeks sought color and form simulta-

neously, for the well-shaped form justifies the color and the appropriate color enhances the form.

But on Mykonos, as on most of the Cyclades, white predominates—except perhaps for the cupolas of churches, which are sometimes painted red, light blue, or even black. Otherwise, white—on houses, staircases, entrances, stone benches—is ubiquitous. The reasons are hygienic, not aesthetic, for whitewash disinfects. Thus, the Mykoniots paint everything but the wooden doors and the tree trunks at least once a year, generally just before Easter, in order to keep their buildings clean in the easiest, cheapest way possible.

This white color is blinding in the strong, clear light of the Aegean, and, like the wind, it may disturb some people. But it repels the heat, as do the white clothes that refresh the body in midsummer. And the whiteness of Mykonos is an integral and symbolic part of the island. The Mykoniots use the same whitewash to cover the stone walls that enclose their fields. These are dry stone walls *(xerolithies)*. The uppermost layer only is mortared together to form a pointed gable, permitting rain water to run off faster, and then whitewashed Looking at Mykonos from afar—when approaching it from Delos on the boat, for example—the viewer is struck not only by the white cubes of the houses and chapels but also by these white, stripelike walls that crisscross the island all the way to the water.

In many fields and rocky spots stand dovecotes, beautifully shaped like little temples. Today, unfortunately, they are increasingly falling into ruin. Windmills nestle comfortably in the landscape, round structures with thatched tops. But even more characteristic of the island are its countless small chapels—some 360 of them—and its one-room houses, these "gracious, silent, much-loved worlds" (from *Erophyle*, a work by the Cretan writer Kornaros) that permit all living functions to take place in a single space. The typical one-room house *(monospito)* is a rectangular structure. On one of the narrow sides, a raised wooden floor serves as a sleeping loft; below it is a pantry. The fireplace in one of the opposite corners is used more as a kitchen than as a source of heat. The walls are made of stone and are up to 20 inches thick. Numerous niches are set into them: one for bread, another for the water jug, others for pots and bowls. Every household object has its special place, ensuring order and beauty.

These tiny houses have flat roofs, which are built of wooden beams, reeds—frequently woven into mats—and seaweed, which absorbs the heat, and finally a weatherproof layer of pressed clay. In front of the entrance, there is generally a tiny forecourt or a beautifully proportioned terrace, a place for the family to sit and often sleep if the sky is clear and the night warm, or if the midsummer heat inside the house is unbearable. This custom is common in other areas of Greece as well. Foreigners are frequently bewildered by the fact that "the Greeks build houses so as to sleep outside." The writer Yannopoulos has written that "life in Greece takes place under the open sky," and so it was in the most ancient times. In the *Iliad*, Homer describes houses that had courtyards because the Greek climate permitted, or even required, an outdoor life.

The small chapels that are strewn across the fields and hillsides are roughly the same size and have the same arrangement of space as the one-room houses. Where the raised sleeping loft is found in the *monospito*, the chapel will have the sanctuary with its screen. And it also boasts the forecourt or terrace in front of the entrance. The only difference is in the structure and form of the roof: the flat roof of the cottage is transformed into a cupola above the chapel. The houses of God and people have developed from the same basic form. Frequently the two stand close together, so that God and man are neighbors. They generally had uniform floor plans: chapel on the left, cottage on the right, and between them a small cistern; rain water available for God and mortals.

Inside, every chapel is a magical world. The choir screen wears the glowing, warm colors that are also used to paint boats. The central opening in the choir wall features colorful cotton curtains of the same material every housewife buys in the harbor shops. In the sanctuary screen or on the walls, lovely icons stand in the glow of lamps that are not permitted to run out of oil. Finally, there are the iron candelabra, whose form and construction seem to be tridents of the sea god Poseidon, taken from the mosaics of Delos.

The chapels are consecrated either to God and the Holy Virgin (Panaghia) or to Nikolaos, the patron saint of seafarers. Whenever a sailor faced destruction at sea, he vowed to donate a chapel. What we now see are kept vows; scarcely one man on Mykonos has not kept his vow *(tamma)* and built a chapel with his own hands. One has used wine in the mortar instead of water because that is what he promised. Another, miserably poor, has built his chapel on the flat roof of his house. The Mykoniots call these rooftop chapels the "holy cats" *(ay gatis)* because of their size.

In the harbor town of Mykonos, the narrow streets are lined mostly with two-story buildings. Stone stairs outside lead to the upper floors. The lower and upper levels often belong to different occupants. Condominiums were known in Mykonos long before there were residential towers in Western cities. The upper and lower dwellings have identical floor plans, the same division of rooms: generally a large salon, a smaller room, a kitchen, and a courtyard.

IN ADDITION TO THE HARBOR TOWN, THE SMALLer settlement of Ano-Meria is worth seeing. Set back from the sea and somewhat above sea level, Ano-Meria boasts lovely houses and two important cloisters, one for men and one for women. Here the visitor comes upon structures of a model architectural beauty, totally in harmony with the surrounding landscape. Everywhere in present-day Greece, native architecture reveals this same quality. Every builder, no matter how modest, proceeds to build not only with the logic that comes from purely technical knowledge but also with the love of old traditions that are lodged in the heart. "With reason and with dream," sang the poet Solomos.

DELOS

DELOS LIES IN THE MIDDLE OF THE CYCLADES, which possibly owe their name to the circle *(kyklos)* that they describe around this island. It is reached by motorboat from Mykonos in under an hour. Delos is tiny; a bit more than three miles long, it measures no more than eight-tenths of a mile at its widest spot. Its highest elevation is the 367-foot Mount Cynthus, which explains why the seafarers of legend frequently lost sight of the island. The coasts are inhospitable, precipitous, and undercut by the stormy seas. Delos has little water, and its former fresh-water stream is now a swamp. Due to the nature of the ground—sandstone on top of granite—rain water collects between the two layers in wells and cisterns. The small harbor that was bustling in antiquity is still in use today, though only by the caïque that regularly brings new visitors to the island in the summer months, otherwise only in good weather.

When first becoming acquainted with Delos, you should head directly for the summit of Mount Cynthus. From it, at every hour of the day, you can see all of Delos

Bust of a satyr.

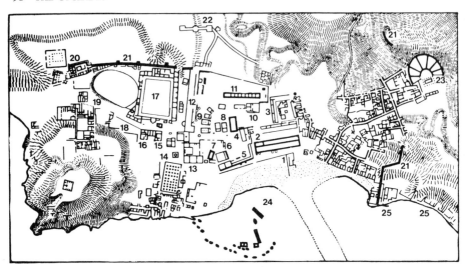

*Map of the sacred precinct on Delos: (1) Pilgrimage way; (2) Philip's portico;
(3) south agora; (4) building of the Naxians; (6) Keraton; (7) Artemision;
(8) temple of Apollo; (9) Four treasuries; (10) Prytaneion; (11) Shrine of the bull;
(12) stoa of Antigonus; (13) Thesmophorion; (14) great hall of columns;
(15) temple of the twelve Olympian gods; (16) temple of Leto; (17) agora of
the Italians; (18) Lion Street; (19) sacred lake; (20) Lake Palaestra;
(21) Triarius wall; (22) museum; (23) theater; (24) sacred harbor; (25) dockyards.*

and, on the horizon, the other Cyclades glistening in the sun.

ACCORDING TO LEGEND, POSEIDON ONCE thrust the mountains into the sea with his trident. They promptly sprouted roots in the depths, preventing them from ever turning to the mainland. This was the origin of the Cyclades. Then, as Homer, Callimachus, and Pindar relate, a young woman, Asteria, leapt into the sea in order to escape the stormy wooing of the father of the gods, Zeus. She floated about in the Aegean, and seamen would spot her now in the Saronic Gulf, now in the Strait of Europos, on the same day in the waters off Chalcidice, along the Attic coast, near Chios or Samos. She simply let herself be carried along on the current, and no one was able to stop her. But one day, the distressed cries of an expectant mother moved Asteria, and she finally held still. This second woman was Leto, who was carrying a child by Zeus and was being pursued by the jealous Hera, Zeus's wife. Asteria defied the angry Hera, offered asylum to Leto, and asked in exchange that Leto's child protect and honor her in the future. Leto promised in the name of the unborn child, Apollo, that Asteria would get a most magnificent sanctuary. At that, as Asteria stood still in the middle of the Cyclades, four pillars rose up from the floor of the sea to anchor her, and Zeus made her visible to all *(delein epoiesen)*; since then the island has borne the name Delos. Finally, at the foot of Mount Cynthus, Leto gave birth to her son Apollo beneath a palm tree.

This mythic tale is obviously a poetic version of natural phenomena that occurred in the Aegean Sea. It also explains why this small and infertile island was chosen as the religious center for the Ionians in the eastern Mediterranean. Remains of earlier sanctuaries, not apparently connected with any specific deity, have been excavated. Presumably the cult center of a Mycenaean goddess already existed here.

The flora of the island today consists of shrubs, wildflowers, a few wild fig trees and some cultivated ones, and fields of melons. Ancient inscriptions attest, however, that grapes, olive trees, and figs used to flourish here. And ancient leases reveal that there were a number of local farmers. Other inscriptions indicate that there were gardens near the shrine to Leto, a grove within the sacred precinct, and estates called Phoenix (palm) and Laurel. The only palm tree growing on Delos today was planted at the beginning of the excavations.

Delos has probably been inhabited since the third millennium B.C. The first seafarers to make the long journey from the coast of Asia Minor to the Greek mainland used it as a refuge and a base. Later a few fishermen who were pirates on the side settled here. According to Thucydides, these were Carians from Asia Minor who established the first settlements, which have been found on Mount Cynthus.

The other Aegean Islands, far more fertile and richer in minerals, developed a lively trade with the coast of Asia Minor and the Greek mainland, while excavations on Delos indicate that an upswing did not take place until early in the fourteenth century B.C. At that time, the inhabitants grew wealthier and moved their dwellings from Cynthus toward the sea, on the site of the later sanctuary of Apollo.

It is assumed that the Apollo cult was brought to Delos by Ionian seafarers around the turn of the first millennium B.C., when the Ionians gained supremacy over the Mediterranean. Their young patron god, who was already revered at sanctuaries in Asia Minor, came to Delos as a newborn, the son and brother of Eastern deities, the Lycian Leto and the Lydian Artemis, respectively, successors of a pre-Hellenic fertility goddess worshipped everywhere in the Aegean. The mythical pursuit of Leto by the jealous Greek goddess Hera may reflect the difficulty with which the Eastern deities attained their places in Greek worship.

Probably in the eighth century B.C., Apollo advanced from being the focus of cult worship on Delos to enter the pantheon of the Olympian gods. He became one of the most important gods, and in time, he came to express most perfectly the Greek spirit. He was also the only one to keep his original name through the Roman Empire.

The eighth century B.C. also marks the beginnings of the rise of Delos, which bound its own fate with its god's. The former barren refuge of sailors became the religious center and the commercial and naval power of the Aegean. For centuries, Delos enjoyed a respect that diminished only when other gods displaced Apollo.

Ancient sources describe the Delia, splendid festivals that took place annually

Apollo slaying the Python.

on Delos to celebrate Apollo's birth. Ionians from throughout the Aegean and the west coast of Asia Minor would come to these popular cult ceremonials.

Beginning in the time of the tyrant Pisistratus (sixth century B.C.), the Athenians developed a strong interest in Delos and fostered their own legends of Apollo's shrine—most notably, the Theseus legend. Theseus's return from Crete to Athens signified the beginning of Athenian political predominance over Delos.

The control of Delos by the Athenians began with the first *katharsis* (purification) that Pisistratus ordered, obeying an ancient oracular pronouncement. As a result of his decree, it was henceforth forbidden to bury the dead on Delos, for Apollo hated death. At first, the *katharsis* applied only to the sanctuary, not the whole island.

The actual hegemony of Athens over Delos began in the fifth century B.C., when the Athenians took over the administration and accounting of the temple treasury. Athens thus gained a foothold on Delos, supporting itself on the Apollo cult in order to expand and maintain its naval supremacy in the Aegean, a blatant example of the alliance of religious and political power.

In the second *katharsis*, in 426 B.C., the Athenians strengthened their position on Delos. They now removed all earlier graves and moved them to neighboring Rheneia, Thucydides wrote. Rheneian finds can be seen in the Museum of Mykonos today.

After this, no one was permitted to die or give birth on Delos. The Delians had to build country houses on Rheneia, and inscriptions relate the measures that had to be taken if a drowning victim was found on the shore of Delos. The only graves left in place were those from mythical antiquity.

In 422 B.C., presumably for political reasons that are now unknown, the Athenians removed all the inhabitants of Delos, completing the *katharsis*. After the Delians had spent considerable time in Asia Minor and some of them had been slaughtered, the Athenians revoked their cruel edict and permitted the survivors to return "by order of the Delphic god." Athens's defeat in the Peloponnesian Wars in 404 B.C. heralded an independence for Delos that was not actually attained for another century. Most of the buildings seen as ruins today were constructed at that time.

During the Hellenistic period, the population of Delos was large and diverse; the major groups were traders and seamen from all over the Mediterranean. The traditional gods lost none of their power. On the contrary, Apollo's sanctuary became wealthier and wealthier thanks not only to the gifts presented to the god by the faithful and by cities courting the favor of Athens, but also to loans that the temple treasury made to merchants. The Delian Apollo sanctuary was unique in that it originated and developed in the midst of an ordinary residential area—first a modest fishing village, then a cosmopolitan center.

The greatest building activity occurred when Rome, having conquered Greece in 166 B.C., returned the island to Athens. Not even half of the buildings from that period have been excavated so far. However, numerous attacks by pirates, the raids of mercenaries of Mithridates of Pontus (first century B.C.), and above all the development of new trading centers in the eastern Mediterranean brought on the slow decline of Delos.

Entering the ruined city of Delos today, the visitor is struck by the remains of beautifully constructed houses with mosaics in their courtyards. The mosaics, which have not been disturbed since they were uncovered, have geometric patterns and poly-

Mount Cynthus: drawing from Olfert Dapper's Naukeurige Beschryving, *1688.*

chrome pictures, such as those of the dolphin, the trident, the masks, and Dionysus riding the panther or tiger.

In the northwestern part of the island, immediately adjacent to the ancient harbor that still exists today, lies the sacred precinct of Apollo and the public buildings surrounding it. It appears to be utterly confusing, for different periods of construction lie atop one another. The first building we come to is that of the Naxians, constructed in 560 B.C. Its name derived from the votive gift from the island of Naxos, the gigantic statue of a young man, which was discovered next to it. The sacred way leading to the three temples of Apollo is lined with the pediments of votive offerings.

It is interesting that the temples of Apollo on Delos were the simplest of all shrines dedicated to the god. Elsewhere in Greece, the most splendid masterworks were lavished on his temples.

To the east stands the prytaneion from the fifth century B.C. This served for gatherings and banquets of the *prytanes,* or magistrates. The archives of the shrine were also housed here. Behind the prytaneion, there is a particularly uncommon, mysterious structure, the famous bull monument. Its use is still unknown.

To the north lies the stoa (hall with columns) of Antigonus, the son of the Macedonian king Demetrius Poliorcetes, from the third century B.C. Here, too, there are ornamental bulls. Standing in front of the stoa is the famous Theke mentioned by Herodotus. Mycenaean ceramics have been discovered here. Tradition has it that the Theke was the tomb of Opis and Argis, the Hyperborean virgins who came from the north and assisted Leto at Apollo's birth.

Farther east lies the most sacred altar of Delos, the Keraton. Theseus sacrificed here, and here people danced the traditional Delian crane dance. Apollo supposedly constructed this altar at the age of four from the horns of goats slain by his twin sister, Artemis. The Artemision, west of the sanctuary of Apollo, was the site of her cult. It is the oldest shrine on Delos.

North of it, near the lake, we see the archaic temple of the twelve Olympian gods, the shrine of Leto, and the renowned Lion's Way—a masterpiece of archaic art that was probably a votive gift from the island of Naxos. This is the only sculptural sequence of wild animals in all of Greece, an Eastern inspiration. The lions guarded the way to the shrine of Leto. The granite palaestra, a public athletic ground, stands on the edge of this precinct.

To the northeast, in the stadium precinct, we come upon the Archigesion, a shrine to the mythical progenitor of the Delians, Anius, a son of Apollo. Only the islanders were permitted to worship him. Nearby, there was a synagogue, a rectangular structure built in the first century B.C.

You must not overlook the group of buildings between Apollo's temples and the entryways. Here are the Aphrodision, the fourth-century B.C. temple of Aphrodite, and, along the now-swampy Inopos River, the terrace of the foreign gods. Gathered here are the Serapeion, the temple of Isis, the Samothrakeion, the monument to Mithridates, the shrine of the Syrian gods, and the temple of Hera. The remains of spacious, three-story dwellings, such as the house of Hermes, also stand here.

A stairway to the summit of Mount Cynthus leads to the prehistoric remains of the oldest settlement on the island. Nearby is the opening of the Antron, a cave that sheltered a shrine to Heracles in Hellenistic times.

Delos is forever associated with Apollo, a cheerful god who took possession of the island with his birth, not by force, as he did at Delphi. Here, he was a god who hated death and was celebrated in song and dance. This serene image of the Delian Apollo might be explained by the fact that it was created by peaceful, openhearted islanders in a gentle, rolling landscape drenched by the pure light of the Mediterranean. The priests of Apollo on Delos also corresponded to this image and bore no resemblance to their austere counterparts at Delphi. Moreover, they administered the god's finances expertly. The lively trading city owed its success to Apollo. Leto kept the promise she had given to Asteria.

SERIPHOS

SHIPS LEAVE REGULARLY FROM PIRAEUS AND LAND in the small harbor of Livadi, where a splendid sand beach awaits. At first glance, Seriphos appears to be barren, but the farther inland one goes, the more this impression is belied. Valleys filled with fruit trees

Danäe, Perseus, and the Chest:
detail from a vase painting.

stretch ahead. Early tomatoes ripen on sunny slopes protected from the wind. Grapevines thrive on the hillsides, and the ancient writers often praised the island's wine. The ground is rich in iron that was mined even in antiquity. The iron mine still operates a day shift, providing a modest wage for some twenty workers.

Tourlos, the island's highest peak, rises some 1,920 feet into the blue sky. The main village of Chora, or Seriphos, lies on a conical hill and can be reached by car in a few minutes on the island's only asphalt road. It is believed that the ancient city was also located here, but no excavations have yet been undertaken. Small white houses now grow like mushrooms out of the rock. Above them, on the top of the hill, stands an old Venetian fortress. The three most interesting Late Byzantine churches (sixteenth to eighteenth centuries) are Aghios Eleutherios, Aghios Ioannis Theologos, and Aghios Athanasios. The little town is surrounded by caves and strangely fissured steep cliffs. They recall a famous myth from antiquity. The legend of the island's origin relates that the brothers Dictys and Polydectes, with Ionians from Thessaly as vassals, were the first residents of Seriphos. And with these two island kings, one enters the great body of sagas relating to Danaë and Perseus.

Danaë was the daughter of the powerful King Acrisius of Argos. An oracle had prophesied to the king that a son born to her would be his murderer. Therefore Danaë was forbidden ever to marry. One day Zeus, the father of all the Greek gods, caught sight of Danaë, fell in love with her, and came to her in the form of a golden rain. Acrisius soon saw that his daughter was expecting a child. Beside himself with rage, he ordered his carpenters to make a wooden chest. He then placed Danaë and her newborn son, Perseus, in this chest and had it pushed out to sea. The waves carried it to Seriphos. Some fishermen pulled it ashore and reported their unusual catch to the island's two kings—the brothers "good" Dictys and "bad" Polydectes. The royal brothers were dazzled by Danaë's beauty and welcomed her and her son willingly to their court. While Dictys remained kind-hearted as always, Polydectes began to spin intrigue. He wanted Danaë for a wife, but she kept refusing him. So he set out to get her by cunning.

At that time, King Oenomaus was reigning on the Peloponnesus, and he had a daughter. Polydectes announced that he intended to marry her and sent his vassals to Oenomaus with lavish presents in order

Medusa: an ancient marble.

*Perseus freeing Andromeda:
an ancient relief.*

to make his courtship appear authentic. In truth, though, his goal was to separate Perseus and his mother, so she would be left without a protector. To obtain the wedding present for his supposed fiancée, Polydectes instructed Perseus to bring to Seriphos the head of Medusa—a fearsome creature (her hair was a mass of writhing snakes, for example) who was so ugly that anyone who looked upon her turned to stone. Scarcely had the young man set out on this dangerous adventure when Polydectes forced himself upon the defenseless Danaë. She raced to the asylum of an altar in order to save herself. At the very last moment, Perseus returned with Medusa's head, and the grisly sight worked its magic on the evil king and his accomplices. The twisted cliffs near Chora are held to be

their bodies. Euripides used this saga in his tragedy *Dictys,* and the comic poet Cratinus depicted it ironically in his play *The Seriphioi.*

Seriphos has only scant remnants of its checkered history. Following the Ionians from Thessaly, the next to arrive were other Ionians from Athens under Eteocles. The island did not take part in the Persian Wars at first, but its men later fought alongside the Athenians at Salamis (480 B.C.) and Plataea (479 B.C.). Otherwise, Seriphos had a relatively uneventful life. "... The frogs on Seriphos are mute," said the Roman scholar Pliny, presumably alluding to the awkward, taciturn nature of the islanders; furthermore, the coins of Seriphos were called frogs. We assume that these coins were minted from ore taken from the island's iron mines.

The first of the foreign conquerors came from the successors of Alexander the Great. Then came the Romans. Seriphos allied itself with King Mithridates of Pontus against Rome, and its inhabitants were severely punished for doing so in 84 B.C. Seriphos entered a long period of decline and finally became only a place to which the Romans banished people.

Crusaders and their families, generally known as Franks to the Greeks, appeared on Seriphos, and on the rest of the Cyclades, beginning in 1204. The island also received its share of raids by pirates. The infamous Chaireddin Barbarossa proclaimed himself lord of Seriphos in 1537, and the Russians ruled it briefly in 1770. In light of all the oppression they had suffered under foreign rule, it is no wonder that the people of Seriphos were among the first of the freedom fighters against the Turks in 1821.

Today, Seriphos is a typically quiet Cycladic island. The yellowish sand beaches of Aghios Ioannis and Psili Ammos sparkle like ribbons between the stark lines of the hills and the crystalline sea. The small village of Pyrghois offers a splendid panorama, while Kentarchos is the most picturesque village, nestled in the middle of a splendid green valley.

The island's oldest church is in the village of Panaghia. Its wall frescos date from 1300 and are well worth seeing. The festival of the Holy Virgin goes on for three days, August 14–16. A bit farther, near Valsamos, is the church of Aghios Stephanos, which also has a few frescos.

The religious center of the island is the monastery of the Taxiarchis ("archangels"), from 1600, in the north. It stands some 330 feet above the sea and resembles a fortress. A 25- to 30-foot wall surrounds the monastery. In its center stands the church of the archangels Michael and Gabriel. The cloister has a fascinating history, and—in spite of numerous sieges by Crusaders, pirates, and Turks—the monastery treasury, including interesting manuscripts, is still partly intact.

The patron saint of the peasants of Seriphos is Tryphon, who fends off mice and rodents. This saint represents Apollo Smintheus, who used to protect people from these nuisances 2,500 years ago. Other traditions also survive from antiquity. On the Tuesday after Easter, for instance, swings are set up in the narrow streets for the young girls, and the young men crawl beneath them, each making a wish that is supposed to come true. This custom is rooted in an ancient festival called the Aiora; the word in Greek means "I swing through the air." Another example occurs during the grape harvest in July and August. Since the wine of Seriphos is highly prized today, this harvest is celebrated with special fervor. Then on Aghios Minas Day, in November, the casks are opened. And when the farmers plant their vines, fifty helpers come and pour wine on the roots, just as was done in antiquity. All then go to church and light candles before dancing outdoors until far into the night.

SIPHNOS

IN THE SIXTH CENTURY B.C., SIPHNOS WAS SO rich in gold and silver that its inhabitants built a famous treasury for the Delphic Apollo, which equaled in magnificence the most precious votive offerings from the powerful Greek city-states. The tables turned, as traditional legend has it, when the Siphnians, blinded by greed, ceased to tithe to the Delphic Apollo out of the income that their mines produced. Punishment was swift: the sea broke into the gold and silver mines and took away the island's source of wealth. At about the time of the birth of Christ, the miserable condition of the island was compared to the thorny furze bush; this Siphnian shrub became synonymous with poverty.

Modern expressions such as "one olive and its stone provide a shoe for the Siphnian" and "a Siphnian's wages are two olives and one onion" attest to the importance of the island's 60,000 olive trees and the modest living they provide. In addition to agriculture, the Siphnians live from their skill at handicrafts; their potters and weavers are renowned for their skill.

When approaching the 31-square-mile island on the western edge of the Cyclades by scheduled ship, you arrive in the harbor of Kamares. Here, taxis are lined up to take tourists to the various villages. Apollonia, Artemon, Exambela, and Katavati lie in the foothills, surrounded by olive groves. Oleander and wild figs grow in clusters in the ravines, while almond trees and fig trees thrive especially in the high valleys. In the spots where the trees grow best, wood and water nymphs were worshipped in antiquity, and they are still believed in today. All over the island one sees dovecotes, looking like little castles, where doves are fattened for the cooking pot. Equally typical of the landscape are windmills and half-ruined Roman and Venetian watchtowers. At first glance, Siphnos certainly does not make as dramatic an impression as Thira (Santorin), for example. Its charms become apparent to the visitor only gradually. A soft light suffuses its gentle contours without blinding.

The name of the main village, Apollonia, preserves the memory of the ancient cult of Apollo. But no temple ruins have been discovered so far. In the village square, you can sit in front of the *kapheneia* in the shade of ancient trees. Here, you are likely to be offered mild, air-dried sheep's cheese (*xynomitsithra*) with your ouzo or a sesame-and-honey paste (*pasteli*) with coffee. On Sunday morning, right after church, you can have a marvelous chick-pea soup that was taken to the baker's in tightly sealed pots on Saturday evening and has stewed overnight over wood coals. Though

there is little *haute cuisine* on Siphnos, it happens that the best Greek chefs are Siphnians.

The churches of Aghios Soson in Apollonia, the Panaghia Gournia near Artemon, and the Panaghia in Katavati are worth vis-

Women of Siphnos: drawing by J. B. Hilair, c. 1782.

iting for their murals. There is an interesting legend connected with the eleventh-century monastery of Theologos Mongou. In the Middle Ages, a beautiful nun from Byzantium sought refuge in this cloister. A nobleman, known as the Baron, courted her and built a church at the spot where he could best catch sight of her. The nun remained true to her vows, so he turned to countless village beauties, who all bore him children. Finally there were so many that a whole quarter of Apollonia was named after the Baron, his church, and his children. Today, it still bears the name Barou.

Most of the medieval Orthodox monasteries are located on hilltops where you can look far out to sea. On the 2,200-foot Mount Prophitis Elias stands the monastery of the same name; the residents go here on pilgrimage in times of drought to beg the saint for rain. The monastery of Panaghia tis Vrisis has an interesting collection of old books and maps. In some of the monasteries, tourists can find lodgings at very low rates—for example, the Prophitis Elias, the Taxiarchis, near Vathy, and the Panaghia tou Vounou. Guests at the Panaghia tou Vounou, which stands on the slope above the large, sandy bay of Platys Ialos, can enjoy the loveliest panorama. Below it, on the beach, is the Xenia Hotel. On the south shore of the island, near Apokofto, ten monks' cells in the monastery of Panaghia Chrysopighi are rented out at modest prices. The icon of the Holy Virgin that is revered at this monastery is supposed to have saved the island from plague in 1676 and freed it of locusts in 1928. It also demonstrated its miraculous powers when it preserved the virtue of some local maidens. The girls had gone to the church at night to bring oil to the Panaghia's oil lamps. Corsairs lay sleeping in front of the church, but instead of returning home, the girls simply stepped over the sleeping men. At this, the pirates woke up and attacked the girls. In order to spare them, the Panaghia caused a crevice to open up and swallow the pirates. A bridge spans the cleft today.

Next to the sea, slightly more than 2 miles east of Apollonia, lies Kastro, the island's oldest settlement. Because of its connecting courtyards, passages, wooden balconies, terraces, and staircases support-

ed by flying buttresses, it gives the appearance of a single large dwelling. Entering the village, you first come upon a row of houses, with tiny windows, that have grown together to form a single solid wall. A broad, high gateway leads through this defense wall, inhabited by poor people, into the inner town. On either side of this vaulted entry, which used to be closed at sunset, the residents were accustomed to sitting on benches and telling stories. Behind it, along the narrow alleys, stand fine houses and churches bearing the coats of arms of their owners or founders. From their balconies hang geraniums and reed baskets full of drying cheese. The church roofs are inlaid with pebbles from the sea, which can also be found in the Venetian fortress and in the interiors of the whitewashed houses.

The impact of history is more visible in Kastro than in other parts of the island. In Herodotus, Kastro is called Asty, or "town." Archeologists have not yet found its prytaneion, market halls, or theater. However, it is possible to see a portion of the ancient city wall and architectural fragments that have since been incorporated into the walls and façades of houses.

SIPHNOS EXPERIENCED ITS HEYDAY IN THE SIXTH century B.C., when the gold and silver mines were most productive. At that time, every citizen enjoyed a share of the wealth. But when some Samians who had been driven from their island came to Siphnos and asked to borrow money, they were refused. Enraged, they plundered the town and took far more than they had originally requested. This event signaled the beginning of the decline that was sealed by the flooding of the mines by the sea. (The inhabitants still point out inundated mine shafts near Aghios Sostis.) The Samians' re-

Siphnos: drawing by J. B. Hilair, c. 1782.

venge was also interpreted as a punishment for the Siphnians' failure to follow the advice of the Delphic oracle, which warned them of "a wooden company and a red herald"; the Samian fleet and the red ship that carried its leaders appeared without the Siphnians' recognizing the omen.

The Siphnians resisted Persia's demands for the island's surrender early in the fifth century B.C. Instead, they sided with the Athenians and joined them in the sea battle of Salamis. In the time of Alexander the Great, the Macedonians used the island's harbors as a base for their fleet. Pirates from Crete repeatedly raided Kastro in the second century B.C., and in the first century B.C., the Romans dispatched a governor to Siphnos; he established his headquarters in Kastro. The Romans left numerous marble sarcophagi that were found strewn about the vicinity of Kastro. This city remained the island's capital under the Byzantines, Venetians, Crusaders, Russians (1771–

1774), and Turks (1617–1771, 1774–1829).

The Crusaders, who visibly influenced the character of the island, conquered it in 1307. One of them, Antonio da Coronia, came from a Spanish family and appointed himself lord of the island, though Siphnos actually belonged to the dukedom of the Aegean. His great-granddaughter Margarita was given the entire island as a dowry when she married Nicola Gosadino of Bologna. The Gosadino family then ruled until 1617, also controlling the islands of Kythnos, Cimolus, Pholegandros, and Sikinos.

The inhabitants of the island learned from the Crusaders how to weave wool, cotton, and silk fabrics and how to weave straw hats in the Italian style, a skill that they once turned into a flourishing trade. Today, though, few of their woven goods are exported. Another centuries-old island craft is pottery. The chemical composition of the Siphnian clay permits high firing

White marble tomb on Siphnos: drawing by J. B. Hilair, c. 1782.

temperatures, so pots made here come out of the kiln virtually fireproof. For nearly 300 years, Siphnos has supplied not only all of Greece but also a number of other Mediterranean countries with earthen cookware. The potting communities today lie in the bays of the picturesquely folded shoreline, near Kamares, Vathy, Platys, and Valos.

The Turks, who replaced the Crusaders as rulers of the island, had only a slight influence on its culture, for they only visited it from time to time to collect tribute payments. Near the end of the seventeenth century, the sultan twice sent Jewish experts to test the mines for lead. The Siphnians, afraid of being forced to work even harder for the Turks than they already did, bribed French corsairs to sink the ships that were carrying the experts and the lead samples they obtained back to Constantinople.

Pitton de Tournefort, counselor to the king of France and a botanist and physician, visited Siphnos on a tour of the East at the beginning of the eighteenth century. He observed that the climate of the island obviously was conducive to long life, for he found men as old as 120. Further, he noted that the women looked like walking mummies, wrapping themselves so tightly—in order to protect their complexions from sun, wind, and dust—that only their mouths and noses were visible. He linked their reserve in dealing with men to this unattractive fashion, noting that the heavily made-up women on the neighboring Melos and Cimolus openly took up with the corsairs. Tournefort was discouraged to see that no one seemed concerned about the preservation of the ancient monuments he visited. He found ruins of a temple to Pan and sarcophagi that the cows drank from.

But those interested in antiquity can now visit recent excavation sites. On the hill of Aghios Andreas, southwest of Apollonia, are the double ring walls of a pre-Hellenic acropolis that is accessible from the south. The outer ring is narrower than the inner one and has projections at irregular intervals, like those at Troy. The inner wall is more than 13 feet thick at its widest point and is interrupted by square defense towers. Its lower sections are built of small stones; the upper part, of massive stone blocks. The main purpose of the excavations, under the leadership of the Greek archeologist Barbara Philippakis, is to date the acropolis precisely. Eight buildings from the Geometric period have been uncovered inside the 325- by 360-foot fortress. Two of these buildings contained eight rooms each. Among the uncovered shards are fragments of vases and oil lamps that cover an era stretching from 3000 B.C. to the Hellenistic period. Near Vathy and Mavro Chorio, there are pre-Hellenic burial grounds with both single and double graves.

PAROS

ANCIENT TEXTS EVOKE IMAGES OF THE BARE, smooth cliffs, fertile pastures, rustic life, and Dionysian festivals of Paros. And, in fact, Paros differs from the other islands of the Cyclades in its soft lines and peaceful appearance. The ridge of Marpessa, in the island's center, gives way to gentle hills that roll down to the sea, permitting relatively large plains on three sides. Two deeply cut bays, Naousa in the north and Paroikia in the west, as well as the smaller bay of Marmara in the east, provide harbors that are protected from the wind. Countless lesser bays also offer refuge from the stormy sea. Only in the northwest are there steep cliffs. The plains have plenty of water, and the hills contain layers of marble between the gneiss and the granite.

Recent excavations on the small island of Saliangos, which was at one time attached to Paros, prove that the island has been inhabited since the end of the Neolithic period, or the fifth to fourth millennium B.C. A

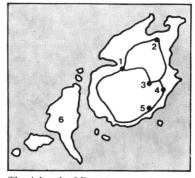

The island of Paros.
1. Paros (Paroikia)   5. Dryos
2. Naousa   6. The island
3. Lefkes   of Antiparos
4. Marpessa

The church of Katapoliani.

first flowering, attested by finds at numerous burial sites near the coast (including Abyssos, Galana, and Gremna), occurred during the Early Bronze Age (third millennium B.C.), and at the beginning of the second millennium B.C., the first settlement arose on the site of the present capital. On the low hill that was crowned by a Western castle in the Middle Ages stood the acropolis and the lower town. A Mycenaean settlement was discovered in 1981 near Naousa. In the course of the Ionian migration at the end of the second millennium B.C., settlers from Attica arrived on Paros and built a city that is unusual for the Cyclades in that it surrounds a hill and is situated near the sea. (Generally major settlements were established atop steep slopes at that time.) There, the acropolis and its fortifications were built. The choice of this site must be assumed to have been determined by the existence of the prehistoric settlement and the desire to follow tradition.

When you approach the town of Paros by ship today, you are greeted by a typical Cycladic town with whitewashed, cubical buildings, picturesque narrow alleys, countless small Late or post-Byzantine churches and the famous Church of the Lower Town, the Katapoliani, which is also called the Church of a Hundred Doors (Hekatontapyliani). Until a few years ago, this church bore the marks of numerous resto-

rations that were performed over the course of the centuries. Recently, however, these later additions have been removed, and the legendary Katapoliani now stands once again in the form that it had during the Early Christian period.

The fertile valleys of Paros have always supported agriculture, vineyards, and especially olive trees. The main craft of the townspeople has been ceramics. Shipping, however, has been the most important source of income.

The chief reasons behind the wealth of the island in antiquity were trade and the colonization of the gold-rich island of Thasos. The Parian colony on Thasos was founded in 680 B.C., and it always preserved close ties to its parent island. After the introduction of a money economy—the emblem on the island's first coins was a dolphin—Paros, with its central location, developed into the most important trading center of the Aegean, just as Delos was during the Hellenistic period and Syros is today. In close association with Miletus, Paros expanded its commercial connections as far as Egypt. Typical of the enterprise and energy of the Parians was their founding of the colony of Pharos on an island off the remote Dalmatian coast at a time of political stagnation in Greece.

Another source of wealth was the marble quarries. Great quantities of the stone were taken from the north side of Marpessa, and it was used as a building material at numerous shrines in Greece (Delos, Epidaurus, and Delphi) and later in Rome during the empire. One variety of light, white marble, the so-called Lychnites, was especially famous. This marble, when cut to a thickness of up to 3.5 millimeters, is the most translucent of all known types. Carrara marble is only translucent up to a thickness of 2.5 millimeters. Strabo wrote that "Parian mar-

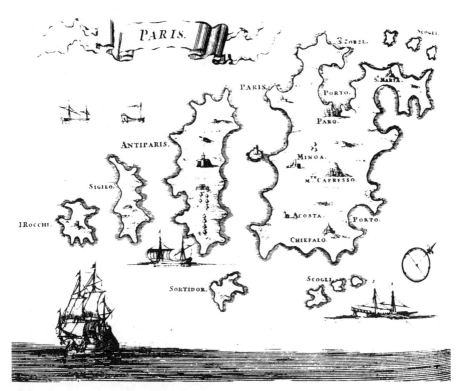

Map from Olfert Dapper's Naukeurige Beschryving, *1688.*

ble is the best for sculptors," and a poet called it "the adornment of the immortal gods." The mine shafts are still visible in the Marathi Valley, northeast of Paroikia. At the entrance to the quarry, there is a votive relief in honor of the nymphs.

The meddling of Paros in Aegean political alliances in the seventh century B.C. and the island's rivalry with neighboring Naxos led to long years of war and a number of defeats. In later times, though, Paros avoided such warlike adventuring and followed a more moderate policy that strove to safeguard a certain autonomy and preserve prosperity. In the fifth century B.C., Herodotus spoke of Paros as an island "in

which one can easily find a lot of gold." In the fifth and fourth centuries B.C., it is estimated that the number of free citizens of the island was about 12,000. In 490 B.C., the campaign of the Athenian Miltiades met with strong resistance here, so the offensive collapsed. After the sea battle of Salamis (480 B.C.), Paros joined the Attic League, and it participated in the second Attic League in 374 B.C. The Parians had no particularly friendly feelings toward the Athenians, but unlike citizens of other islands, they did not revolt.

Except for brief phases during which Athens influenced the island's internal affairs, a moderate oligarchy ruled Paros. The social structure of the island and the distribution of its wealth avoided any drastic inequalities, so there were no major class wars here. The spread of Pythagorean philosophy at the beginning of the fourth century B.C. can be observed in the political trends that dominated the island. Its domestic equilibrium and the expertise of its political leadership led other cities to attempt to follow the Parian model in settling their quarrels. This sense of fairness on Paros is attested by a comment about a judge from the second century B.C., a certain Cillus, son of Demetrius, "who concerned himself just as much for the wage-earner as the employer in the attempt to see that injustice was done to neither the one nor the other."

The Attic League dissolved in 338 B.C., and an independent Paros became a member of the Island League in the third century B.C. In the first century B.C., Paros came under Roman rule. The decline that led to the overall desolation of the Cyclades seems to have been felt somewhat less on Paros; an inscription from the fifth century A.D. referred to "the splendid city of the Parians."

THERE ARE NO IMPORTANT REMAINS OF THE AN-cient city. Two fixed points determined the layout of the original town: the hill of the acropolis (and later the fortress) and the sea. The walls, from the sixth century B.C., were 1½ miles long and formed a nearly complete circle. The city had harbors on both sides of the hill. When the weather is clear and the sea is calm, you can still see the jetties of the eastern harbor and even part of the quayside. The town was dominated by the archaic *hekatompedos naos,* the "hundred-footed" temple in the Ionic style that stood on the hill and was probably dedicated to the town's patroness,

Athena. The marble foundation of its vestibule (*pronaos*) and a portion of the 50-foot-wide cella (*sekos*) have survived. Most of the temple, however, sank into the sea. Some fragments from it, including portions of marble doorway and some Ionic egg-and-spindle moldings, were incorporated into the Crusaders' fortress. Also used as building material for the castle were architraves from the rectangular stoa (col-

Marble quarry on Paros: from The Mediterranean Illustrated, *1877.*

umned hall) that stood in the agora, the marketplace east of the hill, and was restored in the days of the emperor Hadrian.

The apse of the castle chapel is based on architectural elements from a round structure from the fourth century B.C. Of the other public buildings—the Prytaneion, Agoranomion, and Demosion (archive) mentioned in the inscriptions—all traces have been lost. Nor do we know where the theater and the temple of Dionysus and Kore (Persephone) stood. The temple consecrated to "Kore in the City" was decorated with sculptures and restored as late as the fourth century A.D.

Mosaics belonging to a Late Ionic gymnasium were discovered beneath the floor of the Katapoliani. In the center of the ancient city, scholars have located a public building from the Roman period, but nothing specific is known about its use. Here, too, was found a fragment of the so-called Marmor Parium, a list on marble slabs of historical and cultural dates and events from prehistoric times until 264 B.C.

Elements of a pre-Hellenic nature cult survived on Paros, the result of the attitudes of the Parians toward life. The two most important cults on Paros centered on the divinities of the earth and of fertility, Demeter and Dionysus.

THE ASCLEPIEION AND THE DELION ARE THE chief among the known sanctuaries. The Asclepieion, from the fourth century B.C., lies on the terrace of a hill northwest of Paroikia. It is a rectangular building in the Doric style and measures 147 by 55 feet. Columned halls were attached to each of its narrow sides and a number of rooms to the back of it. Its central focus was the open-air altar and an open colonnade connecting it with the sacred spring beneath the cliff. Two semicircular platforms lay nearby. A lesser spring and the remains of an elongated courtyard with various rooms belong to an earlier period. Above the cliff lie scant remains of the shrine of Apollo Pythios.

The Delion was discovered at some distance from Paroikia, on an elevation to the north, on the site of a prehistoric sanctuary. Its marble enclosure (90 by 87 feet), with a small gate and a stone altar dedicated to Apollo, are remnants from its earliest phase. The ground around the altar is paved, for religious dances were performed here. In the mid-sixth century B.C., a small marble temple (31 by 20 feet) was erected on the northeastern corner. This Doric temple includes a vestibule *(pronaos)* and cella *(sekos)* and a second altar, consecrated to Artemis. A dining hall (15 by 17 feet) with a vestibule and marble

benches running around its walls was used for cult banquets and dates from the same time. Outside the enclosure lay a small building where the priests lived. Behind the temple, somewhat downhill, there is a terrace to which two flights of stairs lead. This terrace (29 by 16 feet) offers a splendid view across to Delos. It probably served as a watch post from which the priests scanned the horizon for a fire signal or a flash of lightning before beginning a celebration.

PAROS ENTERS INTO THE HISTORY OF THE GREEK spirit during the first half of the seventh century B.C. with the explosive personality of the poet Archilochus, a native of the island. He himself related something of his adventurous life: "I am a follower of Ares, the stern commander in war, and I am familiar with the gracious gift of the Muses." According to one legend, the Muses gave Archilochus the gift of poetry when he was quite young. As the story goes, his father, Telesicles, sent him into the country to bring a cow to the city to be sold. When he was returning home with his charge, he came to a place called the Lissides ("Slippery Spots"), where he saw a group of women. They merrily asked him if he was leading his cow to market. When he said he was, they offered him a fair price. But no sooner had they done this than both they and the cow vanished. Archilochus, however, saw a lyre at his feet. When he recovered from the shock of this event, he realized that it was the Muses who had appeared to him and given him the gift of the lyre.

In the poetry of Archilochus, the individual first liberates himself from the bonds of tradition and then consciously confronts the problem of uncertainty about the world at large and his own fate. Archilochus led a passionate search for new criteria for an active approach to life freed from illusions. Because he recommended personal answers to moral questions, he tied himself both to the individual and to the community. His contemporaries occasionally reprimanded and criticized his works, but the Parians considered him the guide to proper thought. From the fifth century B.C., he was accorded the honors appropriate to a hero. Somewhat later, his grave was adorned with a sphinx atop an Ionic column, the capital of which has been found. The slabs of a frieze from the sixth century B.C., which depict a funeral banquet, quite likely stem from an older tomb monument to the poet. The Archilocheion lay outside the city to the northeast, near Elita.

A SCHOOL OF SCULPTURE DEVELOPED ON PAROS whose influence extended not only to all of the Cyclades but also to the great art centers of Athens and Argolis. Ancient sources provide us with the names of a long series of sculptors from the sixth century B.C. until the Roman period: Aristion, Euphron, Agoracritus, Thrasymedes, Scopas. The origins of Parian sculpture, to judge from the works that survive, go back to the middle of the sixth century B.C., when organic life began to pulse within the stone figures. The statues of Parian youths *(kouroi)*, slender, cheerful, firm in their outlines, seem to breathe the fresh air of the sea and the mountains. Movement and an inner tension are combined with a delicate treatment of the surfaces. The figures of young maidens *(korai)* are characterized by a sensual depiction of their bodies. The markedly linear drapery only intensifies the elasticity of their youthful forms.

In the second quarter of the fifth century B.C., when the Parian sculptors diverged from the archaic canon, they created pow-

Demeter, Triptolemus, and Proserpina: an ancient relief.

erful works with complicated torsion that radically advanced the representation of movement. The delicacy of the forms of the transfigured deceased on a series of splendid tomb reliefs became a model for Attic funeral sculpture in the Classical period. Following the high classicism of Phidias, the solidity of inner construction relaxed and the figures appear to be captured ethereally in a dance movement or a dreamlike state. The unique art of Paros enriched these new trends with new means of expression: radiant lightness, flowing movement, and a linear construction of drapery folds.

Agoracritus, Phidias's favorite pupil, who collaborated on the sculptures of the Parthenon, introduced this rich style to Athens. The art of Scopas, the sculptor from

Interior of the grotto of Antiparos, from The Mediterranean Illustrated, *1877.
(The small island of Antiparos is just off the southwest coast of Paros.)*

the second half of the fourth century B.C., when powerful Greek forces set out to conquer Asia, basically adheres quite closely to the austere Parian style. The strong passion and tempestuous movement that give his works such expressiveness and the compositional development of his figures in space make this master the most important representative of the so-called Alexander Baroque, the precursor of Hellenistic art. Of the works of Scopas, his ecstatic *Maenad* most impressed antiquity.

The various manifestations of the creative spirit on Paros reveal certain polarities: unbridled individualism side by side with a commitment to the state, deep inner passion as well as surface movement. In fact, a temperamental vitality is paired with a happy relationship with the forces of nature. The iambic poems of Archilochus, for example, are rooted in a rustic devotion to the gods that suffused his nature: "I can strike up a beautiful song about the god Dionysus—wine struck in me like lightning." The conception of the animal world that is expressed on Parian vases of the Orientalizing phase is unparalleled in the art of the Greek vase.

On Paros one must not look for mathematical regularity, abstract ideas, or great spiritual verve. For that reason the Parians were not innovators but rather renovators. Its two most important personalities, Archilochus and Scopas, appeared in times of transition, when creative forces were freeing themselves from tradition.

An ancient poet named Paros "the Wooded Isle" *(byleessa)*. When Greece gradually turned into the art center during the Roman period, however, it was Parian marble that dominated the world's image of the island. For Ovid, Paros was *marmoreamque Paron* ("Paros of the marble cliffs"); in Virgil, Aeneas passes "snow-white Paros" *(niveam Paron)* as he sails from Troy.

Eighteenth-century classicism took over this image. Paros became a symbolic name and a concept of mythical proportion, one that captures the light of the Aegean, concentrates it, condenses it. For example, André Chénier, the French poet who was born in Constantinople, wrote:

Diamond surrounded by azure, Paros, eye of Greece,
Gleaming star in the wave of the Aegean.

NAXOS

NAXOS, PERHAPS THE MOST FAMOUS ISLAND IN the Cyclades, has a heroic appearance. Powerful Mount Zas, which rises to a height of 3,280 feet, dominates the entire landscape. It is composed of layers of gneiss and mica-slate on its lower slopes and strata of ancient limestone at its higher elevations. West of Zas, in the center of the island, near Traghaia, stretches a high plain planted with olive groves. A second, lower plain, the Livadi, extends southward to the sea. Ships can find little shelter along this coast; the cliffs along the shore are too steep. The island's harbors are Apollon in the north, Moutsouna in the east, Panormos in the south, and, most important, Chora, the main town, in the west.

Conditions here have always been more favorable to agriculture and raising cattle than to trade: there are few harbors, while the soil is unusually fertile. The island's religious cults corresponded to its agrarian character: Zeus Melosios, the protector of sheep; Apollo Poimnios, protector of herds; Tragios, protector of goats. The most important cult was that of Dionysus. His priests ranked among the *archons* of the town. The coins of Naxos bore symbols of Dionysus: the *cantharus,* or wine vessel, the thyrsus, the grape. According to myth, Nysa, on Naxos, was Dionysus's birthplace. Ariadne, the pre-Hellenic fertility goddess worshipped in Minoan Crete, is related to him. Also appropriate to the heroic landscape of Naxos was the cult of the giants Otus and Ephialtes.

THE TOWN OF CHORA STILL HAS A MEDIEVAL appearance. The buildings of its castle surround a Gothic tower on a hill at the end of a fertile plain. The multistoried buildings, many of them nearly towers themselves, bear coats of arms above their entrances and combine Byzantine and western European elements; the large estate owners, the lords of the island, lived in feudal splendor from the Middle Ages on. However, as one goes from the castle down toward the harbor into the Borgho quarter, the buildings become simpler and less imposing.

When Constantinople fell into the hands of the Crusaders in 1204, the Venetian Marco Sanudo founded the duchy of the Aegean and made Naxos (Chora) its capital. His descendants and later the Crispi family ruled Naxos until 1566, when the island came under the dominion of the Turks. Reminiscent of those days are the castles of Potamia and Apaliros and also the unusual rustic tower dwellings erected for protection by the estate owners.

AS EARLY AS THE SEVENTH AND SIXTH CENTURIES B.C., Naxos was a wealthy island whose land belonged, just as it did much later, to an aristocracy, which Herodotus referred to as "the fat ones." Later came the rule of the tyrant Lygdamis. Lygdamis, himself an aristocrat, stirred up the people against the nobility, seized power with the help of the tyrant of Athens, Pisistratus, and ruled Naxos during the second half of the sixth century (550–524) B.C. Much earlier, in 735–734 B.C., landless emigrants from Naxos joined with similar people from Chalcis in Euboea and founded a colony in Sicily at the foot of Mount Etna.

In his description of the heyday of ancient Naxos, Herodotus related that it surpassed all the other islands in "bliss" and owned 8,000 shields and countless warships. He also mentioned slaves. Struggles for superiority in the Aegean, chiefly with neighboring Paros and the Ionian city of Miletus, continued for a long time. Howev-

The island of Naxos.

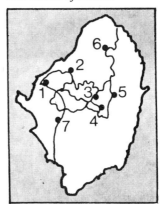

1. *Naxos (Chora)*
2. *Engarai*
3. *Moni*
4. *Philotion*
5. *Apeiranthos*
6. *Koronis*
7. *Ano Sanghri*

er, after forming an alliance with Chalcis, Naxos succeeded in securing a leading role for itself by the end of the sixth century B.C. Testaments to its power are the monuments preserved even today on Delos: the pan-Ionian Apollo sanctuary (640–540 B.C.), the porticoed House of the Naxians, and the famous Lions' Way opposite the sacred lake.

Naxos repulsed the Persians in 501 B.C., but twelve years later it was destroyed by them; the island has never recovered from this tragedy. During the Battle of Salamis in 480 B.C., Naxian ships fought with the Greek fleet. In the following year, the Naxians took part in the Battle of Plataea against the Persians and joined the Delian-Athenian League. But thirteen years later, Naxos revolted against the league, which had developed in opposition to the Persians but had since come under the hegemony of Athens. As a result, after a long siege, the Naxians lost their independence and were forced to take in settlers from Athens who were drawn by lots and known as cleruchs. The Athenian strategist Chavrias defeated the Spartans in the strait between Naxos and Paros; thereupon, in 376 B.C., Naxos entered into the second Attic League. At the time of the Diadochi, the generals of Alexander the Great, who divided his empire among themselves when he died, Naxos was a member of an island league under Egyptian, Macedonian, and Rhodian influence. Finally, in 41 B.C., the island was incorporated into the Roman Empire.

DURING THE FIRST DECADES OF THE CHRISTIAN era, a number of the islands of the Cyclades lay deserted. During Strabo's lifetime (63 B.C.–19 A.D.), only Naxos, Paros, Tenos, and Andros had some significance. After Constantine the Great in the fourth century,

the Cyclades formed a part of the Byzantine Empire. They belonged to the administrative region of Asia. The ninth century brought the Saracens to Crete, and the Cyclades were also subjected to their attacks.

The Byzantine epoch had profound influences on Naxos. In small and large churches strewn across the island, it is possible to trace the development of Byzantine architecture and fresco painting from the sixth century until its decline. Outstanding frescos were recently discovered in Drosiani, near the village of Moni. They include a number of rare examples of early Byzantine art from the sixth and seventh centuries, the period before the battle over images, during which the Iconoclasts destroyed countless pictorial representations in the name of orthodoxy. However, various wall paintings from this tumultuous period of the ninth century survive on Naxos in the churches of St. Artemios, near Sanghri, and of St. Kyriaki, near Apeiranthos. Well worth seeing are the frescos from the thirteenth century in the churches of Lathrino and Kaloreitissa, also near Sanghri, and of the Panaghia Yiallou, near Aghiasos. Particularly fine is the eleventh-century church of the Protothroni, in Traghaia.

APPROACHING NAXOS FROM THE SEA, YOU SEE A small island connected to the coast by a sandbar. On it is an imposing marble gate. This was the western entrance to an archaic temple from the end of the sixth century B.C. Only the foundations of the temple itself have been preserved, but they clearly reveal the outline of the whole complex. The building—114 feet long and 44 feet wide—consisted of a *pronaos* (vestibule), an *opisthodomos* (hall with double columns), and a three-aisle cella. In addition, a portico running around the four sides of

Inhabitants of Naxos: drawing by J. B. Hilair, c. 1782.

the temple was planned; if it had been completed, the temple would have been the largest in all of Greece. The work was never carried out, however. The deity worshipped here was presumably Apollo Delios.

The ancient city, near Chora, dominated the hill and extended from the northern slopes, the present-day castle, down to the sea. None of its buildings have survived, except the remains of the porticos that surrounded a vast square (about 165 by 154 feet), doubtless the marketplace, or agora. These date from the third century B.C. A theater is mentioned in inscriptions, but we do not know where it stood. Another temple has been located outside the city on a north-facing elevation now called Kaminaki.

The remains of a square Ionic temple near Sanghri are of greater importance. This temple was roughly 42 feet square. Its unusual shape, reminiscent of an ancient banqueting hall, supports the assumption that it was a shrine to Demeter, possibly constructed on the site of an older temple of Apollo from the eighth or seventh century B.C. It must have been restored somewhat later, for architectural elements from the fifth and fourth centuries B.C. were found among the ruins.

The massive tower of Cheimarros in the southern part of the island dates from the Hellenistic period. Other remains of towers can be seen in Tripodes and Avlona. These less imposing defense structures, also to be found on other islands in the Cyclades, were built as a means of protecting the fields.

Like Paros, Naxos is rich in marble. In

*Athena Velletri:
an ancient
marble.*

contrast to the fine, translucent Parian variety, however, the marble of Naxos is rather coarse and riddled with crystals. It is found right on the surface throughout the island. Even today, marble is one of Naxos's most profitable exports. In antiquity this marble was worked by artisans who came from other islands, Attica and Boeotia. Legend has it that Vyzes, the inventor of the marble tile, was a native of Naxos.

A local school developed on Naxos that played a most important role in the monumental sculpture of the seventh century B.C. and reached its height between 650 and 550 B.C. One of the traits of this school was the tendency toward monumental forms such as we can see in the colossus of Apollo on Delos or in the nude figures of young men, the *kouroi*, that are preserved in the quarries of Melanes on Naxos. The statue of Dionysus near the fishing village

of Apollonia is another such figure, a marble giant some 36 feet high. The marble cracked, however, and the artist had to leave the sculpture lying in the quarry. The oldest surviving monumental work of art in Greece is the famous statue of Artemis, the votive offering of a woman of Naxos, in the temple of Artemis on Delos. This figure, 5 feet 9 inches tall, dates from the first half of the seventh century B.C. We know the name of a Naxian sculptor, Euthycartides, from the end of the same century. His figure of a youth (*kouros*), more than 6½ feet tall and dedicated to the Delian Apollo, stands on an uncommonly shaped base.

Naxian sculpture on Delos is represented by a series of figures of youths and maidens; among these are the oldest examples surviving in all of Greece. There are others not only elsewhere in the Aegean Islands—for example, on Thira—but also in Athens and beyond; the influence of Naxos on the sculpture of Boeotia was strong indeed. The most impressive of the works discovered far from the Cyclades is the sphinx dedicated to Apollo that stood on a tall Ionic column in Delphi, a votive gift from Naxos from the first half of the sixth century B.C.

The sculpture of Naxos, when compared to other works of Greek art from the same period, is rather lyrical and passive. The Ionian art of those days shows a wealth of motifs from the animal and plant worlds, while Naxos created still, almost abstract figures with sharp outlines. In the overall framework of Ionian art, the simplicity of Naxian sculpture expresses an attitude that is appropriate to the Doric spirit of Greece. However, it also reflects qualities of an agrarian society.

We encounter the same simplicity, columnlike height, and spare modeling on grave steles from the school of Naxos up until the middle of the fifth century B.C. One example is the Alxenor Stele, from Boeotia, in the National Museum in Athens. Grave steles from as far away as the Black Sea indicate the extent of the influence of Naxian art.

Only recently a burial site from the so-called Geometric period was discovered in Traghaia. Standing on a barren, rocky plateau are some thirty round or elliptical graves, some from 32 to 40 feet in diameter. Towering above the entrance to the burial ground was a gigantic, unhewn monolith. It marked the boundary between the tomb area and the site of the cult of the dead. This grave site, from the ninth and eighth centuries B.C., indicates that the inhabitants of the island presented the souls of the dead with figs, grapes, nuts, bracelets, metal sheets with pictures in relief, rings, and everyday objects.

The ceramics of Naxos played an enormously important role until the mid-seventh century B.C. Naxian vases were extremely precise and elegant, with a wealth of painting. The vertical axis is stressed so that the depictions appear to be elongated: lions' heads, horses' heads, and the deity who protects wild animals were commonly portrayed.

IONIANS FROM ATTICA SETTLED ON NAXOS TOward the end of the Mycenaean period, or the later part of the second millennium B.C. They did not come voluntarily but were refugees. The expulsions, attacks, and battles that led to the collapse of the Mycenaean cities on the Greek mainland spurred a flowering of Naxos, for the cultural center of Greece then shifted to the Aegean.

In those early days, an important settlement developed on the west coast of Naxos. It became the hub of the island while its inhabitants set about transforming the plains into arable fields. Excavations reveal that the Mycenaean city, surrounded by a wall, extended along the northeast edge of the Grotta, where the Hellenistic city later proceeded to develop further.

Nearby barrow graves have produced rich finds: vases with a wealth of decorative motifs and depictions of birds, sea creatures, and even men. Gold jewelry has also been unearthed. Such vases, gold, and gems document the unusual variety of the Mycenaean style.

The picture presented by Naxos in the third millennium B.C., the earlier phase of Cycladic prehistory, is quite different. In that remote period the population was distributed among small, independent settlements. At that time, the sea was more important than the land. A number of tiny islands lie off the east and south coasts of Naxos: Donousa, Karos, Kouphonissia, Sinousa, Iraklia. They extend nearly into the region of the Dodecanese, forming a small archipelago dominated geographically by Naxos. These islets were densely populated, as attested by burial sites. The more important settlements of Naxos, Grotta, Panormos, and Spedo all lay on the coast. Two acropolises that have been excavated, at Panormos and at Karos, a city now abandoned, prove that hills with steep approaches were preferred. The settlements were protected by walls. Their primitive buildings, comprising only one or two rooms, were built of ordinary fieldstones or adobe. A flat roof constructed out of some light material was appropriate to the thin walls. And once again the graves: there were both simple, traditional ones and others of two or three stories; the multistoried ones accommodated a number of bodies. The main votive gifts were marble idols and clay vases, daggers or lances, occasion-

Town of Naxos (Chora): drawing by le Comte de Choiseul-Gouffier, c. 1782.

ally silver objects and jewelry.

The Cyclades owed their striking economic progress in antiquity to metals and metalworking as well as increasing trade with the East and the Greek mainland. Copper mines are spoken of on Naxos, as is the presence of lead and silver. Its hardy seafarers sailed as far as the islands of the Adriatic. Most impressive, however, was the artistic creativity of this legendary people. The famous, early Cycladic idols reveal the unique talents of their creators. Hewn of marble, these figures were the product of a remarkably abstract sensibility. From 4 inches to 5 feet high, they depict female figures almost exclusively. They are brightly painted and generally show the figure standing with her arms crossed below her bosom. They do not have bases. A rich collection of this type is housed in the Naxos Museum, as are idols of seated women and one of a man holding what appears to be a cup in his raised hand. In the archeological collection at Apeiranthos, there are some particularly interesting stones that were recently discovered. Simple slabs that are otherwise unworked, they bear representations of everyday scenes, dances, hunts, animals, and ships.

The poet Archilochus compared the wine of Naxos to nectar. Pindar called Naxos "Lipara" because of its fertility and wealth. And indeed, Naxos has been rich and fertile through endless centuries.

Page 129: Religious procession on Karpathos. (© Joseph F. Viesti)

Pages 130–131: Harborside, Mykonos. (© Marvin E. Newman)

Page 132: Fisherman on Paros. (© Charles Feil)

Page 133, top: Woman working with yarn on Paros. (© Susan Shapiro)

Page 133, bottom: Fisherman in green rowboat, Mykonos. (© Marvin E. Newman)

Pages 134–135: Old man in street, Mykonos. (© Morton Beebe)

Page 136: Clothes drying, Rhodes. (© Marvin E. Newman)

Page 137: Woman spinning cotton. (© H. Armstrong Roberts)

Pages 138–139: Church bell on Thira. (© Adam Woolfitt/Woodfin Camp and Associates)

Pages 140–141: Lindus Acropolis on Rhodes. (© H. Armstrong Roberts)

Pages 142–143: Harbor entrance, Rhodes. (© Joseph F. Viesti)

Page 144: Statues on Delos. (© Morton Beebe)

CIMOLUS

OF VOLCANIC ORIGIN LIKE NEIGHBORING MELOS, the small island of Cimolus has long been known for its light "cimolian earth." Travelers from the West and seafarers named the island Argentiera, "the Silver One," because of the silver-white color of its chalky limestone, which the ancients used for washing clothes, for medicinal baths, and for cures. The island is generally barren and poorly watered. In the fertile valley of the Deka, however, there are vineyards and olive and fig trees. The figs of Cimolus were famous in antiquity.

The ancient sources are almost completely silent about the history of the island. The modest tax that was levied on Cimolus by the Athenian League attests to a very limited prosperity. The few coins from the third century B.C. suggest that there were cults of Athena, Artemis, and Poseidon on the island.

Cimolus had close ties to Melos, from which it is separated by only a narrow arm of the sea (see p. 146). In fact, its southwest coast, which lies opposite Melos, was the first part of the island to be inhabited. This early settlement was located on a hill, Aghios Andreas, or Daskaleio, which is a separate island today but was connected to Melos in antiquity by a narrow strip of land; at that time, Melos still bore the old names Ellinika and Limni. On the island of Aghios Andreas, there are remains of walls and ruins that one can follow beneath the shallow sea. These belonged to the late Hellenic city.

This city was inhabited from the beginning of the first millennium B.C. until well into the Christian era, perhaps even until the Middle Ages. Since Mycenaean and even prehistoric shards have been discovered here, it is likely that life on Cimolus began much earlier, possibly even in the second millennium B.C., when the nearby Mycenaean center of Phylakopi, on Melos, was flourishing.

Its graves stretch along the coastline, carved out of the soft stone or sunk into the sandy soil. Some lie in rows facing the interior. The objects buried with the dead suggest that trade took place between the island and Corinth in the Archaic period (seventh–sixth centuries B.C.); later, until well into the Hellenistic period, Cimolus traded with Athens as well. An inscription tells of a judgment by Argos during a quarrel between Cimolus and Melos over the

Cimolus. Plan of the Kastro. (Drawing from the Archives of the Archeological Office, the Cyclades.)

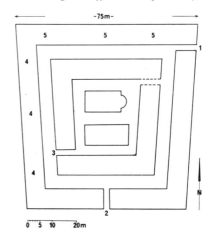

1. *East gate*   4. *Seventeen houses*
2. *South gate*   5. *Fourteen houses*
3. *West gate*

ownership of the uninhabited island of Polyaigos (Polybus). In the Geometric period, a local pottery produced a number of quite provincial but very lovely ceramics. A grave stele made of tufa (from the seventh century B.C.) numbers among the most important finds on Cimolus. The upper body of the female figure depicted on it is in relief, while below her waist the stele is left flat and was surely painted at one time. It is believed to be one of the very oldest representations of a human being in stone from that period.

After the spit of land sank and Aghios Andreas became an island, the danger of attacks by pirates increased and the people living near the shore probably moved further inland.

Thus, during the Middle Ages, the main settlement was northwest of this earlier one, high atop the mountain. On a steep cliff on the western coast, difficult to approach, which the islanders know as Palaiokastro, lie the ruins of a medieval castle (*palaio kastro* means "old castle").

After the conquest of the island by Western Europeans in the fourteenth century, a fortified settlement, the Kastro, was founded on the southeast side of the island, not far from the sea; the small harbor nearby is called Psathi. The Kastro was built on a plateaued hill in the sixteenth century, using a plan that is still discernible. Row houses formed a slightly trapezoidal quadrangular wall. Two gateways provided entry from the east and south. There were originally towers at each corner, only one of which survives today. Inside the wall, there was a second quadrangle composed of double rows of houses. The outer rows contained from ten to seventeen dwellings; the inner ones, five houses each. The only access here was to the west. In the center lay the church square and five houses. The connecting alleys inside the city ran parallel to each other, were mostly covered, and were frequently no more than 8 feet wide.

Today the Kastro lies abandoned. The new town of Cimolus has grown up around it in a vital, primitive architectural style that makes it one of the most picturesque towns anywhere in the Cyclades. Twisting alleys with steps and arcaded passageways form a simple unity with the buildings themselves. There are also numerous Late and post-Byzantine chapels, many of which boast lovely icons. Cimolus is not a grand place, but it has a unique charm. Only the jaded or hurried visitor will fail to be touched by it.

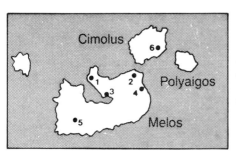

The islands of Melos and Cimolus.

1. Melos (Plaka)
2. Phylakopi
3. Adamas
4. Voudia
5. Mountain of Profitis Elias
6. Cimolus

MELOS

MELOS, WHICH IS ALSO KNOWN AS MILOS OR Milo, is divided into two parts by a deep, horseshoe-shaped bay some 4 miles wide. Countless smaller bays punctuate the multicolored volcanic stone cliffs that line the shore. Unexpected contrasts of landscape occur as steep elevations like the Kastro and Halakas give way to plains bordering the sea or the curve of the bay. Here, volcanic fires created a number of warm sulphurous springs, the well-known *thermae,* which have served as medicinal baths since antiquity. Melos's countless minerals—among them sulphur, alum, and pumice, all of which were known to the ancients—are also a product of the volcano. The amazing Glaronisia (Seagull Islands) off the north coast are doubtless the result of some additional bit of volcanic whimsy: gray rocks, like giant, barren tree trunks, thrust out of the blue sea up toward the sun.

MELOS HAS BEEN INHABITED SINCE THE THIRD millennium B.C. The entire island appears to have been strewn with settlements in those earliest times. From remote Halakas on the wild west coast to Pelos and Theiafi, the mining villages of the east coast and Phylakopi in the north, one can find trape-

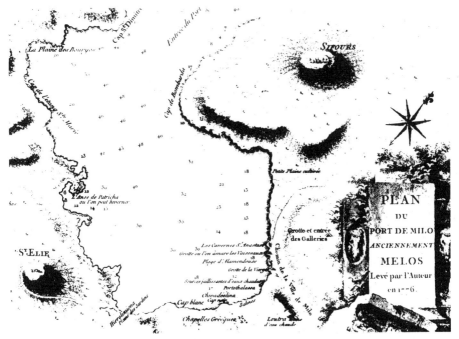

Chart of port of Melos: drawn by J. Perrier, 1782.

zoidal tombs that house the dead in a crouching position. Next to them, there are frequently marble vessels and even more often handmade clay vases with a lovely black or red glaze. At one site, a limestone model of a house with a vaulted roof was discovered. A steatite vessel now in the Munich Museum is a model of another dwelling that comprised seven rooms in a circle around a courtyard with a covered entry. The funeral gifts from that period always included sharp blades of obsidian —the smooth, hard, easily worked volcanic glass that was used to make all kinds of everyday utensils in prehistoric times. Melos was the only island that exported obsidian to the rest of the Aegean, and this trade appears to have continuously contributed to the development of the island.

MELOS EXPERIENCED A FLOWERING AT THE SAME time as the high point of Mycenaean culture; the island's position midway between the Peloponnesus and Crete may have been a decisive cause. This heyday, during the second millennium B.C., is attested by excavations in Phylakopi, where the ruins of a prehistoric city were uncovered by English archeologists in the nineteenth century. Here there are clear traces of uninterrupted habitation in three phases from the third until the end of the second millennium B.C., or through the entire Bronze Age.

Phylakopi lies on the north coast of Melos between high, gray-blue cliffs that fall steeply into the sea. In antiquity, the island extended much farther into the sea, and the harbor lay a considerable distance from the hill on which the city stood. Originally the city had no walls. Its houses were constructed of whatever materials were at hand, and their ground plans were marked by odd angles. The vases of this phase are distinguished by lovely black or brown glazes with geometric motifs etched into them or painted on.

During Phylakopi's second phase, the city was surrounded by walls. It had proper streets and stone houses with right-angled walls, rows of columns inside, and occasionally a second story. Completely miss-

The port of Melos: drawing by le Comte de Choiseul-Gouffier, c. 1782.

ing here was the central fireplace that characterized contemporary dwellings on the Greek mainland. Frescos here depicted flowers, birds, and winged fish.

This second phase of Phylakopi coincided with the Minoan rule of the sea, and connections with Crete were very close. In fact, it is assumed that Phylakopi was under the dominion of Cnossos and accepted Cretan settlers because Melos is the only place in Greece where the fine, multicolored vases from Crete were introduced and where certain frescos betray the techniques of Cretan painters. This Cretan in-

fluence led to a new style of ceramics on
Melos, where marvelous vases were decorated with crocus and iris blossoms, animals, swallows, and fishes. A portion of a
vase with rows of fish can be seen in the
National Museum in Athens.

The second city of Phylakopi was destroyed. The third one, larger and more
strongly fortified than the earlier two, was
built upon its ruins. Two massive walls ran
parallel to each other and were 19 feet
thick, widening to nearly 32 feet near a
gateway that still exists. The plan of the
city seems quite modern: rectangular
blocks of dwellings stood between parallel
streets that were connected by flights of
stairs. In the northeast corner of the city
stood the Mycenaean *megaron* of the ruler
and his court. This structure consisted of a
vestibule (*prodomos*), the main hall (with
a hearth and a covered corridor leading to
small storerooms), and, above these, the
bedrooms. At this time, Phylakopi appears
to have liberated itself from Cretan rule
and to have been incorporated into the Mycenaean cultural sphere. Also at about this
time, if not earlier, tombs were carved into
the bedrock. These were single or double
graves (*thalamoi*) that were approached
by a corridor. Aside from those in Phylakopi, such graves were also dug near Zephyria and on Cape Spathi, the southeastern point of the island. The few
inhabitants of that area today call them "little ovens." At Phylakopi, earthquakes have
reduced the cliffs, along with the chambers
of the dead they contained, to rubble.

The close of the Bronze Age signaled the
demise of Phylakopi. And like a number of
other centers of the Mycenaean world, it
was never again inhabited.

In about 1200 b.c., Dorian emigrants left
the valley of the Eurotas. Bound for Crete,
they stopped on Melos and settled down.
The Dorians selected a site that was protected by its natural surroundings and from
which they could oversee the entrance
into the great bay—a steep, conical hill
roughly in the center of the northern arm

A cave on Melos: drawing by le Comte de Choiseul-Gouffier, c. 1782.

of the sea next to the bay. This hill was protected on the north and south by precipitous slopes; a stream had cut a deep valley
into its east face. The Dorians built their
city on the plateau of the hill, guarded to
the north by the elevation of Pyrgiantes. As

if these natural defenses were not enough,
the new arrivals erected ring walls of the
native black and red stone, with rectangular towers at regular intervals, encircling
the town and running down to the shore.
The city could be entered through the still-

The Venus de Milo.

was the marketplace and focus of activity. Not one of its structures is left. However, the theater, carved into the hillside to the east, survives in the form given it by the Romans. The nine lowest rows of seats have been excavated, as has part of the *skene*. Somewhat above it, there still stands the imposing, 130-foot wall of a building that has not as yet been identified. The ruins of what was presumably a large gymnasium have been found to the east of the theater, and somewhat farther to the north, the traces of the *odeion* ("concert hall"). Ruins of temples to various unknown deities are also visible. At the base of the north side of the hill, a columned hall (*stoa*) from the Roman period has been located. It contains beautiful mosaics and an altar consecrated to Dionysus.

This city, Melos, experienced a flowering in antiquity due to its favorable location and the value of its minerals. We know that Melos continued to export sulphur, alum, and pumice into the Roman period. Wine, oil, honey, and olives also contributed to the island's prosperity; olive trees are rare in the Cyclades except on Melos and Naxos. The wealth of Melos is attested by the fact that silver coins were minted here from the Archaic period on. Pictured on them is an apple, a visual symbol of the island's name; the Greek word for "apple" is *melo*. Historical sources tell us that, in the fifth century B.C., Melos was obligated to pay 15 talents annually to the Athenian League, a relatively large sum for a small island; Naxos and Andros, the great powers of the Aegean, were levied the same amount.

Monuments to the cultural life of Melos in the Archaic period (the seventh and sixth centuries B.C.) include the slender *kouros* (inventory no. 1558) and a pair of marble heads that adorn a gallery in the Na-

preserved gateways, one on the east with a round tower and another on the west with a rectangular tower. Some 325 feet inside these gates, one came upon the agora, which, like the agora of every Greek city,

tional Museum of Athens as well as the lovely Melian vases whose decoration reveals an Eastern influence and draws its motif from the world of plants and the realm of mythology. Although these works were created on an island whose inhabitants were of Dorian descent, they show that Melos was influenced considerably by Ionian culture. There is no marble at all on Melos, yet here, just as on the neighboring marble-rich islands of Naxos and Paros, there were native workshops. Melian sculptors are mentioned on an inscription from the sixth century B.C. now in Berlin and on another from the fifth century B.C. preserved in Olympia. The name in each case is Grophon, suggesting a family of sculptors in which the technique of carving in marble was passed down from father to son. Ionian influences continued into the fifth century B.C., as can be seen from a very beautiful head of a woman, probably Aphrodite, on a relief now in the Athens Museum (no. 3990) and from the small clay reliefs with lively figures, a genre of their own, with which wooden trunks and chests were ornamented.

During the Peloponnesian War, according to Thucydides, the Melians hoped to remain free rather than bring themselves under Athenian rule. They tried to maintain their independence for a full year before they were forced to their knees by hunger and perhaps by betrayal as well. Then, Thucydides wrote, "The Athenians executed all adult Melians they could get their hands on; the women and children they sold into slavery."

Ten years later, when Athens had lost its hegemony, the surviving Melians returned to their homeland. They drove out the 500 cleruchs, a band of Athenian citizens who had been drawn by lot to settle conquered lands. Remains of porticos and some wharves now visible beneath the water reveal that the city of Melos reached down to the sea during this period.

A second period of prominence, which extended well into the Early Christian era, is represented by some important sculptures. The best known is doubtless the Aphrodite from the first century B.C.—after a fourth-century original—that is today in the Louvre. This statue is famous worldwide as the *Venus de Milo*, but other works from Melos equal it in quality if not in reputation: the splendid head of Asclepius in the British Museum, after a fourth-century original and in the manner of the famous contemporary sculptor Bryaxis; the colossal Late Hellenistic statues of Poseidon (no. 235), Amphitrite (no. 236), and an unknown goddess whose headless torso survives (no. 238) in the Archeological Museum of Athens; and finally the Hermes of Antiphanes in Berlin. They all reveal a rare and exalted artistic style not normally encountered in smaller cities such as Melos.

We know from inscriptions which deities were revered on Melos. Some, such as Athena, Zeus, and Heracles, followed the new settlers from their Dorian homeland. Others, like Hermes or Poseidon, were already worshipped on the island. Dionysus Trieterikos, Asclepius, and Hygieia probably came to Melos with later cult migrations. There may also have been a cult of

A mother disciplining her son.

Aphrodite, since her statue was discovered here.

The graves of the city lay outside the walls to the northeast, and they could be seen until the nineteenth century. The area that surrounded them, Trypiti ("the perforated"), takes its name from them. The first archeological researcher of the Cyclades, Ludwig Ross, who came to Greece with King Otto of Bavaria, described them. He tells of rooms with many graves, carved out of the soft stone, on either side of a central corridor. A tomb from the fourth century B.C. recently discovered near Phylakopi conforms to this description. After burial, the coffins had been hermetically sealed with stone slabs, and the funeral gifts, including vases and currycombs, were placed on top of them and in the adjacent niches.

Heathen customs of dealing with the dead doubtless influenced the architecture of the Early Christian catacombs: the extensive complex of catacombs in Trypiti, which is so impressive for its mysterious tranquility, attests to the continued settlement of this region. So too does the baptistry inside the ancient city. The baptistry has the form of a cross; its arms are carved out of the earth, and stairs on all four sides lead down into it. A similar baptistry can be seen inside the wall of the small Byzantine church of the Panaghia in Kipos, on the south coast of the island.

Ruins and remains strewn everywhere prove that the entire island was settled in antiquity, just as the written sources suggest. For unknown reasons, the ancient harbor was vacated in the Early Byzantine period, the fifth and sixth centuries A.D., and the Melians later inhabited the northeastern area of Zephyria. Today one sees in Zephyria, or Palaiopolis, quite a number of ruins dating from the Middle Ages to the seventeenth century and often incorporating materials from ancient buildings.

The area of the ancient harbor was not resettled until the fourteenth century, by which time living conditions had changed. The Melians were no longer economically independent. Farmers by nature rather than seafarers, they had adopted a more modest life style than they had enjoyed in antiquity. In order to protect themselves against pirates, Crusaders, and Turks, they huddled their houses together on the highest hill at a respectful distance from the sea. They thus did not require walls. Neither doors nor windows open toward the outside of the settlement. In the center of the city, the Kastro, rises the tower of the former rulers of the island. The only access to the town, on the west side, was protected by a massive gateway. The Kastro was constructed after Melos had been incorporated into the Duchy of the Aegean. Marco Sanudo, the nephew of the doge of Venice, was the founder of this political entity, whose capital was Naxos, when the Crusaders conquered Constantinople. The Duchy of Naxos lasted on Melos until 1580, when after much uncertainty the island fell under the far more rigid control of the Turks. In the seventeenth century, the small, unprotected villages outside the Kastro joined to form a small town, today the central portion of the modern city of Melos, which continues to owe its economic prosperity to its minerals.

Thousands of years of history are still in evidence here. Passing through the covered walkways of the Kastro and past marble doorways and Crusaders' coats of arms that keep company with ancient grave steles on numerous corners of the city, the visitor to Melos is left with the impression of having explored a truly heroic landscape.

PHOLEGANDROS

NEARLY FORGOTTEN BETWEEN MELOS AND SI-kinos, the little island of Pholegandros sits calmly in the Aegean with its legendary cliffs of chalk and its numerous bays. The visitor lands on the east coast, in Karavostasi, which is the chief harbor. Snow-white buildings line a beach of immaculate sand. Up above, on the summit of a modest hill, is the chapel of the prophet Elijah and, toward the north, the church of Aghios Artemios. Grapes used to be cultivated near Livadhi, but today most of them are allowed to grow wild. Toward the southeast, a fine, white gravel beach rings a tiny bay and a path leads to the chapels of Aghios Modistos and Aghia Kyriaki. They present an odd sight, for they lie hidden among the ruins of a sheep stall. The village consists of only a very few houses, and most of them are closed up. A few of them open their shutters in the summertime, when they shelter the farmers who come here from Athens to plow the fields.

The capital of Pholegandros is Chora, which can be reached from Karavostasi in an hour on foot or on the back of a mule. The road runs along the Nychiti, a fast-flowing brook (*potamia*). If you have no desire to ride or to hike, you can also find a car on Pholegandros—but only one.

Chora stands at the top of a cliff. Venetians built the buildings of the Kastro, a fortification that offered protection against pirates. Until a few years ago, the castle gate stood near the Three Fountains. Now all that can be seen are marks in the pavement where the great door swung open and shut; the inner and outer courtyards have been merged into a single square. In addition to the main gate, there once was a *paraporti*, a second, smaller gateway.

Doubtless it was fear of attacks that led the inhabitants to build their small houses so close together. The town grew up without a plan, but the paved alleyways were laid out in such a way that the houses provided shade for each other, protecting the inhabitants not only from enemies but also from the burning summer sun.

There are only a few churches in Chora, and all of them have the simple Aegean form. Worth mentioning is the Pantanassa church, from roughly 1700, which stands at the northwest corner of the Kastro; it was restored only recently. Its wooden iconostasis is exquisitely carved. The lovely icons, depicting Christ and the Holy Virgin, were executed by painters of the Cretan school. St. George is depicted on the south wing of the altarpiece.

Eastward along the street called Rua is the church of Holy Wisdom, Aghia Sophia, which dates from the beginning of the eighteenth century. Most impressive here is the icon showing the baptism of Christ and the ascension of Mary. An uncommon theme is the wisdom of God; Christ is depicted teaching the wise.

At the east end of the Kastro, sandwiched between two houses, is the oldest church on Pholegandros, which is consecrated to Aghia Eleousa and the Aghioi Anargyroi. It contains splendid icons from the seventh century, as well as examples of the Cretan school of painting. Its roof is made out of a rare wood, called *Phida*, that today is found only on the nearby island of Kardiotissa.

The part of town outside the Kastro was developed after 1780, when the Aegean had been cleared of pirates by Lambros Katsonis. Even the houses in this newer section are small and look hastily built.

NEXT TO THE THREE FOUNTAINS, THE SO-CALLED Dunavides, lilacs bloom and acacias offer welcome shade. If the traveler wishes to visit the private church of the archangel, from 1618, it is necessary to pick up the key from the owners. In this church, one may view, by the mystical light of oil lamps, still more icons by painters of the Cretan school. The main altar has one wing toward the south, and here stands the archangel Michael in a passionate pose. The bell tower of the church of the Cross (*Stavros*), with its primitive icons by a nineteenth-century painter from Siphnos, reaches up into the blue sky.

On the square of the Dunavides lies the church of Aghios Nikolaos, the cathedral of Pholegandros. The iconostasis is carved of wood and is decorated with pictures painted by island artists. Well worth seeing here is the *Awakening of Lazarus*. The church of Aghios Antonios stands "surrounded by the gentle gossip of the birds," as the people put it. Its windows are fitted with frames from the eighteenth century. Nearby is the double church of Aghia Aikaterini and Aghios Fanourios. Finally, there is the church of the Theoskepasti with the loveliest of iconostases, unfortunately half-ruined.

There is a hill east of Chora called Palaiokastro, for here the ancient city of Pholegandros once stood. Passing by the cemetery and the church of the Panaghia, which stands on the ruins of an ancient Greek temple, you turn up the narrow, serpentine street that leads to the summit. There is little to be seen here from antiquity except for some collapsed walls and the fragments and shards of clay that lie all about. Inscriptions have been discovered that mention the temple of Artemis Selasforos and Apollo, the one beneath the church of the Panaghia. The signs of antiquity may be scanty here, but the indigo blue of the sea is captivating as waves foam against the cliffs.

Again on foot or by mule you reach the largest village, Epano Meria, north of Chora. The road is partially paved. One moment you are gazing at the barren interior of the island, the next moment at the churning surf of the sea. As everywhere, there are cliffs, occasional chapels and whitewashed rectangular buildings, and low walls (*xerolithies*) of unworked stone, which prevent the rain from washing precious soil from the cultivated terraces down into the sea. Just outside Epano Meria, next to the chapel of Aghia Paraskevi, a path leads down to a tranquil bay called *Angali* ("embrace"). This tiny harbor with a *kapheneion* and a few houses protects ships against the north wind.

At the intersection at Aghia Paraskevi, instead of descending to Angali, you can proceed into Epano Meria. There you can sink down on the stone bench next to the Aghios Ghiorghios church (1904) and simply enjoy the splendid view of the settlement and the sea. Here and there you can see a farmhouse or a well-kept villa.

The air is wonderful, smelling of thyme, oregano, and sage; this is a place of rustic tranquility. The farmers take their time in going to work under the morning sun. And so it has always been. The history of Pholegandros is equally simple; there are no tales of heroic deeds and ancient glories, but of simple people who endured whatever fate their rulers of the moment determined for them.

STILL, THERE IS NO GREEK ISLAND WITHOUT A myth. Tradition has it that a son of King Minos of Crete was the first to settle Pholegandros. According to this legend, the island was once dependent on Crete, presumably during Cretan naval supremacy in the middle of the second millennium B.C. It is equally probable, though, that Pholegandros was already inhabited at this time by people of the same race to which the Cycladic culture owes its development. The Dorians came later. Inscriptions in the Doric dialect have been discovered.

Herodotus reported that remote Pholegandros surrendered to the Persian king Darius. Persian rule must have been brief, however—namely, until the defeat of the Persians at Salamis. In 478 B.C., Athens founded a sea league to which Pholegandros belonged. Fifty-three years later, an inscription on the Acropolis noted that the island had paid tribute to Athens. It appears that the Macedonians paid little attention to Pholegandros; likewise, the Romans only used such poor islands as places to send their exiles. As was customary at that time, the Pholegandrians worshipped the Caesars as divinities, as inscriptions attest. In 1204, Byzantium was conquered by the crusaders, whereupon the Venetian Marco Sanudo occupied Pholegandros at the same time as he took possession of Naxos. The island, then called Poly Gandro, a bowdlerized name, remained under Venetian rule until 1566. In that year the Turkish crescent was raised over Pholegandros, but in 1829 it became a part of the new, independent Greece along with the rest of the Cyclades.

Your visit is ended. The boats that are to take you to your ship are moored in the darkness. You have waited on the pier for a long time, and now at last the ship has dropped anchor out in the sea. No one knew exactly when it would arrive, and no one was bent on finding out. People on Pholegandros wait patiently. And anyway the steamship can come only when the wind permits it, about once a week.

But now you are off. In the distance the light-colored cliffs and their black recesses fade away. This heroic image may remind you of the geographer Aratus, who called Pholegandros the "iron island."

Woman at ancient Greek street fountain.

SIKINOS

NOTHING OF THE PREHISTORY OF SIKINOS IS known. The first known mention of the island occurred in a speech given by the lawgiver Solon in the agora at Athens in the sixth century B.C. In calling on his fellow citizens to conquer the island of Salamis, which had belonged to neighboring Megara until that time, he chose the tiny, insignificant island of Sikinos as the most striking contrast to powerful Athens. An inscription found on the Athenian Acropolis from 425 B.C. reports that Sikinos had paid Athens a tax: the first written information we have on the island.

As the centuries went by, Sikinos continued to be mentioned only infrequently. The Romans designated it a place for their exiled citizens. In Byzantine times it was plundered by pirates, as were most of the Cyclades. After the fall of Byzantium, Venice was practical enough to permit the Aegean to be conquered by private individuals. Beginning in 1207, any Venetian citizen could outfit a ship with his own money and take possession of any island in the archipelago that he wished. In this way, the famous Marco Sanudo won Naxos in 1208 and the neighboring islands, including Sikinos, four years later. At that time, the island was called Sikandros, and on maps of that period it also bears the names Zetine, Setine, or Setia. The Turks arrived in 1566 and stayed until 1828, when the war of independence brought Sikinos and its neighbors into the new Greek territory.

Buondelmondi called the island desolate in 1420. Tournefort estimated the population at scarcely 200 in 1700. The Dutch philologist Pasch van Krienen spoke of some 700 inhabitants in 1773, as did Ludwig Ross, the German archeologist and philologist, in 1837. Today, Sikinos numbers from 300 to 400 residents.

The charm of this unimposing spot of land in the blue Aegean seems to be its blissful silence. You feel certain that you are the first visitor to tread its paths in years, such as the difficult trail to what was once called the temple of Apollo Pythios, an hour from Chorio, which Ludwig Ross in 1837 was quite probably the first Westerner to traverse after Pasch van Krienen in 1771. The light is like honey at times, especially at sunset. It is accompanied by a deep silence; the only sound is a faraway, silvery tinkling of the bells of animals.

Perhaps the wine does not live up to the ancients' praise. But the figs melt on your tongue, the olive oil on the island is excellent, and, as ancient descriptions attested, the fine-seeded grain of Sikinos is among the best in the Aegean. It is grown with difficulty, but the *xerolithies,* or dry walls, prevent the scanty soil from eroding; industrious people continue to cultivate the land even today.

Sikinos appears in old copper engravings and travel descriptions as a high country with raw and rather steep slopes in which there are caverns that seem as though they had been blasted out of the rock. But this image is true only of the northwestern part of the island. The southeast coast boasts capes like Malta, Kastelo, or Kuras, as well as a series of picturesque, peaceful bays, notably the one at Alopronoia, which was called Aghios Bouronios in the eighteenth century. Here, low hills with a few

View of the island of Sikinos.

balconied houses ring the sandy beach where the steamship drops anchor with its wares and, rather rarely, visitors to the island.

Mules carry you quite comfortably over the paved stones to the main village of Chora in roughly an hour. Chora has two halves—Chorio, the village, and the Kastro, the fortress. The two communities are 325 yards apart. The Kastro, as Pasch van Krienen proclaimed in 1771, is one of the most picturesque island villages in the world. It was a medieval fortress intended to provide protection from pirates. Therefore, the façades of its houses, pressed close together, never face outward, only inward. The walls of the houses are simulta-neously fortifications, broken only by two thick wooden gateways along their entire length. Most of the houses have a hiding place, a crypt in the cellar. The Late Byzan-tine church bears the name Tou Stavrou ("of the Cross").

In Chorio, which lies higher than the Kastro, only a single tower offered protec-tion to the citizens when danger threat-ened. Here the church is consecrated to Aghios Basileios. The nunnery of Zoodo-chos Pighi ("Holy Virgin as Life-giving Fount") stands on a hill close to Chorio, protected by high walls. Today this massive structure is abandoned. It appears not to be very old, but it is impossible to date pre-cisely. It is old enough, though, that the nuns had loopholes in the walls to shoot through.

If you are up to a hike of at least an hour, a sometimes difficult walk both along the cliffs above the sea and inland, you can visit a well-preserved monument from antiquity (second–third century A.D.). In 1837, Ludwig Ross was convinced that this was a shrine to Apollo, and his opinion was reinforced by an inscription found near the ruins (now incorporated in the wall of the school) that referred to Apollo Pythios. Today, though, it is believed that the white marble building was erected as a tomb by some rich citizen of Sikinos. Its dimensions suggest that this was a more probable function, as do the crypts beneath the cella, which still have traces of wall paintings, and the stations that line the approach and lead off to more modest ancient graves. However, the ground plan of the bluish stone monument does resemble that of an Ionic temple with double column and Doric capitals. Visitors could rest on its stone terraces. The imposing marble gateway, carved from a single block of stone (7 feet 9 inches by 2 feet 9 inches) leads from the vestibule down into the crypt. There is an interesting verse inscription above the entrance and to the right. In it a dead woman is called into eternal life by the gods, into the immortality of famous women from the past.

It is not difficult to imagine why the builder chose this spot with its view of the endless sea and the landscape of his homeland as a last resting place for himself and his family. This ancient tomb was transformed into a church in the seventh century A.D. The church was soon destroyed, presumably by an earthquake, and then rebuilt. In 1688, a large monastic complex called Episkopi took shape around it.

The ancient city of Sikinos, which was mentioned by Solon but by no travelers after him, lay in the west on a steep mountain. The remains of a staircase and countless shards of vases have been discovered on the southern slope, attesting to an early burial site. In the south the terrain has been leveled artificially. Was it here that the temple to Apollo Pythios perhaps stood? Dionysus was also revered on the island; coins that have been discovered depict his head, and the dance performed at Dionysian festivals was called the Sikinis. Archeology has so far been unable to shed any additional light on the mysteries of that remote past. The only thing standing on the summit of the mountain above Sikinos is the small church of Aghia Marina, abandoned in its otherworldly solitude.

$I\mathrm{os}$

IOS IS A GRAPHIC EXAMPLE OF HOW A HAPPY blend of landscape and architecture and a harmonious relationship between native inhabitants and summer visitors can be quickly and brutally destroyed. Here the fault does not lie with wealthy entrepreneurs who elsewhere spoil landscapes with boxlike hotels, seeking to make money from the vacationing public's desire for local charm. In this case, young people of all nationalities have descended on Ios in search of unspoilt nature and robbed the island of its peace. All they want is to live cheaply, and they are quite satisfied with a small space on the roof terraces for their sleeping bags and knapsacks. Though each one spends little, together they have brought an unexpected fortune to the residents, who thus increasingly neglect to keep up their houses, streets, and fields— for they are not displeased by their new-found wealth.

Ernle Bradford, who is the author of a book on the Greek islands, wrote during the 1960s that Ios was one of the cleanest spots he had ever visited—and at that time it was. The houses used to be freshly whitewashed several times a year, but this is no longer the case. The streets too are becoming dirtier all the time. The scent of rosemary and cooking herbs has vanished from the backyards; instead a faint aroma of hashish now hangs in the air. The sewers and the garbage removal service are not up to the task of keeping the town and beaches free of litter.

The backpackers began their mass invasion in 1970 and encountered an untouched and unprotected virgin country. By 1973, about 400 were staying through the winter. In the summer months, 4,000 people or more were staying here, and only 500 of these were sleeping indoors. The tourist onslaughts of summer are responsible for several unfortunate side effects: (1) the streets of the upper town are crowded every evening; (2) the islanders no longer produce *askotyri*, the widely sought-after, rather sour goat cheese; (3) the water from the Desis spring no longer fills the cisterns, and in the summer months there is frequently an acute water shortage; and (4) the islanders increasingly despise the visitors for being content with sloppy service and poor food. Greeks and foreigners who own houses here are in despair over the decline of their favorite island.

The island, also called Nio, has only about 1,000 native inhabitants today, as compared with 3,500 in the nineteenth century. Many islanders have emigrated in search of jobs in industry.

SAILORS PRIZE THE HARBOR OF IOS ABOVE MOST others in the Cyclades because its spacious bay offers splendid anchorage. Stretching away from the harbor is the fertile valley of Kato Kambos, where grain, sesame, olives, and fig trees grow in profusion.

From the harbor village, Ormos Nio, one follows a winding path uphill to the main town, Chora, or Ios, and on to the marketplace through a labyrinth of stairways and roof terraces until the street ends abruptly in front of the mountainside. Despite recent ravages, Chora, like Mykonos, is still one of the most charming small towns in the Aegean when one experiences it in spring or fall.

In addition to the 20 small churches in Chora, there are another 150 strewn about the island. The church consecrated to Aghia Irini, next to the harbor, dates from the seventeenth century. The architecture is particularly admired for its variety of styles, and the primitive wall paintings in the interior delight lovers of so-called naive painting.

The fifteen windmills of Ios, which stand behind Chora in a double row up on the barren mountain ridge, were all in operation as recently as the 1960s. When the northeast wind blew, as it usually does in summer, they ground the grain. Now all but one of them are still.

UNTIL RECENTLY, THE CHILDREN OF IOS PLAYED

Women of Nio (Ios): drawing by J. B. Hilair, c. 1782.

with broken idols from antiquity that they called *koutsounes* ("dolls"). Two particularly beautiful idols made of marble (1500 B.C.) have been taken from the island to the National Museum in Athens and to Copenhagen. A collection in Ireland boasts one such figurine that is made of wood, a type that is now extremely rare. Up to a few years ago, these idols were not counted among the valuable works of art that required special protection, so many were taken out of Greece.

The only systematic excavation done on Ios was carried out in 1904 by the French Archeological Institute of Athens. Sections of walls, inscriptions, fragments of sarcophagi, broken columns, and clay shards are the only remains from antiquity discovered to date.

We know that in the fifth century B.C. Ios belonged to the Attic League, and later

shared the fate that befell most of the Cyclades. In the thirteenth century, Ios fell under the rule of the dukes of Naxos, who were Venetian feudal lords. Later, under Ottoman rule, the young women of the island, who were famous for their virtue and their beauty, were collected regularly, like a tax, by the Turks to serve as slaves in their harems. In a private church on the Pano Piatsa in Chora, there is a Late Byzantine icon with a saint wearing a Turkish turban—a true rarity. Architectural monuments from the Middle Ages have been unfortunately neglected. A Venetian fortress near Aghia Theodoti lies in ruins, for example.

The philologist Pasch van Krienen, a Dutch officer in the service of Russia, came to Ios in 1771 and claimed to have found the grave of Homer. He fanned the enthusiasm of the islanders, for they had always been proud to claim Homer as one of their own. Indeed, ancient authors relate that Homer's mother, Clymene, came from Ios and that the poet himself died there while traveling from Samos to Athens. Homer's portrait was stamped on coins from Ios, as Pausanias and Strabo attest.

The so-called tomb of Homer, which was presumably erected only in Hellenistic or Roman times, lies on the north slope of Mount Pyrghos, the highest peak on the island. Today, only a few stones indicate the existence of an ancient shrine.

ON SUMMER EVENINGS, EVERYONE GATHERS ON a stone terrace below Chora to watch the sunset. Visitors from northern countries are always astonished to discover that there is no twilight here. The moment the sun sinks below the horizon, the stars begin to glow in the night sky. The music of Dvořak, Chopin, and Beethoven provides a suitable accompaniment. An enterprising islander has set up a kind of bar and dance hall at little cost, and every day a different concert is scheduled. The young people listen attentively while they watch the fishing boats and sailboats floating by. One can only hope and pray that a true romanticism without vandalism will return to the island.

AMORGOS

AMORGOS LIES SOUTHEAST OF NAXOS. SHIPS SAIL from Piraeus and Naxos to its two harbors, Katapola and Aighiali. In Katapola you disembark conveniently onto the quay; in Aighiali the ships lie at anchor.

Katapola, on a horseshoe-shaped, commodious bay, boasts one of the loveliest natural harbors in the Cyclades. A fertile valley extends inland from it, giving the impression of a huge green garden. This gentle landscape contrasts with the rocky, barren, and towering mountain chains of the rest of the island. Whitewashed houses, gardens with olive trees, grapevines, fig trees, and flowers give the bay a picturesque appearance. The Cycladic character of the three villages lying on the bay (Xilokeratidi, Rachidi, and Katapola) has suffered considerably under the influx of modern civilization. Steel and concrete are used in the new structures here, in imitation of middle-class housing in Athens.

The earliest history of the island begins along this bay. At its southeast corner, in Katakrotiri, nineteenth-century excavations brought to light countless graves from the third millennium B.C. These contained female idols of marble, the most beautiful examples of Cycladic art. These funeral gifts are now preserved in the Cycladic collection of the National Museum; other marble idols from Amorgos have been strewn throughout a variety of world museums and private collections. Traces of Cycladic culture are also apparent at other sites on the island as well.

We know scarcely anything about the Minoan-Mycenaean period, for there have been no systematic excavations. The Geometric period, however, is represented by

The island of Amorgos:

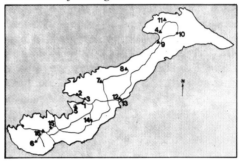

*(1) Katapola harbor; (2) Xilokeratidi;
(3) Rachidi; (4) Aighiali (Giali) harbor;
(5) Mountoulia (Minoa); (6) Arkesini
(present-day Kastro); (7) Terlaki;
(8) Richti; (9) Potamos; (10) Langada;
(11) Tholaria; (12) Chora (Amorgos);
(13) Panaghia Chosoviotissa; (14) Aghios
Ghiorghios Valsamitis; (15) Wrutsi;
(16) Aghia Trias.*

the well-known bronze statuette of a warrior (in Berlin) and by other chance discoveries. Finds of marble fragments and inscriptions permit us to make deductions about the art, religion, and political conditions in the ancient city of Minoa, for which Katapola (*kato-polis* means "lower city") was the harbor. Minoa, today called Mountoulia, was a Cretan settlement to judge from its name, and it doubtless dates back to the second millennium B.C. The numerous shards of Cretan ceramics still to be found in the fields nearby tend to confirm this assumption.

In the seventh century B.C., Minoa was colonized by Samians. This information is supported by the close similarity of the splendid grave steles from Katapola, which are always topped by a palmette, with steles from Samos, by inscriptions, and by the cult of Hera referred to in them. In Katapola, as late as the nineteenth century,

one could still see remnants of the ancient city wall and sculptures and inscriptions that were incorporated into the walls of houses. Today, these remains have either disappeared or found their way into European museums. Some, regrettably, were burned for lime.

It is said that the church of Panaghia Katapoliani, which is well worth a visit, stands on top of the ancient temple of Apollo Pythios. Its fourteen antique columns and various Early Christian architectural elements prove that the present-day church replaced an Early Christian basilica. At some distance from the Katapoliani you can still see some tomb vaults, known to the inhabitants as *tholaria,* from Late Hellenistic and Roman times. The antiquities preserved in the school of Katapola, mostly sculptures and inscriptions, provide a survey of art on Amorgos from the Geometric period up until the Early Christian epoch.

The remains of Minoa, on Mount Mountoulia, above Katapola (a 45-minute hike), are better preserved. On the eastern edge of the steep slope you can still see foundations, remains of gateways in the city wall, and some larger buildings from the Hellenistic and Roman periods. These ruins represent only a faint reflection of the glory of the ancient city.

The other two ancient cities of Amorgos to which ancient sources and inscriptions refer, Arkesini and Aighiali, lie at a considerable distance from each other. Arkesini is located in the southern portion of the island (called Kato-Meria, meaning "lower part"). The considerable ruins of this ancient city are now known as Kastro ("small fortress"), and the church of the Panaghia, which stands on a huge cliff that towers above the sea, is called Kastriani. Some extremely important inscriptions have been found here. They speak of the cults of Aphrodite Urania on the Aspis, Dionysus Kissokomes ("the ivy-wreathed"), Hera, Artemis, Zeus, and other deities. They also tell about the constitutions of Amorgos, the histories of the island's three ancient cities, various treaties in the Classical and Hellenistic periods, and the flowering of the island in the second century A.D., at the time of the Roman emperors Antoninus and Commodus. The city wall, constructed of huge blocks of blue marble schist, is still preserved at a number of spots up to a height of nearly 20 feet. Everywhere you can see the foundations of various buildings, gates, baths, and so on. Not far from Kastro, on the site of the church of Aghia Trias, stands a tall, well-preserved watchtower from the Hellenistic period. Two similar towers, though not so well preserved, can be seen on the other side of the island—not far from the main town of Chora—in Terlaki and Richti.

The third ancient city, Aighiali, which still bears the old name in shortened form, Giali, stands in the northeast part of the island. The ancient sources referred to Aighiali as a colony of Milesians. It is possible to find traces of the ancient city at a number of spots: at the southeast corner of the bay that serves as a harbor for the three villages (Potamos, Langada, and Tholaria); a bit farther inland; and above, on the huge, steep cliffs. In the lower part of the city (next to the bay) are foundations—partly covered

Artemis: an ancient marble.

by water—of ancient buildings, probably from Hellenistic times, the remains of Roman baths, and other walls. To the north of the village of Tholaria, a 45-minute walk from the harbor, there is a fortress called Vigla ("watchtower") on a steep hill, with the remains of walls, foundations, and a stadium. The cults of Hermes and Zeus are also documented at this site. In the same vicinity, statuettes of Serapis and Isis have been found, suggesting the existence of a Serapeion in the time of the Ptolemies. Other finds from the Hellenistic period, doubtless of Alexandrian origin, refer to the connections between Amorgos and Alexandria, the capital of the Ptolemies. Other discoveries here—sculptures, reliefs, vases, and inscriptions—range from Archaic times until the Roman period. Many inscriptions of historical significance are still contained in the walls of houses and churches. Tomb vaults from Roman times in the village of Tholaria are well preserved.

No buildings from the Byzantine period are known in any of the three ancient cities; however, one meets with Late Byzantine and especially post-Byzantine structures in the modern-day capital of the island, Chora, and at the neighboring monastery of the Panaghia Chosoviotissa. Chora lies 1,200 feet above sea level, some 2½ miles from Katapola. A road, still unpaved, makes it accessible by car. The drive in the only passenger car on the island takes roughly 20 minutes. The town is built around a huge rock that looms over the roofs, and it is exposed to the north wind at all times of the year. The 210-foot rock, called To Kastro ("the fortress"), was fortified by the Venetians in the thirteenth century. Tradition holds that Jeremia Ghisi had a fortress built with crenelations, embrasures, and secret approaches so that the inhabitants of the island could flee here during attacks by pirates. An integral feature of To Kastro is the small white church of Aghios Ghiorghios at its northeastern approach.

Unlike Katapola, Chora has remained completely untouched by modern civilization. Here the traditional whitewashed Cycladic houses, which have become rather scarce elsewhere on the island, are all about. Surrounding Chora are bare, rocky, reddish-gray summits, windmills, and a few brave olive trees struggling against the north wind and the arid soil. The town itself is made up of narrow alleys, somewhat wider paved sreets, vaulted passageways, squares both large and small surrounded by lovely houses, some of which are no longer inhabited, and more than forty churches. Its inhabitants are known for their wit; they delight in expressing criticism, whether political or personal, entirely in verse.

Most of the churches, especially the smaller ones, have only one room, covered by a barrel vault and adorned with primitive paintings on the walls. According to surviving inscriptions, the majority of them were renovated in the seventeenth century; thus they must have been originally built a good deal earlier. The church of Aghioi Pantes (All Saints) at the edge of town incorporates Early Christian columns and capitals and in all probability was built on top of an earlier basilica. Older elements are also visible in the Mitropolis, or cathedral. Many of the small churches, following Byzantine tradition, are family churches. In them, Early Christian capitals and bases serve as altars or candelabra.

Both in Chora and in the open countryside are found a number of double or twin churches, which are typical of Cycladic church architecture: Aghioi Pantes, Aghios

Antonios and the church of the Presentation at the Temple, the Mitropolis in Loggia (the Venetian name has survived), the church of the Annunciation and the Ascension near Loggia, and finally the Christos church, which belongs to the monastery that is located in the part of town called Photodotis (meaning "light giving," because the grammar school and high school are there). One distinctive characteristic of the local church architecture is the stepped façade with the bell structure, which is encountered at Zoodochos Pighi, Aghioi Pantes, Treis Ierarches, and others. In the church of Treis Ierarches, a lovely late antique relief has been incorporated into the wall beneath the bell housing. But to designate only specific churches as worth seeing would do an injustice to the rest of the town, which, as a whole, stands as a monument to the Venetian, post-Byzantine, and modern periods.

The visitor should also be sure to see the important collection of antiquities that is temporarily housed in the school. Here are examples of Geometric art (bronze fibulae, shards, and so on), Archaic sculpture (a *kouros* torso and numerous fragments of feet and hands), grave steles with the typical palmette on top, severe tomb reliefs from the early fifth century B.C., fragments from the Classical period, heads and reliefs from Hellenistic times, Roman reliefs and quite important inscriptions from the Hellenistic and Roman periods, altars, and other remains. Two inscriptions have been set into the wall of the town hall in Loggia.

ONLY 45 MINUTES FROM CHORA IS THE FAMOUS monastery of Amorgos, Panaghia Chosoviotissa. After climbing down a steep path toward the sea, you find yourself in the utterly solitary surroundings of the cloister, which is visible from afar. It lies in a cave in the cliffside, at a dizzying height of 984 feet above sea level, on the east side of the reddish-gray mountain of the prophet Elijah, which hangs steeply and threateningly above it. The blinding white architecture of the monastery contrasts strikingly with its stone background. The structure belongs to the so-called Golden Age of Byzantine monasteries and was probably constructed in the eleventh century, at the same time as the cloister on Patmos. The monastery of Panaghia Chosoviotissa was supported and granted special privileges by Emperor Alexius Comnenus, who was then (1088) on Patmos. A number of travelers (Tournefort, Ludwig Ross, and others) were still able to see a portrait of the emperor, painted on wood, that hung there.

There is also a theory that Emperor Alexius Comnenus only renovated the monastery, which had been founded by monks from Palestine in the ninth century. This dating roughly coincides with a legend of the monastery's founding that is still generally known. It maintains that a pious woman from Chosova—a village in Asia Minor or Palestine that cannot be identified—threw three icons in the sea at the time of the Iconoclasm in the ninth century to save them from the destroyers of images. One of the icons showed up in Athos and a second in the small bay, not far from the monastery, where the church of Aghia Anna now stands. The Panaghia (Holy Virgin) gave a sign from above—by placing an iron nail that the monks still show visitors—precisely where the monastery should be built. The monastery was named Panaghia Chosoviotissa, after the town of the icon's origin.

The most important holdings of the monastery include precious icons, including one of the Panaghia covered with silver, sacral objects, priests' robes, and especially some hundred manuscripts. The informative inscription on one of the silver objects, dating from about 1682, refers to the "renovation of the monastery by Alexius Comnenus." Among the priestly garments are a few gold-embroidered pieces of Russian origin, doubtless consecrated by the Orthodox Russians, to whom the island belonged for three years (1771–1774). Copies of the evangelists on parchment (eleventh–thirteenth centuries), codices on paper (thirteenth–sixteenth centuries), seals, and documents are of great significance for the history of Byzantine manuscripts. Other treasures of the monastery are wooden iconostases, a badly corroded wall painting in the refectory, and a marble relief of a standing lion, the emblematic animal of the Venetians, on the floor of the church of the Panaghia. The coat of arms was placed in the monastery by Guilelmo Sanudo in 1309, when he conquered the island.

From the monastery, you can follow a goat path to the Kapsala district, where tombs from the Cycladic period (2500–2000 B.C.) have been discovered. Here too stands the small one-room church of Aghios Ioannis (probably from the sixteenth century), whose interior is decorated with lovely frescos that are rapidly deteriorating due to humidity and neglect.

Strewn about the entire island are numerous churches that contain primitive frescos and icons bearing the signatures of their painters (for example, those by Moschos and Nomikos, both from the seventeenth century, in Chora). Other churches incorporate portions of ancient buildings. Worthy of special mention is the small church of Aghios Ghiorghios Valsamitis, near the village of Skopoi, where the remains of a Venetian tower are also visible.

To reach it, you must hike southward from Chora for about an hour and a half. The church of the Valsamitis, which, according to an inscription next to the door, was renovated in 1688, is widely known because of the "sacred" spring nearby. This spring, called Laloussa ("the babbling one") by the inhabitants, used to be consulted as an oracle by people not only from Amorgos but also from neighboring islands. An Orthodox priest elucidated the babbling of the spring, and his interpretations were accepted by the faithful with great awe. Since that time, some "pious" soul—in truth, a narrow-minded and uneducated one—cemented over the spring, thus silencing the only water oracles that survived from antiquity with the blessing of Christianity.

The path leads on to Kato-Meria. Here, in the village of Kamari, is the small church of Aghios Nikolaos, which was probably built in the sixteenth century and is decorated with beautiful wall paintings that have been well preserved.

AMORGOS HAS ALL THE ADVANTAGES AND DISADvantages of a spot isolated and remote from the center of things since antiquity. Among the advantages is the survival of ancient customs and traditions that can be traced back to Homeric times. A number of ancient words, for example, are preserved unchanged in the local dialect.

The island shared the fate of the rest of the Cyclades. After the Crusades, it fell to the Venetians; in 1537, Turkish rule began under Chaireddin Barbarossa. In the 1770s, it experienced a Russian occupation. Both in Late Byzantine times and in more modern ones, the islanders have been at the mercy of pirates. The folksongs of Amorgos, which commemorate attacks by pirates, are famous.

From the Roman period until very recently, the island served as a place of banishment, often for political prisoners. The hospitality of the Amorgines and their friendly manner have served to ameliorate the hardships of such exiles.

Today, the exiles have gone, and the inhabitants are leaving in increasing numbers. Mostly, they go to seek their fortunes in Athens. Hundreds of houses, especially in Chora and around Kastro, are falling into ruin and are closed up. They stand as testimony to the former prosperity of Amorgos, and to its present-day neglect.

THIRA (SANTORIN)

FROM A DISTANCE, ALMOST NOTHING APPEARS TO distinguish ancient Thera, modern-day Thira (Santorin), from the rest of the islands in the Cyclades. But when drawing closer by ship and entering the bay, the visitor is struck by the aggressiveness of the place. Cliffs fall proud and straight, down into the calm sea. The wall of stone, which is more than 650 feet high and has been broken twice by faults, describes a circle, broken by the bay, that continues on the twin island of Thirasia. Thirasia blocks the horizon. There appears to be no way out into the distance, no view of the other islands that appear to link the Greek landscape together.

This gigantic, round wall of stone gives one a feeling of oppression. In its center lie two tiny islands of black, ragged, hardened lava—disturbing reminders that Thira was a volcano and that its bay is a crater. Leaning against the railing of the ship, the visitor instinctively scans the water with mistrust. It is said that the water is too deep

Volcanic islands off Thira: a 1782 drawing.

The island of Thira.

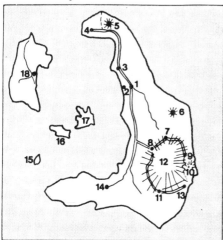

1. *Thira*
2. *Skala anchorage*
3. *Skaros*
4. *Oia*
5. *Mount Megalo Vouno (1,092 feet)*
6. *Monolithos*
7. *Apano Gonia*
8. *Pyrghos*
9. *Kamari*
10. *Mesavouno, ancient Thera*
11. *Emporeio*
12. *Mount Aghios Elias (1,856 feet)*
13. *Beach of Perissa*
14. *Akrotirion*
15. *Islet of Aspronisi*
16. *Islet of Palaia Kaimeni*
17. *Islets of Nea and Mikra Kaimeni*
18. *Islet of Thirasia*

here to permit anchorage, and superstitious sailors prefer to keep at a distance from the island. They know that something monstrous lurks in the depths of the bay. At the moment, it is calm. But the banner of smoke rising from one of the tiny islands reminds one of its presence.

The list of its terrible acts has not been concluded. The history of the island consists of catastrophes, eruptions, and deadly earthquakes. The capital town still bears the pitiless scars of the last quake, which occurred in the 1950s. From the ship, it resembles a white crown, standing out against the sky. At this distance, the eye cannot distinguish the houses from the ghostly layers of limestone that cover the entire length of the rocky wall. Donkeys stand on the quay, waiting to carry visitors upward over dizzying paths to the town, whose unusual character strikes one immediately. It is too new. It has nothing of the antiquated disarray of the usual Aegean villages. It was almost completely rebuilt after 1954; only occasionally does a collapsed wall serve as a reminder of the catastrophe.

But the tragedy *is* recalled impressively by the coldness, otherwise unknown in the Greek islands, of these all-too-prosperous buildings all too carefully arranged. Though undeniably picturesque, something of the soul of the town has been lost. The visitor is only too glad to get away from this chilling modernism and head for the open fields.

Here too, though, one receives an immediate surprise and shock: the unrelieved gray earth, which is found nowhere else in Greece. The ground is fertile, but it wears the color of death. There is an air of death over the entire island of Thira. It is beautiful, this strange rock, eerily beautiful, but without historical resonance. The movement so typical of Greece is here frozen into a mournful passivity. The passion of Greece here becomes an oppressive and formless menace. A silence betraying a kind of anxious expectation is all-pervading.

Everyone who lives on Thira can feel it. The comic opera for which every Greek village provides a setting is also performed

The village of Nebrio, on Thira: drawing by J. B. Hilair, c. 1800.

in Thira. But the residents' hearts are not really in it. The peasants are hiding something similar to resignation. In a way quite uncommon in Greece, they appear to bow before the inescapable. Death has announced itself to them quite often, and quite recently. They know that it will appear again apocalyptically. One day the earth will tear open anew, and the volcano will be reactivated. Misfortune and desolation will fall upon Thira once more.

Few of these people know that their home was the scene of a massive cataclysm in antiquity, the first and also the most important of those that have cast a pall over them. Once blessed by the gods, the island bore the name Kalliste, "the Very Beautiful One"; it was also called Strongule, "the Round One." In about 1500 B.C., it was shaken by a series of earthquakes. Then the volcano exploded. Suddenly, the center of the island literally burst into pieces, leaving a huge hole a few miles wide in its place. The raging sea promptly rolled in to fill the crater. All that was left of "the Very Beautiful One" was a heap of smoking ruins and lava. "The Round One" now assumed the form of a crescent that was supplemented by Thirasia, "the Witness Island." Nowhere in the world have the traces of a natural catastrophe been more visible than here.

Experts are of the opinion that this eruption was by far the most violent in antiquity and even in historic times. A natural catastrophe of such magnitude occurs only once in 10,000 years. The roar of the explosion was audible thousands of miles away. The clouds of smoke that streamed forth from the crater plunged the neighboring regions into utter darkness. Astonishing amounts of molten material poured out of the volcano. Many scholars believe that the seismic wave that resulted from the collapse of the center of the island devas-

tated the Cyclades, the coasts of Greece, Asia Minor, and most of Crete.

At the time of this cataclysm, Crete was radiant in the glow of Minoan civilization. Original and mysterious, brilliant and refined, this culture, long lost to us, remains an enigma. Its origins, its founders, and its collapse present us with many questions. Archeologists have reconstructed a significant number of its unique creations. However, they have not been able to piece together a single fragment of its history. We know only that in about 1500 B.C., Crete was struck by a devastating tidal wave. All of its palaces (except Cnossos), its villas, and its harbors were destroyed.

Thira: engraving by Orrin Smith, c. 1844.

Experts disagree about the cause of this catastrophe. Some believe that this cataclysm was linked, given the relative dates, to that of Thira. The awesome tidal wave is supposed to have been followed by a series of earthquakes that also struck Crete.

Crete never recovered from this blow. Minoan art spread to the Greek mainland and continued on its stunning career. But Minoan power was forever vanquished. The Minoan fleet, the most powerful of its time, was sunk and destroyed forever. The Minoan empire, which stretched across the entire Mediterranean, collapsed.

Crete was tied by misfortune to Thira, since they were both destroyed at the same time. However, it seems that they were also tied together by good fortune before the disaster. Thira must not only have belonged to the Minoan empire, but must also have been one of the most beautiful jewels in Crete's crown. Professor S. Marinatos, who specialized in Thira and its volcanic explosion, attempted to prove precisely this hypothesis. At the end of the nineteenth century, the German archeologist Hiller von Gärtringen had excavated on Thira. Archaic tombs, a Ptolemaic city, and Byzantine chapels were brought to light—but no Minoan remains.

Further research was hindered by one nearly insurmountable difficulty. The volcanic dust that covered the flatlands had solidified into a layer several yards thick. It seemed impossible that archeologists would be able to remove this layer from an area of any size. Yet in the south of the island, near the village of Akrotiri, a stream had eroded this compact mass somewhat. Marinatos was determined; he dug here, and some Minoan dwellings soon appeared. As excavation continued, the dwellings turned into a village. Oil and wine vessels, a millstone, and a workshop suggested something of its everyday life.

Marinatos could not continue long in this fashion, however; excavation is not the same as mining. He made another sounding elsewhere in the same valley. Paved streets and a stairway appeared. It was again a Minoan settlement. The Minoan presence was confirmed beyond question. But the quality of the finds was mediocre. The buildings were relatively primitive, and the ceramics were unexceptional.

In the summer of 1970, Marinatos attempted to join the two areas he had excavated. Suddenly, the style of the finds radically changed. They became more extensive, more detailed, richer, and finer. The site presented a fascinating and a touching picture. A three-story building had just been exposed. A narrow staircase led underground to some sealed rooms where a secret cult may once have been practiced. Not far away, a wall, only slightly uncovered, extended straight into the untouched volcanic layer. The flawless fitting of its enormous, marvelously hewn stones stood in distinct contrast to the rustic structures previously uncovered. It seemed that the palace was waiting to be unearthed. A valuable collection of ceramics that had been found at various spots had already been moved to a nearby warehouse. In a corner, three bronze vases were

still stuck in the earth. Underneath the corrosion, the delicate ornaments of a sublime frieze could be seen. One tiny fragment displayed a flawless embellishment with lily stems in the form of a vase and swallows. The daylight restored the freshness of the colors and revealed every shading that the artist's brush had given them. In the workshops, specialists were assembling fragments of a fresco that shows blue monkeys swinging from branch to branch in the midst of some luxuriant vegetation. Their movements have the grace of a ballet, and their expressive faces are depicted with a stunning realism. A human form has been discovered: a small head in the shadow of a palm tree, a profile with typically Phoenician features. This miniature serves as an unexpected link between archeology and myth, for it recalls the adventure of the king of Phoenicia, Cadmus, whose sister Europa was abducted by Zeus. Cadmus's search for her led him to Thira, where he left a garrison behind. Could this miniature be a portrait of one of his soldiers?

It seems miraculous that so many unbroken objects survive, despite the earthquakes. The ruins show the most devastating signs of these catastrophes. In one spot, for example, some massive pressure has pulverized the walls. In another, granite floors hang twisted in midair as though made of tin. And yet, by chance, fragile vases are still intact and delicate paintings have escaped the slightest damage.

These masterpieces provided adequate testimony: the size of the buildings, the flawless forms of the ceramics, and the elegant perfection of the paintings proclaim that Minoan art on Thira could compete with the most famous centers on Crete. Kalliste, "the Very Beautiful One," was not only a colony of the Minoans. Its radiance was nearly equal to Crete's before the same

Map from Olfert Dapper's Naukeurige Beschryving, *1688.*

tragic fate destroyed them.

The excavations that Professor Marinatos began in 1970 at Akrotiri are being continued. Visitors are allowed to view the partially excavated Minoan city, now protected by an overarching roof. The above-mentioned frescos, from the second millennium B.C., are now housed in a special department (not yet open to the public) of the National Museum of Athens.

AT ONE AND THE SAME TIME, AN EMPIRE COL-lapsed and an island sank into the sea. This catastrophe summons up an echo of an an-cient legend, the most famous and most highly debated one in history: the legend of Atlantis. Marinatos rekindled a theory that had lain dormant since the beginning of this century and presented the view that the brutal end of that legendary continent could have its historic truth in the downfall of the Minoans. Immediately, adventurous archeologists, enthusiastic seismologists, dilettantes, reporters, and television crews descended on Thira in order to hoist the banner of Atlantis. The future will decide whether their efforts are in vain. Yet this theory has a certain credibility. Atlantis finally has an opportunity to materialize out of the clouds of myth and to assume the reality it has vainly sought ever since Plato first told its story. Thira would then become famous for all time. Known for its cataclysms, attractive to hermits and scientists, frightening in its beauty, gloomy in its blinding light, the island seems to be becoming a bit more human as it relinquishes the delicate marvels that are buried beneath its surface. Though threatened by subterranean fires, Thira will survive in spite of all that might happen to it, linked to a legend that has given humankind something to dream about for 2,500 years.

THIRA: ANCIENT THERA

WHEN DORIC TRIBES SETTLED ON THIRA, DURING their migrations from Laconia to Crete, they avoided the gloomily threatening bay, the crater of the volcano. They chose instead the steep elevation on the southeast point of the island, Mesavouno. This is a narrow saddle of limestone on top of layers of schist. It reaches a height of some 1,200 feet and has only a single access, from the northwest, the Sellada, which joins it with a taller mountain (1,850 feet) named after the prophet Elijah. On all other sides, cliffs fall steeply, almost vertically, down to the plain or the sea. Mesavouno had several advantages: a solid foundation that can withstand earthquakes, two nearby springs, and a natural fortification. Mesavouno also has two small bays at the foot of the cliffs, Kamari on the north side and Perissa on the south, where ships can harbor under favorable weather conditions. Off toward the west stretches the largest plain of the island.

THIRA LIES AT THE JUNCTION OF TRAFFIC FROM THE Saronic Gulf to Crete and Egypt and from the Peloponnesus to Rhodes and the south coast of Asia Minor. From the summit of the ancient city, the visitor enjoys a splendid view of the Cyclades—Ios, Amorgos, Anaphi; somewhat farther off, Astypalaia; and when the air is clear, even the long, mountainous line of Crete.

The large number of imported vases discovered in the graves on Thira attest to lively trade with other centers. The earlier vases arrived from Crete and Paros; in the sixth century B.C., they came from Attica and Corinth, Rhodes and Ionia. Yet our awareness of the relationships between Thira and these other places remains superficial; we know nothing of the influences of trade and shipping on the island's social structure or cultural life. The elevation of Mesavouno restricted direct contact with the sea. And the extremely fertile soil of the island enabled the inhabitants to be agriculturally self-sufficient. Influenced by the Spartan way of life, the islanders lived in great simplicity in an isolated world and carved their graves and sanctuaries into the naked rock. Until the end, ancient Thera preserved its agricultural character. A surviving land register reveals that its main products were grain and, to a lesser degree, olives and grapes.

The political structure of Thera had much in common with that of Sparta and Crete. The community of citizens was subdivided into the three Doric *phylai* ("tribes") and these in turn into smaller groups. The members of each group would get together for common (all-male) banquets. There appears to have been another class of people living in the countryside, the *periokoi* ("those dwelling in the vicinity"), who had fewer political rights. The kingdom lasted until the fifth century B.C., when it was supplanted by an oligarchy, a rule by noble families, as Aristotle observed. Mention of a more democratic arrangement, with council (*boule*) and a people's assembly (*ekklesia tou demou*), begins in the third century B.C. Even so, the old aristocratic families, some of whom could legitimately claim royal Spartan ancestry, continued to exercise great political influence.

Isolated excavations were begun on Thira as early as the second half of the eighteenth century, but systematic work would wait until 1896–1902, when Hiller von Gärtringen carried on his research with the enthusiasm typical of that heroic era of archeology. The city extended to a length of 2,650 feet and a width of 688 feet on the saddle of Mesavouno. The chief feature of the city's plan was a main street that led from the Sellada and across the slope of Aghios Stephanos through the middle of the settlement. Space limitations made it impossible to combine the political and religious centers. The city thus developed in two separate directions: the agora and its surrounding dwellings to the west, and the temples and the gymnasium to the east. A city wall was unnecessary because the site was so well fortified by nature. The western part of the city is known today in the form it assumed in the Hellenistic and Roman periods. The eastern part preserves older, more venerable structures, permitting an understanding of the uniqueness of the architecture of Thera and the religious life of that time.

The layout of the older, eastern quarter, which was devoted to religious life, is striking. It comprises an *agora theon,* or "assembly of the gods." In a constricted space of 29 by 13 feet, and also somewhat outside it, small hollows, both round and square, were uncovered in the stone. Near them, the names of gods were engraved in an extremely archaic script. The hollows are thought to have been sacrificial basins, sacred thrones, or constructions that were somehow useful in the placement of stone

The 19th-century church of St. Stavros at Perissa, Thira.

fetishes. In any case, they are linked to an ancient, prepictorial cult. It is possible to make out the names of Zeus, his followers the Curetes, Apollo, Athena, and Hermes. Older, less common names also appear: Lochaia, Dameia, the Dioscuri, local deities elsewhere forgotten, and the north wind, Boreas, who tempered the summer heat in the Aegean. In the second half of the sixth century B.C., the space that contained these inscriptions was largely covered over by a

The Palatine Apollo:
an ancient marble.

polygonal structure 50 feet long and 22 feet wide. This was doubtless the *heroon* of Thera, or the tomb of the mythical founder of the colony, to whom funerary gifts were presented each year, as Pausanias relates.

The official religion at this time was the cult of Apollo Karneios. Not far from the *heroon,* to the north, the shrine of Apollo stands on a rectangular terrace (52 by 36 feet) with a beautifully constructed polygonal retaining wall. Through a small propylon (entrance) with two columns, one comes into a nearly square courtyard that partly covers an underground cistern. On the right are two rooms where the priests lived. On the left rises the temple itself (64 feet long by 29½ feet wide). It consists of a closed *pronaos* (vestibule) without columns, two doorways, and a square cella. The floor of the vestibule is composed of embedded gravel, while the cella's is polished stone. Narrow corridors run along either side of the cella. On the south side, there are two rooms, probably treasure chambers, carved directly into the rock. The temple, erected in about 600 B.C., does not display the customary Doric style. A statue of a *kouros* (youth) discovered beneath the retaining wall was the cult image of the god. The tribal cult of Apollo Karneios common to all Dorians here had a rustic character and was mixed with pre-Hellenic elements. The happy festival of the Karneia was associated with the grape harvest and was celebrated in the countryside for nine days in late August and early September. The tradition of the festival included sleeping in huts made of branches and communal banquets. For banquets, contests, and dances, the whole space south of the temple up to the edge of the cliff was laid out as a single open area supported by an imposing retaining wall 174 feet long. Countless inscriptions carved in

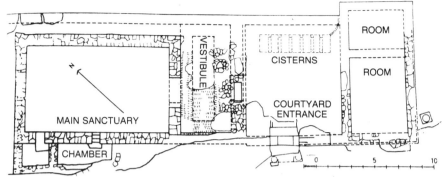

Shrine of Apollo Karneios: floor plan.

the rock relate, often with candor, the exploits of youths who distinguished themselves in dancing or making love.

A few yards in front of the eastern corner of the retaining wall, a cave with squared walls recedes into the cliff; a niche inside it housed the cult image. This cave was consecrated to Hermes and Heracles. Below the square where the Karneia was celebrated stand the buildings that comprised the gymnasium for young men. A courtyard 105 feet long by 69 feet wide and a round building at the northeast corner—probably once housing warm baths—date from Archaic times. A hall with four Doric columns in the center of its façade and a series of rooms along the east side were added in Hellenistic times. A swimming pool with five small cisterns was built on during the Roman Empire.

Another Archaic shrine from the sixth century B.C. cannot even be reconstructed in outline, for its ruins were destroyed when a Byzantine basilica was erected on the same site. From its few remains, one can deduce that this temple had two entrances, which was most uncommon. On the east side lay a large sacred precinct with a propylon. According to an inscription, the shrine was consecrated to Apollo Pythios.

Only isolated walls remain from the houses of the Archaic city that stretched to the west. The agora was given its final form in Hellenistic times. The earlier agora, with its shrine to Athena Polias, must have stood on the same spot. The symbol of Apollo, a marble lion dating from the end of the seventh century B.C., was set up in the agora; this and the two temples recall ancient testimony that Thera was held to be sacred to Apollo.

The cemetery of Archaic Thera lies on the two slopes of the Sellada and next to the street leading down to the Bay of Perissa. The older tomb complexes, from the eighth and seventh centuries B.C., lie in the southern section. The general practice was to cremate the dead and bury their ashes in large vases or stone chests. Crude gravestones of considerable size preserved the names of those who had died. Next to them there was often a funerary table on which food for the departed souls was placed. The newer cemetery (sixth–fourth centuries B.C.) does not contain such massive tombs. It lies along the street that snakes up from the harbor on the north side of the Sellada.

In antiquity, Thera was by no means as great an art center as Paros or Naxos. Nonetheless it developed ceramic workshops whose products were used locally.

Thera's distinctive Geometric style is characterized by monumental forms with only a few decorative motifs, repeated to the point of monotony. This style never evolved any further, and it survived on the island until the end of the sixth century B.C.

Then, during the third century B.C., a colorful exoticism penetrated the closed world of Thera. The Ptolemaic kings of Egypt conquered the island in the course of the battles among the successors of Alexander the Great for control of the Aegean. The Ptolemies occupied the island with a garrison and used it as a base for their fleet. The important complex of quays in Eleusis, now known as Exomiti, on the southern tip of the island, attests to this. Strange cults appeared in the wake of these new rulers—those of the Egyptian deities Serapis, Isis, and Anubis, of the Ptolemaic kings, and of Sabazios.

Army barracks were constructed on the highest elevation of Mesavouno, where it was possible to look down on the city and keep an eye on it. The first side street to the right leads to an interesting two-story building (104 by 59 feet) that served as army headquarters. Through a vestibule with Ionic columns, you come upon a complex of rooms straight ahead, a small courtyard bordered by other rooms to the right, and, to the left, a long corridor leading to a large, covered court with a cistern and rooms along its east side. Across from this structure stands the gymnasium, where the garrison took its exercise. An inscription contains the text of a letter from King Ptolemy VI, Philometor, in which he establishes the fees for oil, for both sacrificial and medicinal use. There follows a listing of the contributions made for the repair of the building by the officers and their companies. Across from the gymnasium, there was a palacelike structure (164 by 108 feet) with airy, imposing spaces arranged in a complicated floor plan.

This colony of foreigners had its religious center in the shrine of the Egyptian gods in the southern part of the city. This sanctuary (51 by 24½ feet) is carved out of the stone cliff. It consists of an open space in which the faithful gathered and a modest cella that contained the cult images. Sacrifices were placed in niches in the rock wall. Water required during the rites was furnished by two cisterns. During the sacred ritual, a priest would descend a small staircase with a vessel of water. The shrine to Serapis was also used by the Basilists, a religious community that worshipped the Ptolemaic kings. A few yards above the temple stood a building whose courtyard was surrounded by columns; this belonged to the Basilists.

INSCRIPTIONS DOCUMENT THE NAMES AND deeds of various foreigners who lived on Thera at this time. One was a commander-in-chief of land forces and naval commander named Hermaphilos, from Raukos, on Crete. He was watching one day as pirates landed in the harbor of Oia and seized hundreds of women and children. During the night he dispatched troops to the harbor. They successfully defeated the invaders and liberated most of the captives.

Artemidorus, the son of Apollonius, managed to immortalize himself in countless inscriptions. He came from Perge, in Pamphylia, far from Thera, and lived here in the third century B.C. As a young man, he was in the service of the Ptolemies. He later joined a group of soldiers who hunted elephants from the Red Sea into the land of the Troglodytes. At last, however, he retired to the peace of Thera for his old age. He performed a number of good deeds for the residents, for which he was on three occasions crowned with a wreath and finally made a citizen. This same Artemidorus built a small temple to Ptolemy III, Euergetes, near the Karneia square. In the sacred precinct he constructed near the city gate, the man and his personality are almost tangible. Here he erected statues and altars and had reliefs chiseled into the rock—an eagle, a lion, and a dolphin with respective dedicatory inscriptions to Zeus, Apollo, and Poseidon—and here we also see his portrait, a medallion depicting Artemidorus with olive branches around his head. It bears the inscription: "As a monu-

ment to Thera, the name of Artemidorus will not be forgotten as long as the stars rise in the heavens and the earth below survives."

HELLENISTIC ARCHITECTURE IN THE CITY EXTENDS over the edge of the slope on a series of terraces between the temples of Ptolemy and Artemidorus. The uneven terrain did not permit a regular arrangement of streets. Two streets run nearly parallel to the main one, while the cross streets, which climb up the steep slope, required ramps and steps.

Women of Thira: drawing by J. B. Hilair, c. 1782.

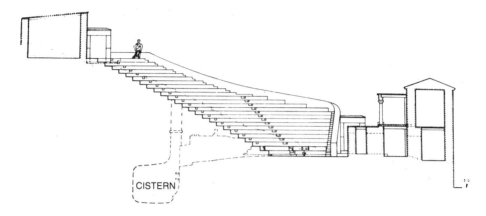

TOP AND BOTTOM: The Hellenistic theater on Thira. The top picture depicts the theater in Roman times.

At the highest point, where the main street widens, lies the agora; it has an overall length of 377 feet and measures 83 feet at its widest spot. Just inside the entrance was the market, with shops that primarily sold foodstuffs. In Roman times, templelike buildings were erected here for worthy citizens of Thera and embellished with commemorative statues.

After the food market comes the state market with its king's hall. This rectangular structure is 164 feet long and 39 feet wide. Ten Doric columns divide the interior into two naves. The long, eastern side has two doorways. One wall boasts two inscriptions that tell of the "repairs by Kleitos-

thenes Claudianos, which he paid for himself" in the second century A.D. During this construction, a space was created in the northern portion where statues of Roman emperors were set up on pedestals. In the same period, a small bath was added to the south side of the king's hall.

Dominating the market is a temple (34 by 22 feet). It stands on a separate terrace, and its façade is enhanced by four Doric columns. Originally, the temple was dedicated to Dionysus. But in the second century A.D., it was taken over by the cult of the Ptolemies and, under Augustus, by the cult of the Roman emperors. An elongated portico (92 by 10 feet) served commercial

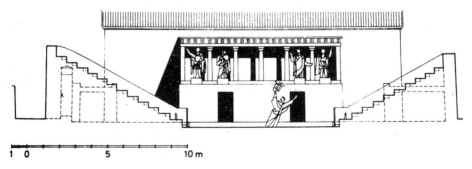

1 0   5   10 m

purposes. Across from it stands the temple of the goddess Tyche. A cross street that leads down over a number of steps to the east brings you to the Hellenistic theater. With an area of 131 by 79 feet, this theater could hold roughly 1,500 spectators. The rows of seats in the auditorium are divided into five blocks and are surrounded by an open portico. In the ancient theater the orchestra was a circle; in the early Roman Empire it was made semicircular. A stage with a wide apron could be constructed in this space.

THE PRIVATE HOUSES OF THERA ARE LAID OUT in the style familiar from Hellenistic structures on Delos with an inner courtyard and, in the larger ones, an ambulatory with columns. They often had two stories, and there were cisterns beneath the courtyard floor. The walls were whitewashed and frequently embellished with polychrome plant motifs. Marble paneling was also used. In general, these houses bear the stamp of prosperity, but they do not display the elegance and luxury found in other Hellenistic centers. Finds on view in the museum reveal something of the decadence of this ancient city, of a striving toward happiness within one's own four walls, where all too often only loneliness and spiritual ennui were at home. Signs of this are the small altars and statues of the domestic cults (Tyche, Hygieia, Agathos Daimon, and especially Aphrodite).

Beginning in Hellenistic times, the dead were no longer cremated. A burial site near the village of Plagades contains sarcophagi hewn out of the cliffs. There are also large tomb chambers near Eleusis, in modern-day Echendra, as well as templelike tombs containing sarcophagi in underground chambers. By the time these were built, the concept of death had also changed; belief in the mortality of the soul led to internment of earthly human remains.

A splendid *heroon* that has survived in Evanghelismos includes a vestibule, an outer hall, and a cella. A smaller *heroon,* consisting of only a single room, is in the church of St. Nikolaos Marmarites, near Emporeio; this structure, including its roof, is quite well preserved. An inscription containing the testament of a certain Epiktete, daughter of Grinnos, tells something of the obligations of survivors and their funeral customs. It mentions a large family cemetery with a garden and ambulatory outside the city. In the midst of this plot stood a temple to the Muses containing a relief frieze and statues of the deceased. Surviving relatives were summoned to an annual three-day celebration at the temple, where sacrifices and wreaths were presented and a common banquet held to conclude the festivities. When the descendants of Epiktete married, they were also supposed to hold their wedding ceremonies in the precinct of the tombs.

THE LATER HISTORY OF THERA MAY TRIGGER AN INTerest in the island's cultural development, but the visitor to the ruins and the museum is most impressed by the Archaic city. Everything here is of a piece: the primeval, austere ethos of monumental art, the simple feeling for life close to nature, and of course the landscape itself. The visitor is immediately transported back to about 630 B.C.

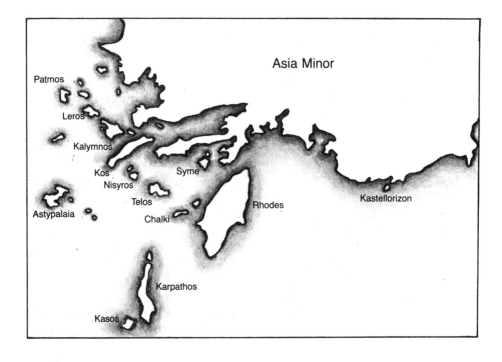

THE DODECANESE

ASTYPALAIA

EVERY ISLAND IN THE AEGEAN, EVEN THE SMALL-est, has a unique image that is similar to that of the neighboring islands only in the main features, just as the faces of people related to each other bear only a general resemblance.

We now know that life on Astypalaia, a stopping point between the Cyclades and the Dodecanese, began in the Mycenaean period. A significant find a few years ago attests to the existence of Hellenic Mycen-aeans. Countless vessels and smaller ob-jects came to light during the excavation of two Mycenaean burial mounds. In the same spot where the graves were discovered, the out-of-the-way village of Armenochori, there are springs that permit us to con-clude that Astypalaia had plentiful water, forests, and fertile fields in antiquity. To-day, the island is barren. Exposed to the drying winds, it only has poor grazing land bordered by low walls. Its three villages are sparsely settled. Visitors, however, are en-chanted by its picturesque houses and windmills.

With a total area of about 38 square miles, Astypalaia is 11 miles long and 8 miles wide. The island is composed of two rocky masses that are barely connected by the isthmus of Aghios Andreas, only 360 feet wide. Around the island are countless smaller naked rocks.

The most imposing attraction of Astypa-laia is a large castle, the Kastro, which was inhabited until World War II. Fragments of the marble wall of an ancient temple on the southeast side of the church of Aghios Ghiorghios offer positive proof that there was a fortified acropolis here in antiquity.

The Venetian Guerini family, who set-tled on Astypalaia in the Middle Ages, ap-parently rebuilt the fortifications, though here, as on many Aegean islands, these con-sisted merely of the back walls of houses built adjacent to one another, not of free-standing walls. Here, these walls are not windowless but broken by balconies and grilled openings so that the inhabitants could look out at the sea. The church of Aghios Ghiorghios was built on the ruins of the ancient temple; the church of the Pan-aghia, above the entrance to the Kastro. Gradually the people moved outside this walled area and constructed large build-ings and churches, such as the Panaghia i Portaitissa (Holy Virgin, Guardian of the Gate), outside the fortification. Small houses are strewn all about the island and

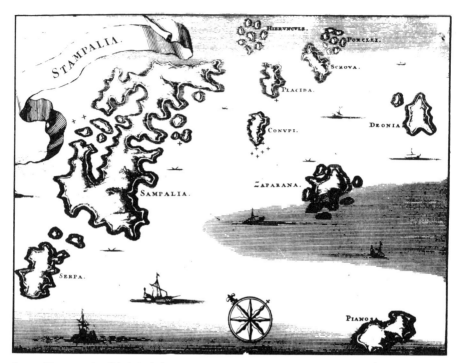

An antique map of Astypalaia.

The island of Astypalaia.

1. *Strait of Aghios Andreas*
2. *Aghios Andreas*
3. *Astypalaia*
4. *Kastro*
5. *Analipsis*
6. *Aghios Ioannis*
7. *Vathy*

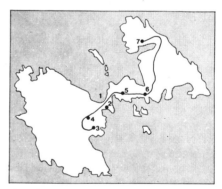

down to Pera Yalo, the harbor, where there are also some modest hotels.

Everywhere too there are blinding white, tiny churches that contain votive offerings from those who have been saved at sea. These churches stand humbly on rough slopes or in the valleys. The tradition of such votive churches dates from Early Christian and Byzantine times, as fragments of mosaic floors attest. Centuries of simple faith have left their traces on Astypalaia.

ARCHEOLOGICAL FINDS SUGGEST THAT ASTYPA- laia was by no means a remote island in antiquity, either in the Mycenaean period or later. Cut off from the world? One has this impression today merely because Astypalaia is so difficult to reach. As so often in the Aegean, one is at the mercy of the steamship lines. In antiquity, sea travel was dependent neither on schedules nor on high oil prices; at that time, it was only a matter of *oureios anemos,* or favorable wind. Small, swift vessels would convey passengers and goods from one Aegean island to another whenever a fresh breeze filled their sails.

NISYROS

The island of Nisyros lies north of the island of Telos and equidistant from the islands of Telos and Kos. Nisyros is round and mountainous; it possesses a city of the same name, a harbor, and a temple of Poseidon. It is thought that Nisyros is a fragment from Kos, having originated in the following manner: during the war of the giants, the god of the sea, Poseidon, is supposed to have given chase to the giant Polybotes; in his rage the god tore off a piece from Kos with his trident and flung it after the giant. This piece was called Nisyros. But the giant continues to live beneath the island even today.

The myth that Strabo related in the first century A.D. is based on the observation that Nisyros, the western part of Kos, and the small island of Yialis among them all have identical rock formations and soil— and on the fact that there was a volcano on Nisyros. Even Homer made a connection between Nisyros and Kos; it would appear that the island really was attached to Kos in early historical times. On Kos there existed a tribe *(phyle)* called Nisyrioi.

Settled at some point by Carians and later by Argives, Nisyros was conquered by Queen Artemisia of Halicarnassus, the sister and wife of Mausolus. Nisyros joined the First Attic League (479 B.C.) as an autonomous city-state. Later, the island formed a *demos* (administrative district) of the island of Rhodes, though it had its own *boule* (council) and *ekklesia tou demou* (assembly). The ruler was here called Demiourgos ("creator"), as in Camirus, while the council of Prostates ("protectors") was analogous to the Prostates of Lindus. Countless coins from the fourth century B.C. have been discovered on Nisyros. From these, we so far know that the gods Zeus Meilichios, Dionysus, Poseidon, Ares, and Hermes were worshipped here.

On a modern map, we discover that Nisyros lies 10 nautical miles south of Kos, 8 nautical miles north of Telos, and 9 nautical miles west of the peninsula of Cnidus in Asia Minor. With a surface area of 13½ square miles, the nearly round island has a diameter of 3.7 miles. Its highest peak is the Diabates (2,296 feet). Its slopes fall roughly and steeply into the sea, with no bays at all. Drinking water is very scarce, though there are various hot springs like those at Thermia and Paloi. The inhabitants, from remote antiquity until today, have dealt with the shortage of water by constructing cisterns. Despite its apparent dryness, though, the island supports vegetation, for its volcanic soil holds moisture.

The first sights to strike the new visitor are the light-colored stone walls *(xerolithies)* that the islanders build to prevent the soil from slipping down the steep slopes. In this way, they secure a little space for their grapevines, almonds, and fig trees. Even the ancients—at least in Classical times—built retaining walls; theirs were larger, however, so as to create modest platforms around

The island of Nisyros.

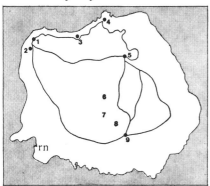

1. *Mandraki*
2. *Spiliani fortress and Early Christian basilica*
3. *Loutra*
4. *Paloi*
5. *Emporeio*
6. *High plain of Lakki*
7. *Alexander crater*
8. *Stephanos crater*
9. *Nikia*

the cliffs to build houses on and to cultivate.

Nisyros has four settlements today: two are in the mountains—Emporeio in the north, Nikia in the south—and two are on the sea—Mandraki, the capital, in the northwest and Paloi in the north. The two mountain villages doubtless developed during the period in which the island was exposed to attacks by pirates, when the inhabitants of all the Aegean Islands fled to their most inaccessible locations.

The capital village of Mandraki can presumably reflect on a past that reaches back into the Bronze Age. A long jetty constructed in antiquity closed off the harbor to the north. The entire harbor basin that Strabo described is completely dried up today. It is here that the main street and the buildings of modern Mandraki were built. Portions of the ancient jetty, which was constructed with a fine clay mixed with lime, have been discovered beneath numerous buildings.

During the Classical period, the settlement stood within the splendidly preserved acropolis of Nisyros. This stands on a hill southwest of the harbor. It seems surprising to encounter such a well-preserved fortification on a volcanic island. The method of its construction explains its survival: gigantic blocks of lava have been piled on top of each other without mortar, sometimes to a thickness of 12 feet; the people who built this fortress did not forget the slumbering giant Polybotes, and the inhabitants spoke of the "Cyclopean wall." One passes through it at an imposing gateway on its northeastern corner. Most impressive is the single, gigantic stone slab, nearly 13 feet long, that covers the gate. It is reminiscent of the stone slab above the entry to the Treasury of Atreus in Mycenae. There is an interesting inscription on the outside of the wall. It explains that this wall belongs to the community and that it is forbidden to build or plant anything within 5 feet of it. Built just as carefully as the wall is the stairway that leads up from the gateway. In the north, the wall extended as far as the medieval castle of the Spiliani, of which a number of remains are visible. In the west, the acropolis was naturally protected, for here the slope is quite steep. Nonetheless additional fortification may have existed. Today, the area within the acropolis is being built up, and except for a few ruins of an Early Christian basilica, there are no longer any signs of ancient structures. The inscription on the wall dates from the fourth century B.C., the basilica from the fifth or sixth century A.D. Thus we may conclude that the settlement within the acropolis of Nisyros was uninterruptedly inhabited from the fifth century B.C. until at least the fifth century A.D.

The ancient cemeteries in which most of the archeological finds have been made lie outside the fortress. The oldest of them (near Aghios Ioannis) dates from the sixth century B.C. It is quite probable that the archaic *polis,* like most Ionian cities, was unfortified and that it stood on the site of present-day Mandraki. Portions of retaining walls discovered near the school in Mandraki reveal the same method of construction as was used in the fortification walls.

The castle of the Panaghia Spiliani was built by the knights of the Order of St. John of Rhodes when they conquered Nisyros. This castle occupies a more exposed site than does the ancient acropolis. In Late Byzantine times, the church of the Panaghia Spiliani (Holy Virgin of the Cave) was fashioned out of a cave in the cliff; this served as the core of a monastic complex. This monastery owes its prosperity to gifts and donations from seafarers and emi-

Poseidon: an ancient marble.

grants, a significant source of income for the impoverished island.

Despite its modest circumstances, Nisyros also felt the influence of artistic movements that came together in the Aegean. Among the earliest finds is a small Cycladic idol, now in a museum in Berlin, as well as three vessels from the Bronze Age. Nothing at all is known of the period from 1500 to 600 B.C. (However, nearly all of the discoveries made so far have been the result of accident; there have been scarcely any systematic archeological investigations.) From the seventh century B.C. until the Early Christian era, the finds indicate that there was an unbroken artistic flowering. Excavations in the ancient cemetery of Aghios Ioannis have brought to light a remarkable collection of flat bowls and vessels, which date from the seventh and sixth centuries B.C., from workshops in Rhodes.

Surviving from the middle of the fifth century B.C. is an especially beautiful Ionian relief that is now in the Archeological Museum in Istanbul. It depicts a standing hoplite whose head is tilted slightly to the right. His left hand is touching his spear, while his right hangs down at his side, just as though the young foot soldier were resting. This stele is admittedly no rarity when one considers how many were reused in Roman times and incorporated into new tombs. Some can be seen on the island itself; others are displayed in the Archeological Museum on Rhodes, where most finds from Nisyros have found their way. These include the finely carved and decorated altars resembling those of Rhodes and dating from Hellenistic or Roman times.

Three Early Christian basilicas have been discovered on Nisyros: one in the ancient acropolis, another near the cemetery of Aghios Ioannis, and the third near Paloi. Capitals of columns, parapet slabs, and portions of mosaic floors strewn here and there are remains from the fifth and sixth centuries A.D. Architectural fragments displaying lovely reliefs and incorporated into the church of the Panaghia Spiliani date from Byzantine days. Shards and pieces of vases from many periods are constantly being found all over the island.

Like the castle of the Panaghia Spiliani, the ruins of fortresses near Nikia and Emporeio recall the monks of the Order of St. John. Everywhere you notice the folk-art quality of structures from post-Byzantine and more modern times—small wayside churches, oil presses, and the houses of Mandraki, Emporeio, and Nikia. Nisyros is rich in traditions, folk tales, and lovely folksongs.

One should not leave Nisyros without seeing its volcano, Mount Diabates, which is an impressive sight. The visitor to Emporeio, roughly in the center of the island, is suddenly confronted with a broad, high plain, called Lakki. The plain was created only after the volcano exploded in 1522 and the mountain collapsed. Today, you can see the craters of the extinguished volcano strewn about the plain like the mouths of streams.

*T*ELOS

THE SLENDER SILHOUETTE OF TELOS STANDS OUT against the coast of Asia Minor to the west of Cnidus and north of Rhodes. This stony island has scarcely any vegetation. In the 1970s, the remains of extinct dwarf elephants were discovered on Telos. They were only 4 feet tall, they lived some 45,000 years ago or more, and they are presumed to have died out in about 4600 B.C. Skeletons, skulls, and elephant teeth lay between limestone layers down as far as 27 to 29 feet. It is believed that further excavations will reveal dwarf hippopotamus fossils and some indication of why such small forms of mammals lived on the Aegean Islands.

The fossilized elephants were found in the cave of Charkadio, near the fortress of Mesaria. This cave is temporarily closed to the public; the finds will soon be displayed in the Paleontology Museum in Athens.

The ancient history of the island, like that of most of the smaller ones, is obscure. Dorians came to Telos in about 1000 B.C. Herodotus relates that the Telians participated in the colonization of Gela (Sicily) in the seventh century B.C. with the Lindians from Rhodes. In the fifth century B.C., they joined the Attic League and allied themselves, after the collapse of Athenian hegemony, with the Spartans. Then, after the sea battle near Cnidus in 394 B.C., they won back their independence. Until the end of the fourth or the middle of the third century B.C., Telos was autonomous. It throve economically and minted its own coins. Erinna, a lyric poetess, was born on Telos during this time. She died young, and only a few of her elegiac verses have survived. An epitaph she wrote for her close friend Baucis reads:

Pillars of death, carved Sirens, tearful urns,

In whose sad keeping my poor dust is laid,
To him, who near my tomb his footsteps turns,
Stranger or Greek, bid hail; and say a maid
Rests in her bloom below; her sire the name
Of Baucis gave; her birth and lineage high;
And say her bosom friend Erinna came
And on this tomb engraved her elegy.

JOHN ADDINGTON SYMONDS

At the end of the fourth century B.C., Telos allied itself to Kos and was ruled by that island. A half-century later it belonged to Rhodes and the Ptolemies ruling in Egypt. Ancient finds reveal that Telos was dependent on Rhodes both politically and culturally. The Romans conquered the island in 42 B.C., and from the Roman period until the early fourteenth century, the history of the island becomes obscure once again. In 1310, the knights of St. John arrived. From that point on, we have only dates associated with catastrophes. When the knights

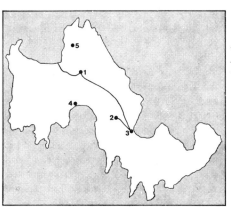

The island of Telos.

1. Meghalo Chorio
2. Mikro Chorio
3. Livadia
4. Eristos
5. Kastro

*Map of Meghalo Chorio
and Kastro.*

1. *The village of Meghalo
   Chorio*
2. *Taxiarchis church*
3. *Ancient city wall*
4. *Modern path*
5. *Cemetery*
6. *Kastro (fortress)*

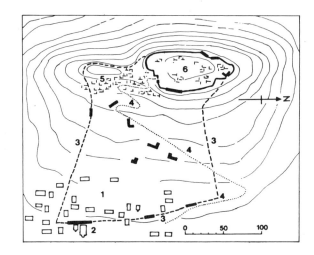

*(After R. H. Sipsen and
J. F. Lazenbyl.)*

feared Turkish attacks in 1475 and 1480, they decided to evacuate the Telians to Rhodes. The Turks did attack Telos in 1479, 1485, and 1504, and they succeeded in conquering the island, along with the rest of the Dodecanese, in 1522. Since then, its fate has been linked to the entire archipelago's.

The hub of ancient Telos lay in the north of the island, always on the same site, which was called Meghalo Chorio ("large village"). The houses stood on the southern slope of the hill of Aghios Stephanos. In front of the north wall of the church of the Taxiarchis, a large segment of the ancient city wall can be seen. Another portion of the fortifications stands amid some houses. On top of the hill there are also retaining walls and ancient ruins among fragments of medieval buildings. In the village there are numerous half-ruined small churches, each only a single room with a slightly curved ceiling and decorated with frescos from the fourteenth and fifteenth centuries. Serpentine streets paved with stone wind downhill from the village.

Like Meghalo Chorio, the cemetery has also occupied the same site since antiquity. Then it took up more room than it does now. There are still ancient graves here, stone slabs with inscriptions, and sacrificial altars. A bronze water-jug (*hydra*) that came from one of these graves now stands in the British Museum, and countless bits of gold jewelry found here, funerary gifts, have been taken to the museum in Rhodes.

ANYONE WHO CLIMBS UP TO THE FORTRESS (*kastro*) will recognize that its imposing entrance and certain portions of the walls date from antiquity. Passing through the gate, one is confronted with an ancient marble staircase. Its steps probably led from the propylaea to the temples of Zeus and Athena, the patron goddess of the city. The islanders took refuge inside the constantly renovated fortification whenever there was threat of war. The overall impression of the place today is that of a fortress of the knights of St. John. Doubtless it is the castle that the Florentine Buondelmondi called Aghios Stephanos in the fifteenth century. Inside the castle, there are a few easily recognized cisterns among the ruins as well as a large one-room church with sixteenth-century frescos.

In the center of the island lies the abandoned Mikro Chorio ("little village"), whose inhabitants left for Livadia or overseas after World War II. There is a medieval watchtower (Kastro tou Lambrou) that may be visited if one wishes to undertake an hour-long hike out of Mikro Chorio to the northwest.

On the northwest coast lies Livadia, a harbor today, just as it was in antiquity. Along the road leading from Meghalo Chorio to Livadia you can make out the ruins of the medieval fortress of Mesaria on a low, rocky summit.

Another point of interest is a ruined medieval castle, Agriosykia, from which one has a lovely view of the sea.

In the north (on the bay of Aghios Antonios) and the west (Eristos), there were presumably ancient settlements that were inhabited up until Early Christian times.

In a rare green valley, in idyllic surroundings, lies the monastery of Aghios Panteleimon, from the eighteenth century, ringed by walls and guarded by a tall, square tower. An abbot by the name of Laurentios built the monastery church in 1703, and some of the frescos that Gregorios of Syme painted in 1776 are still preserved inside. Monks' cells, one above the other, surround the monastery church. Aghios Panteleimon developed into a cultural and trade center and minted its own coinage, which was only valid on the island itself.

The remaining twenty or so churches contain frescos from the thirteenth to sixteenth centuries. After the Turks conquered the island, only small churches were built; their entrances were less than 4 feet high. During Turkish rule, the houses also became increasingly smaller. "A house that one just fits in and a field you can see the edges of" seemed enough to the easily satisfied Telians. Nearly every house had its own oil press and baking oven in its courtyard.

The roughly 400 people who live on the island today lead a quite isolated life. Most of them are old sailors who used to work on the ships of wealthy families from Rhodes or Syme, or farmers whose chief occupation is caring for the artificial terraces that prevent the precious soil from being washed down into the sea by the rain.

KARPATHOS

THE ISLAND OF KARPATHOS IS CHARACTERIZED BY stern contours and intense light. Long and narrow and set somewhat apart from the other islands of the Dodecanese, it is a stepping stone to Crete. Its shoreline is indented with countless bays and beaches. Its mountains offer some protection from the fierce winds. A few remnants from the period of Italian occupation relate Karpathos to the other islands of the Dodecanese: were

The island of Karpathos.

1. Pighadia
2. Menetes
3. Arkassa
4. Aperion
5. Mesochorion
6. Olympus
7. Tristomon
8. The island of Saria
9. The island of Kasos

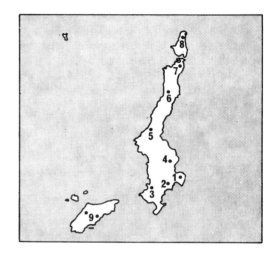

it not for the governor's mansion, a dismal example of the impersonal style of the short-lived Italian rule, Karpathos would have scarcely anything in common with Rhodes or Kos.

Pighadia, the main town, is relatively modern, architecturally indifferent but blessed by nature with a lovely setting. Nestled deep in the bay on a broad sand beach, it enjoys the coolness from the surrounding mountains.

Immediately outside Pighadia, the roads begin to climb, leading to villages perched on the mountainsides like castles. One such village is Menetes, whose old aristocratic mansions have an air of folk-art freshness about them despite their age. Other roads lead out of Pighadia to villages deep in shadow. These routes wind around the slopes of tall mountains standing steeply above the sea and through canyons heavy with the scent of oleander. They lead past sleepy Byzantine churches, ruined fortresses, and barren high plains, where the shadows of clouds on the rock are often the only accents in an otherwise desolate landscape.

The houses of Karpathos are either long and narrow or L-shaped, with a paved and walled courtyard behind. Generally the dwelling consists of the "big house" with a door, a window, and a dormer light, and the "little house" with a window and dormer and the so-called cell with a door and a bake-oven. The "big house" is divided in two: a floor placed roughly 3 feet off the ground with a richly decorated wooden railing forms a kind of balustrade, called a *soupha*. Above this there is a second floor, the *panosouphi*. One climbs two steps to reach the *soupha* and enters it through an archway ornamented with a Byzantine motif. A pillar extending up to the wooden ceiling supports the ridge-pole. Hanging on the wooden railings of the *soupha* and the pillar are the showpieces of the house: gold-embroidered coverlets, colorful tablecloths and towels, and fine embroidery, all the products of long and patient work.

All around Karpathos there are deep-sea caverns and coves, capes where the sea breaks violently, and protected sandy beaches, soft and golden. The sole connection between the two halves of the island is by water. From Pighadia, you may travel to Dhiaphani, the small harbor of the town of Olympus, either in a caïque or on the ship that drops anchor once a week. Farther along the coast, you come to Saria, the small island at the tip of Karpathos with ruins of a Byzantine town, then to Palatia, and from there to the east coast and Vrychounta with its ancient temples. On this mysterious island, you encounter a unique culture with a rich artistic tradition whose center is Olympus.

Olympus is unaltered in both form and spirit. It clings to the mountain and faces the endless sea. In the streets or at the wells, the women of Olympus are always dressed in the elegant costumes whose designs fuse local aesthetic tradition with a utilitarian adaptation to the work that has to be done. These costumes consist of a handwoven white dress with embroidery at the bosom, a wide belt around the waist, and on top of this a simple, long, dark blue vest, which is also embroidered. The women step lightly in bright-colored shoes and stockings, and around their heads they wear three triangular scarves.

The only interruptions to the stoic, dreamy rhythm of the loom, which forms the pulse of life for the women of Olympus, are major events like weddings, funerals, and popular festivals (*paneghyri*). The wedding celebrations of Olympus are famous. Preparations require months, and the celebration itself goes on around the clock for three days.

The event begins in the bride's home, where musicians play in the courtyard as relatives appear with their gifts. The bride sits on a specially decorated couch and listens to improvised songs by the girls of the village, her former playmates. These songs (*mantinades*) speak of the beauty of the bride, of the joy and sorrow that the marriage will bring, and of wishes for the future. Then the groom appears, followed by a wedding parade with musicians and flag carriers, relatives and friends who bear gifts, baskets of flowers, and the groom's costumes. In front of the bride's house, the groom smashes a pomegranate beneath his foot, a symbol of fertility and wealth. The bride and her relatives join the wedding procession. All make their way to the church. Once the vows have been exchanged, there is a banquet at the house of the bride. Benches for as many as 500–800 guests have been set up outside in the garden. The men eat first, and only when they are finished do the women sit down. The feast continues until sunset, when the dancing begins. Songs celebrating the bridal pair are sung, and the Karpathian *syrmatikos* is danced. Beginning with slow, sliding steps in six-eight time, it builds up to a violent whirling circle dance. The entire village joins in the dancing until dawn.

The following day is the "antiwedding" day. The guests betake themselves to the house of the bride's godfather, an important figure in every Greek wedding. There they are served wine in Indian nutshells. The musicians then lead the procession to the newlyweds' house. To get them to open the door, the godfather, whose hands have been tied behind his back, is required to promise the bridal couple a magnificent gift, such as a large, fat lamb. When the door is then flung open, the guests are once more invited to take their places on benches. This time, the men and women sit together. On the third day, only the relatives of the couple continue to celebrate.

Karpathos is governed by unwritten traditions such as this. The girls take their places at the looms to begin to prepare their dowries as soon as they turn ten; the amazing weavings and embroideries that adorn their dwellings on their wedding day represent years and years of work. Tradition also prescribes that only the first-born, boy or girl, inherits the parents' possessions. It almost seems as if medieval, feudal customs were still in force. But during the relaxed, almost wild, celebrations, there is something Dionysian about the place.

KASTELLORIZON (MEGISTE)

KASTELLORIZON IS A SMALL BUT IMPRESSIVE IS-land at the southeastern extreme of the Aegean Sea, only a short distance from the coast of Asia Minor. In fact, it is so close to the mainland that you can swim to it. Kastellorizon lies in a circle of even smaller islands that continue to bear ancient Greek names even today, such as Rhoge and Strongyle ("the round one"). In antiquity, it was called Megiste ("the largest"), for it was the biggest island of this group. It received its modern name in the fourteenth century after the Castello Rosso or Castro Rosso (Red Fortress), erected by members of the Order of St. John of Rhodes on top of the ruins of a fortress built in the fourth century B.C. by Sosikleos Nikagoras. The name also refers to the soil of the island, which is rich in iron and therefore red.

Only one settlement on the island resembles a town. Its multicolored houses and white churches surround a horseshoe-shaped harbor. High above, on the summit of Aghios Nikolaos, stands the medieval fortress. Everything conspires to produce an enchanting vision that you first glimpse

The location of Kastellorizon in relation to the coast of Asia Minor.

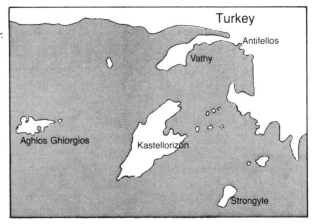

Turkey

Antifellos

Vathy

Aghios Ghiorgios

Kastellorizon

Strongyle

when approaching by sea on the ship that crosses the 72 nautical miles from Rhodes, the island's sole connection to the outside world.

Because of its location, Kastellorizon was repeatedly conquered and occupied, though it has always been poor and lacking in mineral resources that might have made it attractive to foreign conquerors. The visitor will find no luxury hotels, only a picturesque landscape with few traces of modern civilization. Anglers and hunters will discover that it is an ideal retreat.

ARCHEOLOGICAL RESEARCH HAS ALMOST COM-pletely ignored Kastellorizon so far. The remains of Cyclopean walls, Minoan-Myce-naean graves, and prehistoric stone axes,

however, prove that the island was inhabit-ed at a very early date. The first settlers were presumably emigrants who left Crete for Lycia and stayed here instead. The first Greeks on the island were Dorians who set out from Rhodes in the eleventh century B.C. for the coast of Asia Minor, where they later created the famous Dorian *hexapolis* (six-city league)—Lindus, Ialysus, Camirus, Kos, Cnidus, and Halicarnassus. The Dorians left a number of traces of their presence on Kastellorizon—for example, inscriptions and the modern dialect of the people. When the Persians established themselves in Asia Minor, they conquered Megiste in 496 B.C. Since then, with the sole exception of the period 333–304 B.C., when it even minted its own coinage, the

The island of Kastellorizon.

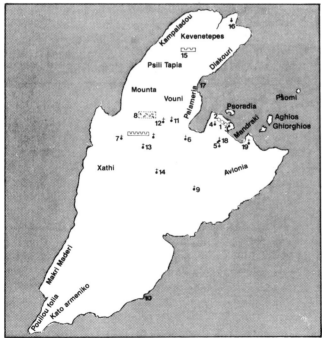

1. *Aghios Nikolaos hill*
2. *Castro Rosso*
3. *Aghia Paraskevi*
4. *Aghios Nikolaos*
5. *Panaghia*
6. *Aghios Merkourios*
7. *Palaiokastro (ancient acropolis and Christian churches)*
8. *Remains of Cyclopean walls*
9. *Aghios Ghiorghios*
10. *Blue Grotto*
11. *Monastery of Profitis Elias*
12. *Monastery of Aghia Triada*
13. *Aghios Panteleimon*
14. *Aghios Ioannis*
15. *Kastreli*
16. *Aghios Stephanos*
17. *Bay of Diakouri*
18. *Aghios Konstantinos*
19. *Aghios Savvas*

(Based on a drawing by Michalis Komninos.)

island has always been under the rule of outsiders, primarily Rhodes, whose general fate it shared until Roman times.

The inhabitants of Megiste worshipped Demeter, Artemis Soteira, the Dioscuri, Hermes, and above all Apollo Megisteus. This Apollo is mentioned on a votive inscription discovered in Kastellorizon and was the Apollo from the oracular shrine of Patara in Lycia, the mainland opposite.

During the following centuries, when Kastellorizon was not plagued by pirates, it developed a measure of commercial activity that secured its inhabitants a good income. These periods of good fortune never lasted long, however, for new conquerors would appear: Arabs, Saracens, and then the knights of St. John, who arrived and built the Castello Rosso after they were forced to leave Jerusalem.

In 1450, Pope Nicholas II presented the island to the king of Naples, Alfonso V of Aragon, as a base for his fleet. Barnardo di Viglia Marino, the commander of twelve galleys of the Aragon fleet, conquered Kastellorizon in the name of the king and had the demolished fortress rebuilt. The Aragon-Neapolitan occupation lasted until 1522, when the island was conquered in turn by Sultan Suleiman the Magnificent. The Venetians held it for a short time in 1570, then the Turks again, then the Venetians once more, and the Russians, under the Greek admiral Lambros Katsonis, took possession in 1789 and fitted it out as a naval base. At that time, many Greeks served in the Russian armed forces so that they would later be able to organize themselves as freedom fighters against the Turks. In 1821, most of the islanders left their homes and fought in the war of liberation on their own ships, only returning to Kastellorizon in 1828. After more than a century of further political adventures, Kastellorizon finally became a part of Greece again in 1947. Today some 20,000 Kastellorizonians live in Australia, 500 in America, 2,000 on Rhodes, 1,000 in Athens, and only 300 on the island itself.

In the main settlement, there is a small museum in the church of Aghia Paraskevi, which the Turks converted into a mosque in the eighteenth century. Here you can see ancient inscriptions, a number of interesting sculptures, votive reliefs, vases, amphorae, oil lamps, capitals, folk art from the Byzantine period, embroidered native costumes, and the work of goldsmiths and silversmiths.

Among the highlights of Kastellorizon are:

1. The metropolitan church, dedicated to Aghios Konstantinos. This is a basilica, dating from 1833, that contains twelve granite columns, each carved from a single block of stone that was taken from

Artemis: from a painting by Correggio.

the temple of Apollo at Patara, in Lycia.

2. The half-ruined church of Aghios Niko-laos from the eleventh century, which stands at the foot of the hill below the fortress and contains some especially lovely wall paintings.

3. The small church of the Panaghia ton Choraphion ("Holy Virgin who watches over the fields"), next to the town, with interesting icons from the seventeenth century.

4. The church of Aghios Merkourios, which blends Oriental and Occidental architec-tural styles.

5. The so-called Lycian barrow grave from the fourth century B.C., which is carved into the mountain below the fortress. This particularly well-preserved tomb is of Greek origin but resembles tombs from the coast of Asia Minor in appear-ance and is therefore designated as Ly-cian by the natives. There is also a Mycenaean grave near Avlonia.

6. The walls of the ancient acropolis, now called Palaiokastro ("old fortress"), with their Dorian inscriptions. The walls en-close ancient ruins and cisterns and some Christian churches.

7. Cyclopean wall fragments at two spots on the island, near Kampos, between Mounta and Palaiokastro, and on the plain near Aghios Ioannis tou Vounnou (St. John of the Mountain).

8. The monastery of Aghios Ghiorghios (1759), with a catacomb, that stands on the mountain of the same name.

IN VARIOUS PLACES ON THE ISLAND YOU CAN STILL find wine and oil presses from antiquity in addition to countless ancient graves and altars.

Of particular interest to the visitor are the island's unexpected and uncommonly beautiful caverns, especially the Blue Grot-to, known locally as Trypa ("hole") or Pho-kiali ("seals' playground"). King Victor Emmanuel of Italy considered this site more beautiful than the famous Blue Grot-to of Capri. Here, at dawn, it is splendid to see the sunlight refracted in the deep blue sea. The entrance is quite small and low. When passing through it in a boat, you may be lucky enough to see the seals that give the cavern one of its names.

The hospitable inhabitants of Kastellori-zon are delighted to see the occasional tourist and are happy to offer accommoda-tions. In addition, it is possible to stay at the Hotel Megisti at the harbor, and in various modest guesthouses.

RHODES

PINDAR WROTE THAT HELIOS, THE SUN, WAS THE first to see the island of Rhodes when it rose up out of the sea. And it is a fact that Helios, who is not to be confused with Apollo, was worshipped primarily on Rhodes and only rarely elsewhere in the Grecian world. Geologists have deter-mined that the island *did* rise out of the sea. Everywhere it is possible to find excellent-ly preserved sea shells embedded in stone.

The three ancient divisions of the island of Rhodes: Ialysus, Camirus, and Lindus.

(Based on a drawing by Grigoris Konstantinopoulos.)

Archeological data clearly confirm that the first inhabitants of Rhodes came from around the Aegean. Minoan peoples settled the island's western coast. Somewhat later, Achaeans came from the Peloponnesus. Full of warlike spirit and energy, these newcomers subjugated the Minoans and erected fortifications near the mountain now called Philerimos. Philerimos, the fortress mountain of Ialysus, was given the name Achaea.

Among the first Mycenaean vases that archeologists unearthed were some examples from Rhodes, the Ialysus bowl being the most representative specimen. We now know that there was a late Minoan settlement near the village of Trianta. Excavations have uncovered portions of a building whose earliest foundations date from about 1550 B.C. The cemeteries of Ialysus and Camirus also date from Mycenaean times. We can also assume that life on Rhodes developed probably without interruption from the Mycenaean to the Geometric periods.

FROM THE HISTORIAN DIODORUS WE LEARN THAT the first inhabitants of the island were the Telchines. According to tradition, they were a rather mysterious race of semi-divine beings. They were outstanding workers in bronze and the first makers of statues. After the Telchines came the Heliades, the sons of Helios, and finally the Heraclidae under their leader Tlepolemos. Some modern-day scholars interpret these three successive waves as the Minoans, the Achaeans, and the Dorians respectively.

Homer implies that by the Trojan War, Rhodes and the surrounding islands were ruled by Dorians—Heraclidae, the descendants of Heracles. The Dorians came from the west of Greece, probably Epirus, and penetrated as far as southwestern Asia Minor and the Dodecanese. This region was named Doris after them. Rhodes was absorbed into the Ionian cultural sphere of this area after the Geometric period. Of its Dorian origins it only preserved—but emphatically—the Dorian dialect, well into Roman times and even until today.

Homer goes on to say that the Dorian Heraclid Tlepolemos divided up the island of Rhodes into the three cities of Ialysus, Lindus, and Camirus, that he took part in the Trojan War, and that he fell in hand-to-hand combat before the walls of Troy. The three city-states of Rhodes, whose boundaries we now know almost precisely, existed in harmony until the end of the fifth century B.C.

The Three Ancient Cities

THE OLDER MYTHS CONCENTRATE ON CAMIRUS, on the west coast of the island. To Camirus came Althaemenes, the grandson of Minos and son of the king of Crete, Catreus. An oracle had told Althaemenes that he would kill his own father. To avoid such a misfortune, he left Crete and landed near Camirus. Althaemenes built the first sanctuary of Zeus Atavyrios on the highest peak on Rhodes, Mount Atavyros; on a clear day, one can see Crete from here. But Catreus set out in search of his son and also landed on the coast of Rhodes, near Camirus. Night had fallen. Believing that they were pirates, Althaemenes attacked his father and his companions. When he realized what he had done, he prayed to Zeus to let the earth swallow him up. And so it did.

Ialysus entered the pan-Hellenic stage in about the middle of the fifth century B.C. Diagoras of Rhodes won fame and honor for Ialysus and the entire island by his victories at the Isthmian Games and at Delphi, Nemea, and above all Olympia, the main centers of athletic competition. To crown his victory, Diagoras invited the great Pindar to Rhodes and requested that the poet commemorate his host and glorify the island in song. Pindar traces Diagoras's ancestry back to the mythical Tlepolemos, the first Dorian king of Rhodes. Other myths connect the worship of Poseidon, which was traditional in Ialysus, with King Cadmus, who came to Greece from Phoenicia, to the east.

Lindus experienced a heyday in post-Dorian times. The inhabitants of the city tried to trace their history back into prehistory and claimed that the famous shrine of Athena had been founded by Danaus when he left Egypt with his daughters and headed for Argos. In truth, the rocky region of Lindus was first inhabited by Lindians during the Geometric period. Probably because of the poor soil, they had to take to the sea, and Lindus developed into a major city of merchants and seafarers by the fifth century B.C. It participated in the extensive colonization of Asia Minor, Sicily (Agrigentum, Gela), and even the Balearic Islands, off the coast of far-away Spain. In the sixth century B.C., Lindus was ruled by the wise Cleobulus, whose personality must have influenced the life of the city strongly. Cleobulus was a man of moderation and self-control. He also led the victorious Lindian troops to the nearby mainland of Asia Minor, erected numerous public buildings, restored the sanctuary of Athena, most probably constructed the aqueduct, and

House in the town of Lindus. (After a drawing by N. Chatzimihalis.)

apparently remained in office for forty years.

The glory of Lindus came to an end with the Persian wars against Greece at the beginning of the fifth century B.C. The city's ships, on which it was wholly dependent, were commandeered by the Persians, who robbed all the other Ionian cities of their fleets as well.

During the Classical and Hellenistic periods, Lindus was only a modest settlement. But the Lindians strove to maintain the monuments of their better days and held the memory of their glorious past in high honor.

The Origins of the City of Rhodes (Synoecism)

RHODES'S PEAK CAME IN 441 B.C., AFTER THE DEfeat of the Athenians in Sicily. Under the leadership of Dorieus, son of the famous Olympic champion Diagoras, a handful of noblemen from Ialysus presented the vision of a great city to the islanders, a city

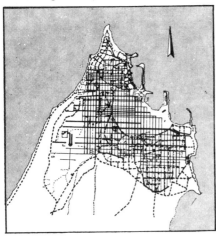

Street grid of the ancient city of Rhodes, designed by Hippodamus of Miletus as confirmed by excavations.

that would replace the now-antiquated settlements of Lindus, Ialysus, and Camirus. A greater *asty* (city-state) was to be founded, one better organized than Athens if not more splendid.

In 411 B.C., representatives of the three cities assembled on the acropolis of Lindus to sign the city's new constitution. The most important feature of this constitution was its provision for a *boule* (council) to be headquartered in the new city. This was to replace the three old *boulai*. The new city was begun in 408–407 B.C. It was designed to resemble the prow of a ship. Its foundations were laid out in accordance with the most modern technical concepts of the time, either by Hippodamus, the leading Greek architect and city planner of the fifth century B.C., or by one of his pupils. The site, on the northern point of the island, was carefully selected. It was excellently suited to accommodate a harbor for ships arriving from all directions. The slope down from the acropolis toward the east offered special opportunities for drainage, the steeper slope to the west for fortification.

The entire city was divided into zones (see figure to left): the zone of the acropolis, with sanctuaries, temples, and groves; the zone of the agora, near the large harbor, which remained through the Middle Ages and until the present; the zone of the docks, near the eastern edge of the city; and finally the residential zone, which was the largest. Nearly all of these ancient divisions have been located by excavation. Next the streets were laid out, straight and continuous from north to south and from east to west, adequately wide and with a prescribed distance between them. The city walls were constructed in a circle 6 miles in diameter, and the harbor was developed.

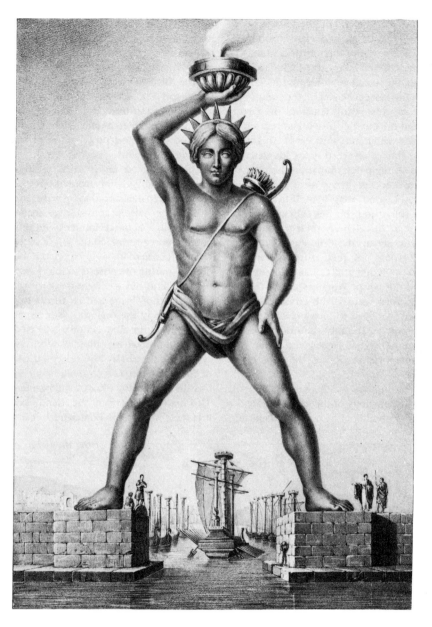

*The Colossus of Rhodes: drawing from Louis
La Croix's* Iles de la Grèce, *1853.*

In this way, the city of Rhodes was born. It soon attained an important position in the Greek world of the fourth century B.C. The city's heroic hour came in 306 B.C. The formidable Macedonian Demetrius Poliorcetes (the Besieger), son of Antigonus, one of the successors to Alexander the Great, attacked the city because it had refused to ally itself with him against Egypt. This siege turned into a severe test for Rhodes, yet thanks to their determination the citizens were victorious. They were aided by a southerly wind that demolished Demetrius's ships, and the Besieger was forced to retreat. To celebrate their triumph, the Rhodians set up the Colossus, a statue of Helios some 98 feet tall. The ancient Greeks included the Colossus of Rhodes among the Seven Wonders of the World. This victory secured the city's fame, and the Greeks began to look on Rhodes as a major power. The city then flourished, it became richer and richer, and it played a most important role in the history of Greece.

An earthquake in 226 B.C. toppled the Colossus, portions of the city walls, and a number of buildings. However, this misfortune gave the Rhodians the opportunity to rebuild almost the entire city in the new Hellenistic style. The city walls were strengthened, massive towers were erected, the fortified city was expanded somewhat, and the shrines on the acropolis were laid out in terraces in harmony with the so-called Pergamum style, though adapted to classical proportions, in keeping with the tradition of Rhodes.

The city lived chiefly from shipping, from trade, and possibly from its open port, where merchants stored their wares in exchange for harbor and storage fees. Its strong walls, its powerful fleet, and its fair constitution guaranteed the safety of these commercial activities. No one dared touch the city during the unrests of the third and second centuries B.C., brought on by the emergence of Rome and its threat to the equilibrium of the region.

However, the first century B.C. was tumultuous. In 88 B.C., Rhodes was unsuccessfully besieged by Mithridates, the king of Pontus. But in 42 B.C., the Roman consul Cassius did occupy Rhodes and plunder it. This marked the end of the island's era of greatness. During the Roman period, it was

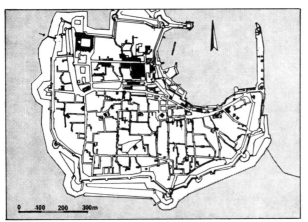

Plan of the medieval city of Rhodes.

(Based on a drawing by Grigoris Konstantinopoulos.)

a province that survived on its memories of a glorious past.

Many of the Roman emperors granted special privileges to Rhodes, but other emperors retracted these freedoms. At the close of the third century A.D., Diocletian, during his efforts to strengthen and organize the empire, placed Rhodes once and for all under the jurisdiction of the province of the islands. This curtailed the special status that Rhodes had maintained under some previous emperors.

Christianity reached Rhodes quite early; tradition has it that the apostle Paul landed near Lindus. The new faith rapidly found countless adherents. We know the name of a bishop from as early as the second century. Recent excavations suggest that a number of large subterranean rooms from antiquity became municipal catacombs.

We have no written documents from the Byzantine period. It is highly probable that, in the sixth century, the Rhodians, who could no longer protect their expanded city and its numerous harbors, retreated into a smaller area. They fortified it and constructed a small city around the fortress. Byzantine Rhodes was only a fifth as large as the city of antiquity.

We do know that the island was plundered by the Goths in the third century, the Arabs and Saracens in the seventh century, and the Seljuks in the eleventh century. Also during the eleventh century, Rhodes allied itself with the Venetians, who then ruled the sea; later it offered its assistance to the Crusaders. When the latter conquered Constantinople, Leon Gavalas named himself the lord, or "despot," of Rhodes. In the mid-thirteenth century, the Genoese took over the island. Genoa's Admiral Viniolo sold Rhodes, Kos, and Leros to the Order of St. John of Jerusalem in 1306, and Rhodes again took its place on

the world's stage.

The confrontation between the Christian and Islamic worlds took place primarily in the eastern Mediterranean and in the Aegean. The knights of St. John underscored the geographical importance of the island as a bulwark of Christendom with the saying "Fortitudo eius qui Rhodum tenet" (The strength of he who holds Rhodes).

Although the number of knights who settled in the fortified Byzantine city cannot have been significant, there was continuous building from the fourteenth until the first quarter of the sixteenth century. The Gothic style seemed foreign to this sunny Aegean island, but it was gradually adapted to local building traditions by native masters, and a charming blend of Byzantine-Aegean and Gothic elements resulted. The western Renaissance also had an effect on the island's architecture.

In 1480, the knights of St. John, aided by the Greeks, repelled the awesome attack of the Sultan Mohammed. In addition to the damage caused by that siege, a devastating earthquake struck in 1481. Contributions from all of Catholic Europe assisted in the reconstruction. By 1522, Rhodes was a lovely, excellently organized, and modern fortified city.

Then the youthful Sultan Suleiman the Magnificent determined to destroy it once and for all. The most terrible siege Rhodes ever experienced lasted for a full six months. The Greeks proved to be true allies to the knights of St. John. Fontano has immortalized the heroic deeds of a courageous woman of Rhodes in his book *De Bello Rhodio*. The Christians of the world were moved, but they provided no material support. The sultan's cannon laid the city in ruins, and hunger and disease were rampant. The last Grand Master of the Order of St. John of Rhodes finally had to capitulate.

The knights abandoned Rhodes, followed by thousands of islanders who had no desire to fall into the hands of the Turks. The resultant foreign rule lasted for four centuries. Turkish soldiers, police, and officials settled on the island, yet the percentage of Turks in the population never exceeded a third of the Greek one. The Greeks gave up the fortress; they built houses in the area or withdrew to villages inland. The Turks converted the Byzantine churches inside the fortress, or Kastro, into mosques, so the islanders built new churches, which gave their names to the new settlements or quarters: Metropolis, Aghia Anastasia, Aghios Ghiorghios, and Aghios Ioannis. The Greeks were permitted to enter the Kastro, which was now surrounded by Turkish

City of Rhodes, with Tower of St. Nicholas at right. View from Adams's The Mediterranean Illustrated, *1877.*

cemeteries, only after sunrise, and the gates were closed again at sunset. The fertile land around the city was divided up among the new masters, and the harbor of Rhodes became a base for the Turkish fleet. The island survived like this until 1912, when the Turks and Italians went to war over Tripoli. The Balkan peoples then united against the Turks and drove them out of the Balkan Peninsula. The Italians saw their chance. Temporarily, or so they said, they occupied Rhodes and the other Dodecanese Islands. Somewhat later, Mussolini decided to incorporate the islands into his empire and named them Isole Italiane dell'Egeo ("Italian Islands of the Aegean"). A new city with large governmental buildings was erected outside the old walls; new

streets were built to connect the Greek suburbs with each other and with the Kastro. The Islamic cemeteries were abandoned. In 1947, Rhodes was reunited with Greece at last, after six centuries of foreign domination.

Points of Interest

THE CITY OF RHODES BOASTS POINTS OF INTEREST from all periods of its history, so the visitor should try to stay at least a week. The ancient remains lie outside the medieval walls, but they have not been completely excavated. The acropolis, a hill with two low peaks in the western part of the city, occupies roughly a fifth of the ancient city.

Ancient sources tell us that the most important sanctuaries stood here; between them ran walkways *(peripatoi)*. The acropolis developed at the same time as the rest of the city, so straight streets led here from the harbors and other districts. The Pytheum, a walled sanctuary containing the Doric limestone temple of Apollo Pythios, occupies the southern promontory of the acropolis. Northeast of the temple, the foundations of a complex building have come to light; the significance of this structure has not been established yet. At the foot of the acropolis is the Stadium, now restored, and the restored Odeum, which served some function in the cult of Apollo. To the east, it is likely

Plan of the modern city of Rhodes.

1. *Aquarium*
2. *Neo-Gothic governmental palace*
3. *St. Nikolaos Tower*
4. *Church of the Knights of St. John*
5. *Nea Agora*
6. *Palace of the Grand Master*
7. *Old city*
8. *Archeological Museum*
9. *St. George's Church (Byzantine)*
10. *Suleiman mosque*
11. *Courts of Trade*
12. *Archbishop's Palace*
13. *Remains of the Gothic fortress church*
14. *Ilk-Mihrab mosque*
15. *Windmills*

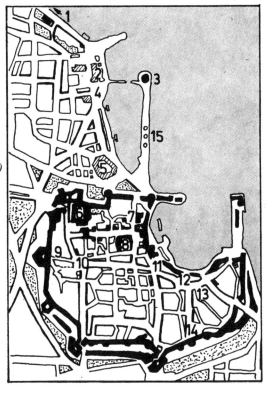

that the Palaestra and the Gymnasterion will be found; neither has been excavated yet. The temples of Zeus Polieus and Athena Polias dominated the northern elevation of the acropolis. Here one has an incomparable view of the sea, and it was here that the astronomer Hipparchus had his observatory. Along the eastern edge of the area sacred to Zeus and Athena lay a large stoa (columned hall) with two side wings, which recent excavations have exposed. Strewn about the margins of the hill are the Nymphaia, large rooms carved into the rock and generally furnished with cisterns. Statues stand in niches. These sculptures were purely decorative, thus evidence of the first "rococo" style. These Nymphaia, from the late Hellenistic period—the second and first centuries B.C.—served as models for the Roman emperors, who imitated such grottos and sculptures in Italy and elsewhere.

Rhodes is fortunate that Ioannis Kontis, the first Greek archeologist responsible for unearthing its ancient monuments, worked extensively with the ancient plan of the city and determined the order of subsequent excavations. Thus, after twenty years of digging, a nearly complete system of city plans—called the Hippodameion, after the city planner Hippodamus of Miletus—has been confirmed on the basis of excavated finds, as well as aerial photographs and written sources.

The ancient streets, running at a distance of 82 and 108 feet from each other, are indeed *dienekeis* (through streets); their width extends up to 52 feet each. You can see the cross-section of such a street in front of the National Bank of Kyprou Square; also the east wall of an ancient building and the covering of a large drainage canal. Remains of the façade of an imposing house are preserved next to the sidewalk on the west side of Sophouli Street. Scattered across the lower floors of new buildings are portions of ancient streets, buildings, and drains; traces of the ancient city wall are also still visible here and there.

The fortifications in the harbor of Akandia are interesting. The ruins of one tower and the foundations of several others suggest how these fortifications must have looked at one time and permit comparison with their medieval successors. In the garden of the present-day Archeological Institute, two avenues were uncovered before World War II. This was the precise point where they intersected, and they appeared in the form they had during the Roman period. Unfortunately a bomb destroyed the greater part of these ruins during the war. However, you can still see the surfaces of the streets themselves paved with stone slabs, steps to the left and right that led up to the porticos that once lined the street, and the bases of several columns.

The necropolis (cemetery) of ancient Rhodes extends to the south, and countless inscriptions there supplement excavations that have been made in the city. The oldest tombs were rectangular trenches dug into the earth or carved into the rock. During the Hellenistic period and afterward, an unusual sort of group grave was preferred. The typical one was a square subterranean chamber with large openings along the walls, where the dead lay, or smaller ones to accommodate urns with their ashes. Luxurious funerals with gifts of silver, gold, and precious stones were either uncommon in aristocratic Rhodes or expressly forbidden.

THE EARLY CHRISTIAN PERIOD IS REPRESENTED by only a few monuments in the city, among them a large basilica, uncovered re-

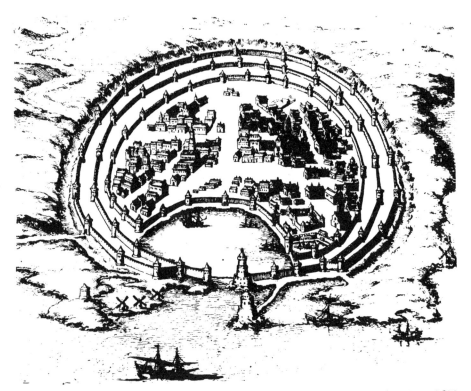

The old city of Rhodes: drawing from Olfert Dapper's Naukeurige Beschryving, *1688.*

cently, at the foot of the ancient acropolis. This is a structure 196 feet long and 82 feet wide, built on the foundations of an ancient shrine.

The Byzantine period, however, is well represented. The Metropolis, the present-day Byzantine Museum, and other churches scattered throughout the medieval city permit us to trace its architecture from the eleventh century to the arrival of the knights, and its painting from the fourteenth century until the conquest by the Turks.

The period of the knights of St. John is uniquely depicted by the complete layout of surviving fortifications. These provide a look at the life and the architectural tradition of Byzantine Rhodes in two stages: one from the fourteenth until the beginning of the fifteenth century; the other from 1481 to 1522. Behind the strong outer city wall stood the inner one, which separated the knights' quarter—the fortress, or Kastro—from the citizens' quarter. In the knights' precinct lay the hostels, or courts, of the contingents from Italy, France, Spain, England, Auvergne, and Provence. Most of these courts are located along the Street of Knights, which begins next to the Byzantine Metropolis, and ends at the palace of the Grand Master of the Order of St. John.

In this quarter of the city, there is also

the first hospital erected by the knights, a fourteenth-century building that now serves as the headquarters of the Archeological Institute, and the large fifteenth-century hospital, where the Archeological Museum has been set up. The statues displayed here have been discovered on the islands of Rhodes and Nisyros since 1912. Here one can also see the vases and funeral offerings from the cemeteries of Ialysus and Camirus. Tombstones of the knights are displayed in the East Hall. Extensions of the Archeological Museum are also planned along the Street of the Knights: one annex for prehistoric finds on the islands of Rhodes, Karpathos, and Astypalaia, and a second for objects discovered during the past twenty years on Rhodes. Also in this vicinity are the Pinakothek, an excellent collection of twentieth-century paintings, and the interesting Folklore Museum, with wood carvings, embroideries, carpets, and ceramics from dwellings in the Dodecanese in centuries past. The Metropolis itself, from the tenth or eleventh century, was transformed into a Gothic church by the Order of St. John. It now serves as an Early Christian and Byzantine museum. Among other things, you can study Byzantine wall painting here.

The façades of nearly all of these buildings are richly ornamented in the medieval taste, especially those along the Street of the Knights. The courts belonging to the knights from Castile and Auvergne, and also the large hospital, show Renaissance influences. Individual marble doorways and window enclosures also have Renaissance features.

The most imposing structure of medieval Rhodes in terms of sheer monumentality is the restored Palace of the Grand Master. It stands on the summit of a hill above the eastern harbor and commands not only the medieval quarter but the entire city of Rhodes. In antiquity, the shrine to Helios must have crowned this site. The façade of the palace has been respected in the restoration. The interior, however, reflects the pompous taste of the Italian Fascists, who ruled the Dodecanese between the two world wars. Despite this, the atmosphere of the Middle Ages has been preserved with magical freshness in many of its corners.

A wide variety of architecture enlivens the medieval citizens' quarter. The boundaries that divided it from the knights' quarter were leveled under Turkish rule. The knights' buildings themselves suffered numerous changes. Today some of them survive in their original form with only superficial alterations, the façades of others were completely restructured by the Turks, and still others have been stamped with the lines of Rhodian neo-classicism. Courtyards embellished with arcades evoke the influence of the knights; others, leading to gardens within the houses, remind us of the Turks. Numerous small green parks adorn the medieval city.

The broad Odos Sokratous, the main street that leads westward from the harbor, deserves particular attention. It runs into the city marketplace, where the agora stood in antiquity. This market thus occupied the same site until World War II. Today the city has burst through its walls, and the centers of trade have developed outside. Nonetheless, quite a number of businesses stayed in the old marketplace. In spite of all these sights, the walls, which constitute a ring nearly 3 miles long, are still the most impressive remnants of the medieval city, with their seven gates and numerous imposing towers.

The city of the knights preserved its character even during the time of the

Turks, who did not alter the layout of the city. They did build mosques, but these added a new, picturesque element to the cityscape. The conquerors were content to take up residence in the dwellings of the knights. Only much later did rich merchants begin to construct neo-classical houses, occasionally paving their courtyard with fine mosaics or ornamenting them with arcades or columns. Their gardens, however small, were planted with palms, bougainvillaea, and groves of banana trees.

The city of Rhodes was demolished in World War II. How should the remnants of the old be integrated harmoniously into the new building that reconstruction requires? The new city, which had already begun to expand during the Italian occupation, extends farther to the west, and its buildings are taller. And large hotels have sprung up in response to the pressure of tourism. Even in Rhodes it is impossible to escape the twentieth century.

Monuments and Points of Interest Outside the City of Rhodes

THERE ARE TWO OTHER CENTERS, IALYSUS AND Camirus, where the visitor discovers a blend of ancient, Byzantine, and medieval remains.

The city of Ialysus once consisted of various separate settlements. It is dominated on the west by the elongated mountain that became known in the Middle Ages as Mount Philerimos. The Achaeans were the first to fortify Philerimos in prehistoric times—hence, the name Achaea appears in old inscriptions and texts. It is possible that the myth of Iphiclus sheds some light on events in this landscape; though narrated only by later writers, the legend could well be based on historical fact. The story relates that Phoenicians lay entrenched on Achaea under their leader, Phalanthos. An oracle proclaimed that the fortress would fall only when crows had white feathers and fish swam in wine vessels. The Greek Iphiclus, who directed the siege, was sly enough to persuade a servant of Phalanthos to throw fish into the wine vessels, while he himself whitewashed a flock of crows. No sooner did Phalanthos perceive these ominous signs than he laid down his arms. Today we know that there were no Phoenicians on Rhodes. But perhaps the warriors behind Phalanthos were Achaeans.

Strabo called the legendary mountain "the fortress." And at its eastern corner stands the Byzantine fortress to which Prince John Cantacuzene withdrew in 1248 in the face of a Genoese attack. The knights of St. John first set foot on Mount Philerimos in 1306, and Sultan Suleiman the Magnificent established his headquarters here in 1522. The mountain was also fortified during World War II.

Today, excavation is in progress at the foot of Philerimos, near the parking lot, and at the summit, near the Order of St. John's monastery. Also near the parking lot, a small church was discovered that once belonged to a Byzantine cloister; today it lies in ruins. It dates from the tenth century and must have once had a cupola supported by four columns.

Excavations in the courtyard of the monastery of the Order of St. John brought to light the remnants of a Doric temple of Athena from the Hellenistic period. In the sixth century A.D., this temple was demolished to make way for an Early Christian basilica. Remains of its baptistry are near the bell tower, from the time of the knights. The floor of the church was laid out in marble slabs, portions of which can be seen in front of the baptistry and in the monastery church.

In Byzantine times a new, smaller church was built on top of the ruins. And precisely on top of this the Order's first Gothic church was constructed, surrounded by chapels. The Italians restored the church and the remains of the monastery. Today they constitute the most important complex of buildings on Mount Philerimos.

On the easternmost spur of Philerimos stands the Byzantine fortress, which also served the knights as a refuge. It was destroyed during World War II but has since been restored. Near the entrance to the monastery precinct stands the small church of St. George. Its wall paintings from the fourteenth and fifteenth centuries have unfortunately been partially painted over.

From Philerimos there is a splendid view of the sea and the coast of Asia Minor. On hills at the foot of Philerimos and in the surrounding area, the cemeteries of Ialysus have been excavated. These finds, dating from Mycenaean times as well as the Classical period, can be seen today in the Archeological Museum of Rhodes.

ALSO ON THE WEST COAST, 21 MILES FROM THE city of Rhodes, lies ancient Camirus. This city was inhabited from the sixth century B.C. until the sixth century A.D. It lies on three separate levels. On the lowest one, resting on a massive retaining wall, a shrine was discovered in which the altars were still in place. West of it is a Hellenistic temple in the Doric style, close to it a well and countless pits containing votive offerings. A street connects the temple precinct with the acropolis on top of the hill. Here, from at least Archaic times, lay the sacred mountain of Athena and her temple. One large cistern survives; it once provided water for the city. In Hellenistic times, the hill was crowned by a stoa (columned hall). The city's houses stretched between the temple precinct and the acropolis. Particularly in the fall, the sea at sunset takes on splendid colors as you look down from Camirus.

IN LINDUS, TOO, THE VISITOR IS OVERWHELMED by the unforgettable natural beauty. Its air and light are of an unparalleled clarity. An infinite horizon encloses a landscape that is

The island of Rhodes.

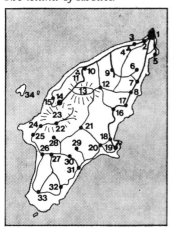

1. *Rhodes*
2. *Ixos*
3. *Trianta*
4. *Ialysus*
5. *Kallithea*
6. *Kallithies*
7. *Afandu*
8. *Kolympia*
9. *Kalamonas*
10. *Kalavarda*
11. *Camirus*
12. *Dimylia*
13. *Mount Profitis Elias (2,618 feet)*
14. *Embonas*
15. *Kastellos*
16. *Malona*
17. *Archangelos*
18. *Kalathos*
19. *Lindus*
20. *Lardos*
21. *Alaerma*
22. *Aghios Isidoros*
23. *Mount Atavyros (3,986 feet)*
24. *Sianna*
25. *Monolithos*
26. *Apolakia*
27. *Arnitha*
28. *Istrios*
29. *Asklipio*
30. *Vati*
31. *Gennadi*
32. *Lachania*
33. *Kattavia*
34. *The island of Almnia*

richly varied. The settlement found at Lindus today originated in the tenth or eleventh century A.D. Lindus truly flowered again in the sixteenth century, after the knights of St. John had left the island. The Lindians became seafarers once more, as they had been in antiquity. And the small city was rebuilt, its houses rooted in the simple Rhodian peasant tradition.

Life in these dwellings is rather plain. Behind a courtyard, where the family often gathers, lies an elongated room, where one greets friends, sleeps, and stores foodstuffs, the family linens, and clothing. In one corner, slightly elevated, stands the bed, spread with a richly embroidered throw, or *sperveri*. Plates from native kilns, icons, and embroidered hangings decorate the walls. In wealthier houses, the ceilings are painted with animals, flowers, and decorative patterns. The façade of the house is embellished

In Greek mythology, the Hours or Seasons were the gatekeepers of heaven.

with reliefs, copies from the knights' houses in the city of Rhodes that the Lindian sea captains admired.

The courtyard is paved with white and black pebbles. To one side lie smaller rooms. What is unusual about the Lindian house is its *pylionas,* or monumental entrance. Vaulting or four arches shelter it and also · support the captain's room above—for the captains, on land as at sea, liked to be high up so that they could see everything. The windows of this room open toward the sea on all sides. The ground floor of the Lindian house has few windows, and they open only onto the courtyard.

The church of the Panaghia (Holy Virgin) dominates the city and dates from the fifteenth century. The well in the center of the marketplace is ancient. The local word for "well" is *krana* (the Dorian form of *krene*). The hill is also called Krana, after the well.

The present-day town· doubtless occupies only the center of the ancient city, which at least in Hellenistic times had large public buildings that faced the two harbors. Next to one harbor, named after the apostle Paul, are the ruins of the ancient theater and a vast structure whose purpose has not been identified. Next to the main harbor, there were numerous administrative buildings.

The famous acropolis of Lindus crowns a steep cliff. The cult of Athena, who was worshipped here, presumably dates from the ninth century B.C. But even during the Geometric period, there was a temple on Lindus, which was restored by Cleobulus in the sixth century B.C. This temple, which was destroyed by fire in 392 B.C., was succeeded by another. The ruins of that temple have been reconstructed. Excavations on the acropolis brought to light the monumental entryway from the fourth century B.C., patterned after the propylaea of the Acropolis in Athens. An extensive portico was also discovered, as well as an impressive broad staircase.

The buildings and monuments from a wide diversity of times lend Lindus its special charm. Worthy of particular mention are the ruins of a Byzantine church, an imposing government building, the walls running around the acropolis, and the prow of a ship that was chiseled out of the rock in 180 B.C.

Those who hike about on the island will also come upon the Byzantine castle of Monolithos, the knights' castle of Kritinia, the Byzantine monastery of Tharri, and the church of Phountoukli.

Syme

IN THE *ILIAD*, HOMER DESCRIBES NEREUS, THE king of Syme, as the handsomest man— "after the flawless Achilles"—among the Danaans who descended on Troy. The island of Syme itself is also well known in myth. Glaucus, a famous seafarer, sponge diver, and shipbuilder, constructed the *Argo* and took part in the Argonauts' expedition in search of the Golden Fleece. Belonging to a family of sea deities, Glaucus turned the heads of more than a few royal princesses. Finally he kidnapped Syme, a daughter of King Ialysus of Rhodes, and brought her to the desolate, barren island known since by her name. Before that time, it was called Metapontis or Aegle, after the nymph who bore Apollo three daughters, the Graces.

But there are other legends to explain the island's name. According to one, it was here on Syme that Prometheus made the discovery that he could make people out of clay and thereby keep the human race alive. When Zeus learned of this, he transformed Prometheus into an ape *(simia)* and kept him on the island until his death. Another tale has it that the fiancé of Syme, a lovely princess, died shortly before their wedding. He was called Lorymon, after the city on the coast of Asia Minor. In her sorrow, Syme died as well. Her last request was to be buried on this island, where she could most clearly see the hometown of her beloved. Even today, the ancient ruins on the east side of Syme are known as "the castle of the king's daughter," in reference to this legend.

THE ISLAND IS 24.5 SQUARE MILES IN AREA AND lies 24 nautical miles from Rhodes. Since the very earliest known times, the fate of Syme has been linked to that of Rhodes. Ruins scattered all across the island bear witness to Syme's former glory.

Arriving in Ghialos, one of the "eight splendid harbors" mentioned by Pliny, the visitor encounters a town that rises up the hillside and even up the slope of Mount Vigla. The clock tower and the tile roofs of the neo-classical buildings along the quay encircle a dance of colorful boats and slender caïques, from whose rigging bundles of sponges hang. The lower town was built mostly in the nineteenth century. Beyond the old bridge lies the shipyard, Tarsanas, where the swift ships that once set out for Venice and the Black Sea were built. Today, it houses the first Greek experimental station for turning sea water into fresh water. A stone bell tower calls attention to the church of Ai-Yannis, constructed in the typical Dodecanese style. It stands on the site of a row of ancient temples that have been destroyed. Somewhat farther along, but still next to the quay, is the small square called the Skala ("steps"), the center of the town's political and commercial life. Five hundred stone steps lead up from this square to the "Village," the oldest settlement on the island. It is dominated by the fortress, or Kastro, whose every stone recalls the past: antiquity, the Roman and Byzantine periods, the days of the Crusades, and the years of Turkish rule. After attacks by pirates—a terrible affliction for the islands—had subsided, the islanders increasingly sought their fortunes in seafaring and trade. Recalling Syme's flowering in about 1700 are the aristocratic houses *(archontika)* as well as the more modest dwellings, built of the local stone, that line the narrow, cobbled streets.

The *archontika* generally bear the names of their owners—for example, the tasteful Peteinaki or the Haska, which is embellished with delicate wood carvings. The one known as the Sala is an exception. It is known not by its owner's name, Hadziagapitou, but by a reference to the fact that it contains the only large hall on the island. Paintings above the four doorways into this hall depict the symbols of the four evangelists. They proclaim that just as the

Prometheus making man: from a sarcophagus.

four evangelists gave a firm foundation to the faith in the four directions of the compass, so shall the Hadziagapitou family stand firm in every direction down to its farthest descendants. One medallion depicts a girl lending a book to a youth; another, a pair being blessed by Eros. In a crypt below the hall, the archives of the elders of the community were hidden, as were the treasury of the Panormitis Monastery, citizens pursued by the Turks, and the family's daughters during attacks by pirates. Here too were kept the decrees *(firmans)* in which the sultans granted the island privileges. The architecture of the Sala resembles a fortresslike Italian villa.

At one time, the mantic custom of the Koukouma was practiced in the spacious, paved courtyard of the Sala. In this ceremony, held on the first of May, young women tried to find out who their future bridegrooms would be. The preparations were complex: the curious young women collected the "silent water"—they were not permitted to speak while doing so—from seven houses where the lady of the house was called Irene ("peace"). They then poured this water into an ancient gold vessel, into which they also threw their rings, and covered the vessel with a red silk cloth. The water was left outdoors on the terrace overnight so that it would be seen and illuminated by the stars. The next morning, the day of the festival of St. Athanasios, the girls would gather again, remove the red cloth, toss lilies-of-the-valley into the vessel, and sing songs in praise of their yearned-for suitors. Each of them would fish one of the rings out of the water and name a man's name.

That afternoon, the young men appeared with musicians, and until late at night they would dance the *susta,* one of the loveliest of Greek dances, in which the men's endurance was put to the test. All the girls kept the same partner as long as they could; then there was a "cut," and the partners changed. The participants ate *pitta,* a heavily salted pastry dish that had to be prepared by a girl whose parents were still living. Since the *pitta* made them thirsty, the girls would dream that night of drinking water. If the name of the host in whose house the girl dreamed of drinking water coincided with the name she had named in the afternoon while taking the ring out of the water, it was certain that her future husband would have the very same name.

Physical strength and endurance were not only required of the young men of Syme in dancing, incidentally. Only those who could dive for sponges at a depth of 100 feet were allowed to marry.

WHEN THE TURKS CONQUERED THE DODECA-nese in 1522, the inhabitants of Syme managed to get the sultan's permission to govern themselves, a right they kept until the end of the nineteenth century. In return, they agreed to pay the Turks a tax. Two elders *(demogerontes)* were chosen by popular acclaim, and these ruled the island together with twelve advisers. Medical and pharmaceutical treatment and education were provided to both rich and poor at no cost.

The former pharmacy, Spetsaria, is one of the loveliest neo-classical buildings on Syme. The island also has more than 100 churches, monasteries, and mountain chapels. All are adorned with wall paintings, gilt or polychrome choir walls, and mosaic floors. The devoted worship of the saints stems from the consciousness of the

danger in which the sponge divers live.

In the bay of the harbor of Nimporeio, you can see the ruins of an Early Christian basilica with marvelous mosaic floors that depict various birds, animals, a soldier, and even a camel driver. Somewhat farther south lie twelve underground vaulted chambers—the Twelve Caves, as they are known to the local residents. Legend has it that during the reign of the Byzantine emperor Theodosius II (408–450) a school of icon painting and sculpture existed here.

To get to the monastery of Roukouniotis, you must hike for roughly an hour. A huge, umbrellalike cypress stands at its entrance. The monastery is a rectangular structure with all the characteristics of Byzantine fortress architecture. The lower church rises above the foundations of a heathen temple. The wall paintings probably date from the sixteenth century. Cretan painters worked in the lower church, native artists in the upper one. Although the monastery is consecrated to the archangel Michael, many of the wall paintings depict scenes from the life and miracles of St. Nikolaos. One remarkable icon portrays the hospitality of Abraham and was painted by a Cretan, Stylianos Geni Kretos. The choir walls here are very delicately executed.

IN THE SOUTH OF SYME LIES THE BEST HARBOR, Panormos. If you approach it by ship, you can hear the geese and possibly the bells before you can discern another monastery, the Panormitis, consecrated to the archangel Michael and bearing the stamp of Byzantine and post-Byzantine times. On the painstakingly executed iconostasis (sanctuary screen), it is possible to see the archangel, the prince of the heavenly hosts, in full figure. Legend has it that the monastery was founded because a small icon was discovered under a mastic bush here.

Panormitis then developed into a pilgrimage site for Christians from all parts of Greece. The faithful throw votive gifts into the sea, even when they are still a considerable distance from the island, as testimony that they have kept their vows. These offerings always manage to reach the harbor of Panormos.

Kos

AN ANCIENT SAYING PROCLAIMS, "IF KOS DOES not provide, Egypt will not provide either," a reference to the fact that Kos has been uncommonly fertile since the earliest times. It is said that the inhabitants of Kos have always insisted on independence, loved peace, and shown both generosity and a special fondness for irony. The people of Kos do not like to travel; this was true in antiquity and it continues to be so today. If they do have to go abroad temporarily or if they emigrate, they are likely to suffer chronic homesickness, as their folksongs relate.

EVIDENCE OF NEOLITHIC HABITATION LIES strewn over the entire island. Finds in a cave behind the village of Kephalos have suggested a peaceful society of farmers, hunters, shepherds, and fishermen. Tombs represent the early Bronze Age. The Mycenaean era (fifteenth–twelfth centuries B.C.) has left behind much richer and more important traces, especially at one settlement and its cemetery, near the modern city of Kos. The Archeological Museum of Kos now houses countless finds from the so-called Geometric style that were discovered on this site. During that early period, the island was densely inhabited, and before the Trojan War, the descendants of the mythical Heracles, the Heraclidae, had landed on its coasts. Under Pheidippos and Antiphus, they proceeded to outfit thirty ships for the campaign against Troy. This was a historic moment, for suddenly the men of Kos learned something about seafaring. Up to that time, their journeys had probably taken them no farther than the islands of Kasos and Karpathos to the south.

According to Herodotus, whose hometown, Halicarnassus, lies opposite Kos on the coast of Asia Minor, Kos, Halicarnassus, Cnidus, and the three cities of Rhodes—Lindus, Ialysus, and Camirus—formed the Dorian hexapolis. This league had its religious center at the temple of Apollo on Cnidus. Herodotus also tells us the name of the first tyrant of Kos: Scythis. Some scholars claim that his name suggests that Scythis was not a native of Kos. He placed authority in the hands of his son Cadmus; Cadmus, filled with a strong sense of justice, willingly surrendered it to the men of Kos and set out for Sicily.

Before the Persians began their march toward Asia Minor and Greece, Kos and the neighboring islands had subjected themselves to the rule of Halicarnassus. Once the Persians were defeated, Kos joined the Attic League. In the course of the Peloponnesian War, Alcibiades built a fortress on the island; this was presumably in the town of Meropis, but it has not yet been located. When the city of Rhodes was founded, the people of Kos determined to build their own great city, Kos (366 B.C.). From then until the sixth century A.D., this city was the center of the island. Its greatest glory was in the three centuries before Christ. The Asclepieion of Kos was world-famous.

To the Romans, Kos was an attractive spot where one could live well. They endeavored to repair the damage of various earthquakes. Kos, along with other islands in the Aegean, reached a second flowering in the Early Christian period. Its basilicas attest to this. In the mid-sixth century A.D., the city must have been destroyed by a catastrophic earthquake and abandoned by its inhabitants. The place lay empty and desolate, with columns, marble fragments, and statues rising above the rubble. It remained in this condition until the end of the fourteenth century. However, in 1391–1396, when the knights of St. John of Rhodes were being threatened by Sultan Bayazid, they hastily erected a fortified city on the site of the ancient agora of Kos. In doing so, they made extensive use of ancient materials. It was like a rebirth of antiquity; for example, the northwestern gate of the new city of Kos was called the Gate of the Forum, which is simply the translation of the Greek word "agora."

In the fifteenth and sixteenth centuries, the knights of St. John of Rhodes constructed the fortress, which still stands near the harbor. It is possible that in antiquity, another island protected the harbor at that spot.

The Turks arrived and settled in the fortified city. They also made their homes in the surrounding countryside amid the Greek population, among whom there were still rich landowners. Even under the Turks there was much rebuilding. Neoclassicism is represented by particularly beautiful structures on Kos. Greek architects used ancient marble in the two mosques in the city and in several private houses that survived the earthquake of 1933, a catastrophe that had dire consequences. From 1933 to 1943, the Italians carried out extensive excavations in the city of Kos. The modern city began to develop at about the same time, expanding day by day. In 1947, Kos became a part of Greece with the rest of the Dodecanese.

The chief products of ancient Kos were agricultural produce, handicrafts, and especially woven goods. Its fine fabrics, known to the Romans as *vestes Coae,* were famous. The island also profited from trade and the income produced by the Asclepieion. From the fourth to the sixth centuries B.C., the capacity of the harbor was very great, and active building went on in the vicinity. The juxtaposition of past and present gives Kos its unmistakable charm. Although only fragments of antiquity remain, five important periods of building can be traced. These lie directly on top of one another.

THE ARCHEOLOGICAL SITE NEAR THE HARBOR LIES where the knights of St. John built their city in the fourteenth century. The Turks also settled here when they conquered the island. Slowly, the city pressed outward beyond its walls. Ruins of ancient public buildings came to light here during excavations after 1933.

In the eastern sector, the wall from the Classical period was unearthed. A portico that backed onto this wall surrounded a sanctuary in which the foundations and the remains of the superstructure of a lovely Hellenistic temple were discovered. There is reason to believe that this was a temple of Heracles. In the Early Christian period, a

The island of Kos.

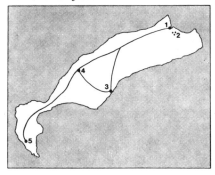

1. *Kos*
2. *Asclepius sanctuary*
3. *Kardamaina*
4. *Antimachia*
5. *Kephalos*

monumental basilica was erected nearby.

Most impressive is a sanctuary of Aphrodite with two entrances *(propylaea)*. It is surrounded by a lovely wall. This complex lay in the center of the city and was visible from the harbor.

In the western sector stretched the columned hall of the agora, 492 feet long and 269 feet wide. Two columns of this stoa have been set up again. The Romans gave the agora a splendid appearance; the city walls no longer served defensive purposes. A broad staircase now led from the harbor to the wall and its vaulted gateway.

THE SECOND ARCHEOLOGICAL SITE OF MAJOR IM-portance lies in the western part of the city, along the Odos Megalou Konstantinou. Here the Roman city can be reconstructed with relative accuracy. Portions of the central east-west paved street have come to light. It was flanked by broad sidewalks and spacious porticos and divided the city into two halves. By studying the remains here, including charming mosaic floors and wall paintings from the houses, you can get a vivid impression of the way of

life here in Roman days.

A road to the west, which intersects the central street at nearly a right angle, leads to the splendid baths and an interesting structure, from the time of Vespasian, that has been restored. Next to it—beneath the Roman buildings, in fact—the portico of the Hellenistic gymnasium was discovered and partially reconstructed. A bit farther to the west lies the equally interesting stadium.

Even a summary description of ancient Kos must include the *odeion* (concert hall) from the Roman period and one restored house, which contains an uncommon number of rooms. These buildings and the countless bathing facilities convey some sense of the economic prosperity that Kos enjoyed during those centuries.

A CONSIDERABLE NUMBER OF AEGEAN ISLANDS were famous then. Apollo had been born on Delos. Rhodes was the island of Helios. Polycrates had lived and worked on Samos. Kos was the island of the god of medicine, Asclepius, and of the greatest physician of antiquity, Hippocrates. His fame continues to survive because he brought to the study of medicine the observation of human nature and its pathological processes, a logical way of thinking, and a strict adherence to scientific research.

Hippocrates lived probably from 460 to 356 B.C. As a young man, he dreamed of a journey that would take him away from the tiny island and out into the world. And Hippocrates did go as far as Thrace, Thasos, Abdera, Cyzicus, and possibly even more remote spots. He died near Larissa, in Thessaly.

Hippocrates first studied rhetoric with the sophist Gorgias and philosophy with the great Democritus. He studied medicine with the Pythagorean Alcmaeon. He thus began to draw away from the purely metaphysical views of that time. Instead, he immersed himself in the precise description of the symptoms of illness, hoping thereby to recognize changes in the body. Not only medication, but diet and psychotherapy played major roles in his treatment. Hippocrates was also the first surgeon.

Hippocrates envisioned the ideal doctor as one who would do much and promise little, one who would use words sparingly, one who would be modest and not greedy for money. To this day, the Hippocratic Oath is taken by those who are about to practice medicine:

I swear by Apollo, the physician, by Asclepius, Hygieia and Panacea, and by all the gods and goddesses, making them my witnesses, that I will carry out, according to my ability and judgment, this oath and this indenture. To hold my teacher in this art equal to my own parents; to make him partner in my livelihood; when he is in need of money to share mine with him; to consider his family as my own brothers, and to teach them this art, if they want to learn it, without fee or indenture.... I will use treatment to help the sick according to my ability and judgment, but never with a view to injury and wrongdoing.... I will keep pure and holy both my life and my art.... In whatsoever houses I enter, I will enter to help the sick, and I will abstain from all intentional wrongdoing and harm, especially from abusing the bodies of man or woman, bond or free. And whatsoever I shall see or hear in the course of my profession in my intercourse with men, if it be what should not be published abroad, I will never divulge, holding such things to be holy

secrets. Now if I carry out this oath, and break it not, may I gain forever reputation among all men for my life and for my art; but if I transgress it and forswear myself, may the opposite befall me.

Hippocrates wrote more than 100 books in the Ionian dialect, which his teacher Democritus also used. Many have survived, not in the original but as reworked by later physicians.

The Asclepieion of Kos lies about 3 miles southwest of the city. It is beautifully situated, and the view from the sanctuary is unforgettable. There was presumably a temple of Apollo in this vicinity from as early as the fifth century B.C. It stood in a grove of cypresses, and accordingly Apollo here had the cognomen Cyparissus. Roughly a century later, the city erected an altar for the Asclepieion on this spot. At the beginning of the third century B.C., it was replaced by a large marble altar that boasted Ionic columns and splendid statues attributed to the sons of the sculptor Praxiteles, who carried on their father's tradition. At this time, if not earlier, the Koans constructed a small Ionic temple of Asclepius nearby, the exedra, and other buildings to the west of the altar.

On the Asclepieion's lower terrace, dat-

Section of a 1688 map of Kos.

ing from the same time, stood the porticos, entrance (propylon), and guest rooms. A staircase led up from here to the altar. The terrace above the altar was begun in the third century B.C. Wooden porticos were erected on stone foundations. The Doric temple, the Doric stoa around the upper terrace, and the staircase leading from the altar to the upper temple followed in the second century B.C.

The Koans patterned their Asclepieion after those of Epidaurus and Rhodes. The latter of these, which once stood in the center of the city, has been lost forever. However, the Asclepieion of Kos survived for nearly 1,000 years. Then, over the next 1,500 years, it gradually decayed, destroyed by time and buried by rubble and dust. Only in 1901 were its remains unearthed—a great moment for archeology. People had searched for it all over the island, and it was finally discovered by the young German epigraphologist and archeologist Rudolph Herzog, who was assisted by the Koan Iakovos Zarraftis, a lover of antiquity.

The Italians researched the Asclepieion and reconstructed it. In its reconstructed form, it corresponds to its Hellenistic appearance with Roman additions. Among the latter are the partially rebuilt temple, the baths outside and beneath the terraces, the retaining walls, and their niches decorated with statues. A modest settlement was established here in the Byzantine period, as indicated by a cemetery and a church that were located above the temple.

The Asclepieion on Kos was founded after the death of Hippocrates. At that time, it was a very modern sanatorium in which the teachings and methods of the master were strictly practiced. Propaganda and advertising were in part responsible for its

Plan of the city of Kos.

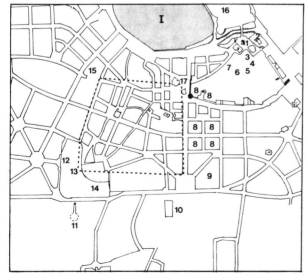

1. *Harbor of Mandraki*
2. *Square with the "Hippocrates" plane tree*
3. *Early Christian basilica*
4. *Hellenistic stoa*
5. *Temple of Heracles*
6. *Small temple*
7. *Shrine of Aphrodite*
8. *Stoa of the agora*
9. *Temple and altar of Dionysus*
10. *Restored house*
11. *Odeion*
12. *Stoa of the gymnasium*
13. *Latrine*
14. *Houses*
15. *Stadium*
16. *Fortress from the time of the Knights of St. John*
17. *Museum*

(The dotted line outlines the Mycenaean settlement. Drawing by G. Konstantinopoulos.)

success. Poems of thanks were commissioned to be read aloud to the public. The poet Herodas, for instance, visualized two Koan ladies leaving the city at dawn with their servants to present sacrifices to Asclepius. The poet skillfully had one of them, the naive Coccale, describe and admire the sanctuary so that listeners might get an idea of what was to be seen within it. It was still small then, but it contained, besides the statues that decorated its altar and other works, the statue of a boy wringing the neck of a goose and a painting of Aphrodite stepping forth from the sea foam by the celebrated Apelles, a work that Strabo was still able to marvel at in Rome in the second century A.D.

The Archeological Museum of Kos, on the central square, contains most of the finds from recent excavations; some others, notably mosaic floors and various statues, have been transferred to the fortress in Rhodes. Statues and reliefs are exhibited in the museum's five galleries. In the west gallery, there are large Hellenistic sculptures, including the torso of a god, presumably a cult figure, female figures in rich drapery, and well-preserved portrait busts. In a special area stands a statue of Hippocrates, which more recent scholarship has determined to be a Late Hellenistic copy of a classical original. Also in this room are an ancient relief depicting a banquet and some charming tomb reliefs.

The small statues on display in the north room of the museum, dating from the Classical period, were discovered in a rural sanctuary near the village of Pyli. They are not exceptional works of art, but they do suggest the degree to which the influence of the classical forms had extended throughout the world of that time. The eastern gallery houses statues from Roman times. However, the most beautiful ones

Page 225: The Street of the Lions, Delos. (© Adam Woolfitt/Woodfin Camp and Associates)

Pages 226–227: The lion statues. (© Fulvio Roiter/The Image Bank)

Page 228, top: Temple of Aphaea, Aegina. (© Marc S. Dubin/Art Resource)

Page 228, bottom: The basilica of Aghios Stephanos, Kos. (© Marc S. Dubin/Art Resource)

Page 229: Amphitheater, Delos. (© SEF/ Art Resource)

Pages 230–231: Roman baths, Kos. (© Marc S. Dubin/Art Resource)

Page 232: Church ruins, Zakinthos.

(© Larry Dale Gordon/The Image Bank)

Page 233: Monastery of St. John, Patmos. (© George Contorakes/The Stock Market)

Page 234: Monks, Patmos. (© John Lewis Stage/The Image Bank)

Page 235: Interior on Skyros. (© John Lewis Stage/The Image Bank)

Pages 236–237: Inside a church on Siphnos. (© John Colombaris/The Stock Market)

Pages 238–239: Monastery on coast, Ios. (© Charles Feil)

Page 240: Panaghia Chosoviotissa, Amorgos. (© Marc S. Dubin/Art Resource)

are in the courtyard, where you can also see the impressive Roman mosaic depicting the reception of Asclepius on Kos.

Out in the flat countryside there are numerous relics from antiquity, enabling the visitor to imagine the prosperity of the island at that time. The small theater in Kephalos, on the west side of the island, offers a stunning view of the bay of St. Stephanos and the remains of temples. Many Early Christian basilicas have been excavated, several, such as those of Mastihari and Aghios Stephanos, in an enchanting landscape near the sea. Above Palero Pyli lie the ruins of a Byzantine fortress and several houses and churches. A visit to the knights' castle of Antimachia, which dominates the southern part of the island, is a definite must. It is highly likely that it was constructed by the Grand Master of the Order of St. John, d'Aubusson, on top of an older Byzantine fortress in 1494. There were no ancient building materials in this vicinity, so this fortress, like the one on Rhodes, was built out of uncut stone. The knights of St. John maintained the castle until 1520, as the coats of arms attest.

KOS HAS WON COUNTLESS FAITHFUL ADMIRERS among those who have visited it, looking for peace and finding it. Although there is an uncommon number of ancient ruins here, there is an ever-present sense of life lived abundantly, enriched by works of art and the blessings of prosperity and spared from tragic upheaval to this day.

KALYMNOS

KALYMNOS LIES NORTHWEST OF KOS, NOT FAR from the coast of Asia Minor. Barren, rocky mountains riven by deep chasms extend across it in all directions and fall steeply into the sea, leaving only a narrow strip of beach here and there. Ovid called the island *"Silvis umbrosa Calymne"* (shady, wooded Kalymnos). Today, however, one could scarcely describe it as wooded, in spite of the brush on the rocky slopes, the few large fig trees, or the famous orange groves in the valley of Vathy. But the lush growth of thyme still suggests why the ancients valued the honey of Kalymnos as highly as that of Attica.

The visitor arrives in the harbor of Pothia, the only town on the island. Its houses, mostly two- and three-story private homes in the neo-classical island style, cling to the hills surrounding the harbor. Here and there a splendid church stands out, testimony to both the prosperity and the piety of the captains and sponge divers who have contributed their tithe in gratitude for having escaped the forces of nature unscathed. For Kalymnos is above all the island of sponge divers; sponges are the main source of income even today. Discouraged by their poor soil, the Kalymnians turned to the sea; under the constant threat of death, they still exploit the floor of the sea in remote waters. The life of the entire island revolves around the departure (April–May) and the return (Septem-

The island of Kalymnos.

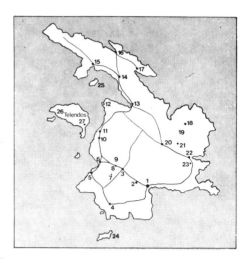

ber–October) of the sponge divers. Their return is awaited with great anxiety and regaled with endless feasts, even though every year a number of families have cause to mourn. Their dangerous life—dependent on the sea, whether they dive for sponges, set out to catch fish, or deal in shipping—has made the men of Kalymnos particularly hardy. The islanders are gifted with an independent, restless, curious spirit that distinguishes them from the other people of the Dodecanese. The endless rocking of the colorful boats in the harbor, the vitality of the people strolling noisily and busily along the quay or sitting over ouzo and *chtapodi* in the *kapheneias*—these are all a delightful welcome to the new arrival.

AFTER THE SEA HAD BEEN RID OF PIRATES, THE population no longer required the protection of the fortress, or Kastro, which lies northwest of Chorio, and they moved nearer to the sea and the harbor, where present-day Pothia began to develop in about 1850. It is clear that this site had been inhabited long before, however, from the five-sided apse of a stone Early Chris-

tian basilica near the old grammar school, from the classical graves in the area, and from the ancient remains uncovered in 1884 in the foundations of the church of Palia Panaghia. Pothia's ancient heritage is thoroughly understandable when one considers that this generous harbor lies directly opposite Kos.

According to Diodorus, the island, like the rest of the Dodecanese, was originally inhabited by Carians. In time it was then settled by Dorians, either under Thessalus, the son of Heracles, or, as Herodotus insists, as emigrants from Epidaurus. In an attempt to give themselves a nobler ancestry, the islanders claimed—and Diodorus also transmits this version—that the companions of Agamemnon landed on Kalymnos on their return from Troy, their four ships having been thrown off course. They then settled here and mixed with the Dorian population.

Archeological investigation confirms that Kalymnos has been inhabited continually since the Neolithic period. The countless grottos in the cliffs above the shoreline provided the island's first settlers with convenient and safe shelter. Fishing, hunting, and, to a certain extent, agriculture encouraged the island's development. Neolithic tools and ceramics testify that a bustling society continued here into the Bronze Age. These remains have been found not only in the cave in Vathy, which will be discussed in more detail later, but in Pothia itself, in the caves on the rise topped by the small church of Aghia Barbara and on the Choiromandres hill. Minoan culture reached Kalymnos at the same time as it spread to other Aegean centers—numerous artifacts have been found in Vathy—and was then supplanted by the culture of Mycenae. Mycenaean remains in Vathy, Pothia, and Chora (Chorio) are extensive and fully equal in quality to those of Rhodes.

Kalymnos is separated from the Ionian island of Leros only by the narrow channel of Diapori, and it is supposedly possible to swim across this strait by way of the Pitaridia, the small rocks dotting its surface. Yet Kalymnos hardly had any ties to Leros. Instead, from the very beginning it oriented itself toward Kos, only an hour and a half away and likewise settled by Dorians, and toward the Carian coast, across from the deep harbor of Vathy. For this reason, the population of Kalymnos was concentrated on the southern part of the island, while the north was always sparsely settled. Kalymnos belonged to the Dorian world in terms of its constitution and political organization, but it played no particularly significant role in history.

As early as 546 B.C., the island appears to have belonged to the satrapy of Caria, and it took part in the rebellion of the Ionian Greek states against the Lydians in 498 B.C. Later, together with Kos and Nisyros, it fell under the dominion of Queen Artemisia of Caria, under whose leadership it was forced to fight on the side of the Persians in the sea battle of Salamis. Kalymnos became independent in about the middle of the fifth century B.C. It joined the Attic League and remained a faithful member despite the defection of other allies; its contribution to the league, 1½ talents, was admittedly anything but princely. The island also participated in the Second Attic league (378 B.C.), but it withdrew a short time later (355 B.C.) and again acknowledged the rule of Caria. It was granted increased liberties and permitted to mint its own coins once more. There had been local coinage since the middle of the sixth century B.C. These silver staters were stamped on one side with the *chelys* (seven-stringed lyre) and on the other with a head with a helmet and beard that some scholars consider to be Apollo Hyacinthus of Sparta; this Apollo is the only one to wear a helmet and beard.

When the successors divided up the empire of Alexander the Great among themselves, Kalymnos fell to the Ptolemies. Shortly afterward, in the late third century B.C., it came under the rule of Kos. In Roman times, it belonged to the province of Asia; under Diocletian, to the Provincia Insularum; and under the Byzantines, to the theme of Aigaion. When trade between the West and East increased after the collapse of Byzantium, the Venetians occupied Kalymnos. They surrendered the island somewhat later to the Order of St. John of Rhodes, which had to give it over in turn, along with Kos, to the Turks.

THE PERA KASTRO IS THE OLDEST OF THE ISLAND'S medieval monuments. It stands to the left of the main road to Chorio, beyond the last houses of Pothia. The Pera Kastro is a small castle on top of a low hill. At the foot of this hill stands the small Christ Church, and on its slopes three ancient windmills. The fortress is also known as Kastro tis Chryso-cherias after the church of the Panaghia (Holy Virgin) sheltered within its walls. Remains of frescos are preserved inside the church; an ancient icon of the Panaghia, with gilt hands, is supposed to have given its name to the church, or so the islanders say. On the walls of the fortress, which the knights of St. John constructed to protect the harbor, you can still make out the coats of arms of the Grand Master de Lastic (or perhaps the Grand Master Fluvian?), of Fantino Guerrini, Adimaro Dupuy, and Giacomo Geltru. However, it is not known exactly when the Pera Kastro was built. In any case, the hill was not inhabited for the first time in the Middle Ages; late Mycenaean shards have been found on its eastern and southern slopes. These, together with Mycenaean graves discovered in the valley of Pothia, have led scholars to suspect that the hill was the site of the acropolis of a Mycenaean settlement that extended along the valley of Pothia near the harbor.

Chora (Chorio) is several centuries old. A castle originally stood here as well, the so-called Kastro. According to tradition it was constructed as early as the ninth century A.D., in Byzantine times, when the inhabitants withdrew to the interior to escape from pirates. The knights of St. John left their coats of arms in the fortress, documenting their renovations and additions. Today, one can see only the coats of arms of del Carretto, of the order itself, and of an unknown knight with the date 1519. Ludwig Ross also saw the coat of arms of d'Aubusson when he visited Kalymnos in 1841. The only approach up the steep hill to this fortress is from the southeast. The houses and cisterns and some of the churches inside it have fallen into ruin. Strewn all about are blocks of stone and shards from the fourth century B.C. and from the Hellenistic period.

Not until the seventeenth century did the inhabitants again dare to venture forth from the fortified Kastro to build their homes at the foot of the mountain; thus, present-day Chorio gradually took shape. Among these structures are several examples of the original form of the Kalymnian house, the *katzia*. This is a rectangular dwelling with a single room in a courtyard with grapevines, a well, and a bake-oven. The raised wooden *kravatos* separates the living area from the sleeping area; beneath it lies the *ampari*, or cellar, in which the harvest was stored. If the family grew larger, additional rooms were built on the second story.

SOUTH OF CHORIO IS MOUNT ARGOS, SITE OF THE Church of the Twelve Apostles. Tradition has it that this church was founded by the Blessed Christodoulos of Patmos in the eleventh century. Ancient ruins and graves have also been found in the immediate vicinity of Chorio. If you take the road leading to the west, you note increasing traces of the past.

NOT FAR FROM CHORIO, TO THE LEFT SIDE OF THE road, you encounter the ruins of the church of Christos tis Ierusalim (Christ of Jerusalem), the most venerable monument on Kalymnos. The west wall of the altar niche of this Early Christian basilica, with its three-part window, still stands, as does the *synthronon* of the presbytery, the semicircular stepped seats of the clergy. The floor of the central nave is paved with marble slabs, while those of the side aisles display mosaics.

The structure is dated to the sixth century A.D., but the majority of the building materials are of ancient origin. Inscriptions in the floor and on the wall of the apse inform

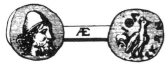

Coin from Ithaca, with head of Odysseus.

us that the basilica was erected on the site of the sanctuary of Apollo Dalios. *Dalios* is the Dorian form of *Delos*. The chief cult on Kalymnos was thus one of the Delian Apollo; his shrine, as in other cities in the Greek world, was a dependent foundation of the temple on Delos. From the fourth century B.C. on, decrees, documents, and contracts were deposited within the sacred precinct. Bits of ceramics and other finds attest that the cult already existed here in the Archaic period. Festivals were celebrated here— the "great" Dalia every four years, the "lesser" one annually—with athletic and artistic competitions. A laurel grove and a cult theater once formed a part of the sanctuary. Inscriptions from the third century B.C. provide the names of its benefactors.

Another Early Christian basilica stands less than 100 yards southeast of the church of Christos tis Ierusalim. This basilica, also with a nave and side aisles, was built somewhat later than Christos tis Ierusalim and apparently outside the grounds of the temple of Apollo. It was consecrated to the Aghia Sophia or the Evangelistria. Here too the floors are covered with slabs of marble and mosaics, and the walls are ornamented with stones from antiquity. A larger-than-life-sized torso of a cult statue of Asclepius was found in the basilica's foundations in 1968; in antiquity, the worship of the god Asclepius and of his daughters Hygieia and Panacea quickly spread across the island alongside that of his father, Apollo. This Torso of Asclepius now stands in Pothia. It is complete from the neck to the waist. In the same space, which serves as a tempo-

rary museum, there are also a number of Neolithic finds from Aghia Barbara and Vathy, Mycenaean vases and shards, as well as extraordinary examples of Geometric and Archaic ceramics of Kalymnos.

If you take the road toward Brosta and Myrties along the lovely sand beach to the northwest of Christos tis Ierusalim, you come into the territory of the Damos (Dorian for *demos*). Here is the site of the Hellenistic necropolis. Charles T. Newton, the British vice-consul in Mytilene, excavated it with the permission of the Turkish pasha in 1854–1855 and sent his finds back to England. Chamber tombs in the cliffs, the foundations of houses, walls, and other remains reveal for certain that there was a city on this site. Presumably the area belonged to the ancient *demos* of Pothaea, which likely comprised the southwestern portion of the island, including the fertile vicinity and harbor of Pothia and stretching as far as the villages of Elies, Linaria, and Kantouni.

At one time, the island was divided into several *demoi*, or municipalities; then, at the close of the third century B.C., after Kos had annexed and reorganized it, their number was reduced to only three: Pothaea, Orcatos, and Panormos. These districts can be located with relative certainty even today.

The *demos* of Panormos is supposed to have extended from Myrties and Sykia as far as Emporeio and to have included the nearby islet of Telendos. The word *panormos* denoted a harbor in which one might drop anchor in all weathers, and it indeed applies to the deep bays of the west coast, which may be reached safely from either the north or the south and are protected by Telendos. The wealth of ancient remains says something about the importance of the entire region. Though difficult to reach, it is possible to find the traces of ancient fortresses in Xerokampos and Vryokastro near the bay of Argynontas. The walls of Anginaries, between Argynontas and Skalia, may date from Carian times. Farther to the north, above the bay of Emporio and some ten minutes from the village, the Kastro stands on a steep cliff; portions of walls and two rectangular towers survive. Its staircases and its gateway are carved out of the solid rock. Inside, there is an ancient olive press with a typical heart-shaped millstone and various cisterns from a later period. The Kastro is almost completely protected to the east by cliffs, and it dominates the passes leading to the sea from the east to the north. Although the Kastro has not yet been researched, the consensus is that it dates from a time when Kalymnos was under Carian rule.

Remnants from later times are strewn about everywhere. Impressive Byzantine frescos are preserved, for example, in the small church of Aghios Nikolaos in Skalia. A small Early Christian basilica stands south of Myrties on a low hill, along with the church of Ai Ioannis Melitzakas. It differs from the other Early Christian basilicas on the island because it has three naves and mosaic inscriptions in the narthex. Its construction, its proportions, and its relatively good condition also distinguish it. Farther north, on the Aspropuntari, the cape thrusting out toward Telendos into the sea, there is still another small medieval fortress, Kastelli, or Palaiokastro. According to tradition, it was founded in the ninth century A.D. by the survivors of a catastrophe in Vathy. Remnants of walls, a few buildings, and ruined cisterns still crown the cliffs, and a line of walls divides the slope from the peak down to the sea. On its west side stands the small church of the Panaghia.

The strait that separates Telendos from Kalymnos was once dry land, according to legend; it supposedly sank in an earthquake. Fishermen tell of submerged columns and structures that they claim to have seen in the depths. It is certain that there are remains of Early Christian walls in the sea all along the east coast—nothing unusual in the Aegean. The boat from Myrties reaches Telendos in ten minutes.

The northern part of Telendos is domi-

nated by the high, steep Mount Aghios Konstantinos. A small church of the same name and a medieval fortress stand on its summit. A few fishing families live around the anchorage on the islet's flat, sandy southern section. Well-preserved Early Christian structures strewn all about attest to better days. For example, there is the basilica of Aghios Basilios, an impressive baptistry, and a complex of aboveground monumental tombs consisting of splendid domed chambers. To the west of these tombs, there appears to have once been a theater, for there are curved terraces rising up the slope. Farther along the coast are the remains of still another small church.

The northern part of Kalymnos was sparsely populated even in antiquity. All

The harbor of Pothia.

that survives here are a few Neolithic or later finds and the frescos of Aghios Petros, in Palionisos. The eastern part, separated from the southwest by steep mountains, presents a completely different picture. The fertile valley of Vathy is filled with lush orange groves. Across from Caria, there is a harbor that is protected on both sides by high cliffs and that cuts deeply into the plain. The inhabitants today are concentrated in three small, neighboring villages: Platanos, Metochi, and Rhina.

At the entrance to the harbor, where a chain blocked the entry of ships in the Middle Ages, yawns the cave of Daskalio, some 40 feet high. Excavations have revealed that people lived here continuously from the Neolithic period up until the Middle Ages. The roof of the cave resembles a cupola, and the water in it is pure and sweet. The cave first served as a dwelling, then as a place of Christian worship.

Neolithic traces have also been found elsewhere in the valley. Guarding the pass toward Argynontas, north of Metochi, is the mountain of Kyra Psili, with a monastery of the same name. On its eastern slope, some 200 or 300 yards above Metochi, lies Kastellas. This spot can be reached only from the west. Here you can still see the ruins of a fortress from the early days of Greece, when the Dorians controlled only the southern part of the island. Its construction resembles fortifications on the Carian coast.

Above the harbor and 100 yards east of Metochi lies Empolas. A wall from the Hellenistic period, still quite well preserved, runs along the ridge. Stone blocks from antiquity were used in the construction of a three-nave Byzantine church and the nearby church of the Taxiarch from the seventeenth century. The entire area, down as far as Metochi, is littered with bits of buildings and loose stones from the Classical to the Roman periods. Hellenistic and Roman graves have also been discovered here. Between Metochi and Rhina, a rectangle that may have been a Hellenistic structure survives. It is now called Phylakes and consists of an entryway and two rooms. Archeologists have identified it as a fortified villa or a watchtower.

In Rhina, which is named after the church of Aghia Irini, are found countless Roman ruins, strongly suggesting that under the Roman Empire, the area was nearly as important as Empolas. More noteworthy, however, are the Byzantine remains: the ruins of a town and churches with frescos. The name of the church of Panaghia Chosti ("sunk in the earth"), which has frescos from the twelfth and thirteenth centuries, is explained by the following legend: One night, when the Resurrection was being celebrated in all of the churches, the Saracens invaded. They broke through the chains blocking the harbor and plundered the city. St. Irene saw her church in danger and asked the Holy Virgin for help, whereupon the earth opened up and the church simply sank into it, along with its entire congregation and its priests. Centuries later, two shepherds watching their flocks in the vicinity heard the Easter liturgy and suddenly saw a brightly lighted church. They joined the congregation and celebrated the Resurrection. When the people of Kalymnos heard the story, they rushed to the spot but saw nothing. Only much later did some of the faithful begin to dig at this spot, where they discovered the buried church and unearthed it.

This story illustrates how history and legend intertwine on Kalymnos. The fishermen and divers have always dreamed of the silence of the depths of the sea, and they live on in a fantastic world in which dream and reality are inseparable. They tell tales that their listeners believe as though they had experienced them personally: sagas of princesses and Persian kings, miraculous stories of buried treasures. The islanders also entertain visitors with such stories; the more incredible they sound, the more they envelop you in an atmosphere of magic.

*L*EROS

THREE MOUNTAIN MASSES, STRETCHING FROM the northwest to the southeast and interrupted by deep bays, make up the island of Leros. The bay of Lakki, in the northwest, is one of the best and most secure harbors in the Aegean today. But, as is the case with most of the Dodecanese, the old harbor on Leros, Aghia Marina, lies on the east coast, facing Asia Minor. It is probable that the ancient city of Leros was situated here.

Strolling about in the small towns of Aghia Marina and Platanos today, you discover here and there, behind rusted iron fences and shaded by lemon trees, a few dilapidated villas. These were built by people from the island who had left and grown rich abroad, especially in Egypt, then returned at about the turn of the century. The local folksongs tell of the homesickness of the islanders, the persistent longing to see Leros's mountains and bays once more.

Leros is a green island that is well supplied with water, but space is limited, so the grain, fruit, and vegetables that can be cultivated here barely suffice for the farmers themselves. The entire island is inhabited, and there are houses everywhere. The most important towns are Platanos, beneath the huge old fortress, and Aghia Marina.

The fortress above Platanos is the most important monument on the island. From its high and impregnable position, it dominates not only the island of Leros but seemingly the entire archipelago. All of the fortresses in the Dodecanese were erected at strategic sites, and they took shape several millennia ago, when the first Hellenes settled here in mythical times. The fortress of Leros is supposed to have been extremely important in the Byzantine period, when the Hosios Christodoulos, the holy abbot, lived here. He arrived in the eleventh century, with the permission of the Byzantine emperor Alexius, and proceeded to destroy all the surviving heathen temples and monuments. Later he moved to Patmos, where he built the monastery of St. John

The island of Leros.

1. *Harbor of Lakki*
2. *Ancient harbor of Aghia Marina*
3. *Platanos*
4. *Kastro*
5. *Lepida*
6. *Xerokambos*
7. *Alinda*
8. *Partheni*

the Theologian, above the cave of the Apocalypse. This foundation still owns the smaller monastery, named Metochia, on Leros. The fortress took on its present form under the knights of the Order of St. John, who settled here in the fourteenth century. These knights, whose headquarters were on Rhodes, were able to rely on the energetic people of Leros to repel the Turks successfully until 1522, when the island capitulated.

The outer walls of the fortress can be seen in the form they were given during restoration work undertaken after World War II. Also standing is the church of the Panaghia tou Kastrou (Holy Virgin of the Fortress). The ruins next to the church are all that is left of the former monks' cells. Various portions of dwellings are still visible, and at the highest point there are the ruined barracks. Cannons were placed here in World War II.

Until the end of this war, Leros belonged to the Italians, as did the rest of the Dodecanese. It was they who built the first concrete buildings on Leros, in the present-day harbor settlement of Lakki, and laid out the first wide streets and gardens. Yet Lakki is unlikely to impress the visitor as much as Platanos, Aghia Marina, or the fortress, where there is a sense of either the remote past or the folkloric atmosphere of the island.

There were ancient settlements near both Platanos and Aghia Marina, as various archeological finds and foundations attest. We can also suspect that after the close of the eighth century B.C., Leros belonged to the great Ionian community that centered in Miletus. Herodotus mentions Leros in connection with the Ionian rebellion against the Persians at the beginning of the fifth century B.C. Sporadic archeological finds prove that the island has been continuously occupied from that time until the present day.

On the southeast coast lies Xerokambos, today only a few scattered farmhouses. The hill above this village contains the remnants of a fortress from the fourth century B.C., with well-cut stones and a mosaic floor that has been badly damaged. The inhabitants speak of the structure as the Palaiokastro, or "old castle."

Partheni, on the northwest coast, was well known outside Greece during the military dictatorship (1967–1974) as a camp for those banished from Athens. It is possible to reach Partheni from Patmos in a small motorboat in an hour and a half. The name *Partheni* is derived from *Parthenos,* or "virgin," and refers to the virginal goddess Artemis. We know from various finds and inscriptions that there was once a

Artemis: from an ancient marble.

shrine to Artemis on Leros. Long before it was possible to confirm this, mythological tradition led scholars to suspect as much: in Calydon, in Aetolia, the sisters of Meleager were thrown into deepest mourning at his death; out of compassion for them, the goddess Artemis changed them into birds and permitted them to fly to her sanctuary on Leros.

On Leros, as is quite common on the smaller islands, names from antiquity are still encountered. For example, the name of the region of Temenia, which lies near Lakki, recalls the ancient Temenos, or sacred precinct, and the name Paliaskloupi comes from the ancient *Palaion Asklepieion*, or old shrine of Asclepius. Ancient names also live on in the place names Alinda, Drymonas, and Lepida.

PATMOS

SINCE THE ELEVENTH CENTURY, PATMOS HAS been dominated by its monastic fortress, a bulwark of the faith. Its bells are famous for their deep sound, which can be heard from a great distance; to foreign ears it is a striking change from the brighter bells generally heard in Greece. Square white houses with gray pumice-stone terraces surround the massive stone fortress like a protective wall.

The monastery of Aghios Ioannis Theologos is unique among Byzantine monasteries in that there is no sharp division between the monks and the islanders. The monks' contemplative life adheres to the strictest Byzantine rituals, but it is not shut in behind the monastery walls. The monks move freely about outside the monastery and are even permitted to spend the night with their relatives. Women and children are allowed to call on the monks with equal freedom.

The peaceful atmosphere has a calming influence on everyone who comes to Patmos and is fortunate enough to find a place to stay in the upper town. In such a recep-

tive mood the visitor is prepared at all times for the unexpected or the unusual. In the summer of 1974, for example, when a Turkish warship was sighted off the coast of Patmos after Turkey invaded Cyprus, vacationers did not react as they did on other islands; despite the threat of war, not one of them thought of fleeing back to Athens. Perhaps the monastery, standing there as a timeless and steadfast presence, eased their anxieties.

For many, Patmos is the most beautiful of the Greek islands, as it was for the taxi driver who went there for two days and stayed on for thirty years. Anyone would feel blessed by fate if he or she had a chance to live here.

The run-down mansions from the sixteenth–nineteenth centuries near the monastery have recently been bought up and restored by Athenians, Greeks living abroad, and foreigners, though unless a foreigner is married to a Greek woman, he has no legal right to buy real estate. Most of these mansions are whitewashed structures with roof terraces reminiscent of the

Cycladic style, but here woodcarvers and stonecutters have embellished the façades with Byzantine doors and balconies and Italian loggias and windows. You can stroll about in these streets for hours without growing bored, constantly discovering new and lovely architectural details. Particularly impressive are the houses owned by the Valvi, Liakopoulou, Konstantinidi, Stephanidi, Photiadi, Ralli, Simantira, and Kalliga families and by Sadruddin Aga Khan and Prince von Schwarzenberg. Since 1946, the island has been placed under state protection as part of the national heritage; local furnishings, such as trunks and cupboards painted with floral designs, finely carved tables, and four-poster beds, may not be taken out of the island. In many cases, the homeowners are willing to admit visitors. If you wish to see a more modest house that belongs to an islander, you should speak to the woman of the house, probably the owner, in accordance with local custom. For on Patmos, the oldest daughter is customarily presented with her parents' house as part of her dowry when she marries, and the parents move to a new house which their son is required to build for them—a most unusual practice in Greece.

The people of Patmos are hospitable but not especially interested in tourists. Visitors arrive at Skala, the harbor town, where there are newsstands, shops, cafés, taverns, hotels, and a post office.

THE ISLAND HAS A SURFACE AREA OF A LITTLE MORE than 13 square miles, and the great majority of it is covered with volcanic rock, including liparite and trachyte. Around the bay of Lambi, in the north, there are quantities of multicolored pebbles that will make anyone a passionate collector. There are no forests, but figs, almonds, lemons, and pears are grown quite extensively. The island's shrubs, chiefly thyme and sage, feed swarms of bees that produce honey of exceptional fragrance.

The ancient name of the island lives on in the local dialect; the islanders do not call themselves Patmians but rather Patinioi or Patiniotes. An inscription dating from the fifth century B.C., preserved in the monastery, refers to the island as Patnos. This

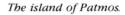

The island of Patmos.

1. Skala
2. Chora
3. Cave of the Apocalypse
4. Kambos
5. Kalikatsou
6. Bay of Lambi

same inscription relates that Orestes was driven here by the Furies after he killed Clytemnestra, his mother, and that this was the most venerable island of all, sacred to Artemis, who dwelt in the deep waters off the Patmian coast. As recently as the early eighteenth century, the French physician and botanist Pitton de Tournefort was able to discern columns in the clear water of the harbor near Skala. These columns are no longer visible today, but near Petra, or Kallikatsou, it is still possible to climb down into the water by steps cut out of the solid rock. A shrine is supposed to have stood here, but it is not known whether it was consecrated to Artemis or to Aphrodite, goddess of seafarers. On Patmos, Artemis resembled the fertility goddess of Ephesus, in Asia Minor, more than she did the virginal Greek protectress of hunters.

Above Skala stand the ruins of a fortress dating from the fourth century B.C., on a hill now known as Kastelli. Ancient graves and shards lie strewn about the whole area.

The ancient historians rarely mention Patmos and then only briefly, for no particular military memories are associated with it. What is known is that Ionians replaced the original Dorian settlers and that the Romans used the island as a place of exile; the Romans preferred to banish unwanted citizens to wild and barren islands. The most famous among these exiles was St. John of Patmos, who may be the same person as the beloved disciple of Christ. The emperor Domitian (81–91 A.D.) may have banished John to Patmos for teaching the new religion in Ephesus. It is also equally likely that John fled to Patmos as an old man in the last year of Domitian's reign to escape the persecution of Christians. Clement of Alexandria relates that John returned home after Domitian died and never returned to Patmos. We will never learn why John chose Patmos as a place of refuge; possibly because Roman galleys rarely landed on the rocky coast of this windswept island; the only sailors who ventured to sail its dangerous waters were pirates who hid their booty in the caves that dotted its steep cliffs. Countless legends have attached themselves to the figure of St. John. It is said, for example, that he brought about the collapse of pagan temples in Ephesus merely by the strength of his spirit. On Patmos, he is said to have turned the magician Kynops into a rock that stands on the southern tip of the island. There you can also see a cave where evil spirits are still thought to lurk. In Skala, a group of stones lies in a semicircle; these are supposed to have formed the fount where John baptized new converts. Legend also has it that the Gospel of St. John was written on Patmos. The Greek Orthodox Church has given St. John of Patmos the cognomen Theologos ("Theologian").

The cave in which St. John received the Revelation (Apocalypse) lies midway between Skala and the upper town of Patmos. To the left, below the road, there is a monastery next to the cave, known as Apokalypsis. To imagine the cave's original state, you must shut your eyes to the many features that have altered it over the centuries: sanctuary screens, icons, oil lamps that hang from the ceiling and have blackened the purplish porphyry walls. If you can do this, you may understand how, in such surroundings, John received his visions of the end of the world after much fasting and praying. The colors with which he depicts the Apocalypse correspond to the scene a visitor comes upon when standing at the mouth of the cave at sunset, watching the light refracted in the high waves that crash against the cliffs.

St. John here dictated the book of Rev-

View of Patmos from The Mediterranean Illustrated, *1877.*

elations to his pupil Prochoros:

> I, John, who also am your brother, and companion in tribulation, and in the kingdom and patience of Jesus Christ, was in the isle that is called Patmos, for the word of God, and for the testimony of Jesus Christ. I was in the Spir-

it on the Lord's day, and heard behind me a great voice, as of a trumpet, Saying, I am Alpha and Omega, the first and the last: and, What thou seest, write in a book, and send *it* unto the seven churches which are in Asia. . . .

Pictures of St. John are to be found not

only in this cave but also in frescos in the vestibule (exonarthex) of the church and in miniatures in the monastery library, which was built as a Byzantine monastic fortress in 1088 in memory of St. John the Theologian. Its cornerstone was laid by the pious abbot Christodoulos, who had founded other monasteries in Asia Minor and on the islands of Kos and Leros. The Byzantine emperor Alexius I Comnenus (1081–1118) had presented him with the island of Patmos. It is said that Christodoulos came upon a statue of Artemis while building the monastery, dashed it to pieces, and buried it in the foundations. The ancient columns in the courtyard permit the assumption that one of the Olympian gods was worshipped on this site. Various capitals and architectural fragments also suggest that an Early Christian basilica once stood here.

A document, preserved in the library, that bears the imperial gold seal of Alexius I contains a list of the privileges granted this and other monasteries. Such foundations were placed directly under the emperor's control. This monastery was granted political autonomy, it was exempt from taxation, and it was permitted to hold land in Crete and Asia Minor and to maintain its own fleet. These privileges were reaffirmed by each succeeding emperor. The Turks brought only very slight alterations to the monastery's status.

The only law in force on Patmos was the strict rule known as the *typikon*, introduced by Christodoulos. The abbot wished to make the entire island a place of spiritual meditation and asceticism, where only men would be admitted.

It proved impossible to maintain a strictly male society for very long, and the families of the lay brothers who worked for the monastery eventually settled on the southern tip of the island; they later moved close to the monastery for better protection. Women took over many of the housekeeping chores, while the men served as soldiers whenever necessary. Above the main entrance to the monastery was a cantilevered balcony known as the *phonias* ("murderer") or *zematistra* ("scalder"). From here, it was possible to pour boiling oil or water and molten lead on attackers.

After passing through the main entrance, one comes into the courtyard, which has been surrounded by arcades since 1698. To the left stands the monastery church with its two side chapels. These buildings, as well as the refectory (*trapeza*), date from the twelfth and thirteenth centuries. The frescos in the Mary Chapel are well worth seeing: the Holy Virgin sits enthroned in the center, holding the infant Jesus in her lap, while the archangels Michael and Gabriel stand on either side (behind the choir wall). In the other side chapel, there is a Byzantine sarcophagus containing the mummified remains of Christodoulos. Proceeding to the refectory, you encounter frescos depicting scenes from various ecumenical councils, subjects extremely rare in the history of Byzantine painting.

From the balustrades and walls of the monastery terrace, you can look down on the town, characterized by church cupolas, narrow streets that become empty and silent in the evening, and houses whose roofs are designed to catch rain water and channel it into cisterns. Beyond the town, you can see a large part of the island and the surrounding sea.

The monastery and the sea have always been closely linked together in Patmos. After the fall of Constantinople in 1453, refugees from there considerably increased the number of seafaring monks; the same thing happened when Crete was conquered by the Turks in 1669. Sailors from Patmos regularly journeyed to Jerusalem, Jaffa, Constantinople, Russia, southern Italy, and even Germany. One of them, Iakovos Meloitis, wrote a detailed account of his travels in 1588. It is now in the library of the University of Tübingen.

The women of Patmos never traveled. But they embroidered and knitted cotton stockings that were much prized in lands as far away as Italy.

Some 800 houses were built during the sixteenth and seventeenth centuries by seamen who had grown rich through trade. Their ships brought fine furnishings back from the East and the West, as well as valuable jewelry and clothing. Native artisans soon imitated and adapted the designs of these imported items in their own work.

The Patmian way of life became so opulent in those times that Silvestros, the patriarch of Alexandria, felt obliged to travel to Patmos in 1580 and appeal to the inhabitants not to concern themselves so much with clothing their mortal bodies in splendid garments, but to be mindful of the not-too-distant day when they would stand naked before God. Outward poverty and inner spiritual wealth should constitute the island's true treasures.

Outward poverty was soon enough imposed upon the Patmians, for the island was destroyed during the Turkish-Venetian War. There is a manuscript in the monastery library, No. 107, in which the event is described as follows: "On June 18, 1659, the Venetian armada arrived and demolished Patmos, on a Saturday; Francesco Morosini made numerous demands, accursed may he be." After the Turks established their hegemony over the Mediterranean islands in 1669, they did not in fact settle on Patmos, but came every year to the monastery to pick up their tribute.

In 1713, the Patmian Makarios Kalogheras, who had studied theology and philosophy in Constantinople, founded a school near the cave of the Apocalypse in 1713. Subjects were taught here that were not taught elsewhere in Greece. It remained a model institution until 1856. Books were

Women of Patmos: drawing by J. B. Hilair, c. 1782.

printed here that are now preserved in the famous library of the monastery of St. John the Theologian. This is one of the most modern libraries in Greece. A special air-conditioning system keeps the valuable manuscripts free of moisture. Anyone wishing to visit the library must obtain a special permit. The core of the collection is the works that Christodoulos brought over with him from his home monastery near Mount Latmos, in the vicinity of Miletus. As he himself stated, he had saved these from the Turks only with the greatest difficulty. A catalogue of the library's acquisitions was begun in 1201. The oldest of the manuscripts catalogued at that time was a section of the Gospel of St. Mark, written in the sixth century in gold and silver lettering on purple parchment. The Russians took part of this manuscript to Leningrad, and a few pages are in the possession of the Vatican, the Vienna Museum, the British Museum, and the Byzantine Museum in Athens. Another of the library's valuable treasures was once taken to England. This is a manuscript of Platonic philosophy from the ninth century A.D. It is now known as the Codex Clarkianus, after Edward Daniel Clark, who bought it from the monastery.

The museum also houses the following: a number of especially beautiful icons; a Book of Job embellished with forty-two miniatures and a commentary from the eighth century; a copy of the sermons of

Patmos: drawing by J. B. Hilair, c. 1782.

Gregory of Nazianzus to his preachers that was written in Reggio di Calabria in 941; tenth-century copies of the *History* of Diodorus Siculus; and early editions of ancient Greek literature. Gospels from the eleventh to the fourteenth centuries, their bindings ornamented in silver and gold, are displayed in glass cases.

The catalogues *(brevia)* show that for centuries the monastery lent codices and, later, books, not only to the smaller monasteries attached to it *(Metochia)*, but to other foundations on the islands and in Asia Minor. It is clear that Patmos was an important cultural center for the entire Mediterranean. The significance of Patmos to Christianity was enhanced in the 1960s, when the Ecumenical patriarch Athena-

goras declared it a "holy island of Christendom."

Certain religious festivals are celebrated differently on Patmos than in the rest of Greece; Christ's washing of feet on Maundy Thursday is one of the most striking examples. The abbot of the monastery takes on the role of Christ, while his monks represent the twelve apostles, the youngest of them portraying Judas Iscariot. A procession, led by the abbot, leaves the monastery and arrives at the main square at about eleven in the morning. There, a platform decorated with carpets and green branches is set up on the square. The whole ceremony revolves around the dialogue between Christ and Peter. The monk representing John provides the

commentary.

JOHN: Before the Passover celebration, when Jesus knew that his time had come to leave this world...he arose from the Last Supper, poured water in a basin, and began washing the feet of his disciples, drying them with the cloth that girded his body.

(Here the foot-washing scene is symbolically enacted.)

JOHN: Then Jesus came to Simon Peter and spoke to him:

PETER: Lord, are you about to wash my feet?

JESUS: What I do you cannot know yet; but you will know it by and by.

PETER: Never should you wash my feet.

JESUS: If I do not wash you, you will have no part of me.

PETER: Lord, not my feet alone, but also my hands and my head.

JESUS: Whoever has been washed requires nothing more than that his feet be also washed—he is completely clean. You are clean, but not all of you.

After the monks and the other participants in the ceremony have prayed before the icon of Christ, the procession returns to the monastery. When this ritual was performed in Constantinople, the capital of the Byzantine Empire, the emperor took the role of Christ in his palace and the Greek Orthodox patriarch did so at the famed church of Aghia Sophia.

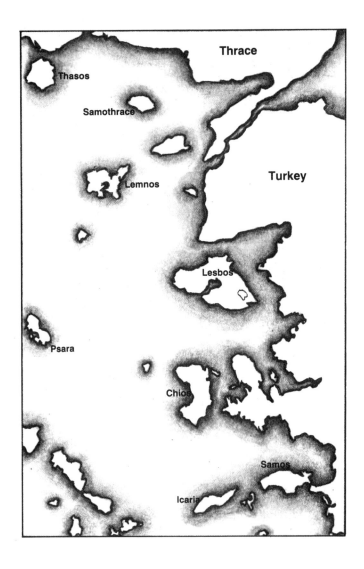

ISLANDS OF THE EASTERN AND NORTHERN AEGEAN

*I*CARIA

THE NAME ICARIA WOULD BE FAMILIAR NEITHER to us nor to the ancient Greeks were it not for the myth of the legendary Daedalus, whose son Icarus fell into the waters nearby. The Icarian Sea was named for him.

Icaria was rarely visited in antiquity and seldom today. It has no harbors or bays to offer shelter from the high winds. The geographer Strabo called the island Alimenos, or "harborless," and Homer, in the *Iliad*, compared the raging uprising in the camp of the Achaeans to the Icarian Sea: "In storm the people raised up like massive sea-waves atop the Icarian flood, which the east and south wind stir up...."

Icaria lies apart from other Aegean Islands and away from the shipping routes between Ionia and the Greek mainland. In antiquity, it was called Makra or Doliche, both of which mean "long"; the island is some 87 miles in length. It was also known as Ichthyoessa, or "rich in fish," an epithet that still applies.

The Atheras Mountains run across Icaria from east to west; the highest peak rises to 3,412 feet. To the south of this range, gray granite cliffs veined with blue-white marble drop steeply into the sea. Vegetation is generally sparse, but wherever a small amount of soil has accumulated, between the rocks or in the folds of the hills, there are hidden gardens where plane trees, myrtles, and fruit trees grow. Each garden is protected by walls made of stones piled on top of one another; in one corner stands a two-story towerlike farmhouse. The Icariots have always lived scattered all over the island as farmers, shepherds, and charcoal dealers. Any spot where there is a school and a church they call a village, and the French traveler Tournefort wrote in 1702 that "to them a village might only be a house standing completely isolated."

In good weather, ships anchor off Aghios Kyrikos. From there, a mule track leads across the saddle of the Atheras Mountains. It leads past Manganitis, along the southwest coast, and then down to an altitude of 2,900 feet, into a barren, rocky landscape.

The island of Icaria.

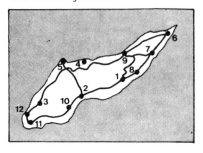

1. *Aghios Kyrikos*
2. *Manganitis*
3. *Langada*
4. *Evdilos*
5. *Armenistis*
6. *Fanari (Drakanon)*
7. *Kataphygi*
8. *Therma*
9. *Miliopo*
10. *Trapalon*
11. *Karkinagrion*
12. *Kalamos*

Occasionally you must hold fast to the furze when the wind rages. But as soon as you climb down the slope of the mountain to the north, you are surrounded by endless pine forests, possibly one of the most impressive landscapes in the Aegean. Ravines turn into valleys, small streams into torrents. The German philologist and archeologist Ludwig Ross remarked that the Icariots lived in this solitude "like the old Germanic tribes." Their habits and customs have been preserved unchanged. The old-fashioned dialect bears Ionian traces. An ancient and vital tradition of folk art survives especially in the western part of the island, in the remote village of Langada.

At one time Icariot sponge dealers traveled as far as Alexandria or Constantinople. But they would always return to their own villages as quickly as possible. The Icariots ascribe their love of their homeland to the wild plants that grow on the Atheras Mountains, which are eaten either raw in salads or cooked as vegetables. Rare species of Greek flora are found in the treeless ravines—certain kinds of wild sage, poppy, sea onion, juniper bushes, and many kinds of mushrooms that are famous throughout the Aegean. Naturally there are poisonous mushrooms as well. Eparchides related that in the fifth century B.C., a whole family died from eating them; the poet, who chanced to be on Icaria at the time, wrote a touching inscription for their tomb.

LET US RETURN TO THE STORY OF DAEDALUS AND Icarus. Icarus is supposedly buried on Icaria. But he was born on Crete, where his father, Daedalus, the first Athenian sculptor and smith, lived in exile at the court of King Minos. Daedalus was a favorite until Minos discovered that the artist had invented a means whereby Queen Pasiphaë could have intercourse with the white bull of Poseidon. The king promptly threw the artist in jail along with Icarus, whose mother, Naucratis, was one of Minos's slaves. Father and son plotted flight and constructed two pairs of artificial wings, one for each of them. They affixed the large feathers with strings, the smaller ones with wax. Ready for takeoff, the father admonished his son: "Fly neither so high that the sun melts the wax nor so low that the sea wets the feathers!" They slipped into their wings, and off they went. "Stay close to me," Daedalus called, "and aim to the northeast." Soon Naxos, Paros, and Delos came into view. Is it not remarkable that even at the dawn of history, men could understand something of the intoxication of flight? For suddenly, Icarus forgot his father's caution and began flying straight for the sun in his excitement. When Daedalus looked back, Icarus had disappeared. The heat of the sun had melted the wax, and his wings had come apart. Icarus plunged into the sea and drowned; Daedalus could see him floating helplessly on the waves. Legend has it that Daedalus

The flight of Icarus.

The revels of Dionysus and his bride Ariadne: from a sarcophagus.

brought his son's body to the nearest coast and buried him there.

According to Pausanias, however, Icarus was supposed to have suffered shipwreck in a sailboat his father had invented and constructed for him. Are the wings perhaps a poetic metaphor for sails? If so, it may be no coincidence that the best harbor of ancient Icaria was called Histoi (Greek for "masts"). Ancient Histoi probably lay in the vicinity of present-day Evdilos.

The first men to fly are remembered on Icaria to this day. The old people of the island tell the story of Icarus in their own version: he was the son of an Icarian king who wanted to kidnap a Cretan princess. The wings, which were to carry the pair back to Icaria, disintegrated in the sun and the lovers drowned in the sea. The island's myths and sagas are continually revised and retold by both educated and uneducated natives.

THE FIRST HISTORICAL INFORMATION REGARDING Icaria is found in Strabo, who wrote that settlers came to the island in the middle of the eighth century B.C. from Miletus, in Asia Minor. During the Persian Wars, it appears that the Icariots subjugated themselves to Polycrates, the tyrant of Samos. In Aeschylus's *Persians* and in Herodotus, we read that Samos had recognized the sovereignty of the Persian King Darius at that time. During the Peloponnesian War between Athens and Sparta and their respective allies at the end of the fifth century B.C., the Icariots were allied with the Athenians, and inscriptions on the Acropolis in Athens and in Delos attest that they were members of the First Attic League. The poet Eparchides, mentioned above, was from Icaria, as were the sculptor Timocles, who worked on the reliefs of the Serapis sanctuary, and his lover, whose beauty and charming intelligence captivated even the priests of Serapis.

From the fourth century B.C. until the first century A.D., nothing is known of Icaria. The geographer Strabo wrote that the island was uninhabited and served as

the Order of Jerusalem), whose deputies fled from the island when pirates attacked. Then Sultan Selim II conquered Icaria in 1567. Turkish rule lasted until July 17, 1912, when the Icariots chased away the Turkish officials. At that time, the Free State of Icaria printed a series of commemorative stamps.

ARCHEOLOGICAL FINDS ON ICARIA HAVE BEEN RELatively haphazard. Only in recent years have scholars become interested in its Byzantine churches. Most of the ancient remains have been found to the north of the Atheras Mountains, on their so-called windy side. Graves with clay votive gifts from the fifth century B.C. have been discovered between the village of Christoton Rachon and the small harbor of Armenistis; to the north of the church of Aghios Charalambos, there are the foundations of an ancient wall. In the nearby woods, there are tombs and grave steles from the fourth century B.C. In the church of Ghialiskari, which is consecrated to the Holy Virgin, there is an inscription in the wall that probably dates from the third century B.C. It announces the fine that would be required of anyone who dared to bury a stranger in the family tomb. Offenders would have to pay tribute to Artemis Tauropolos ("protectress of bulls"), whose sanctuary, which was mentioned by Strabo, stood west of Armenistis.

pastureland for the people of Samos. But at that time, Samians lived on Icaria; this much is clear from inscriptions found on the island. So Strabo's information may be suspect. Like many an ancient traveler, he never set foot on the island. We do know that in the fifth century A.D., Icaria was a bishopric and that in Byzantine times, it formed the seventeenth theme (administrative district) of Aigaion Pelagos and served as a place of exile for members of the imperial family who had fallen into disgrace. Even today, certain Icariots boast of their imperial ancestry.

The Byzantine emperor Isaac Angelus gave the island in fief to the Venetian Siccardo Beationo in 1191. The descendants of Beationo, who ruled until 1333, called themselves barons of Icaria. Then, for a short time, the island belonged to the Italian Maonesi family, who also ruled Chios. From 1362 until 1481, there were counts of Icaria who belonged to the Arangio Giustiniani family. They were followed by the Cavalieri Gerosolimitani (Crusaders of

By boat, it takes an hour and a half from Armenistis to reach the mouth of the Halaris River, where the foundation of a temple with a cella, opisthodomos, and adytum (inner sanctum) was brought to light, along with two elongated bases, which presumably supported altars. In addition, portions of female statues from the fifth century B.C. were discovered, executed in the best Attic style. Countless shards of vases were also found, representing all the periods from the seventh century B.C. until Roman times. One archeologically interesting discovery was a clay shard from the fifth century B.C. with the inscription TAVRO-P(OLO). This, along with other inscriptions and coins, is additional proof that the most important shrine on Icaria was consecrated to Artemis Tauropolos.

The ancient Icarians who lived in Oine depicted the head of Artemis Tauropolos on the faces of their coins, and a bull and the names Oinaion, Oinai, or Oinoi—not Icaria—on the reverse. Another coin shows the head of the god Dionysus, for a myth relates that he was born on Cape Drakonon. Dionysus is also closely associated with Icaria because the island's wine was highly prized throughout antiquity.

Oine (or Oinoe), the Artemis Tauropoulos sanctuary, the baths, and Drakonon are the significant ancient sites on Icaria. Oine was the most important town; it stood between the present-day village of Kambos and the north coast. Kambos, lying in the midst of lush vegetation, has unusual gray-brown farmhouses roofed with local green slate. They resemble nothing else in the villages of Greece: their walls are a multicolored mosaic composed of ancient slabs of marble, reliefs, inscriptions, pebbles, and chunks of granite. Among the embedded fragments, it is possible to make out two particularly noteworthy steles from the fifth and fourth centuries B.C. Both depict female figures whose heads have been lost. On one, it is still possible to decipher the inscription HEROSTRATE. The cemetery of ancient Oine is presumed to be near Kambos. Here, when conversing with the peasants, one hears a great deal about the *tholaria*, which are ancient chamber tombs, or about *kastrakia*, "small castles," the remains of ancient fortifications. The Middle Ages have left the most visible traces in the area around Kambos.

The church of Aghia Irini is the oldest church on the island, constructed on the foundations of an Early Christian basilica. The apse and a portion of the mosaic floor of this basilica can still be seen. The outside walls of the church of Aghios Ghiorghios in Palaiokastro are embellished with ancient marble fragments. Most imposing is the medieval wall with arcades, the portion of the Palatia ("palace") that still stands. According to legend, it was here that exiled sons of the Byzantine emperors lived. A side trip from Kambos leads to the monastery of Aghia Theoktiste of Lesbos, with its evocative, ivy-covered cave. East of the village of Miliopo, there is a small church standing amid ancient fortification walls. It has a vaulted roof, a Doric capital, and lovely icons from the sixteenth century.

On the eastern tip of the island lay ancient Drakonon, now known as Fanari, with a well-preserved tower from the Hellenistic period that was attached to a long-since-destroyed fortress. The Icariots believe that Icarus was once imprisoned here and also that a black man here used to guard a treasure stolen from Constantinople. Holes in the tower made by cannon fire are visible. During the wars of liberation against the Turks, the tower was a target for Admiral Miaoulis's artillery.

Between Fanari and Aghios Kyrikos lies Kataphygi. Here, one of the most beautiful ancient examples of Cycladic art was discovered—a marble relief on which the Parian sculptor Palion depicted a seated woman with a little girl on her lap. In front of her stand two youths, and a young boy lies at her feet. Palion may not have come to Icaria by chance; there were strong ties between Paros and Miletus, and during the sculptor's lifetime, Milesians lived on Icaria.

A road lined with tombs from the sixth

century B.C. leads upward from Kataphygi to the ancient acropolis, which is dominated by Therma, the most important medicinal spring on the island today and one of its oldest settlements. Ludwig Ross visited Icaria in 1841, and he was especially impressed by the ancient remains and aqueducts in Therma. Inscriptions indicate that the baths were called Asclepieis at the end of the third century B.C. At that time, the warm sulphur baths of Icaria were famous throughout the Aegean.

The sulphur bath of Therma (52.5° C) is beautifully situated at an elevation of 3,280 feet and is the greatest attraction of the island. The ancient finds discovered on Icaria are on display in the high school in Aghios Kyrikos, the main town and harbor, which bears the name of the island's patron saint.

Samos

THE ANCIENT WRITERS OFTEN SPEAK OF SAMOS, its beautiful landscape, and its contributions to Greek culture. The poet Menander celebrated the wealth of Samos with an expression that is still common today, saying that there, one could even "get milk from birds."

In antiquity, the island had many names, several of which were derived from trees and shrubs that constitute its flora; for example, Elaiousa, the Olive Island; Dryousa, the Isle of Oaks; Cyparissia, the Island of Cypresses. But the best known and presumably the oldest of the island's names was Parthenia, the Virginal One, referring to the myth that the goddess Hera, the wife of Zeus, was born here.

The first inhabitants of Samos were Carians or Leleges. They were succeeded by Ionians. In about the middle of the seventh century B.C., Perinthus, on the Propontis, was established by Samians. However, Milesian colonists settled more extensively here; there were as many as ninety Milesian colonies along the shores of the Pontus, all of them settled between 650 and 550 B.C. The pharaoh Amasis (569–525 B.C.) was well disposed toward Greeks and permitted more Greek merchants to settle in Naucratis in addition to the Hellenes already there, even allowing these temporary residents their own cult precinct. Thus, among other shrines erected in Naucratis, the Samians built one to Hera. In the sixth and fifth centuries B.C., Samos and Miletus were the most important cultural centers in the eastern Mediterranean.

The tyrant Polycrates ruled Samos beginning in 537 B.C. and made it world famous. Herodotus relates that no other Hellenic tyrant could compare with Polycrates in power or splendor. He made the capital, Hieron Asty (Holy City), now called Pythagoreion, into one of the most magnificent cities of the time. In addition, he surrounded himself with poets, musicians, architects, workers in bronze, and scholars: Herodotus, who wrote part of his historical work on Samos; Aesop, who is said to have composed some of his fables here; and Anacreon, who came from Teos, in Ionia, and celebrated youths and maidens in verse. According to the inscription on a seated statue dedicated to him, Polycrates "collected booty from Hera"; in other words, he engaged in piracy in the service of the goddess, at the same time steadily increasing his own wealth and power. After his death—the satrap of Sardis had him crucified on the mainland opposite—the island was temporarily ruled by the Persians. Then, in the fifth century B.C., it joined the First Attic League.

The Samians fell away from Athens in 440–439 B.C., and the Athenians took revenge by devastating the island. Later, during the Peloponnesian War, the Samians supported Athens against Sparta and were thus awarded Athenian citizenship. In Roman times, Samos was a base for legions dispatched to Asia Minor, and the emperors themselves came to recuperate on the island. Antony and Cleopatra spent several months here together.

In Byzantine times, Samos belonged to one of the two administrative districts of the Aegean (the theme of Thalassis). The island's pine forests supplied building material for its fleet. At that time, Samos was plagued by pirates just as often as were the other islands of the Aegean. After the fall of Constantinople in 1453, the Samians fled to Chios. In the sixteenth century, they returned and founded new villages. During the rebellion of the Greeks against the Turks in 1821, Samos served as a bulwark in the eastern Mediterranean. The powers who supported the new Greek state—France, England, and Russia—permitted Samos a kind of self-government. Between 1834 and 1912, its rulers were Orthodox Greeks with Ottoman citizenship; they were named princes and governors by the sultan and later ruled with a parliament. Most public funds were invested in cultural institutions. In the summer of 1912, the Samians successfully rebelled against the Turks under the leadership of Themistokles Sophoulis (the prime minister of Greece after World War II), and joined the new nation of Greece on November 11, 1912.

NEARLY ALL OF THE MONUMENTAL WORKS NOW found on Samos, partially in ruins, date from the reign of Polycrates: the jetty, designed to protect the city from the waves in high storms; the Amphistomon Orygma, an aqueduct, fed by mountain springs, that not only provided water for the city's wells but, in summer, spilled water down across marble steps to cool the inhabitants; massive walls, more than 4 miles long, that were never breached by enemies; and the

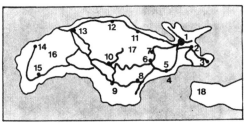

The island of Samos.

1. Samos
2. Palaiokastro
3. Klima
4. Pythagoreion
5. Site of ancient Samos
6. Chora
7. Mytilenioi
8. Myloi
9. Spatharaioi
10. Pyrghos
11. Kokkarion
12. Aghios Konstantinos
13. Neon Karlovasion
14. Drakaioi
15. Aghia Kyriaki
16. Mount Kerketefs (4,701 feet)
17. Mount Karvouni (3,782 feet)
18. Asia Minor

huge temple of Hera, the largest temple of antiquity, which could have held four Parthenons. Even today, the walls and the harbor works of Pythagoreion are excellently preserved.

Herodotus described the technical achievements and the great temple of Samos:

> I have spoken at greater length of the Samians because of all the Greeks they have accomplished the three greatest projects. First they have created a tunnel through the base of a mountain some 150 spans high from one side to the other. The tunnel is 7 stadia long [.8 mile] and [8 feet] in height and width. For its entire length there is a ditch [20 yards] deep and [3 feet] wide. Through this the water is led from a large spring and fed into the city's pipes. The architect of this conduit tunnel was Eupalinos, the son of Naustrophos, from Megara. That is one of the projects. The second is a jetty built out into the sea and curved around the harbor; this jetty is some 20 spans deep, and its length is somewhat over 2 stadia [nearly 440 yards]. Their third creation is a temple, the largest of all temples so far as I know. Its first architect was Rhoecus, the son of Phileus, a Samian.

The measurements given by Herodotus do not entirely conform to the facts, but he does describe the layout of this remarkable aqueduct correctly.

The German Archeological Institute has carried out excavations on Samos for decades and uncovered, among other things, the greater part of the ancient aqueduct, nearly 2 miles long, of which roughly 3,300 feet (.6 mile) were led through the mountain. In the past decade, Ulf Jantzen has investigated this water tunnel, or Eupa-

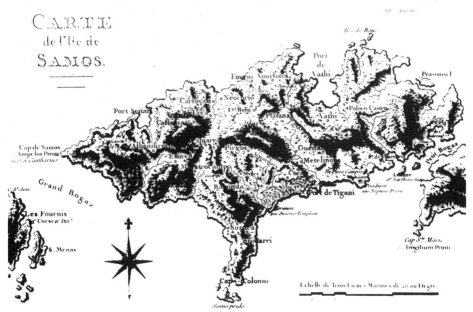

Map from Choiseul-Gouffier's Voyage Pittoresque dans la Grèce, *1782.*

lineion, named for its builder, Eupalinos of Megara (sixth century B.C.). It was cleared, the conduits leading to and from it were sounded, and the plan behind the placement and construction of the pipes was made evident. Excavation of the Eupalineion unexpectedly revealed that the tunnel served the population of Samos as a refuge during attacks in early Byzantine times. Also of particular interest are countless inscriptions and graffiti in red on the walls of the tunnel. These indicate something of the ancient methods of surveying and construction of the aqueduct and are thus of great value.

In the temple of Hera, or Heraion, which was excavated under the direction of the German archeologists Buschor, Wiegand, and Homman-Wedeking, quite valuable finds were made, even though it had been plundered continually since Roman times. The Roman governor Verres spirited splendid statues away to his capital, a sacrilege to which Cicero strongly objected in the Senate. Antony also gave Cleopatra some sculptures he had stolen from the temple of Hera. An inscription on a stele now in the museum, reading KOSMOS THEAS ("wealth of the goddess"), suggests that the countless votive gifts housed in the temple caused it to be referred to as an art gallery as well. Of this temple and its forest of columns, which Herodotus compared to the pyramids and the temple of Artemis at Ephesus, only bases and a few isolated standing columns remain. Excavations here have been under the direction of Kyrieleis since 1976. One particularly exciting recent find was the excellently preserved torso of a gigantic *kouros*, originally 17 feet tall, the largest statue of a youth that has been found in Greece, apart from the colossus of Naxos. It is a Samian masterpiece from about 580 B.C.

Opposite the propylaea, you can still see a portion of the altar standing where there is also the petrified trunk of the sacred Lygaria (from *lygos,* or "willow tree") in whose shade Zeus was said to have celebrated his marriage to Hera. The Greeks held this tree, so Pausanias relates, to be the oldest of plants, still sprouting green leaves though having stood since mythical

Temple of Hera: drawing by J. B. Hilair, c. 1800.

times. Hera was supposed to have grown up in its leafy shade, and Zeus was said to have met her there in secret in the days when Kronos still reigned. Archeologists did in fact rediscover the stump of this tree during excavations.

SAMOS GAVE THE ANCIENT WORLD A LARGE NUMber of famous men. The astronomers Aristarchus, Aristides, Aristilos, and Conon were born here; the most famous of these was Aristarchus, whose observations of the skies led him to deduce a sun-centered solar system 1,800 years before Copernicus. An artist family on Samos included Rhoecus, the architect of the temple of Hera, his sons Theodorus and Telecles, and one of his grandsons, Theodorus. The philosophers Pythagoras, Melissus, and Epicurus were born here, as was a certain Dioscurides, who created splendid mosaics in Pompeii (now displayed in the Naples Museum). Other Samians were the seafarer Colaeus, who was said to have been the first to sail through the Pillars of Hercules (the Strait of Gibraltar), and the poet Creophylus, who inscribed the Homeric epics on wooden tablets. According to Plutarch, Homer was stranded on Samos during a sea journey from Chios to Athens; Creophylus took Homer into his home, asked his guest to recite from the *Iliad* and *Odyssey* each evening, and wrote down his words. One of Creophylus's descendants, Lycurgus, the king of Sparta, supposedly brought the tablets from Samos to Sparta and thereby to all the Hellenes.

THOSE WHO ENJOY BROWSING IN MUSEUMS have a choice of six different collections:

1. Many finds from the Heraion are displayed in the Archeological Museum in the main town of Vathy, on the north coast of the island, including the base of the Genelaos portico, countless reliefs of funeral banquets, a famous sarcophagus in the form of a temple, unique wooden statuettes and tools, ivory carvings, and bronze figures.
2. Other finds from the Heraion and a statue of the emperor Augustus are housed in the museum in Pythagoreion.
3. The Museum of Religious Art in Vathy contains interesting icons, old books, and manuscripts.
4. The library in Vathy boasts an extensive collection of old books donated by various patriarchs and princes of Samos.
5. The Pinakothek of Vathy contains portraits of Greek freedom fighters, works by Nicephorus Lytras, a famous Greek painter, and documents from recent Samian history.
6. The Museum of Paleontology contains animal skeletons that are 13 million years old. They include bones of ancestors of our modern rhinoceros, elephant, gazelle, giraffe, and hyena and skeletons of samotheria, an animal so named because its fossils have been found only on Samos.

VARIOUS MONASTERIES FOUNDED IN THE SIXteenth century are definitely worth a visit: the monastery of the Meghali Panaghia (Holy Virgin), the Zoodochos Pighi (Lifegiving Fount), the Zoopoios Stavros (Lifegiving Cross), and the Panaghia tou Vronta.

The monastery of the Meghali Panaghia, which stands in the interior of the island, was built on the site of a shrine to Artemis by monks from Asia Minor. Other monks, who came from the monasteries on Mount Athos, decorated the walls of the monastery church with frescos. These well-preserved wall paintings are marvelous to behold. The monastery must have been extremely wealthy at one time; the Samians relate that once, when its treasury caught fire, so many gold and silver objects melted down that they formed a gleaming stream.

From the monastery of Zoodochos Pighi, there is a view of the strait between Samos and Mykale, where the Greeks defeated the Persians in the fifth century B.C. and the Turks in the nineteenth century.

THOSE WHO MERELY WISH TO RELAX ON SAMOS will find sand beaches and a clear sea on the south coast. It is well worth taking a motorboat around the island or exploring the interior by car. Especially beautiful are the villages of Platanakia and Koutsi, with chestnut trees, ancient plane trees, and many splashing fountains.

CHIOS

EXCAVATION ON CHIOS, THOUGH NEVER SYSTEM-atically undertaken, has unearthed settlements from the Neolithic period (fourth millennium B.C.) and cities some 2,000–3,000 years later. The Ionians came from the Greek mainland in the eighth century B.C. and settled on Chios and the coast of Asia Minor, bringing a great culture with them. The freedom-loving, restless spirit of these people created the flourishing cultural and commercial centers of Asia Minor, where natural science, philosophy, literature, and the fine arts were either born or given new forms. The city of Chios, which has stood on the same site since antiquity and remained the capital of the island, was laid out under Ionian influence.

The sixth century B.C. was the golden age of Chios. The island was then a place of po-litical stability, a sense of moderation, economic prosperity, and a comfortable, cheerful way of life. Even in antiquity, familiar expressions referred to the typically serene and plentiful life of the islanders: "a Chiotic life," "a Chiotic laugh," "a Chiotic banquet." At the feasts of Chios, slaves poured a famous wine into equally famous beakers (numerous examples survive in the museums of Europe), and rhapsodists accompanied these revels with singing. The sculptures created in this peaceful landscape in the sixth and fifth centuries B.C. are masterpieces. The few that survive, such as the graceful marble *kore* (statue of a young maiden) known as the Maiden of Chios in the Acropolis Museum, attest to the Ionian sense of elegance. The Persians attacked Chios in 493 B.C. This is the first

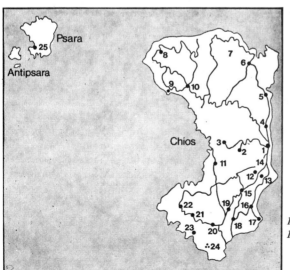

The islands of Chios and Psara.

1. Chios
2. Nea Moni monastery
3. Anavatos
4. Brontado
5. Langada
6. Kardamylla
7. Mount Pelinaion (4,255 feet)
8. Aghios Galas
9. Aghia Markella
10. Volissos
11. Lithi
12. Vaviloi
13. Neochori
14. Kambos
15. Tholopotami
16. Kataraktis
17. Nenitas
18. Kalamoti
19. Armolia
20. Pyrghi
21. Olympoi
22. Mesta
23. Fanoi
24. Emporeio
25. Psara

catastrophe known to have struck the island.

In Byzantine times, especially in the eleventh and twelfth centuries, the island regained a high degree of civilization and culture. At that time, the city was surrounded by fortification walls that still stand, and it was then that the Nea Moni (New Monastery)—a majestic building and an internationally significant work of art—was created.

The Genoese ruled the island from 1346 to 1566 and encouraged agriculture and trade in silk. At that time, even the villages were fortified—a system of defenses that is still visible. Marble sculptures from this period, now on display in the local museum, reveal that the arts were also championed.

The first phase of Turkish rule, beginning in 1566, brought numerous privileges to the Chiots, and the eighteenth century was an era of particular economic success for them. The Chiots produced silks and cottons, and they shipped damasks, satins, and taffetas, ladies' stockings, and shawls— along with their main products, mastic, oranges, and lemons—to faraway ports. The wealthy traders who came to constitute the upper middle class built the Meghali Scholi (Great School), villas, and countless churches, and they sent their sons to Western European universities. The French writer Chateaubriand called the city of Chios a fairy-tale place, and other foreign travelers have celebrated the happy, charming, and polite Chiot women in their elegant costumes: a kind of miniskirt, white stockings, and delicate shoes. Even the peasant girls dressed in the Ionian style, wearing artistic hairdos and selling the tourists hand embroidery, flowers, and what is called "the wine of Homer."

In 1822, Chios was struck by a second catastrophe. In the previous year, the war of liberation against the Turks had broken out on the Greek mainland. The sultan, perhaps encouraged by the authoritarian domestic policies of the European courts, was determined to squelch the revolutionary movements of the Greeks by force. The Chiots had locked the island's Turkish garrison in the fortress, and rejoiced. In Constantinople, the sultan's harem was especially offended by the Chiot rebellion; the island had furnished these women with its famous mastic gum, which they chewed incessantly and did not wish to be deprived of. Possibly at their urging, the sultan commanded that all Chiots living in Constantinople be beheaded, that Turkish ships besiege the island and bombard it, and that thousands of Turkish soldiers be landed there. The city and forty villages were torched, 25,000 natives were executed, and twice as many were imprisoned. The tragedy of Chios demonstrated to Europe the extent of Turkish cruelty contrasted with European humanitarianism, and it gave a new thrust to pro-Greek feeling: Victor Hugo's long, sad poem "L'Enfant de Chios" circulated in pamphlet form, and Eugene Delacroix's *La Massacre de Chios* (now in Paris in the Louvre) was endlessly reproduced.

Nonetheless, Chios remained under Turkish rule until 1912. The inhabitants were permitted to resume their occupations. Farmers planted the countryside with orange, lemon, and mastic trees, and traders put to sea again in new ships.

The conservative, industrious Chiots have always chosen peace rather than warfare and have never been interested in colonies or conquest. Throughout history, their trading genius has led them to the ports of the known world. Even today, there are traders, shippers, and bankers from Chios all over the world. The Greek

Women of Chios: drawing by J. B. Hilair, c. 1800.

expression *Oi Chiotes pane dhyo-dhyo* ("The Chiots always walk in pairs") refers to the islanders' inborn solidarity.

YOUR SHIP DROPS ANCHOR IN CHIOS, A LIVELY harbor town lined with coffeehouses and small shops. The stores sell an extremely sweet confection made of mastic, a specialty of the island, in small clay vases that are imitations of ancient beakers. This town is the capital, in sight of the coast of Asia Minor. Not a single building from the past has survived. Everything that withstood the devastation of 1822 was destroyed in the earthquake of 1881. The town is now filled with hideous structures. The most refreshing spot is the expansive central square, shaded by old plane trees. A bronze statue of the freedom fighter Admiral Kanaris from Psara, the work of the sculptor Tombros, marks its center, and a stele com-memorating the notables hanged here by the Turks in 1822 stands at its northern corner. Nearby, a marble fountain, dating from 1768, in the baroque Turkish style, recalls the centuries of Turkish rule. In the mosque next to this square, built in the nineteenth century, art works from antiquity and the Middle Ages are temporarily stored, waiting to take their places in the new museum. Here, you can see Neolithic finds from the cave of Aghios Galas, early Helladic ones from Emporeio, two especially beautiful *kores* from the sixth and fifth centuries B.C., fragments of Ionic architecture, and a particularly rich collection of marble architectural fragments from Early Christian and Byzantine churches. The Genoese Renaissance is represented by reliefs and sculptures. Finally, interesting works by unknown folk artists depict how the art of marble carving was handed down

The shrine of Cybele: drawing by le Comte de Choiseul-Gouffier, c. 1800.

from father to son in the villages of Latomi and Thymiana from the seventeenth to the nineteenth centuries. One can still discover especially finely carved marble reliefs all over the island, built into the walls of churches and houses and on the wells of the villages of the Kambos ("plain").

In the northern part of the city of Chios rises the Kastro, its massive walls interrupt- ed by towers. It was first erected in Byzan- tine times; additions by the Genoese and the Turks kept it an effective fortress well into the nineteenth century. During Byzan- tine and Genoese rule, towers, palaces, vil- las, and churches of the ruling class stood here (it is difficult to distinguish between remains of Byzantine and Genoese build- ings). The Turks, though, lived in small

Greek scholar Korais, who was born here. Next to it stands the Folk Art Museum.

A RECOMMENDED ATTRACTION OF CHIOS, EVEN for those who may not be captivated by Byzantine art, is the Nea Moni monastery. Nea Moni lies in the center of the island on Mount Provateion, about 7½ miles from the city of Chios. The architecture and painting of Nea Moni represent the official imperial art of the mid-eleventh century, especially the renaissance during the Macedonian dynasty.

The monastery is surrounded by a high wall. Surviving from the original buildings are the monastery church, the cistern, the rectangular tower in the southwest, and the refectory, which has been considerably altered through the centuries. In the irregular courtyard, dominated by a modern bell tower (1900) and huge cypresses, stands the monastery church. Except for the new cupola, which is a faithful reproduction of the original, and the exterior paint, only very slight changes have been made to the building since the middle of the eleventh century.

Nea Moni was known throughout the Aegean and attracted numerous visitors. Its troubles began during the destruction of Chios in 1822, when the monks were murdered and the church was set on fire. The relics and the library's manuscripts were scattered when the Turks plundered the complex. New damage was caused by the earthquake of 1881. The central cupola, the barrel vaulting of the chancel, and the bell tower collapsed; in many places, the mosaics were destroyed. The monastery began to fall into ruins. In recent years, the Greek Archeological Service has endeavored to restore it.

The church of Nea Moni, like other churches on Chios and Cyprus, is an insular

houses separated by narrow streets and protected by the fortress walls. At that time, the Greeks lived outside the fortress where the present-day city has spread. The main street of the modern city, the Aplotaria, is lined with shops; a very steep street intersecting it leads to the nineteenth-century Metropolis and to the fourth-largest library in Greece, named after the modern

Port of Chios: drawing by J. B. Hilair, c. 1800.

octagonal church. Eight hanging spandrels on eight arches support the cupola. The fronts of four major flat-walled apses and four somewhat narrower apses bridge the corners.

The mosaics of Nea Moni are among the most important examples of mid-Byzantine monumental painting. Despite the damage they have suffered, they are extremely impressive for their use of uncommonly lively colors. What we see is the balanced interplay between a hieratic style and the academic style of antiquity. The compositions are simple but nonetheless splendid, thanks to the rhythmic arrangement and in-

dividuality of the figures. At times, their gestures are highly dramatic. Vivid shading appears beneath an apocalyptic light. A wealth of color, deliberately chosen, often creates daring combinations standing out against the gold background or pierced by golden rays of light. These mosaics have been compared by art historians to the mosaic of the Zoë Monomachos in Hagia Sophia in Istanbul, those of the Vatopedi monastery on Mount Athos, and other treasured examples.

South of the capital the Kambos begins. The roads crossing it lead between high, yellowish, monotonous stone walls. For

miles the traveler sees only these impersonal walls and the sky. But behind them extend small paradises of lemon, orange, and mandarin groves. Splendid villas once stood among them, but these were destroyed in 1822 and 1881.

In the south of the island grow the famous mastic bushes, which thrive only in this spot. All attempts to transplant them to other areas have proven fruitless, even when the local soil was also taken along. The "tears" dropped by the mastic bush dry into transparent "diamonds" only on Chios, where for centuries they have been gathered by the farmers three times a year. It is still a mystery why the "tears" dry into "diamonds" only here; everywhere else in the world they remain fluid, and even 100 yards from the twenty-four so-called mastic villages it is no longer possible to get "diamonds" from the bushes. The lentiscus, or mastic bush, is an evergreen shrub or small tree that grows from 3 to 9 feet tall. Its twin leaves, leathery and shiny on the upper side, are slightly reddish initially but later turn a brilliant green. Its pea-sized, pitted fruits are scarlet at first but black when ripe. The aromatic sap, which issues from the bark of the stem as a thickish, light yellow juice, is called *mastiche* (from *mastazo,* meaning "chew," because the bark was chewed) and gave the bush its

An ancient Greek piper with his dog.

name. The ancients used this substance as a medicine for chronic cough and stomach ache, processed it into facial salves, or simply chewed it to lend a pleasant aroma to the breath. Men chewing mastic were considered ill-bred by the ancients, just as perpetual gum chewers are today. The wealthy mastic villages, which lived from and owed their prosperity to the mastic harvest, also harvested the envy of conquerors and were heavily fortified.

One of the roads through the Kambos leads to Neochori, whose church consecrated to the Panaghia (Holy Virgin) is an example of local nineteenth-century peasant architecture. The road then leads past the village of Kato Kataraktis, which boasts two small Byzantine churches. It is well worth stopping in the village of Nenitas to admire an especially finely constructed *templon* (sanctuary screen). Six-tenths of a mile farther lie the ruins of the Kyra Panaghia church from the thirteenth century.

Another road across the Kambos goes to the village of Vaviloi, where a path leads off between gardens and olive groves to the church of the Panaghia i Krina, a masterpiece from the twelfth or thirteenth century. It is quite well preserved, and its perfect proportions give it an unforgettable charm. The dating of the church is based mainly on the style of some of its frescos.

The church of the Aghioi Apostoli stands in the center of the old and interesting village of Pyrghi. Its harmonious cupolas date from the thirteenth century, while the frescos on its walls and in its vaulting were done in the eighteenth century. The architecture of Pyrghi is unusual for Greece; slender two- and three-story houses line the narrow, spiraling streets, and buttresses stretch across from one side of the street to the other. The façades are especially fascinating, for they are covered with geometric designs in black and white paint. After leaving the medieval village of Olympoi, you drive through a green landscape to the ancient harbor of Fanoi, once an important center but now in ruins. Those interested in medieval island architecture will not want to miss the village of Mesta, which has a Byzantine church consecrated to the Taxiarchis (archangel Michael).

THE CHIOT CAPTAINS, SHIPPERS, AND SAILORS come almost exclusively from the northern part of the island—from Brontado, for example. The best of the island's ships have been built here as well. The inhabitants boast that Columbus came to Brontado to recruit the famous Captain Andreas for his voyages of discovery. On the cliffs above the shore at Brontado, there is a bronze monument commemorating the men who have died at sea, the work of the modern Greek sculptor Apartis.

Farther to the north, beyond Brontado, one encounters the so-called Stone of Homer. The Chiots claim that Homer was born on the island. For centuries, the people of Brontado have pointed with pride to a huge rock in which seats have been chiseled out. According to them, this is where Homer taught his pupils. Scholars disagree; they believe that the polished rock is a shrine of the goddess Cybele. Even more northward lie the harbors of Kardamylla and Delphini, where the ancient Greeks hid their warships and where the islanders now keep their boats.

In one of the northern villages, Aghios Galas, Neolithic artifacts have been discovered, and the Byzantine period is represented by churches with fine frescos and sanctuary screens. In northern Chios, which is wooded and has ample water, the villages are not laid out like fortresses, as they are in the south. Here the scattered houses are plain and small, with simple wooden roofs.

PSARA

HOMER CALLED THIS REMOTE AND TINY ISLAND Psyrie, but he said nothing more about it. And nowadays, by no means every Greek can tell you where it lies (see page 273). Psara, as the island is now called, was ignored by history for centuries. Then, all of a sudden, it became famous. When Greece finally rebelled against the Turks in 1821, after centuries of oppression, the men of Psara were the first to fight for freedom. And though many Greeks do not know where to begin to look for the island on a map, they know the name Psara as a synonym for the desire for liberty.

In the sixteenth and seventeenth centuries, Greeks from the mainland came here to escape oppression and persecution. Psara has more rock than soil, and the dwellings and fishing boats built by these refugees were extremely modest. But adversity made these new settlers hardy and industrious, and, by about the beginning of the nineteenth century, Psara had become the third greatest sea power in the Aegean, out-

ranked only by the islands Hydra and Spetsai. Its ship owners, captains, and traders had attained great wealth.

And they sacrificed all of it in the earliest hours of the war of liberation. Abandoning their lucrative ventures, they led the pursuit of the Turkish fleet. Their forty-five ships carried gunpowder for ships' cannon, and their victorious exploits inspired all Hellas. It was they who developed the *bourlotieris*: a man would guide an old

A Dutch map from 1688.

boat full of explosives up against an enemy ship at night; as often as not, he was blown to bits along with his target.

The losses were so great that the Turks determined to exterminate the *bourlotieris* and destroy Psara. Fourteen thousand Turkish soldiers landed on the island. But rather than capitulate, the islanders blew themselves up. The heroic self-sacrifice of Psara, an inspiration to poets and writers, was a powerful boost to pro-Hellenism in western Europe.

EVEN RECENTLY IT ALMOST SEEMED AS THOUGH the Psariots had not yet got over the shock of their self-destruction, though it had occurred about 150 years ago. You can climb the tedious path to the Black Slope (Mavri Rachi), to which the modern Greek poet Dionysios Solomos dedicated one of his loveliest stanzas:

On the charred earth of Psara,
Glory roams alone,
musing on her warrior-heroes,
wearing a wreath on her hair

made of a few dry weeds
left on the desolate earth.

RAE DALVEN

IT WAS HERE THAT THE PSARIOTS BLEW THEM-selves up by igniting their powder magazine. And what can the visitor see? All about lie black tiles, but on top of them, completely unexpectedly, fragments of Mycenaean vases. Mycenae here as well? A shadow of that magnificent culture?

The barren terrain is covered with sharp rocks that cut like knives. And suddenly a valley opens before you. Vegetables and watermelons grow there, and in the sand next to a small harbor Mycenaean tombs lie half-exposed—after 3,000 years.

Homer and his Psyrie. The *Odyssey* and the Trojan War. These ruins make one wonder whether the Achaeans—the men who set out for the coast of Asia Minor with Agamemnon and Menelaus to fetch back the lovely Helen—might also have put ashore here. The island of Psara has so far not been investigated by archeologists.

*L*ESBOS

LESBOS, IN THE NORTHEASTERN AEGEAN, IS THE third largest island in Greece. It has an area of 630 square miles and some 140,000 inhabitants, and the nearby coast of Asia Minor is visible day and night.

The city of Mytilene is located on the east side of the island. It boasts a proud castle, softly rolling hills that reach down to the sandy shore, and a huge statue to freedom in the harbor. With its picturesque and bustling quays, it managed not only to develop gradually into the capital but to give its name unofficially to the whole island. Most Greeks traveling to Lesbos today will say, "We're leaving for Mytilene."

In the fourth century A.D., Longus wrote his famous pastoral romance *Daphnis and*

Chloe, which is a hymn to the beauty of the island. He said:

> On Lesbos there is a city called Mytilene, which is large and beautiful. Canals cross through it…and these are crossed by lovely bridges of white, polished stones. One has the impression not of a city but a group of islands. It happened that some 200 stadia from this city of Mytilene there was the estate of a wealthy man, a marvelous property: mountains filled with game, fields laden with grain, hills covered with vines, and pastures supporting splendid herds. The tide washed against the soft beach of the extensive coastline. The seacoast had numerous harbors adorned with impressive buildings. One could also find countless baths, parks, and groves, some the work of nature, others created by man's art, and all adapted to pleasurable pursuits….The park was quite beautiful, similar in extent to the royal gardens. It extended across a slope for the distance of nearly a stadion, and was some 4 plethra in width. One might have thought it a wide glade. All kinds of trees grew there, apples, myrtles, pears, also pomegranates and figs and olives; also there were tall grape vines embracing the apple and pear trees with their ripening grapes as though competing with them to produce even lovelier fruits.

The landscape praised by Longus vanishes

The island of Lesbos.

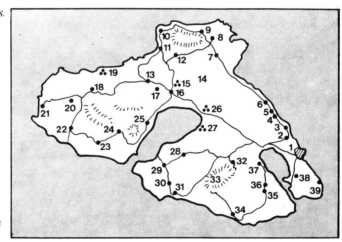

1. Mytilene
2. Moria
3. Pamfilla
4. Thermi
5. Loutra
6. Mistegna
7. Mantamado
8. Klio
9. Sykamia
10. Molyvos
    (Methymna)
11. Petra
12. Stypsi
13. Filia
14. Aghia Paraskevi
15. Arisbi
16. Kalloni
17. Limonos
18. Antissa
19. Site of ancient
    Antissa
20. Ypsilou
21. Sigri

22. Eresus
23. Mesopotos
24. Agro
25. Parakila
26. Mesa
27. Pyrrha
28. Vasilika

29. Polychnitos
30. Vrisa
31. Vatera
32. Aghiassos
33. Mount
    Olympus
34. Plomation

35. Skopelos
36. Papados
37. Kato Tritos
38. Loutra
39. Kratigo

in the vicinity of Sigri and Eresus, near Mount Ordymnos. Here, there is no vegetation at all. Instead, thick trunks of petrified trees stand 20 to 35 feet high, and around them lie their petrified branches. The boiling fluids that transformed them into stone created countless nuances of black, gray, and brown.

Roads that begin in Mytilene lead to the island's ninety villages, which are either exposed to the sea or are protected by mountains and cliffs. While the other Aegean Islands, especially the Cyclades, have common features linking them, Lesbos has a unique charm. Greens of all shades soften the light, distinguishing it from the white of the Cyclades. The towns and buildings are different, too. They have nothing in common with those of the other islands in the Aegean. On neighboring Chios, for example, there are still structures standing from the Middle Ages. On Lesbos, by contrast, the buildings are modern. Their architecture resembles that of the Greek mainland. All buildings are roofed with tiles and have no roof terraces, unlike those of the Cyclades. The painted ceilings in Molyvos (Methymna) are characteristic of Macedonian architecture. Preserved in the village of Petra is the dwelling of the Barelzidena, a nineteenth-century villa in the style of western Macedonia, with frescos and ceilings carved of wood. Particularly beautiful wooden chests, adorned with carvings in various patterns, are products of artisans of the older generation. Today, these, along with bronze household objects, can be admired in the museums of Mytilene. The bronze workers of the nineteenth and early twentieth centuries were quite famous.

Another type of folk art still flourishing on the island is ceramics. In two large villages, Aghiassos and Mantamado, there are workshops where peasants work their clay with potter's wheels. The water pitchers of Mantamado preserve their ancient form, with white decorations on a natural background. The workshops of Aghiassos, however, have abandoned their own tradition in favor of the polychrome decoration of modern Greek pottery. Aghiassos is an interesting, picturesque village lying on forested Mount Olympus. Its church preserves an ancient, reputedly miracle-working icon of the Virgin Mary. On Assumption Day (August 15), this church is visited by pilgrims from all over the island. From August 1 until this day, men, women, and children all wear black. In doing so, they are fulfilling an ancient vow. Aghiassos can also boast of its improvising poets, whose satiric verses are reminiscent of bawdy and biting passages from classical Greek comedy. During Carnival, groups of masked men mock everything and everyone.

ONE RELIGIOUS CUSTOM REMINISCENT OF ANcient sacrificial feasts is the "Paneghyri of the bull" in the village of Aghia Paraskevi. On this holiday, a picturesque procession of costumed men and women, including horsemen on colorfully decorated mounts, proceeds to the village chapel. After Mass, the priest sacrifices a bull raised especially for this day. The sacrifice is followed by a banquet with a great deal of drinking and finally a horse race. The winning rider is adorned with a silken scarf, and, with his friends, he goes from house to house to be waited upon by the young women.

Each village has unique historical or mythical attraction. In Thermi, the inhabitants point out the warm medicinal baths that were dedicated to Artemis Thermeia in antiquity and the old buildings they call the "towers." In Mantamado, the visitor is shown a wax relief portrait of the archangel Michael; in Sykamia, the small harbor that inspired the novel *Panaghia i Gorgona* by the modern Greek writer Stratis Myrivilis; in Petra, it is the cliff with a notable church and artists' dwellings that visitors must see.

And in Antissa, the people talk about Orpheus. In ancient times, according to local residents, Orpheus wandered through Thrace and enchanted people with the tones of his lyre. His song calmed the sea, made nature more lush, tamed animals, and caused men to forget their passions. The whole world listened to him as though under a spell. But the Maenads killed Orpheus and threw his head and his lyre into the river Hebrus. The river carried them down to the sea, whose gentle waves brought them to the north coast of Lesbos. Sand covered the singer's magnificent head, but the lyre stood upright and the wind played on its strings. A sweet, sad melody could be heard across the island. The nightingales learned the tune, and the wind echoed it when it rustled in the leaves of the trees. The inhabitants of Antissa—which then lay on the shore—buried the head of Orpheus at a spot they named Orphikia and presented the lyre to the sanctuary of Apollo. This is a myth that glorifies the beauty of the landscape of Lesbos and the birth of lyric poetry.

ANCIENT TEXTS TELL ABOUT THE PRE-HELLENIC tribes on Lesbos. The endings of certain place names, such as Antissa and Methymna, bear witness to the presence of these peoples. Other place names refer to legends whose protagonists were among these first settlers. For instance, one lush valley in the bay of Kalloni is called Makara, after the island's mythical ancestor, Macar, whose wife was named Lesbos. Prehistoric relics are strewn across the whole island, waiting for systematic excavation. The oldest prehistoric settlement, from the close of the Neolithic period or beginning of the

Orpheus and his lyre.

Bronze Age, lies near the village of Polychnitos, at a spot called Chalakies.

In the village of Thermi, outside Mytilene, an extensive prehistoric site has been discovered. It was inhabited throughout the entire Bronze Age; a succession of five cities stood here. It seems to have been inhabited by peace-loving peoples, for there are no fortification walls. Finds suggest that these people lived in well-built houses, kept pets, cultivated the fields, fished, hunted, and wove. Though not particularly advanced metalworkers, they were excellent potters. Their vases of gray clay were unpainted; a few were embellished with incised grooves. This type of gray-glazed ceramic is known as Lesbian bucchero.

In the Heroic period, in about 1100 B.C., when their fleet sailed for Troy, the Achaeans dropped anchor off various islands to take on provisions and water. One of their stops was said to be the island of Psara; another was, according to the *Odyssey*, "resplendent Lesbos, where Odysseus challenged all to a fight and wrestled with Philomeleides. He threw him to the ground with great force, so that all of the Achaeans rejoiced." After Odysseus had killed Philomeleides, the Achaeans plundered the island, and their booty was impressive, even to Agamemnon. Nonetheless, Agamemnon had to surrender his share to Achilles in order to soothe his wrath: "He gives you seven women skilled in numerous arts/Lesbian ones that he chose himself when you conquered the blossoming island...." Today, the inhabitants of Petra point out a well outside the town where Achilles is supposed to have quenched his thirst. In Makara, in a rocky area near the sea, huge graves are found; legend has it that the dead left behind by the Achaeans were buried here.

In the twelfth century B.C., when the Dorians invaded the Greek mainland and the original inhabitants had to search for new homes, the imaginative, industrious Aeolians from Thessaly settled on Lesbos. They brought with them the Aeolian culture, language, and customs, and Lesbos became their second home. Powerful cities developed, including Mytilene, Methymna, Eresus, Antissa, Pyrrha, and Arisbe. The first four still exist. Pyrrha, once famous for its harvest from the sea, disappeared beneath the waves. When the sea is calm, you can still see faint traces of it at the bottom. The impressive ruins of Arisbe, which fell victim to attack by neighboring Methymna, are decaying more and more as time goes on.

THE SOIL OF LESBOS IS WELL-WATERED AND FERtile and has always provided bountiful harvests. The olive oil of Lesbos was much sought after in ancient times, and even today the olive harvest is all-important, determining each year whether people live in wealth or poverty. The olive groves seem endless, climbing up the mountainsides and clear down to the sea. Once the olives are ripe, women fan out across the whole island to pick them off the trees and gather them off the ground. The barley of Erisus and the excellent wines of Methymna were also renowned in antiquity. Large landowners constituted the elite of the island; they led a very comfortable life and cultivated the fine arts extensively.

In time, the people of Lesbos became traders and seafarers, exporting the island's products. In the eighth century B.C., they colonized the opposite coast of Asia Minor, giving rise to a new Aeolian homeland, the "Lesbian country" (*lesbia chora*), with Lesbian language, customs, songs, and costumes. This link has persisted until the present. The emigrants to Asia Minor and their descendants retained strong ties to Lesbos; they often returned to recuperate or to sacrifice to the gods. In Christian times, more recent descendants of these people came here to pay homage to either the Holy Virgin, in the church of Aghiassos, or the archangel Michael, in the church of Mantamado.

THE SEVENTH AND SIXTH CENTURIES B.C. brought the first "Lesbian Spring." Lesbos entered into poetic competition well prepared, for the lyre of Orpheus had revealed the secrets of poetry and music to the islanders, and their folksongs were known far and wide.

In the seventh century B.C., a singer and a poet found renown beyond the island: Terpander of Antissa and Arion of Methymna, respectively. Surviving earlier Greek poetry—notably Homer, the Homeric cycle, and Hesiod—is largely epic, dealing with myth and celebrating the deeds of heroes. Now, though, surviving poetry begins to be more individual, often expressing personal feelings and impressions. The rhapsodists who recited epic poetry intoned their texts, with the lyre playing only a secondary role. But in lyric poetry, the lyre was not used only as accompaniment, and poets also had to become composers. This poetic genre took its very name from the lyre (*lyra* in Greek), becoming known as lyric poetry and its practitioners as lyricists. It is said that Terpander increased the number of the strings on the lyre from four to seven and constructed his melodies around the octave. Arion's fame, however, was based on his poems. Both of them became celebrated on the Greek mainland at the time when trade was first developing there, the first coins were being minted, monarchical forms of government were disappearing, and the Geometric style was flourishing in

Orpheus and Eurydice:
painting by Lord Leighton.

the fine arts. Terpander left for Sparta, while Arion went to Corinth. In Corinth, Arion gave a new form to the dithyramb, the hymn sung at festivals in honor of Dionysus. His contribution to the development of the Corinthian cult of Dionysus influenced the birth of Greek tragedy in Athens in the fifth century B.C.

SOMEWHAT LATER, NEAR THE CLOSE OF THE SEVenth and the beginning of the sixth centuries B.C., Lesbos gave us the splendid poetry of Sappho and Alcaeus. Sappho, the daughter of an ancient aristocratic family, was born in Antissa but lived in Mytilene. Her clear verses, full of intellectual and emotional energy, were written in the Aeolian dialect; the lyric poets tended to write in their local tongues. Her meters and linguistic form are exquisite. Sappho was also bold enough to speak of the passions. Wealthy and aristocratic women on Lesbos enjoyed more freedom than elsewhere, and from all over the island, in some cases from even farther away, young girls came to study under Sappho at a kind of finishing school, where they learned to dance, perform music, comport themselves and move correctly, dress with taste, and master the social conventions. The beauty and youth of these girls are praised so passionately in many of Sappho's poems that she later became a symbol of homoerotic love between women, giving rise to the term "lesbian love." For example:

Peer of the gods he seemeth to me, the blissful
Man who sits and gazes at thee before him,
Close beside thee sits, and in silence hears thee
Silverly speaking.

Laughing love's low laughter. Oh this, this only
Stirs the troubled heart in my breast to tremble!
For should I but see thee a little moment, Straight is my voice hushed;

Yea, my tongue is broken, and through and through me
'Neath the flesh impalpable fire runs tingling;
Nothing sees mine eyes, and a noise of roaring
Waves in my ear sounds;

Sweat runs down in rivers, a tremor seizes
All my limbs, and paler than grass in autumn,
Caught by pains of menacing death, I falter,   .
Lost in the love-trance.

JOHN ADDINGTON SYMONDS

Sappho's contemporaries sang her songs throughout all of Greece. On Lesbos, they minted coins bearing her image. Numbers of modern Greek women and girls proudly bear her name today. A few years ago, two statues of the poetess, commissioned by foreign women who were admirers of hers, were erected in Mytilene. One of these shows Sappho in classical form and stands in the center of the city. The other, a modern work, is alien to the artistic sense of the islanders; it is not their Sappho. After long wrangling, the committee responsible for the statue decided to remove the controversial work from Mytilene to a pine grove near the sea—doubtless a spot that Sappho would have chosen. The next day, however, it was found blackened with coal dust, the Mytilenians' revenge for the desecration of their heroine.

Alcaeus lived on Lesbos at the same time as Sappho. He was a poet and warrior whose verses in the Aeolian spirit celebrated feminine beauty, war, and politics. (At this time, Lesbos was shaken by a rebellion of the peasants, merchants, and seafarers against the aristocracy, the large landowners, such as Alcaeus himself, who had held extensive tracts for two centuries, and by vicious strife among the various groups of aristocrats.)

The visual arts did not share in this surge of creative activity on Lesbos. During the sixth century B.C., the prelude to the triumph of Classicism, while the rest of Greece was producing Geometric and later Archaic vase painting, and while the Doric and Ionic styles were being developed in architecture, the island was relatively inactive. Its only art works still known to us today are the uniquely delicate Aeolian capitals, whose volutes rise up out of the column above the constriction of the echinus like vegetable forms. These were a part of a large Archaic temple near the village of Klopede. The Lesbians continued to make their gray-glazed bucchero pottery, which followed the tradition of prehistoric monotone pottery and contrasted totally with the work being produced everywhere else in Greece.

An Ionic temple from the fourth century B.C. has been excavated in Mesa, which was the political and religious center of the island. A sanctuary in this city, where there were altars to Zeus, Hera, and Dionysus, was the focal point of the Koinon of the Lesbians, a league of cities. There was an annual festival at which all the allied cities took part. Poetic epigrams confirm the local legend that contests were held in the temple of Hera between the most beautiful maidens of the island. Numerous historical sources and inscriptions in the Mytilene Museum tell of cults of Asclepius, Apollo, and Artemis and of the temples adorning each city. Some of these may still be waiting to be discovered.

Lesbos maintained its importance through the Classical period and even later. Other cities were eager to stay on friendly terms with this respected sea power. The island's fate became firmly linked with that of the rest of Greece, and Mytilene became the island's wealthiest and most powerful city and its political capital.

While the classical, Attic spirit was triumphant in Athens, a distinct philosophical school was flourishing in Aeolian Mytilene. Philosophers, historians, rhetoricians, and poets made great names for themselves here. The philosopher and natural scientist Theophrastus (372–287 B.C.) came from Eresus. Aristotle came to teach in the school of philosophy in 384 B.C., as did Epicurus in 341 B.C. The city's music academy was also widely known. The theater of Mytilene, an important classical building, had been built earlier, in the fifth century B.C. It is one of the very few ancient structures on Lesbos that has been excavated.

AN ACTIVE ARTISTIC AND INTELLECTUAL LIFE PERsisted on Lesbos through Roman times. The island's location, its mild climate, and its beautiful landscape attracted many visitors, and it became one of the Romans' favorite vacation spots. During the Roman Empire, Mytilene underwent a great deal of construction, especially in the third century A.D., when the theater was rebuilt and the city's water supply was assured by an aqueduct, still visible at various spots. On the north edge of present-day Mytilene, below the theater, there are wonderfully beautiful mosaic floors in the so-called house of Menander, from the third century A.D. They show scenes from twelve of Menander's comedies and a portrait of the poet. The Athenian Menander lived from 342 to 293 B.C., but eight centuries later his comedies were still being presented in the theater at Mytilene—an unusual tribute to a poet.

Mytilene also continued as a center of philosophical study. Scholars from Lesbos became advisers to some Roman emperors. For example, the Stoic Diophanes taught the Roman statesman Tiberius Gracchus (168 B.C.), the historian Diophanes became a friend and adviser to the general and triumvir Pompey (106–48 B.C.), and the rhetorician Potamon instructed the emperor Tiberius (42 B.C.–37 A.D.) in the art of speaking. Lesbos was indebted to many of these men for laws that favored the island and preserved its political autonomy. The lenience of the Romans evoked excessive gratitude from the islanders, who observed the cult of the Caesars. On numerous inscriptions, which are now on view in the museum, the Caesars are elevated to gods.

IT HAS BEEN SAID THAT THE CULT OF THE CAESARS prevented the rapid spread of Christianity on Lesbos, but the great number of Early Christian churches from the fifth and sixth centuries—some fifty have been discovered—appears to belie this speculation. Compared to the number of Early Christian monuments on the island, there are only a very few churches from the Byzantine period—only six, in fact. This is astonishing, for Lesbos experienced a new flowering in the Byzantine era and enjoyed the favor of the Byzantine emperor. In fact, many notables lived on Lesbos at this time.

Among the ruins in the foundations of an old church in Kratigo, the so-called treasure of Mytilene was discovered. To whom did it belong? Who brought these marvelous golden ornaments, silver ecclesiastical objects, and coins—all dating from the seventh century A.D.—from Constantinople to Lesbos? And why? Today, the treasure is preserved in the vaults of the Mytilene Museum.

Lesbos experienced hard times when pirates began to plague the Aegean, and Saracens, Crusaders, Venetians, and Genoese all conquered the island in turn. Under the rule of the Genoese Gattilusi family, Lesbos enjoyed another period of prosperity. Maria, the sister of the Byzantine emperor John V Palaeologus, brought the island to her bridegroom, Francesco Gattilusi, as part of her dowry in 1355. (Genoa had shown an interest in Lesbos since 1261 and had taken charge of protecting the island from attack by the Turks.) The rule of the Gattilusi lasted for a century, until 1462, and was a mild, tolerant administration. The Gattilusi respected the Orthodox faith of their subjects, learned Greek, and took an interest in the history, archeology, and literature of the island. The walls surrounding Mytilene were strengthened by the construction of numerous towers, and many fortresses were built in the villages. The large castle crowning the green hill of Mytilene still bears above its gateway a shield that combines the Gattilusi coat of arms, the emblem of the Palaeologus, and the eagle of the Byzantine emperor.

The island was conquered in 1462 by Sultan Mehmed II, nine years after the fall of Constantinople. Lesbos assumed a special significance for the Ottomans. At the junction of major trade and military routes, it became an important supply base for the Turkish fleet. Most of the island's inhabitants emigrated; those who stayed were reduced to being poor, uneducated peasants. But at the end of the eighteenth century, the admiral of the Turkish fleet, Hassan Pasha Tsesaerli, built up the shipyard of Mytilene, and shipbuilding developed into a major industry. Hundreds of islanders found employment, and the nineteenth century saw yet another rise in the fortunes of Lesbos. A great number of lovely eighteenth- and nineteenth-century churches, large and small, adorn the villages and are scattered across the island.

The revolutionary spirit of liberation from Turkish rule reached Lesbos in 1821: a Turkish frigate was blown up in the harbor of Eresus. This success proved inspiring: the fleets of the small islands of Hydra, Spetsai, and Psara set out for battle and defeated the Turks in the Aegean. Lesbos remained under Turkish dominion, however, until November 8, 1912. Today, the islanders still celebrate that day, which happens to coincide with the feast of the archangel Michael, by making a pilgrimage to the village of Mantamado to light a candle in front of the icon of the archangel.

When the Turkish-Greek War ended in 1922, whole waves of uprooted and persecuted Greeks from the opposite Turkish mainland, the former Aeolian homeland, came back to Lesbos to find refuge. Since the beginning of the twentieth century, a new Aeolian school has grown up around the poet Ephtaliotis and the writer Bernardakis, who used the *demotiki* (folk language) instead of the *katharevousa* (literary language). The book *The Teacher with the Golden Eyes* by Stratis Myrivilis was first printed on Lesbos, and many modern Greek writers, including Venesis, have come from here. The famous modern Greek poet Odysseus Elytis (winner of the Nobel Prize in 1979) comes from Mytilene. The famous art critic Thériade, who made a name for himself in Paris, also came from Lesbos. Thériade, in turn, made the folk painter Theophilos internationally renowned. Theophilos would paint on the walls of houses and cafés, on doors, old cloths, containers, boxes—anything that he could get his hands on—only in exchange for a meal. He died in poverty in 1934. In recent years, however, art dealers have even removed frescos from the walls of village coffeehouses in order to sell them for high prices in the international market. Thériade also established a lovely museum in Vareia, a suburb of Mytilene, where Theophilos was born. Many of Theophilos's pictures hang here, in the midst of the olive trees, the little churches, the tavernas, and the simple people he painted in such a singular manner.

*L*EMNOS

LEMNOS IS AN ISLAND OF PLAINS AND GENTLE hills, a sparse amount of green, and yet a uniquely impressive landscape. Its highest point is the Skopia, at 1,541 feet. With an area of 183 square miles, Lemnos is the eighth largest of the Greek islands, only very slightly smaller than Samos.

Its abundance of agricultural products doubtless made Lemnos self-sufficient in antiquity. Today, the island's produce is distinguished more by its quality than its quantity: excellent wines, figs, fruit, tobacco, long-fiber cotton, sesame, grains, nuts, and a honey that owes its fragrance to the

The island of Lemnos.

1. *Myrina*
2. *Thanos*
3. *Kontias*
4. *Kaspakas*
5. *Kornos*
6. *Sardai*
7. *Mount Skopia*
8. *Atsiki*
9. *Lichna*
10. *Moudros*
11. *Skandalion*
12. *Poliochni*
13. *Kontopoulion*
14. *Plaka*
15. *Palaiopolis*
    (Hephaisteia)
16. *Bay of Pournia*

native thyme, fennel, and dill. Hunters have their choice of hare or partridge, and fishermen almost never cast their nets into the dark blue, crystal-clear sea in vain. In the spring, fish migrate northward into the Black Sea, and they return south in huge numbers in the fall. And Lemnos lies in the middle of their route.

The island's medicinal springs are also important. There are radioactive springs near the village of Plaka; the spring bubbles up out of the sea in an especially beautiful spot with deep green cliffs. The sulphur springs in Thermia were well known to the ancients, and the famous *lemnia ge* (Lemnian earth) was claimed to have healing properties. In antiquity, it was provided with a guarantee, the so-called Lemnian seal of Artemis, and exported. Chronic stomach complaints and even snakebite could be treated with Lemnian earth, as was attested by Dioscorides in his pharmaceutical work and by Galen, who twice visited Lemnos, in 162 and 165 A.D. Lemnian earth came from Mount Moschylus, and it was credited with healing the god Hephaestus and his son Philoctetes, who was wounded en route to Troy. The warm springs on the western side of the island are supposed to have sprung from the once-active volcano Kournos. Moschylus, so closely linked to mythological tradition, is also said to have been a volcano in the remote past.

The Lemnian landscape inspired the island's inhabitants to worship earth and fire, and the god of blacksmithing so closely associated with them, Hephaestus. This deity had a shrine near Moschylus. Whenever the ancients saw smoke rising from this peak, they believed that Hephaestus was in his workshop, where he created such wonders as the throne of his mother Hera and the shield of Achilles. In the *Iliad*, He-

phaestus tells Hera how Zeus once grabbed him by the leg and flung him into space. He fell all day long and finally crashed on Lemnos, unconscious. There he was cared for by the Sinties, the first inhabitants of the island, according to Homer. Hephaestus, Homer says, loved Lemnos more than any other spot on earth, and his was the most important cult on the island. The largest city, Hephaisteia, was also named for him.

Later, the Minyans are said to have settled on Lemnos. Herodotus, Thucydides, and Aeschylus called the inhabitants of Lemnos Pelasgians or Tyrsenoi, and some scholars connect them to the Etruscans.

The Argonauts stopped on Lemnos on their adventurous trip to Colchis to capture the Golden Fleece. A great tragedy had occurred on the island in the previous year. The women had neglected to give the prescribed votive offerings to Aphrodite.

In revenge, the goddess afflicted them with an extremely noxious odor so that their men no longer wished to touch them. Instead, the men set off for the coast of Thrace to bring women from there. The women of Lemnos proceeded to slaughter not only their unfaithful husbands but every single male on the island. The ancients referred to this frightful deed as *Lemnia kaka* (the Lemnian sacrilege), which became a common figure of speech.

Princess Hypsipyle was an exception among the women of Lemnos. She hid her father, Thoas, in a chest that she set afloat on the sea. Hypsipyle was punished for this deed by the other women, but Thoas was the only man of Lemnos who was spared. Then when the *Argo*, the ship of the Argonauts, became visible from afar, the women donned their husbands' armor and prepared for battle. Ultimately, however, they followed the advice of one of Hypsipyle's old nursemaids and welcomed the strangers. Hypsipyle allied herself with Jason, to whom she offered the throne of Lemnos. The women of the island lay with the Argonauts so that the Lemnian race would not die out. At the splendid wedding feast, the Cabiri also returned and supposedly filled the amphorae with wine. Hypsipyle bore Jason two sons, Eueneus and Thoas. But the Argonauts had to sail on in search of the Golden Fleece. The pain of parting felt by Jason and Hypsipyle inspired Euripides to write a tragedy that has since been lost. Eueneus became the king of Lemnos; he is supposed to have supplied the Greeks with wine during the siege of Troy. In order to purify Lemnos from all the blood that had been spilled, he devised rites that were performed at annual festivals of the Cabiri: every fire on the island was extinguished

Jason steals the Golden Fleece: from an ancient relief.

for nine days, then new fire was brought from the altar of Apollo on Delos.

JASON AND THE ARGONAUTS, THE DIOSCOURI, Heracles, and Orpheus—all of these heroes became connected to the cult of the Cabiri, who were considered protectors of seafarers. Lemnos had an important shrine to the Cabiri, as did Samothrace, Thebes, Imbros, Anthedon, and various other cities in Asia Minor. As with many of the cults of antiquity, the cult of the Cabiri remains enigmatic. It is certain that the Cabiri were chthonian divinities who were somehow linked to the fertility of the soil and the protection of seafarers. Their name has a Semitic root and signifies "the great ones, the strong ones." Accordingly, the ancients referred to them as the Great Gods.

On Lemnos there was a greater Cabirus, who was frequently identified with Hephaestus; according to another tradition, Hephaestus was the father of the Cabiri. The younger Cabirus was associated with Hermes. Their cult seems to have developed in Classical and Hellenistic times. In addition to the two male Cabiri, two female deities were worshipped. North of Hephaisteia, near Chloe, to the east of the Pournia bay, the Lemnian shrine of the Cabiri was excavated in 1937. Its oldest portions go back to Tyrsenoi times. The sacred precinct extended across two hills, and its most hallowed structure consisted of a three-aisle hall with an apse. Excavations also located a large stoa (columned hall) and an extensive telesterion on the northern hill, which was presumably erected to house the increasing number of pilgrims. Inscriptions there also provided interesting information about how the cities of Hephaisteia and Myrina, the two largest and most important cities of ancient Lemnos, were governed. Hephaisteia is now known

as Palaiopolis ("old city").

The location of Lemnos has made the island strategically important ever since antiquity; the island lies only 24 nautical miles from the entrance to the Dardanelles. It maintained relations with Troy, which lay opposite it, and, in prehistoric times, especially with Thrace. As Polybius tells us, the island was first called Aethalia. It was rechristened Lemnos after a prehistoric fertility goddess of that name.

Excavation on Lemnos has been undertaken by the Italian Archeological Institute since 1926. Its finds can be seen in the local museum in Myrina and in the National Museum in Athens. Lemnos enjoyed a flowering during the Bronze Age that shows some relation to those of Thermi, on Lesbos, and Troy. Countless settlements from this period have been discovered: Axia, Trochalia—where you can see ruins of small dwellings—Vriokastro, Mikro Kastelli, and so on.

One settlement that has been systematically researched is Poliochni (Polyochne), which lies along the sea on the bay of Vroskopo, near the village of Kaminia. It stood on a hill where successive layers some 30 feet deep were discovered, making it possible to reconstruct the topography of the spot during the Bronze Age. It seems to have been established before Troy, and was destroyed by the same earthquake that struck Troy. The heyday of Polyochne began between 2700 and 2200 B.C. and continued with some interruptions until 1600 B.C. Especially noteworthy here are the ceramics and gold jewelry, which vie with Troy's. Early Polyochne was an important center, with buildings of the Megaron type and a ring wall. It appears that there were warehouses for grain. No metal objects were discovered in the first phase, but the second phase reveals that the inhabitants

Heracles and the Hydra.

Heracles bringing home the boar of Mount Erymanthus: a Greek vase painting.

were able to work metal quite well. Close trading ties to Crete and the Cyclades at this time were also detected. In the third phase, the city expanded, covering the western slope of the hill, and was surrounded by a larger wall. The fifth phase of Polyochne contains larger residential structures, public buildings, wide streets crossing it from north to south, and two large squares.

All that is known of Lemnos until the sixth century B.C. is something of its rich mythology, which suggests that the inhabitants were not Greek. In 1885, an extremely interesting grave stele from this pre-Hellenic era accidentally came to light in Kaminia. Chiseled on it are the figure of a warrior and some inscriptions that use Greek letters but are in an unknown language. These inscriptions run around the head of the warrior and along one side of the stele. This stele fascinated archeologists, who recalled Herodotus's statement that in his time, "Pelasgians who spoke a barbaric language" were living on Lemnos and on the Hellespont. After its discovery, the stele had a curious history. In 1885, it was still mortared into the wall of a small church, but by 1902, it had disappeared; the islanders had hidden it to protect it from the growing interest of foreigners. A French warship actually dropped anchor near Lemnos in order to decamp with the stele, and foreign collectors were becoming more and more insistent that the sultan sell it. The stele was taken to Alexandria, where the Greek scholar Apostolides submitted information on pre-Hellenic inscriptions on Lemnos to the Egyptian Archeological Institute, and it was then brought to the National Museum in Athens. It proves "in writing" that the pre-Hellenic tribes actually existed and that the Archaic art of Lemnos was related to the contemporary *anatolisousa* (Eastern-influenced) art of Greece and Asia Minor.

In the sixth century B.C., Herodotus tells us, Lemnos was conquered by the Athenian general Miltiades. Afterward, it came under the rule of the Persians, and following 479 B.C., Lemnos became a member of the First Attic League. Athenian *cleruchs* settled on Lemnos; in the middle of the fifth century B.C., they donated the world-famous Lemnian Athena, a masterwork in bronze by Phidias, to the Acropolis in Athens. For a time, Lemnos fell away from the Athenian alliance—after the Peloponnesian War, for example—but the Athenian general Conon recaptured the island from the Macedonians. In 307 B.C., the Macedonian general Demetrius Poliorcetes reconquered Lemnos, and it remained under Macedonian rule until 202 B.C., when it was occupied by Romans. After 166 B.C., the island once more fell to Athens. In the second and third centuries A.D., four important rhetoricians and sophists, Verus, Flavius Philostratus, Philostratus Lemnius and his grandson, came from the famous Lemnian family of the Philostrati.

During the Byzantine era, Lemnos belonged to the theme (administrative district) of the Aegean and was a bishopric. Later the island was conquered by the Navigaiosa, a Venetian family who held it until 1269, when the Byzantine admiral Likarios won it back in the name of Emperor Michael Palaeologus. Then it was turned over to the emperor's son-in-law Francesco Gattilusi. Because the Gattilusi were hated here, the Lemnians at first put up no resistance to a Turkish invasion. Later, however, in 1475, Sultan Suleiman dispatched 300 ships to Lemnos to lay siege to the island, since reconquered by Venetians, and the islanders sided with the Venetians. In this battle, a Lemnian heroine named Marula distinguished herself. She took up the shield and spear of her fallen father, placed herself at the head of the demoralized garrison, and drove off the Turks. The Turks finally reconquered Lemnos in 1478, but it

belonged to the Venetians again for a short time in 1665. In 1770, the Russians attacked Lemnos in vain. The islanders, who sought to help them, were cruelly punished by the Turks. In 1912, the Greek ships under Admiral Pavlos Koundouriotis won a decisive sea battle against the Turks in the waters of Lemnos, and the island was finally free to join modern Greece. You can still see half-ruined medieval Venetian and Turkish fortresses on the island near Kastro, near Kotsino (Kokkino), and elsewhere.

MYRINA, WHICH WAS FIRST RECOGNIZED AS being the site of ancient Myrina by the archeologist Alexander Conze in 1858, today contains a particularly nice bungalow settlement for summer guests. Its traces of ancient walls, buildings, staircases, and streets are discernible only to an archeologist. A number of terracottas depicting a female deity have been found here, as well as inscriptions indicating that there was once a shrine of Artemis in the area. Myrina has preserved its ancient name, which was that of an Amazon. Coins, even those from Roman times, depict the Amazon with a huge diadem on her head.

The larger ancient city, Hephaisteia (modern-day Palaiopolis), lies in northern Lemnos. It too was inhabited by pre-Hellenes. In antiquity, there was a *phryktoria*, a station that relayed fire signals, on the once-fortified hill that rises behind the city. At the beginning of the fifth century B.C., this city surrendered without a fight to the victor at Marathon, Miltiades. Italian archeologists have here discovered a number of dwellings, a shrine, and a large necropolis where the dead were cremated. The graves date from the eighth to the sixth centuries B.C. The shrine was destroyed near the end of the sixth century B.C. The weapons, gold coins, clay idols, and vases found here were produced in local workshops and reveal a Creto-Mycenaean artistic heritage. On certain shards can be made out the same unknown language that appears on the above-mentioned stele. The finds at Hephaisteia further demonstrate that Lemnos traded with Corinth, Attica, and Macedonia. Later graves, from the fifth century B.C., clearly show an Athenian influence, doubtless thanks to the *cleruchs* from that city, who also brought the cult of the goddess Athena to Lemnos; her shrine stood near Komi, northeast of Hephaisteia. Remains of a Roman theater have also been uncovered in Hephaisteia. Settlements from Hellenistic and Roman times have been found in the village of Kaminia, near the Aghios Nikolaos church.

SAMOTHRACE

THOSE WHO WISH TO VISIT SAMOTHRACE MAY embark from Alexandroupolis in northern Greece or from Piraeus. Boats from both ports dock on the west coast of the island, in the bay of Kamariotissa. From here, a good road leads to Chora, the only town on the island today. Another road from the harbor leads to the complexes of ancient ruins. The ancient city, now called Palaiopolis ("old city"), lay on the north coast, near a cape where its acropolis stood. Palaiopolis was founded in about 700 B.C. near the famous sanctuary of the Great Gods.

The name of Samothrace has become world famous thanks to the *Winged Victory* now in the Louvre in Paris. The island, though, is peaceful and only rarely visited. Owing to its countless springs, it is covered with lush vegetation. Mount Phengari (Moon Mountain), rising to a height of 5,406 feet, is generally capped with snow in winter, and on its slopes, where wild goats clamber, are found stones of the most varied colors. There are few areas of level ground, so Samothrace has a scarcity of fields and pasturage. However, it produces fruits and vegetables, including especially good onions that have been exported since antiquity. More profitable was the export of wood, iron, and a black local stone that was used in jewelry. The warm sulphur springs in the north (Loutra) were frequented by convalescents until Byzantine times.

Because of its location in the northeast corner of the Aegean, a spot where the waves tend to be high, Samothrace was a place of refuge for smaller vessels in antiquity, and seafarers came to think that the gods placed it here for that express purpose. Until the time of the apostle Paul, Samothrace was a stopover for travelers between the Black Sea or the coast of Asia Minor and Greece.

IN THE LATE NEOLITHIC PERIOD, THE ISLAND WAS inhabited by unknown peoples. Then, in about 1000 B.C., Thracian tribes from the mainland opposite landed and mixed with the original inhabitants and founded the island's cult. Greek settlers arrived here in about 700 B.C. from the nearby coast of Asia

Minor (from the region of Aeolis). The Greeks brought with them the cult of Athena, who became the protective deity of the city-state they founded.

The raw mountain landscape of the island and its dense, dark woods were unsettling to the imagination of the ancient Greeks and helped to foster the mysterious cult of the Great Gods. Though the origins of this cult go back to pre-Greek times, the Hellenistic element was decisive in its development. A pre-Greek tongue was still used during its rites, possibly until as late as the fourth century B.C., as attested by inscriptions and vases. Various bits of information from ancient writers and from excavation finds provide a general but still superficial overview of the cult of Samothrace.

The central figure was the Great Goddess, the powerful mistress of the woods and mountains. Local Hellenistic coins depict her seated between two lions. She corresponded roughly to the great female deity worshipped throughout ancient Anatolia, the Phrygian Cybele, and other nature goddesses. The Greek settlers identified her with their Demeter, the goddess of the earth and of fertility. Yet until the end of antiquity, her pre-Hellenic name, Axierus, persisted, as did those of the other Great Gods. The goddess's power, it was believed, lay in the rock and the ore that were so plentiful on the island. It was thought that the goddess would protect the faithful if they wore iron rings made of native metal, amulets that were customarily dispensed at the sanctuary.

Alongside Axierus stood Cadmilus, her partner. He was a youthful god who represented the fertilizing power. The Greek inhabitants equated him with Hermes; his attributes, a sheep's head and herald's staff, were also borne by Hermes. These divine

The Winged Victory.

symbols were depicted on the coins of Samothrace.

In addition to this divine pair, there were the Cabiri, two young demons, familiar to us from statuettes. Later Greeks identified them with the Dioscuri (the twins Castor and Pollux) and gave them a snake and a star as attributes. The Cabiri later became the protective deities of seafarers, and sailors filled the sanctuary of Samothrace with votive gifts. Also belonging to the circle of the Great Gods were two deities known in the island's pre-Hellenic language as Axiocersus and Axiocersa. They corresponded to the Greek Hades and Persephone, the god of the underworld and his consort.

The riddles of the cult of the Great Gods are further clouded by the fact that there were also sanctuaries of the Cabiri—for example, on Lemnos, on Tenedos, and near

Thebes—where these deities were quite differently construed. In general we can say that the cult of the Cabiri and the Eleusinian mysteries shared certain similarities. The initiates in both cases were seeking earthly happiness and a better afterlife. As at Eleusis, there were two stages to the initiation in the Samothrace rites: the *myesis* (initiation) and the *epopteia* (revelation). On Samothrace, men and women, citizens and slaves, Greeks and foreigners, and even children could be initiated; the ceremony was performed whenever a believer wished it. In contrast to Eleusinian practices, no specific waiting period was required between the first and second stages of initiation; one could even receive both on one and the same day. We know that the *epopteia* required a special moral cleansing, which was a kind of confession of sins. As at Eleusis, the celebration was accomplished at night by the light of torches. Every participant had his own clay lamp on which the initials of the Great Gods were generally inscribed. The priests presented the faithful with purple *taenias* (sacred fillets) which were then tied around the body as a protection against shipwreck and death.

The sanctuary of the Great Gods on Samothrace was never wholly destroyed, and a number of ruins from antiquity are still visible. In 1444, the Italian humanist Ciriaco Pizzicoli di Ancona copied ancient inscriptions there. Occasional digs were later undertaken on Samothrace, but the Austrians began the first systematic excavation near the end of the nineteenth century, followed by the Americans in 1938. The entire precinct was uncovered only recently.

There is a Cyclopean wall from pre-Hellenic times, portions of which still stand (No. 2 on map, p. 302). Once the Greeks assumed care of the sanctuary in the sixth century B.C., they erected special buildings for the performance of the rites. It was then that the Anaktoron (palace; No. 1) was built. Here, the initiation was accomplished. Part of the building contained a room called the "holy apartment," where the faithful clothed themselves in white robes. They then entered the main portion of the Anaktoron, where the ceremony took place in public. After it was completed, the initiates entered a chamber at the north end of the building, where a priest known as the hierophant (revealer of the sacred) explained specific divine symbols to them. The initiates wore wreaths in their hair, and sacrifices, processions, invocations, and prayers to the Great Gods followed one another in succession.

Built at the same time as the Anaktoron was a large hall (No. 3) for gifts, where a variety of votive offerings was housed. Ranging from splendid donations from the rich to modest ones from the poor, all of them showed gratitude to the Great Gods for saving their donors from shipwreck.

Also constructed at this time was the building where the *epopteia*, the second stage of initiation, was conducted. Various remains are still recognizable (No. 4). Its façade was redone in the fourth century B.C. in the monumental style of that time. Two hundred years later, a pediment was added. The interior, with an apse, consisted of a hall and, on either side of it, a narrow room with benches along its walls. In 1956, two rows of Doric columns forming its façade were restored.

Through an Ionic propylon (entry gate; No. 5), you enter the building (No. 7) in the center of the sanctuary, where dances were performed in honor of the Great Gods and an annual mystery play was presented. The Arsinoeion (No. 8), named after the queen who financed it in 189–

181 B.C., was the largest circular structure of its time in Greece. It supported a conical roof made of clay tiles. The smoke created by the sacrificial fires was able to escape through an opening in this roof. Turning south from the Arsinoeion, you encounter a monumental altar with Doric columns (No. 10). Opposite lies a theater from the second century B.C., constructed of white limestone and native porphyry (No. 11). Behind the theater lay a portico (No. 12); portions of it and of the theater are still visible. The existence of this large theater shows that performances of the so-called sacred drama were an important part of the sanctuary's ritual. One play showed how the god of the underworld kidnapped the goddess of fertility. The marriage of Cadmus to Aphrodite's daughter Harmonia was the subject of another mystery play. It is assumed that this festival took place in July each year; it may be coincidence that the present-day islanders celebrate Paneghyri (a local church festival in honor of St. Paraskevi) in July as well.

During the last few years, the American Archeological Institute has uncovered a number of buildings (Nos. 15–18). We do not know what they were used for. Building No. 19 was the gift of a Milesian woman sometime between 250 and 200 B.C. One building from the fourth century B.C. (No. 20) was set up for ritual banquets. The spectators taking part in the festivities stood or sat on stepped risers laid out in a circle in the fifth century B.C. Also interesting is the ancient cemetery (No. 14), with its graves from the seventh through second centuries B.C.

In antiquity, visitors came in great streams, among them the ceremonial embassies of the Greek city-states. Herodotus and the Spartan general Lysander came to Samothrace in the fifth and sixth centuries B.C. to be initiated into the mysteries, which even Plato spoke of with reverence.

In Hellenistic times, the sanctuary enjoyed world-wide fame. The successors of Alexander the Great revered it especially, recalling that King Philip II of Macedonia had here met and fallen in love with Princess Olympias from Epirus. Olympias, who happened to have come to Samothrace at the same time as Philip in order to receive initiation, became Philip's consort and the mother of Alexander.

Samothrace maintained its importance as a naval base during the tumultuous battles among the Diadochi. The reputation of its religious rites caused the island to become a place of asylum for political refugees. Even the last unfortunate king of Macedonia, Perseus, sought refuge there after being defeated by the Romans. Because of the connection between the cult of Samothrace and Dardanus (who was from the race of Aeneas, the mythical founder of Rome), the Romans held the sanctuary in high esteem. Even Piso, Caesar's father-in-law, had himself initiated here. The last famous visitor to the "holy isle" was the emperor Hadrian.

During excavation, it was discovered that the island had been devastated by a severe earthquake in about 200 A.D. Through the following centuries, the inhabitants withdrew from the coast into the interior, seeking refuge from attack by pirates. They retreated to the Byzantine fortress, now known as Chora. In the fifteenth century, the Byzantine emperor turned over the island to the Gattilusi from Genoa, who further fortified it, using some building materials from the ancient shrines. The towers that Palamede Gattilusi built in the fifteenth century are the best-preserved ruins of the old city. After the Turks had conquered Constantinople, the people of

Samothrace were forced to emigrate there. Only in 1912 did Samothrace become Greek once again. During World War II, its inhabitants suffered greatly under Bulgarian occupation forces who had gained a foothold in northern Greece along with Nazi Germans.

IN ADDITION TO THE SANCTUARY OF THE GREAT Gods, the local museum in Chora, and the

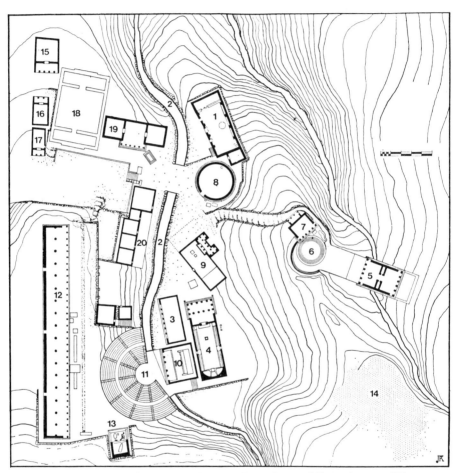

Plan of the sanctuary of the Great Gods on Samothrace: (1) Anaktoron; (2) Cyclopean wall; (3) hall for votive gifts; (4) building for the second step of initiation; (5) propylon; (6) round building on the stream; (7) Doric structure presented by Philip III and Alexander IV; (8) Arsinoeion; (9) Temenos; (10) monumental altar; (11) theater; (12) ambulatory; (13) niche of the Nike; (14) ancient cemetery; (15–18) buildings for unknown uses; (19) building of the Milesian Woman; (20) banqueting hall. (After John Kurtich.)

medieval ruins, there are two outings worth recommending:

1. Anyone who is fond of hiking can climb Mount Phengari in six hours. After two hours, you can rest at the sulphur springs of Therma before undertaking the major part of the climb to the summit. From the peak, there is a splendid view, which Homer described in the *Iliad*. When the air is clear, it is possible to see the Thracian coast, the islands of Thasos and Lemnos, and the Ida Mountains beyond Troy.

2. By boat, you can go along the south coast as far as the bay called Ammos ("sand"), which is especially beautiful and where a waterfall plunges from the steep cliffs into the sea.

*T*HASOS

AT THE NORTHERNMOST EDGE OF THE AEGEAN, not far from Kavalla and the eastern Macedonian coast, the island of Thasos rises up out of the sea. Aleppo pines, plane trees, olive and nut trees, prickly palms, mulberry and myrtle trees, a wealth of wild and cultivated fruit trees, bushes, and aromatic plants compose the lush vegetation that covers the ravines and slopes of the island, extends down into the valleys and up to the mountaintops, and borders the shore, where the waves spray it. Spring water is plentiful in the northern and eastern parts of the island, flowing in swift streams through the idyllic meadows. The sea penetrates deep into the land in many places, creating picturesque bays with lovely beaches. The harmonious combination of sky, sea, and cliffs, of mountains and green valleys, makes Thasos one of the most enchanting places in Greece.

A mountain range runs from the northwest to the southeast across the island's 154 square miles. Though steep on the northern and northeastern slopes, these mountains are quite approachable on the southern and western sides, where they blend into low rows of thickly forested hills. The peak of Hypsarion is 3,947 feet high. Its lower regions are rich in white marble, which the ancient Greeks used for both buildings and sculptures. Of the known ancient quarries on the island, the most impressive and noteworthy are those near Halyke in the southeast, on the site of an important ancient settlement. Nearby are an ancient shrine consisting of two similar structures with porticos, two cult caverns, graves, and two Early Christian basilicas.

Thasos had a wealth of precious metals, including gold and silver. According to Herodotus, the mines were located on the eastern side of the island. The Phoenicians were the first to discover and exploit these deposits. Tradition has it that the Phoenicians first came here following Thasus, the son of Cilix, or Agenor himself, or even Poseidon in the search for Europa, who had been kidnapped by Zeus. Ancient mine

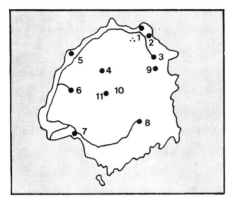

The island of Thasos.

1. Thasos
2. Makriammo
3. Panavia
4. Prinos
5. Ormos Prinou
6. Kallirachi
7. Limenaria
8. Theologos
9. Potamia
10. Mount Ipsarion
11. Maries

shafts can still be found in numerous places. Pliny mentions that there were also semiprecious gems like amethyst and opal on the island.

Thasos has been inhabited since the late Neolithic period and the Bronze Age. Two particularly interesting prehistoric settlements were located in 1969 near the village of Maries and near Kastri, where Greek archeologists recently uncovered a prehistoric acropolis, late Helladic necropolises and countless Neolithic finds. Along the coast, the evidence of habitation in antiquity and in the Byzantine period is numerous: mines, marble quarries, retaining walls, terraces, an Archaic monument, simultaneously a tomb and a lighthouse, to the nobleman Akeratos on Cape Pyrghos, the Roman baths near the village of Soteros, grave steles and inscriptions, fortified manor houses with watchtowers, the foundations of ancient buildings, Early Christian churches, and Byzantine and post-Byzantine settlements. In later centuries, the inhabitants withdrew from the coast into the interior to escape the pillaging of pirates. There, not visible from the sea, they created picturesque villages, whose tile-roofed houses can still be seen. Among the most important villages of the seventeenth and eighteenth centuries is Panaghia, with a lovely village square, fountains, and tall plane trees. Another is Theologos, where the dwelling of Hadzigheorghis, the ruler of the island during the war of liberation in 1821, still stands among the old houses. Between Theologos and Panaghia another charming village, Potamia, was founded more recently. Its roofs are covered with red tiles. The bay of Potamia has an exceptionally lovely beach, the Chrysi Akti ("golden coast"), which is covered for miles with fine, blond sand. Near the village, there is one charming building in the Athos style preserved from the nineteenth century. Today, Thasos has ten settlements.

IN ANTIQUITY, THASOS WAS PARTICULARLY WELL situated for trade and shipping because it lay on the routes connecting Asia Minor, the Cyclades, and southern Greece with the coast of Thrace. The legendary wealth of precious metals on the island fascinated the Greeks.

Toward the end of the eighth and beginning of the seventh centuries B.C., the people of Paros, in the Cyclades, conceived the plan of colonizing Thasos. According to Pausanias, the greatest painter of Thasos, Polygnotus, is supposed to have depicted the leaders of the immigrants in a painting that adorned the building of the Cnidians in Delphi. It showed Tellis, a young man of Paros, in a ship with a priestess of Demeter, Cleoboea, bringing the cult of Demeter to

Thasos. A generation later, in about 600 B.C., Tellis's son, Telesicles, obeyed the Delphic oracle and announced to the inhabitants of Paros that he had been told to build a city on the island of Hierie ("the holy") that would be "visible from afar" (*eudeielon asty*). Having arrived, Telesicles first had to survive fierce battles before he could found his settlement, on the site of the present-day city on the northern shore of the island.

During the early part of the first millennium B.C., Thasos was inhabited by barbarians who were members of Thracian tribes. The old name of the island, Edonis, or Odonis, probably derived from the Edones, a Thracian people from Pangaeum who were related to the Saiers mentioned by Archilochus (see below).

Twenty or thirty years after Telesicles landed on Thasos, in about 660–650 B.C., the conquest of the opposite mainland coast began with the help of reinforcements from Paros. This coast became known as the "continent of the Thasians." Two men who participated in this campaign were the lyric poet Archilochus, the son of the founder Telesicles, and his friend the *strategos* (general) Glaucus, the son of Leptines. Glaucus fell in battle, and his cenotaph has been discovered in the agora of Thasos. Fragments from the songs of Archilochus show how difficult the conquest of the "continent of the Thasians" must have been. The poet himself was nearly captured, but he saved himself by running away and throwing down his weapons:

> Let a Saier glory in my shield;
> I left it in the battlefield.
> I threw it down beside the wood,
> Unscathed by scars, unstained by
>   blood.
> Escaped, I keep my forfeit breath;

> I soon may find, at little cost,
> As good a shield as that I've lost.

At about this time, or perhaps later, the Thasians founded a series of *emporia*, fortified acropolises and trading posts, in Thrace, on the mainland opposite. It is certain that the cities of Galepsus, Oisyme, Neapolis, Stryme, and Crenides were colonies of theirs, and Pistyros, Akontisma, Antisara, and Apollonia probably were colonies as well. In the sixth century B.C., the Thasians penetrated to the vicinity of Scaptestyle in the Pangaeum Mountains, where the famous gold and silver mines were located.

Thasos enjoyed its heyday in Archaic times. An important political, commercial, economic, and artistic center arose. With the profits from the mines on the island and in the Pangaeum Mountains, which amounted to 200 or even 300 talents a year, the Thasians constructed powerful warships and a formidable trading fleet. During roughly this period, important buildings and shrines were constructed, and a wealth of architectural, sculptural, and ceramic works attest to a flowering of culture. In the last quarter of the sixth century B.C., the first Thasian coins came into circulation. They showed Silenus kidnapping a nymph, who resists him mightily.

This first phase of the flowering of Thasos ended with the Persian Wars. The Persian king Darius commanded the Thasians to tear down their city walls and surrender their warships. The banquet that the Thasians held for the army of the Persian king Xerxes in 480 B.C. in order to save their colonies cost a staggering 400 talents.

After the Persians withdrew from Greece, Thasos became a member of the First Attic League in 477 B.C. and contributed some thirty triremes to it. An attempt by

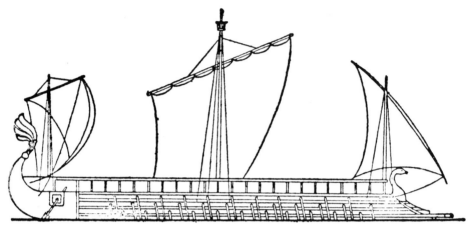

An Athenian trireme.

Athens to gain control of Pangaeum led Thasos to secede from the league. In 465 B.C., the Athenian general Cimon undertook a campaign against Thasos, and he besieged the island for three years. Exhausted by the long siege, the Thasians had to accept the extremely harsh conditions set down by the Athenians: they would tear down their city walls, pay a huge sum as tribute, and give up the "continent" with its profitable mines. From then on, Thasos was under the influence of Athens.

Thasos again became a major trading center in the last quarter of the fifth century B.C. This is clear from coins minted at the time, from the significant export of amphorae filled with the excellent Thasian wine that Aristophanes mentions, and from the duties imposed by the city over an uncommonly large area: from Mount Athos in the west to the mouth of the Hebrus River in the east. In the local museum, two laws regulating the sale of wine from this period are on display.

During the last phase of the Peloponnesian War, the city suffered heavily under a civil war with its colony Neapolis as well as

from conspiracies, rebellions, and the interference of the two great powers, Athens and Sparta, in its internal affairs. In 405 B.C., the Spartan general Lysander conquered the city and commanded that all partisans of Athens be murdered in the shrine of Heracles. But the Athenians drove the Spartan garrison from Thasos between 390 and 388 B.C. Somewhat later, in 375 B.C., Thasos became a member of the Second Attic League. The harbor of Thasos now became a base for the Athenian flotilla.

Simultaneously, the Thasians attempted to reconstruct their ancient state. The culmination of these efforts was the founding of a new colony, Crenides, in 360–359 B.C. at the instigation of the Athenian Callistratus, who was living in Thasos as a political refugee. Crenides lay in the fertile Daton region, where some very rich gold deposits had recently been discovered. At about this time, the Thasians circulated a new coin with the inscription THASION EPEIRO ("continent of the Thasians").

The expansion of the Macedonians to the east of the Strymon River crushed the Thasians' dream of rebuilding their state.

King Philip II of Macedonia conquered all of Thasos's colonies and the most important cities of Thrace. In about 340 B.C., he appears to have gained political control of Thasos through the representative of the pro-Macedonian party, a certain Aristoleon.

During the Macedonian dominion, the Thasians preserved a limited political autonomy, maintaining connections with various cities and engaging in trade. Thasian wine was exported in great quantity. Handles of amphorae in which the wine was shipped bore various symbols, names, and the designation THASION. These have been found not only in Macedonia and Thrace, but from the shores of the Hellespont to as far away as Egypt, Sicily, the Adriatic and Illyrian coasts, and central Asia.

After the Macedonians were defeated at Cynoscephalae, the Romans declared Thasos a free state. A new phase of economic prosperity and extraordinary trading activity began. New silver tetradrachmas—with the ivy-wreathed head of young Dionysus on one side and Heracles and the inscription "Heracles, the savior of the Thasians" on the other—circulated during the second century B.C. through the whole Balkan region and as far away as central Europe. During the Romans' wars with Mithridates, the king of Pontus, Thasos remained true to the Romans, and it thus suffered greatly under siege by Mithridates. The Romans rewarded the Thasians' allegiance by granting them various privileges and returning their colonies to them. During the battles near Philippi in 42 B.C., the democratic leaders Brutus and Cassius used Thasos as a supply depot for their troops. In the Roman period, the Thasians' power and wealth were concentrated in the hands of only a few families; these formed a new bourgeois class that was divided into "friends of the caesars" and "friends of the homeland" (*philokaisares* and *philopatrides,* respectively). They also founded an oligarchical governing body, the senate.

During the Byzantine period, Thasos first belonged to the theme (administrative district) of Macedonia and later to that of Thrace, and it was the seat of a bishopric. Three Early Christian basilicas have been discovered in the ancient city. There are also ruins of Early Christian and Byzantine churches in other parts of the island. During the Middle Ages, the island fell successively to the kingdom of Bonifatius of Montferrat of Thessalonike, to the Byzantine empire, to the Genoese, and to the Venetians. In 1414, Thasos was given to the Gottilusi family of Genoa by Emperor Manuel II Palaeologus. The Genoese fortifications and buildings on the acropolis date from this time.

The Turks conquered the island in 1455 and drove away almost all of its inhabitants. From then until 1813, Thasos belonged to a Turkish admiral, who had to pay a tax for it to the sultan. During the war between the Russians and the Turks (1770–1774), a Russian flotilla used the harbor of Thasos as its base. The Russians used the island's wood to build and repair their ships. In 1813, the sultan gave Thasos to the Egyptian Mohammed Ali, who was born in Kavalla. He founded the Egyptian dynasty, which was virtually independent of the Ottomans, under which Thasos was permitted a free administrative system.

In 1821, during the Greek war of independence, the Thasians snatched up their weapons and rebelled against the Turks under the leadership of Hadzigheorghis, but shortly afterward they negotiated a peace treaty with the pasha of Thessalonike. Toward the end of the nineteenth century, the economic situation of the island was miserable, and unrest followed on the

Egyptian government's decision to surrender the exploitation of the island's forests to an English company. The Turks intervened in 1902 and annexed Thasos again, but only briefly. The Greek admiral Pavlos Koundouriotis liberated Thasos on October 17, 1912, and returned the island to Greece.

THE FRENCH ARCHEOLOGICAL INSTITUTE IN ATHens began systematic excavation on Thasos in 1911, and this work has continued, with only brief interruptions, until the present. Major portions of the ancient city have been brought to light, and many significant buildings and shrines have been discovered, as have a great number of art works now housed in the museum here.

The city developed gradually over a period of about 1,000 years, from the seventh century B.C. until the third century A.D. It first began to develop near the sea, at the western foot of the hill of the acropolis. There, the oldest hutlike dwellings were uncovered. One important group of houses from the Archaic and Classical periods has been excavated in the northern part of the city (No. 12 on map, p. 310). The older dwellings were constructed in lovely polygonal masonry and form regular residential blocks separated by straight streets. French archeologists recently discovered mine shafts dating from the sixth century B.C. on the acropolis. Hardly tall enough to stand in, these show that the ancients mined iron and other ores here.

At the eastern end of the agora (No. 2 on map), the oldest of the city's monuments was discovered, the cenotaph of Glaucus; the inscription from its base—the oldest on Thasos—is in the local museum. When the Parians erected the city, they founded shrines on the heights for their deities: Athena Poliouchos (protectress of the city) (No. 18) and Apollo Pythios (No. 17), whose oracle had led Telesicles to found the Parian colony on Thasos. The large marble temple of Athena replaced an older temple at the beginning of the fifth century B.C. Erected on a lovely walled terrace on the central hill of the acropolis, it dominated the entire settlement. Today, only its foundations remain. The temple of Apollo Pythios doubtless lies beneath the Genoese fortifications. An unfinished statue of a *kouros* (youth) from this temple was found in the east wall of the acropolis. Some 11½ feet tall, this *kouros* from the seventh century B.C., whose slender proportions were clearly influenced by Ionian sculpture, can be seen in the Thasos Museum.

Dating from the sixth century B.C. is the temple of Heracles, with its polygonal masonry. This particularly noteworthy shrine was given its final form during the fifth century B.C. (No. 27). It includes an ambulatory with a monumental propylon, a broad entryway, an assembly hall, a peripteral temple, and five cult rooms. Among the most important finds at the site are the statue of a leaping Pegasus, the head of a Silenus, the head of a horse from a pediment, and the torso of an athlete. These sculptures belong to the austere Archaic style and are now on display in the Thasos Museum. The sanctuary of Artemis, east of the agora, also goes back to the sixth century B.C. (No. 8), but finds attest that the goddess was already venerated at this site a century earlier. Relics of this shrine include a wealth of beautiful votive offerings on display in the museum, exquisitely painted plates—such as a polychrome depiction of Bellerophon astride Pegasus and battling the Chimaera—gold jewelry, finely worked bronze mirrors, and ivory sculptures. Other sixth-century B.C. shrines are the sanctuary of the Patrooi Theoi (paternal gods) (No. 15) and the anonymous temple in Arkuda (No. 29).

The city wall, more than 2 miles long, was erected toward the end of the sixth and the beginning of the fifth centuries B.C. Its remains are still impressive. It was constructed of marble slabs, sometimes alternating with schist ones. The city wall encloses the three highest hills and a large portion of the valley. The gates of the city wall are not simply gatehouses but more like small temples, with wonderful relics depicting gods, heroes, and the demons who were the "guardians of this city," as an Archaic inscription on one of the gates attests. Five of these gates have impressive relief ornament: those of Silenus (No. 22), Heracles and Dionysus (No. 23), Zeus and Hera (No. 24), the "goddess with the chariot" (No. 11), and Hermes and the Graces (No. 13). On a slab next to the Parmenon gate (No. 21) are carved two gigantic apotropaic eyes (intended to ward off evil) in the Archaic style.

The ancient city had two harbors: the commercial harbor (No. 14) and the "closed" or military harbor (No. 1). The jetty of the commercial harbor, near the Evraiokastro (Jews' fortress) at the site of a picturesque shipyard, is now submerged but still visible. The military harbor, repeatedly repaired, has preserved its ancient form to the present day. This harbor is the most charming part of Thasos. Tall plane trees shade the shore. Bright-colored boats and small ships are moored here, and fishermen spread their nets along the quay to dry or mend them. On the east side of the harbor stands a large, handsome building with many windows and a tile roof. It dates from the close of the nineteenth century and is owned by the Vatopedi monastery on Mount Athos.

The passage of the Theoroi (ceremonial

*Bellerophon and Pegasus:
an ancient relief.*

officials) (No. 6) was built facing the east side of the agora in about 470 B.C. Altars, votive inscriptions, votive sculptures, and reliefs attest to the sanctity of this complex. It was here that the reliefs depicting Apollo Musagetes and Hermes with the Graces, now in the Louvre, once stood. A list of the names of the *theoroi* was carved into the marble slabs of the passageway (now in the Louvre and in the Thasos Museum).

The great physician Hippocrates stayed on Thasos for three years, and he mentioned the city's theater (No. 16) in his *Epidemics* in about 410 B.C. Its present structure dates from later times: the proscenium from the beginning of the third century B.C., and the stage and the seats from the second century A.D.

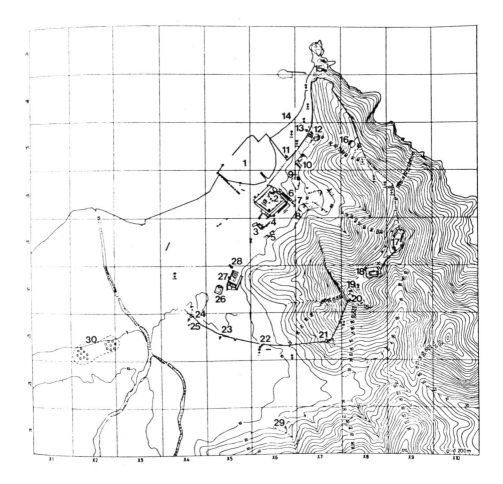

*The ancient city of Thasos: (1) closed or military harbor; (2) agora (marketplace);
(3) Roman building; (4) main street; (5) Odeion; (6) passageway of the Theoroi
(ceremonial embassies); (7) well; (8) shrine of Artemis; (9) shrine of Dionysus; (10)
shrine of Poseidon; (11) gate of the Goddess with the Chariot; (12) the northern
quarter; (13) gate of Hermes and the Graces; (14) commercial harbor; (15) shrine of
the Patrooi Theoi (paternal gods); (16) theater; (17) acropolis—shrine of Apollo
Pythios; (18) shrine of Athena Poliouchos (protectress of the city); (19) shrine of Pan;
(20) stairs carved into the rock; (21) gate of Parmenon; (22) gate of Silenus; (23)
gate of Heracles and Dionysus; (24) gate of Zeus and Hera; (25) marble sarcophagus
from the Roman period; (26) monument to Thersilochos; (27) shrine of Heracles;
(28) triumphal arch of Emperor Caracalla; (29) unidentified shrine from the Archaic
period; (30) cemetery from the Hellenistic period. (Plan from the Athens City
Planning Office.)*

BY THE BEGINNING OF THE FOURTH CENTURY B.C., the city had assumed the form it would preserve through the following centuries. The splendid agora (No. 2) was begun at this time and was not completed until the second century A.D. This political, religious, and commercial center of Thasos, the pulsing heart of the city, was constructed near the "closed" harbor, 15 feet from the sea wall. The large courtyard, roughly 325 feet on each side, was surrounded by a complex of buildings serving religious, administrative, and social needs. The oldest buildings included the shrine of Zeus Agoraios (Zeus of the marketplace), an administrative structure, the 320-foot northwest stoa (portico), and the circular altar of the Thasian athlete Theagenes, one of the most famous athletes of antiquity; Pausanias relates that he won some 1,400 victory wreaths in various Panhellenic games. In sections of the city beyond the agora, the shrines of Dionysus (No. 9) and Poseidon (No. 10) were built in the fourth century B.C. Two interesting monuments donated by patrons of the drama were erected near the shrine of Dionysus in the early third century B.C. A number of remarkable sculptures came from them, including the head of a young Dionysus, a tragic mask, statues of Dionysus, and a muse wearing a peplum, a personification of comedy. At the shrine of Poseidon, a charming group from the third century B.C. was discovered: Aphrodite atop a dolphin on whose tail fins a little Eros is riding. This is now in the Thasos Museum.

Municipal construction in Thasos continued into late Roman times. Various porticos and other structures were added to the agora, and the area outside the agora and around its southern end was expanded. An odeum was constructed (No. 5), and a portico with an inner row of columns (No. 3) was built across from it. The main street (No. 4) leading from the shrine of Heracles to the agora was paved. Along it, the exedra of Tiberius Claudius Cadmus was constructed. The last of the known public buildings was the great marble triumphal arch, which was set up between 213 and 217 A.D. to honor the emperors Caracalla and Septimius Severus and the latter's wife Julia Domna (No. 28).

Then came the advent of Christianity. The city of Telesicles that was "visible from afar" with its splendid marble buildings surrendered its prominence after 1,000 years and sank to the level of an unimportant Byzantine town. The churches of the new faith replaced the ancient sanctuaries, often being erected on the same sites and incorporating ancient building material.

Today the main harbor of the island is Limenaria, and the main town is Chora.

Dionysus: an ancient marble.

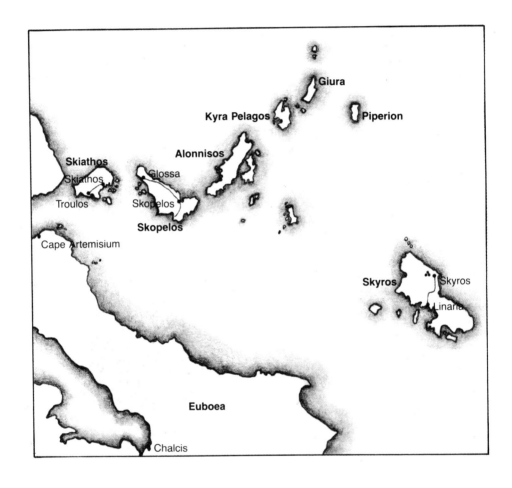

Giura

Kyra Pelagos

Piperion

Alonnisos

Skiathos

Glossa

Skiathos

Troulos

Skopelos

Skopelos

Cape Artemisium

Skyros

Skyros

Linaria

Euboea

Chalcis

THE SPORADES

SKIATHOS

THE NAME OF THE ISLAND OF SKIATHOS PRESUM-
ably means "shade of Athos" (*skiá* =
"shade"). Mount Athos, in fact, lies some
90 nautical miles away, but when the sky is
clear, its 6,550-foot peak can be discerned
in the distance. Scholars trace the names of
all the Sporadic islands, Skiathos, Pepar-
ethos (now Skopelos), and Icus (now
Alonnisos) to pre-Greek origins.

A wealth of trees also casts a welcome
shadow on the island. One large bay, Kou-
kounaries, is named for the umbrella pines
that line its shore. Poplars grow in the lower reaches, and in the undergrowth are
found pink and violet heather, arbutus, ane-
mones, wild orchids, and various types of
iris. In addition to the many chestnut and
lemon trees, there are some 600,000 olive
trees, which provide the main source of income for the islanders. Tourism, however,
is now vying for prominence with the olive
oil and fish trade; during the 1960s, a number of villas and vacation homes were built
on the island.

The island, 7½ miles long and 5½ miles
wide, used to be a holiday resort primarily
for Greek families from nearby Volos and
for all those who love to lie on soft, yellow,
sandy beaches and swim in a sea that is
calm and crystal clear, not just made to appear so in travel folders. Large, and generally ugly, high-rise hotels and a paved 6½-
mile coastal road have resulted from the
tourist invasion, considerably detracting
from the peacefulness of the island. But
even during the peak season, you can still
escape to one of about sixty solitary bays in
a little boat.

Approaching Skiathos by ship, you can
discern from a distance white houses with
bright red roofs and one of the loveliest
natural harbors in the Aegean, which,
during the summer months, is protected from the fierce *meltemi*, or north
wind.

It is quite easy to get to Skiathos. You can
take a ferry from Volos, a 3-hour crossing,
or you can go by bus from Athens to Aghios
Konstantinos and take a ferry from there,
6½ hours in all. It is also possible to fly
from Athens in 45 minutes.

Throughout the centuries, the island lay
mostly outside the mainstream of history.
Only rarely were its inhabitants disturbed.
Skiathos is first mentioned by Herodotus
in connection with the events surrounding
the sea battle near Cape Artemisium in
480 B.C. The Greeks, who were arrayed off
Cape Artemisium, received fire signals
from Skiathos that kept them informed
of the Persian troop movements on land
(in Thessaly·) and of the advance of
Persian warships toward Euboea from the
north.

Skiathos: harbor and capital.

Watchers probably sent their signals from Pyri, where an observation tower was later erected. Just before the battle began, Herodotus relates, "The Persians separated 200 ships from their fleet and sent them around Skiathos so that the Hellenes would not see them sailing off Euboea." At Cape Artemisium, the Greek fleet was able to deal a severe blow to Persian naval power.

FROM ANCIENT TAX RECORDS, IT WOULD APPEAR that Skiathos was not a prosperous island; it paid Athens only one-seventeenth of what neighboring Skopelos paid. Philip of Macedonia conquered the island in 338 B.C. When his successors were forced to leave Skiathos in 200 B.C., they pulled down all of its buildings in order to hinder the advance of the pursuing Romans. In 88 B.C., an admiral in the service of the king of Pontus hid his booty, acquired through years of piracy, on Skiathos. He was pursued by the Romans, and after his escape, they avenged themselves on the people of the island.

Marc Antony gave Skiathos to Athens in 42 B.C., and the emperor Hadrian declared its independence in 128 A.D.

In about 530 A.D., Skiathos became a bishopric, and the ruins of the Saint Sophia monastery near Troulos date from that time. When the Byzantine Empire was divided after the Fourth Crusade, the island was ceded to the Ghisi family of Venice. Then, from the thirteenth to the eighteenth centuries it was alternately ruled by Venetians, Turks, and Byzantines. Skiathos was a refuge for thousands of Greeks during the War of Independence, and it sheltered the escaping Allied soldiers in World War II. When Skiathos was occupied by the Italians in 1941, fishing boats from Skiathos would carry refugees, whom the islanders had hidden, farther east for safety. Some of the sailors who organized these nocturnal rescue trips are still living today. But they do not boast of their heroic acts, and strangers rarely manage to get them to speak of their wartime adventures.

THE ONLY TOWN ON SKIATHOS IS THE HARBOR town. Private houses, hotels, or villas built by foreigners, some of which are available for rent, lie strewn all over the island. Everyone gathers in the harbor to shop, to stroll, or to relax. The new town was built over the ruins of the ancient one in 1829, when Skiathos was returned to Greece at the end of Turkish rule. At that time, a shipyard was added, and the overall impression of the place has scarcely changed since.

Between the harbor's two bays—the ferries dock in the eastern one—lies the island of Bourtzi, overgrown with pines, where people stroll at sunset and look at the remains of the Venetian walls. Fishing boats, sailboats, and yachts are anchored along the long Paralia ("waterfront"), and

you can look at them for hours, sitting in one of the numerous coffeehouses and restaurants. Here there is a constant coming and going, a friendly throng of people, and loud conversation. On the landings of steps, parallel to the waterfront, there are chairs and tables in front of tavernas, which are occupied from early morning until late at night. The farther you penetrate into the town, the steeper the narrow, twisting alleyways become. The most noteworthy church is situated in the upper section of the town and is the one consecrated to Aghios Nikolaos, the patron saint of seafarers. Foreigners flock to two antique shops, the Castello and the Archipelago, and quite rightly, for they are both located in beautiful old houses, carefully preserved. Greek tourists are certain to visit the modest dwelling of the writer Alexandros Papadiamantis (1851–1911), who died here after having written what is known as provincial literature in the best sense. He also wrote fine journalistic essays.

VISITORS INTERESTED IN ARCHEOLOGY WILL BE disappointed by Skiathos; excavations have never been undertaken here. And history buffs must also be good hikers in order to reach the medieval capital of Kastro ("fortress") and the monasteries of Evangelistria, Kechria, and Kounistria. A guide to these various routes, edited by J. E. Causton, is available in the island shops. It is also possible to hire a donkey and a guide or even go part of the way by motorboat before setting off to the interior.

The Evangelistria monastery lies about halfway between the main town and Kastro in a charming landscape some 1,300 feet above sea level. With a spacious courtyard and a nearby spring, the monastery was a refuge for the leaders of the Greek fighters during the 1821 War of Independence.

Also well worth visiting is the seventeenth-century monastery of Kounistria, from which you can see Mount Pelion on the Thessalian coast, and the monastery of Kechria, where frescos from the seventeenth century are preserved.

Kastro, which was built near the sea and was protected on three sides by steep cliffs, was the capital of the island between 1300 and 1830. Today, only a portion of the massive fortifications, a half-ruined drawbridge, and three of the original thirty churches—the Church of Christ is the most interesting—remain. Kastro is said to have been laid out as a refuge from pirates. One of these was Chaireddin Barbarossa. Barbarossa was a Greek who converted to Islam. He assembled a fleet of Algerian and Tunisian pirates in North Africa, and he terrorized the entire Mediterranean for years. On one of his voyages, in 1538, he conquered Skiathos. He had hundreds of people killed and sold about 4,000 into slavery. The islanders subsequently refortified Kastro and rebuilt the Church of Christ. Today, Kastro is a ghost town, quite unlike the rest of the island, which seems the picture of serenity and contentment.

SKOPELOS

SKIATHOS AND SKOPELOS IN THE NORTHWEST, Skyros in the southeast, and Alonnisos, Kyra Pelagos, Giura, and Piperion in the northeast constitute a group of islands that dominates the northern Aegean and forms a natural bridge between northern and southern Greece and between the east coast of the mainland and Thessaly and the shores of Asia Minor. The ancient Greek name for Skopelos was Peparethus. It is under this name that the island is mentioned in ancient texts and descriptions. The first person known to have called it Skopelos was the geographer Ptolemy, in the second century A.D.

Skopelos is 12½ miles long and has an area of 37 square miles. The island is widest in the southeast and narrows to a point in the northwest. Mount Dhirphi (2,257 feet) in the west and Mount Palouki (1,784 feet) in the east divide the island into two halves. Along the north coast, the winds strike magnificent steep cliffs that are dangerous in bad weather. Toward the east, the cliffs give way to a generous harbor that was a hiding place for pirates for centuries. Here lies the island's capital, ancient Peparethus and modern-day Skopelos.

Unlike the north shore, the south coast has beaches that are sheltered from the wind; farther inland, there are small valleys and rolling hills covered with olive trees and pine forests. Today, the island's second town, known as Glossa (Platana), lies in the southwest, in the midst of vineyards and olive groves, on the slopes of a range of schist mountains. It encompasses the villages of Ano, Kato Klima, Machalas, and Loutraki. The population of Skopelos is estimated at 6,000, and the island is part of the province of Magnesia.

EARLY ARCHEOLOGICAL EXCAVATIONS ON SKYROS and more recent ones on Alonnisos prove that important settlements existed on the Sporades as early as the Neolithic period, so it is possible that Skopelos and Skiathos, which lie close to the coast of Thessaly, were also inhabited then. In 1936, Skopelos's history was illuminated when archeological investigations uncovered an extremely rich grave. It contained golden jewelry, seals, copper utensils, lance points, double axes, copper, silver, and stone vessels, idols, and, most important, a sword handle decorated with gold—all dating from late Helladic times. The presence of so many funerary gifts (especially the weapons and the largest Mycenaean sword heretofore unearthed) suggests that this was the tomb of some royal personage who died roughly when the Cretan settlement of Peparethus was founded. This sword may even have belonged to the Cretan hero Staphylus, who is mentioned as the founder of Peparethus (and whose name was given to the place where the grave was discovered). In its material and execution, this sword is certainly worthy of a ruler. According to Apollodorus, Staphylus was the son of Dionysus and Ariadne. The Athenian hero Theseus left Ariadne, Minos's daughter, on the island of

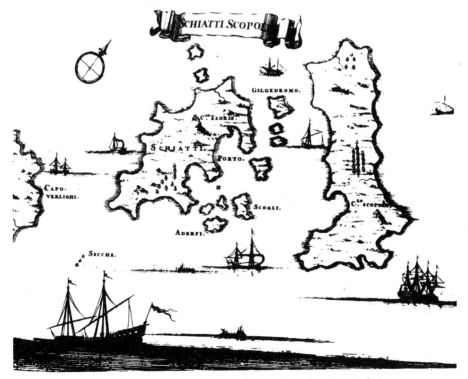

Map from Olfert Dapper's Naukeurige Beschryving, *1688.*

Naxos when he returned from Crete. On Naxos, the god Dionysus fell in love with her. He took her to Lemnos, where she bore him four children: Thoas, Oenopion, Staphylus, and Peparethus.

The Cretans are said to have introduced the cultivation of grapes and olives to some of the Aegean Islands. For many centuries, the island of Peparethus was famed for its olives and its wine. According to legend, Staphylus discovered the first vine, and tradition connects him with the cultivation of the grape on the island.

Although Peparethus was a Minoan colony, its character was closer to that of Mycenae. It is possible that the first Cretan settlers allowed themselves to be influenced by Mycenaean Greece and became less dependent on their homeland. Staphylus and Peparethus were revered as heroes, and coins bearing the heads of Dionysus and Staphylus were minted during the Classical period.

After the Mycenaean period, Peparethus was a base for pirates, the Dolopes, for centuries. In about the eighth century B.C., settlers came to the island from Chalcis and founded three colonies: Panormus, Selinous, and a third on top of the ancient city of Peparethus. The mixture of these new inhabitants and the old spurred a financial and cultural upswing. Trading ships from Peparethus sailed as far as Kos, Lesbos, Chalcidice, and Sicily. Silver coins were minted—a sign of flourishing wealth—and votive gifts from the people of Peparethus were sent to the sanctuary at Delphi. The runner Agnontas, who was victorious at Olympia in 569 B.C., was from Peparethus. A picturesque harbor on the south coast still bears his name.

During the Persian Wars, Peparethus remained neutral. Once the invaders had been driven away, the city became a member of the First Attic League. Peparethus's wealth is suggested by the fact that it contributed 18,000 present-day drachmas (3 talents) to the Delian coffers, while neighboring Skiathos was paying a mere 1,000–1,500 drachmas. Influenced by the political and cultural rise of Athens, Peparethus became a large city with a democratic form of government and a role in the political life of Greece. Its relationship to Athens remained virtually undisturbed throughout antiquity. After the Peloponnesian War, though, it suffered the fate of the conquered. It was forced to adopt an oligarchical government, and its decline began. It later struggled desperately to escape conquest by the tyrant Alexander of Pherae, subjugating itself first to the Macedonians and later to the Romans, under whom its democratic government was restored. Despite high tariffs, its trading also resumed, and wine making again became a chief source of income.

Christianity spread across Peparethus in the third century A.D., and in about the middle of the fourth century, the island became the seat of a bishopric that existed until 1842. In the third century, the new name of Skopelos also became prevalent. There are very few documents relating to the life of the islanders through the Byzantine period. Apparently the city of Peparethus, like all of the island's other ancient towns, was abandoned. Small settlements grew up at various spots across the island. When the Crusaders conquered Constantinople, the Venetians occupied many islands of the Aegean, and Skopelos became the seat of a succession of Venetian barons.

Numerous conquerors followed until 1538, when the Turkish pirate and admiral Chaireddin Barbarossa took possession of the island with 150 ships and plundered it, killing the inhabitants. Skopelos remained desolate for years. Later in the sixteenth century, new settlers arrived. The Turkish administration granted them self-government and some privileges. A noteworthy intellectual movement emerged at the beginning of the eighteenth century at the school founded and financed by Stephanos Daponte. A spirit of independence survived throughout the entire Turkish domination, and persecuted freedom fighters from the Greek mainland found refuge on Skopelos. The islanders took an active part in the struggle for independence, and, with the signing of the London Protocol in 1830, Skopelos became part of the new Greek nation.

Ancient Greeks gathering an olive harvest.

SKOPELOS HAS PRESERVED NEARLY ALL OF ITS ANcient place names, but only a few antique monuments have managed to survive destruction or be uncovered by archeologists. The most important testaments to Bronze Age life on the island are the tomb of Staphylus and the Cyclopean wall at the edge of the town of Skopelos, which dates back to the time of the pre-Hellenic settlement of the island. Remains of walls from the historical period are preserved in Panormus and around Glossa, as are the foundations of shrines from the fifth and fourth centuries B.C., such as the sanctuary of Asclepius near the town of Skopelos. Some sarcophagi, coins, and a number of statues and inscriptions also survive.

The islanders constructed their bishop's see some 550 yards outside the town of Skopelos, and its remains can still be seen. On a hill to the south of the city stands the church of the island's patron saint, Reghinos. St. Reghinos was the first bishop of the island (mid-fourth century) and was martyred by soldiers of Emperor Julian the Apostate. He was buried in a small fourth-century sarcophagus in the courtyard of the church later consecrated to him. The island has a number of small Byzantine churches, such as Aghios Athanasios and Aghioi Apostoli from the eleventh century, Aghioi Taxiarchis, and Aghios Nikolaos. There are also churches from the time of Turkish rule; several preserve frescos from the seventeenth century. The many churches attest to the deep religiosity of the inhabitants of Skopelos. Placed on picturesque cliffs or gentle shorelines, they give the island its own distinctive charm.

Visitors to the island will also find its monasteries interesting. One of the most important is the Evangelistria monastery. Standing at a considerable height, it offers a magical view of the town to the east. Its founding in 1712 is credited to the great island family Daponte, and it is a dependency of the Xeropotamos monastery on Mount Athos. Another monastery earlier occupied this site, and Stephanos Daponte constructed the present one on the old foundations. Its nave is built in the style of a four-column church. Particularly noteworthy is its iconostasis, which depicts the Holy Virgin and Child and is covered with wood carvings. The most impressive of its icons portrays the Virgin Mary; it is covered with silver and is framed by relief scenes from the Old and New Testaments. Tradition has it that this is a work from the time of the Byzantine emperor Nicephorus Phocas II (963–969).

In the eastern part of the island stands the Prodromos monastery, which was renovated by the monk Philaretos in 1721. Nearby lies the older monastery of Aghia Varvara—the date 1648 is inscribed on the door to its nave—which is presently unoccupied. An hour from the town of Skopelos is the oldest monastery on the island, the Transfiguration of the Savior, which was founded in the sixteenth century. Among the seals it preserves on patriarchal documents is that of the patriarch Kyrillos II from 1636; there is also one of the patriarch Gabriel III from 1702. A third seal, that of Sophronios II in 1775, proves that the monastery continued to thrive during the first centuries of Turkish rule.

In the church of the Panaghia Livadiotissa monastery (seventeenth century), which used to belong to the Sinai monastery of St. Catherine, there is a wonderful icon of the Holy Virgin that is the work of the Cretan church painter Antonios Aghorastos (1671). In the forecourt of the Aghioi Taxiarchis monastery you can see the remains of an Early Christian church (672). The monastery of the bishop's see, located in the courtyard of a Venetian building, was burned when the Turks retreated.

NOW AS BEFORE, THE INHABITANTS OF SKOPELOS are dependent on the sea. A large percentage of the population goes to sea, and the rest are farmers. Pears and almonds and, especially in recent years, plums from Skopelos are widely sought.

At annual folk fairs and on holidays, the women of Skopelos still wear their traditional costume: a silk sleeveless dress with

Page 321: White-washed alley, Ios. (© Peter Tenzer/Wheeler Pictures)

Pages 322–323: Brightly painted houses, Nisyros. (© Marc S. Dubin/Art Resource)

Page 324: Afternoon in Mytilene, Lesbos. (©Marc S. Dubin/Art Resource)

Page 325: Birdcages, Mykonos. (© Adam Woolfitt/Woodfin Camp and Associates)

Page 326: Bridge, Delos. (© Adam Woolfitt/Woodfin Camp and Associates)

Page 327: Entranceway in Chora, Andros. (© Marc S. Dubin/Art Resource)

Pages 328–329: Castle of the Knights, Rhodes. (© Marc S. Dubin/Art Resource)

Page 330: Street scene, Skopelos. (© Marc S. Dubin/Art Resource)

Page 331: Wall with black cat, Hydra. (© Lisl Dennis/The Image Bank)

Pages 332–333: Stacked boats, Syme. (© Marc S. Dubin/Art Resource)

Pages 334–335: Aghia Marina harbor, Leros. (© Marc S. Dubin/Art Resource)

Page 336: Boat by door, Mykonos. (© Linda Wagner/The Stock Shop)

pleats and an embroidered hem; beneath it, a soft silk jacket richly embroidered in gold and with sleeves to the elbow. They also wear a small cap decorated with gold coins. Their everyday working costume is simpler: a white blouse and a bright blue dress, which is more reminiscent of the folk costumes of the mainland than of the other islands. The dialect, too, is that of northern Greece. Similarly, they do not dance the island *ballos* on Skopelos but rather the *tsamikos* and the *kalamatianos*. Formerly, the islanders—"bell carriers," as they call themselves in their dialect—would dress in lambskins and a belt hung with bells during Carnival, dancing in the streets an unusual dance known locally as "the hop." This custom goes back to an ancient tradition that may have had its roots in the orgiastic Dionysus festivals.

As mentioned before, the town of Skopelos occupies the same site it did in antiquity and in Byzantine times. It climbs up the flanks of a hill that is crowned by a fortress. It has countless churches—one in almost every street. The houses are tall and slender, the streets winding and narrow. The only broad street leads down to the harbor. With their tile roofs, wooden balconies, and bay windows, these houses resemble the architecture on Mount Pelion in Thessaly more than the Aegean type on neighboring Skyros. Unfortunately, many of the town's buildings have been destroyed by earthquake. Standing in their place today are unattractive concrete structures with marble façades. Though the town of Skopelos has lost its unified architectural style, it still boasts a number of picturesque sections. The beauty of its landscape is enchanting, as are its 350 white churches, its houses, alleys, colonnades, and harbor.

SKYROS

SKYROS, THE LARGEST AND SOUTHERNMOST OF the Sporades, can be reached by ferry from the harbor town of Kymi, on the east coast of Euboea. After a crossing of an hour and a half, one lands at the small town of Linaria. Like the other best natural harbors on Skyros, Tris Boukes and Kalamitsa, Linaria lies on the west side of the island, which offers the most shelter from wind and waves and where the sea is calmest. The east side, by contrast, is exposed to the open Aegean. The southern part of the island is dominated by the peak of Panoftis, 2,591 feet high. In this region of steep treeless slopes, gigantic razor-sharp rocks, and coastal caves, one encounters small wild horses, a type of pony descended from an ancient species. These are only one of the tourist attractions of this picturesque island. The northern part of Skyros is more fertile. Here, along with pines and cedars, there are gardens and vineyards. The few grave steles, inscriptions, and sculptures from various parts of the island now displayed in the museum here also reveal that Skyros was never heavily populated, and written sources confirm this.

The steep, rocky acropolis, which was

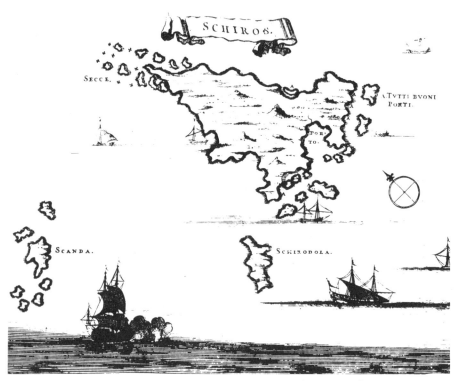

Map from Olfert Dapper's Naukeurige Beschryving, *1688.*

fortified in antiquity, rises above the north-east coast. Now it is known as Kastro, and the huddled houses of the present city of Skyros climb up its slopes. Their walls and thresholds are a blinding white, while their terraces, the so-called *dhomata*, glow a grayish blue. The view of this small city from the height of Kastro is one of the most charming sights in the Aegean. In addition to the houses and alleyways below, one can also see the hills and valleys to the north. On the horizon to the west are the Mavrouna Mountains, whose rich springs feed the Kephissos River. In the northwest rise Mount Notes and Mount Kalomastos; between them lie the ancient marble quar-

ries, which are still in use today.

Some thirty years ago, a Paleolithic tool, a hand-axe made of flint (*pyritholithos*), was discovered on the northeastern slope of Kastro. Others, made of obsidian, were then unearthed on the Vaftistera, in the western part of the town, and many more flint tools were found near the bay of Achilli (known as Achilleion or Achilleios Limen in antiquity), 3 miles northwest of the city. The Spiliotissa cave proved to be another rich source of finds: Mesolithic (pre-Neolithic) flint and obsidian tools were recovered here. On the northeast spur of Kastro, at a spot now called Tou Papa to Choma ("the soil of the priest"), traces of a Neolithic settlement, dating to the fifth millennium B.C., were discovered: clay vessels, shells, animal bones, and obsidian disks. Prehistoric shards have also been found on the Fourka hill and near the Kephissos River.

The area of Kastro was inhabited in Mycenaean times as well. On its southern extension, Basalos, traces of a cemetery were discovered, as were vases now on display in the local museum. Particularly noteworthy is an amphora that depicts an octopus (*krake*) and a ship with a bird-shaped prow. The pieces of the Skyros Museum reveal that the period between 1050 and 900 B.C. was a flourishing one for the island. The forms and decoration of the vases suggest close ties with Thessaly, Euboea, and the other northern Sporades. Graves from the Geometric period have been located not only at the ancient cemetery of Basalos but elsewhere on the island.

In mythology, Skyros is associated with Theseus, Achilles, and Neoptolemus, an indication of how important the island was during the Mycenaean period. Thetis hid her son Achilles on Skyros to keep him out of the Trojan War. Dressed as a girl, Achilles stayed at the palace of King Lycomedes until Odysseus convinced him to fight in Troy. Odysseus brought gifts—jewelry, fine fabrics, and bright-colored ribbons—and the female playmates of Achilles pounced on them. Achilles, however, had eyes only for the splendid weapons among the gifts. Achilles met a hero's death outside the walls of Troy. Neoptolemus, or Pyrrhus, the son of Achilles and the king's daughter Deïdameia, was born on Skyros. And Theseus found asylum here after being driven from Athens. Legend has it that he was killed here by being flung off the acropolis. The general and statesman Cimon transported the bones of the legend-.

Diomedes (left) and Odysseus (right) take Achilles from Skyros: wall painting from Pompeii.

ary king to Athens in the fifth century B.C., where they were buried with great ceremony.

IN ARCHAIC TIMES, IT APPEARS THAT A MARBLE temple dedicated to Apollo was built on the summit of Fourka hill. The rock was leveled to support its foundations (79 by 58 feet). The structure was completely destroyed; only a few vases remain, along with an Archaic marble hand and the handle of a vessel, with an inscription stating that a certain Silanodoros had consecrated the vase to Apollo.

Ruins of another large temple, 75 by 45 feet, lie on Cape Markesi on the northern tip of the island. Nothing definite is known about it, but it was presumably consecrated to the sea god Poseidon and seems to

Lithograph after a drawing by Lemonnier in the Benaki Museum, Athens.

date from the Classical period. The remains of an apse in its interior suggest that it was transformed into a church in the Middle Ages. Near the bay of Aghios Phokas, there are fallen towers and retaining walls from antiquity.

After Cimon came to Skyros, the island, which was also known as Pelasgia or Dolopia, was inhabited and administered by Athenians. The fortification of the acropolis dates from the fourth century B.C. and was probably done by Macedonians, who held the island until 166 B.C. At that time, it was conquered by the Romans, who presented it to Athens.

Under Roman rule, Skyros was known chiefly for its multicolored marble. In the Byzantine period, it belonged to the theme (administrative district) of Hellas, and it was the seat of a bishopric until 1837. In

895, the church of the Episkopi (bishop's see) was erected on Kastro and dedicated to the Assumption of Mary. An earthquake destroyed it in 1840.

The Saracens were never able to conquer Kastro, though they launched repeated attacks in 900. Nevertheless, it became a base for pirates for a brief period. In 1204, after the fall of Constantinople, Skyros, like Lemnos and Tenos, became the personal possession of the new Latin emperor of that city. Eighty years later it fell to the Ghisi family. The new fortifications of Kastro were constructed by the ninth ruler of the archipelago, Francesco Grispo (1383–1397). In the mid-fifteenth century, Skyros became a Venetian colony, and the Turks arrived in 1538. The ancient Hellenic island remained Turkish until 1821.

In the main town and strewn about the

island are noteworthy churches from the fifteenth to the early eighteenth centuries. The church of Aghios Ghiorghios, inside the monastery on Kastro, houses interesting wall paintings. In the sanctuary of the church of the Panaghia Eleimonitria (merciful Virgin Mary), which, according to an inscription, was built in 1680, one should particularly note a lovely head of Christ and a procession of saints that bears a striking resemblance to the procession of angels in the church of Perivleptos in Mistra. In the churches of the Panaghia tou Tselepi and Panaghia tou Theodori, the sculptural quality of the wall paintings is astonishing. Especially in the female figures, there is no trace of the severe Byzantine style; rather, Western influence has been at work. The church of the ruined monastery of Aghios Demetrios, which lies halfway between the main town of Skyros and the harbor at Linaria, is well worth a visit. An inscription on the half-destroyed outer wall tells us that this wall was completed by a Master Nikolaos on October 10, 1611. The message is rife with touching spelling mistakes. In the entryway, there is a Roman statue, headless and draped in a toga.

Those who are interested in folk arts and crafts will find Skyros a treasure-trove. Nearly every house has old clay pots, plates painted in gleaming colors, and embroidered towels, sheets, and shirts boasting original designs and color combinations. And practically every house has some distinctive architecture, whether it be the fireplace or the *patari* (raised part of the room), along with copper utensils and beautifully carved chests, chairs, and benches. In some, a Venetian mirror or a piece of French porcelain also recalls the past.

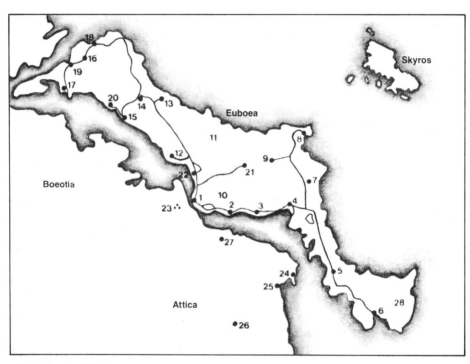

The island of Euboea.

1. *Chalcis*
2. *Eretria*
3. *Amarynthos*
4. *Aliveri*
5. *Styron*
6. *Karystos*
7. *Aulonari*

8. *Kymi*
9. *Manika*
10. *Vasilika*
11. *Mount Dirphys*
12. *Politika*
13. *Mantoudi*
14. *Strofilia*

15. *Limne*
16. *Istiaia*
17. *Aidipsos*
18. *Cape Artemisium*
19. *Oreioi*
20. *Rovies*
21. *Steni*

22. *Kastelli*
23. *Aulis*
24. *Rhamnous*
25. *Marathon*
26. *Athens*
27. *Oropos*
28. *Mount Ochi*

THE GREAT ISLAND, EUBOEA

*E*UBOEA

EUBOEA IS ONE OF THE SEVEN LARGEST ISLANDS IN the Mediterranean, along with Sicily, Sardinia, Corsica, Crete, Cyprus, and Majorca. Its elongated shape gave rise to several of its ancient names (which included Euboea), such as Makris, Makre, and Doliche. Euboea runs parallel to the Greek mainland for nearly 100 miles, from the Gulf of Mallis in the north to near Sounion in the south. Its greatest width, between Chalcis and Kymi, is 31 miles. Between the bays of Koralides in the east and Styron in the west, though, it is only 3.7 miles wide.

The highest elevation is Mount Dirphys (5,757 feet), an impressive massif. In the north rises Mount Telethrion, locally known as Kantili; in the south, Mount Ochi (4,593 feet) surrounds the plain of Karystos. There is a Mount Olympus on Euboea; it is one of the southwestern spurs of Mount Dirphys, which forms a backdrop to the valley of Eretria. The Lelantine Plain (Lelanteion Pedion) between Chalcis and Eretria, through which the Lelas River flows, is the source of the island's agricultural wealth.

In antiquity the islanders lived primarily from raising cattle. Other sources of in-come were forestry, agriculture, and fishing—just as they are today.

The island's prehistory dates back to the Stone Age, as remains at thirty-two sites, all of them apparently from the Neolithic period, attest. The most important finds have been at Chalcis, Limne, Barka, Aidipsos, Rovies, Amarynthos, Vasilika, and Moula. These settlements are equally represented in the interior and along the coast. The people of that time were familiar with seafaring, as were their Early Helladic successors (2600–2000 B.C.). There are some fifty settlements from this period on Euboea. Only a few have been systematically investigated—among them Manika, north of Chalcis, Aulonari, Oreoi, and most recently Lefkandi, between Chalcis and Eretria. The largest collection of Early Helladic settlements is in the central and western parts of the island, especially between modern-day Aliveri and Psachna.

Trade has been attested to through the whole Early Helladic period. At that time, Euboea imported astonishing numbers of objects from the Cyclades—or Euboean artists used Cycladic patterns when making their vases and pots. In Manika, vases in the style of the region of Troy (now in the Chalcis Museum) were discovered. Connections to Troy at about 2000 B.C. are particularly numerous.

The Middle Helladic period lasted from 2000 to 1600 B.C. Settlements from this epoch were largely peaceful farming communities in the flatlands.

The Euboean plains were thickly settled in Mycenaean times (1600–1200 B.C.). Lefkandi was an important center not only in the Mycenaean but also in the Geometric period. This town has been thoroughly excavated by the British Archeological Institute and reveals much about life and death through the centuries; one cemetery from the ninth century B.C. came to light here.

Fourteen villages in central and northern Euboea traded actively with Thessaly but also with Athens and the southeastern Aegean at the beginning of the first millennium (1000–850) B.C.

In historical times the island was divided up in the Greek fashion into independent city-states. Their relations were not always peaceful.

Chalcis

GREEK AND ROMAN WRITERS CALLED CHALCIS the "metropolis of the island." The city lies on the Strait of Euripos and was connected to Boeotia, on the mainland, by a bridge as early as 410 B.C. For centuries, the Strait of

View of the city of Chalcis.

Euripos was used by every seafarer who sailed north or south and wanted to avoid the dangerous cliffs and currents on the other side of the island. Passage was controlled by Chalcis, so the city's position was strategic in times of both peace and war. For this reason, Chalcis was much courted and often attacked, and, at least in the fourth and third centuries B.C., it was heavily fortified. Its acropolis, some of whose ruins are still standing, crowned the hill of Vathnovounia, near the sea. There were also fortifications on that part of the Boeotian coast that belonged to the city of Chalcis—for example, on the present-day Karababa hill.

Recent excavation has revealed that the ancient city of Chalcis extended to the east of the present one. The bay of Aghios Stephanos was its harbor, and the agora lay nearby. Unfortunately, little is known for certain about the various buildings and villages in and around the city that the ancient writers mention. Five huge capitals from the temple of the Olympian Zeus are on display in the Chalcis Museum. These date from 500–470 B.C. We can assume with reasonable assurance that the temple stood where the Byzantine church of Aghia Paraskevi, which can still be seen today, was later built. Inscriptions indicate that Chalcis housed shrines to Athena, Apollo, Delphinus, and Dionysus. Arethusa was the name of the city's major spring.

The oldest traces of human habitation in Chalcis date from the early Neolithic period. Shards of monochrome vessels from that period have been found. The most important finds from 2600–1200 B.C. were made on the peninsula of Manika, north of Chalcis, and in the villages of Trypa, Vromousa, Tris Kamares, Panaghitsa, and Pei.

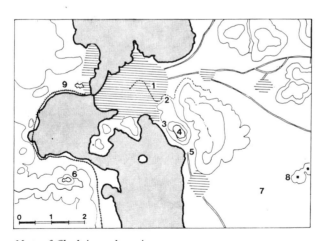

Map of Chalcis and environs.

1–2. *Venetian aqueduct*
   3. *Arethusa spring*
   4. *Acropolis*
   5. *Ancient suburb*
   6. *Hellenistic fortress*

     of Aulis
   7. *Lelantian Plain*
   8. *Phylla*
   9. *Karababa*

Various cemeteries with Mycenaean vaulted tombs and rich funerary gifts have been unearthed. Near the Arethusa spring, a number of vases were found in tombs from 1000–900 B.C.

In the eighth century B.C., Chalcis was a powerful and influential city. It became a considerable colonial power at an early date. Together with other city-states on the island it founded the first Euboean colonies in Italy and on Sicily as well as on Chalcidice, a peninsula in northern Greece. The Samnites, Latini, and Etruscans adapted the Chalcidian form of the alphabet of Kymi and created the Latin alphabet from it. Chalcis's colonial ventures led to the development of a well-to-do middle class that demanded a voice in public affairs from the aristocracy; they were not successful until toward the end of the sixth century B.C.

At the end of the eighth century B.C., various disputes about colonization, trade, and control of the local agricultural region led to war between Euboea's two largest city-states, Chalcis and Eretria, and their allies. The main object of this battle, which has gone down in history as the Lelantine War, was the conquest of the fertile Lelantine Plain. It is assumed that Chalcis was victorious, though with great loss of power; definite information about the outcome of this long conflict is scarce. Athens conquered Chalcis, which was then ruled by an oligarchy, and its ally Boeotia in 506 B.C. Four thousand Athenian *cleruchs* settled around Chalcis and divided up the land among themselves. After this, the city never again had any particular significance.

On their first campaign, in 490 B.C., the Persians left Chalcis alone; after destroying Eretria, they headed straight for Attica. Ten years later, the ships of Chalcis fought alongside those of the Athenians in the sea battle at Salamis.

The most important events in Chalcis's history after the Persian Wars are as follows:

446 B.C.: Euboea rebels against Athens. Athens conquers Chalcis, and the wealth of the local aristocracy is divid-

The Strait of Euripos: drawing from The Mediterranean Illustrated, *1877.*

ed up among Athenian *cleruchs.*

446–411 B.C.: The inhabitants of Chalcis become tax-paying subjects of the Athenians.

411–410 B.C.: Chalcis liberates itself from the rule of Athens.

410 B.C.: The Chalcidians build the fortified bridge across the Strait of Euripos with the help of the Boeotians.

378–377 B.C.: Chalcis becomes a member of the Second Attic League.

335–334 B.C.: Chalcis expands its fortifications across the hill now known as Karababa, in Boeotia.

333 B.C.: Chalcis serves as a base for the Macedonian fleet.

323 B.C.: Aristotle flees from Athens to Chalcis, where he lives in exile until his death in 322 B.C.

308 B.C.: Chalcis joins the Boeotian League.

302 B.C.: King Demetrius Poliorcetes (the Besieger), one of the Diadochi of Alexander the Great, assembles his army in Chalcis before marching against Cassander in Macedonia.

209 B.C.: Philip V of Macedon fortifies the city.

196 B.C.: Philip V is forced to surrender the city to the Romans.

3rd century A.D.: The temple of Olympian Zeus and Athena Archegetes is restored.

359: The Roman vice consul Poulius Ambelius decides to restore the public buildings of Chalcis, including a columned hall (stoa), certain of whose architectural fragments (capitals with inscriptions from the time of Augustus) were recently discovered in a wall from the time of Justinian in the center of modern Chalcis.

527–565: At the time of the Byzantine emperor Justinian the bridge across the Euripos was restored, and a new, fortified city was constructed on the site of modern Chalcis.

880: Osman, the emir of Tarsus, attacks the city with thirty galleys and is beaten by the Greek general Oiniatis.

1204–1470: Chalcis is ruled by the Venetians.

1338: The walls of Chalcis are newly fortified.

1436: Cyriacus of Ancona lives in Chalcis, at that time renamed Negroponte, and occupies himself with copying ancient inscriptions.

1465: The Venetian admiral Vittore Capello again fortifies the walls of Chalcis.

1470: Chalcis is conquered by the Turks.

1821: Chalcis is liberated from the Turks and incorporated into the modern Greek nation.

A VISIT TO THE CHALCIS MUSEUM IS HIGHLY RECommended. Here, among other artifacts, the pediment sculptures of the Archaic temple in Eretria that was dedicated to Apollo Daphnephoros ("the laurel-bearer") are on display. The most beautiful of these is the statue of Theseus kidnapping an Amazon.

Eretria

ERETRIA'S INTERESTING HISTORY CAN BE READ from its ruins. It is one of the rare places where a great ancient city has not been covered by a later settlement. The city walls from the Classical period and countless shrines and public buildings are largely preserved. Only recently has the rapid expansion of the modern city of Eretria, also known as Nea Psara, threatened to erase the traces of antiquity. Thanks to the work of the Greek Archeological Authority and of Swiss archeologists, the ruins of important buildings continue to be excavated, and countless new finds are added to the local museum.

Recent investigations date the earliest settlement on the site to the Early Helladic period (2600–2000 B.C.). This settlement was located at the northwestern edge of the present-day swampy area, which was then presumably a bay of the sea. In addition, shards from the third to the middle of the second millennia B.C. have been found in Pesonisi (now known as the Isle of

Dreams, Nisi ton Oniron), on the acropolis of Eretria, and beneath the temple of Apollo Daphnephoros. A number of Mycenaean shards have come to light on the northeastern side of the acropolis and on its southern spurs. To date, not a single find has

been unearthed from between the twelfth and tenth centuries B.C.

The founding and flowering of historic Eretria falls in the eighth century B.C. Countless important finds attest to a fortified city with an active commercial life.

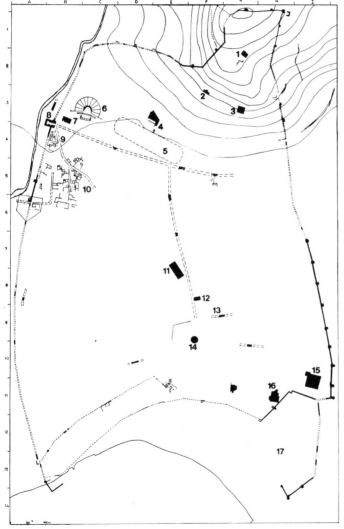

Plan of Eretria.

1. Hellenistic structures on the acropolis
2. Shrine of Demeter Thesmophoros
3. Shrine of a goddess, presumably the Olympian Artemis
4. Gymnasium
5. Probable location of the stadium
6. Theater
7. Temple of Dionysus
8. Western gate
9. Dwellings of the nobles
10. Private dwellings
11. Temple of Apollo Daphnephoros
12. Wells
13. Site of a prehistoric settlement and fifth-century B.C. street
14. Tholos in the center of the agora
15. Palaestra and shrine of Eileithyia
16. Shrine of Isis
17. Site of the harbor

Some scholars believe that the Mycenaean Eretria that was known to Homer is to be found east of the modern city, near present-day Amarynthos. However, others insist that it lay to the west, near Lefkandi, where, as mentioned above, recent excavation uncovered an important settlement continuously inhabited from 2600 B.C. until toward the end of the eighth century B.C. Presumably, the last inhabitants of Lefkandi settled in Eretria after leaving their own homes, as it was already a well-organized community. It is possible that Lefkandi was destroyed in the Lelantine War (eighth century B.C.) against Chalcis.

As previously mentioned, Eretria, when it was at its economic and cultural height, participated with the other Euboean city-states of Chalcis and Kymi in intensive colonization. The transition from an oligarchical regime to a democratic one occurred near the end of the sixth century B.C. In 490 B.C., in revenge for the burning of the temple of Sardis, the Persians destroyed Eretria on their march toward Attica and took many of its citizens as hostages. Nonetheless, the city rapidly recovered; within ten years, it was capable of sending seven triremes to Salamis to combat the Persians. As a member of the First Attic League, the city enjoyed a peace that lasted many years. But after a vain attempt to free itself from Athenian hegemony in 446 B.C., Eretria was forced to surrender its lands to Athenian *cleruchs.* In 411 B.C., the Athenian fleet suffered a devastating defeat in the harbor of Eretria while battling the Spartans and Eretrians. By 394 B.C., relations between Eretria and Athens were friendly once more, and between 377 and 357 B.C., Eretria belonged to the Second Attic League. During this time, it was ruled by local tyrants: Themiston, Menestratos, Ploutarchos, Pleistarchos, and Cleitarchos. In 341 B.C., the Euboean Alliance was founded. Under the subsequent rule of Macedonia, Eretria regained autonomy for a time. In the fourth, third, and part of the second centuries B.C., Eretria controlled most of central and southern Euboea, which had been divided into *demes* (communes), after the Attic model. From inscriptions, some fifty *demes* that were subordinate to Eretria are known about.

In 198 B.C., the Romans devastated the city. After having been rebuilt, it was leveled again in 87 B.C., and it never recovered from this catastrophe. In 21 B.C., Emperor Augustus finally removed Eretria from Athenian control. It was already a ruined city, and it remained sparsely inhabited until the fifth century A.D., when it was finally abandoned. And so it remained until 1834, when the few refugees who had escaped from the island of Psara, which had been devastated by the Turks, made homes for themselves here. Hence the official but seldom-used name Nea Psara (New Psara).

The museum on present-day Eretria is small, but it contains works from all epochs of the city's history. It includes Mycenaean and Geometric finds from Lefkandi—especially interesting is a proto-Geometric centaur from the tenth century B.C. that was a funeral offering—as well as vases from the Geometric, Archaic, Classical, and Hellenistic periods, idols, bronze vessels and weapons, jewelry, countless inscriptions, and votive gifts. A series of amphorae, from the fourth century B.C. and discovered here, are temporarily housed in the National Museum in Athens.

Kyme and Other Cities

THE ANCIENT CITY OF KYME HAS NOT YET BEEN located with certainty, though in the vicinity of present-day Kymi, on the east coast, there are still several unexamined settlements that date back to Mycenaean times.

HISTIAEA (OREIOI), ONE OF THE OLDEST CITIES OF Euboea and one that is mentioned in the *Iliad,* lay near the present town of Oreioi. It was continuously inhabited from Early Helladic times until the Middle Ages. A storeroom in an administration building contains a small collection of tomb inscriptions and votive reliefs, fragments of sculptures and architecture. A huge marble bull from the fourth century B.C. that was found at the bottom of the sea stands in the main square of Oreioi.

AIDIPSOS IS NOW A SPA WITH THERMAL SPRINGS. It occupies the same site as the ancient city of the same name (Aedipsus), which was especially popular in Hellenic and Roman times because of its medicinal baths. It has not been researched by archeologists. Accidental finds, including some statues and inscriptions from the Roman period, are housed in the town hall.

KARYSTOS, IN SOUTHERN EUBOEA, WAS BEST known for its marble quarries in antiquity, just as it is today. Remains of its ancient acropolis survive in Palaiochora, beneath the medieval Castel Rosso. Inscriptions, sculptures, and architectural fragments that have been found strewn about the vicinity are collected in the building of the Giokala Foundation. The famous building called the Drakospito ("dragon house") on Mount Ochi, above Karystos, was once commonly thought to be prehistoric. However, recent opinion is that it is a Late Geometric cult building. Systematic excavation is yet to be done to resolve this question.

DYSTOS IS A MASSIVE FORTRESS FROM THE CLASSICAL period that crowns a conical, rocky hill near a lake. It is definitely worth a visit.

*E*UBOEA, OFF THE BEATEN TRACK

YEAR AFTER YEAR, MORE AND MORE GREEKS AND foreigners travel to Euboea to relax, to swim, or to go mountain-climbing. This increasing popularity has evolved gradually. It seemed that Chalcis would always retain its charm, with its old houses and warm, populous neighborhoods, that Eretria would always be a sleepy, one-street town, that Aidipsos, with its shoreline promenades and old-fashioned, upper-middle-class hotels, would continue to decay. The chestnut forest on the summits above Karystos, the ancient plane trees near Steni, and the firs on Mount Dirphys—a rarity in Greece—it seemed that these would live forever. But this was not to be; in the past few years, widespread fires destroyed many of the island's forests; more and more factories and concrete houses sprouted up in the once peaceful landscape. Industrial development also left its mark on the Mantoudi area, while the west coast has

The sacrifice of Iphigenia:
a wall painting from Pompeii.

become marred by the tourist invasion, with its hotel complexes. It also seemed that the change of tide in the Euripos channel near Chalcis was a totally inexplicable phenomenon. But geologists are now coming up with a highly complicated theory, explaining why the tide in the Euripos channel changes several times a day, flowing back and forth at a speed of six to eight nautical miles an hour, and remains calm for only a few minutes before changing again to the opposite direction. According to one local legend, Aristotle drowned himself in the Euripos channel out of sheer frustration at not being able to solve the mystery.

At Aulis, across from Chalcis, before the Trojan War began, the Greek ships waited for months for a favorable wind so that they could sail out to the open sea and head for Troy to retrieve Helen. Now that there are motorboats, it is easier to navigate the Strait of Euripos, but even today, however, the retractable steel bridge allows ships to pass only when the current is favorable.

IT IS POSSIBLE TO VISIT AULIS EN ROUTE FROM Athens to Chalcis (whose name recalls the mineral wealth of copper ore—*chalkos*—on Euboea). Fifty-three miles from Athens, a road branches to the right and leads to Aulis, where, near a cement factory, lie the remains of a shrine dedicated to Artemis; this is the spot where Iphigenia was sacrificed.

This site also recalls one of the earliest of the Greek poets, Hesiod, who crossed the Strait of Euripos on his way from Thebes in about 700 B.C. to take part in the funeral games in honor of King Amphidamas, who fell in the Lelantine War. Poetic and gymnastic contests took place at these festivities. Hesiod, who had been invited by the late king's sons, competed with the *coryphaei* of his time and won the first prize, a tripod, as he relates in his *Works and Days*.

SEEN IN THE MORNING SUN FROM THE HILLS OF Boeotia, Chalcis appears to be a beautiful white city. A second look proves disappointing. Scarcely anything is left of the old city, which must have been particularly charming between the sixteenth and the eighteenth centuries, when it boasted Venetian and Turkish houses richly ornamented with wood carvings, Venetian fortifications, marble fountains, a Jewish quarter with its synagogue, and numerous Orthodox and Catholic churches.

So much of Chalcis has been ruined, razed, and rebuilt that the few remains of the past do not evoke an adequate picture of it. The Early Christian basilica now known as Aghia Paraskevi was remodeled in the fourteenth century, and its Gothic interior is interesting—if only because the Gothic style is extremely rare in Greek architecture. Also standing are the former Venetian governor's palace (Spiti tou Bailou), the church of San Marco di Negroponte, which was converted into a mosque by the Turks in 1470, and portions of an aqueduct on the eastern edge of the city.

HOWEVER, SOME TRACES OF EUBOEA AS IT ONCE was awaits visitors who leave the main roads. For example, if you turn off the highway connecting Chalcis and Eretria at Vasiliko and head northeast toward Phylla, you pass three watchtowers that the Venetians built out of dark gray stone. They were part of a whole network of towers from which watchmen relayed fire signals of warning when pirates attacked from the sea or enemy forces approached on land. The watchmen near Phylla also had to see that no water was stolen from the conduit, laid out in antiquity and rebuilt by the Venetians, that led from near Mount Dirphys to Chalcis. On either side of the road toward Phylla there are vegetable gardens and orchards; this area is part of the fertile Lelantine Plain.

In the summer of 1975 in the course of a village feast, the modest birthplace of the Greek freedom fighter Andreas Miaoulis was made a national monument. At that time, countless Greeks who had scarcely heard of Phylla before flocked here. In its narrow alleyways, the visitor comes upon delightful houses painted blue, green, and vermilion.

When the Byzantine Empire was dissolved, during the Fourth Crusade (1204), Euboea was surrendered to three noblemen from Verona who divided up the island between them. The capital continued to be Chalcis, which was renamed Negroponte ("black bridge"). Near Phylla, the fortress now known as Kastelli (designated as Lilanto Castle on medieval maps) stands on an outcropping. This well-preserved fortress was captured at the end of the thirteenth century by Licario, who grew up in Karystos and was descended from the lesser Italian aristocracy. When two of the lords of the island forbade his marriage to Felisa, the widow of the third ruler, he sought revenge. Leading a force of Byzantines, he drove these princes from their fortresses and, after heavy fighting, managed to conquer the island. For nearly two centuries, the Byzantines and Venetians fought over Euboea until, in 1390, the Venetians captured all of its key positions. The three former princes of Euboea were confined to their estates, and the Venetians shipped most of the island's products—such as timber, grain, and olives—to Venice, so the islanders fell into dire poverty.

THOSE WHO GO TO EUBOEA CAN REDISCOVER the Middle Ages, whose remains are not much appreciated in Greece as a rule; yet they vividly evoke a colorful and little-known period of Greek history. When driving from the small factory town of Aliveri to Kymi, on the east coast, you can admire from afar the ruined fortresses and watchtowers on the low foothills.

In Chani Avlonariou you can visit the twelfth-century church of Aghios Demetrios. It stands right beside the road, and its windows and doors have a distinct Romanesque quality about them; its side walls incorporate the bases of ancient columns. Another church well worth visiting for its beautiful though badly damaged fifteenth-century pastel frescos is Aghia Thekla. It stands in the cemetery of the village of the same name, some 6 miles from Chani Avlonariou.

After returning to Chani Avlonariou, you can proceed along the main road and then turn off toward Vryses. This route leads through an enchanting, hilly landscape where cypresses, olives, and fruit trees alternate with vineyards. Oleanders line the banks of numerous streams, most of which dry up in summer. Planes and poplars grow next to weathered stone bridges. From here you can move on to Kymi. Kymi is the only harbor on the otherwise steep east coast that permits ship connections between Euboea and the Sporades. Ancient Kymi was significant to world history: through its ancient colonies in Sicily and southern Italy, its alphabet, in Chalcidian form, and Greek culture in general were disseminated in the West. The area around Kymi is famous today for its fossils, shells, plants, insects and leaves from the Tertiary period.

Not all the routes into the interior from the main roads are pleasing to the eye. Near Aliveri and Mantoudi, the visitor cannot help feeling depressed at the sight of whole mountains eroded through mining and at the clouds of cement dust that blow across the countryside from Chalcis.

In the small fishing harbor of Amarynthos (Kato Vatheia), which is crowded

Chalcis and the Strait of Euripos: drawing by S. Pomardi, 1819.

in summer, fresh fish is available from spring until fall. These fish are not the noble varieties preferred by connoisseurs, but there are plenty of delectable fish such as whitebait and fresh sardines. Here, fresh fish is a staple culinary item, unlike many of the other islands, where everything the fleet catches is shipped off to Athens, or frozen and exported abroad.

From Amarynthos, you can take a meandering country road out to the isolated monastery of Aghios Nikolaos, which stands on a slope of Mount Serbouni. From this spot, there is a spectacular view out across land and sea. The exterior of the exquisite monastery church is decorated with colorful glazed tiles. Inside the church, there are interesting frescos painted in 1555–1565.

From Eretria, where several Greeks, especially artists, have built summer houses, it is worth a trip inland to see the ancient theater. Unlike other Greek theaters, this one has vaulted underground corridors

Chalcis (Negroponte). Engraving by P. Coronelli, 1686.

leading up to the stage, from which the players—primarily those portraying figures from Hades—could climb up onto the stage. Eretria is the most important archeological site on Euboea (see p. 349). In recent years, a number of goldsmiths' workshops dating from about 700 B.C. were unearthed here. The temple of Apollo in Eretria housed the pediment sculpture of Theseus ravishing the Amazon Antiope—a masterpiece of sculpture from 520 B.C. that makes a trip to Euboea worthwhile even if you are not a connoisseur or art historian. The way Theseus lifts Antiope onto his chariot suggests not so much an abduction as an embrace; you can almost feel the warmth of the couple's skin and feel their

breath. The pair form an integral whole, as if they had always belonged together.

EUBOEA IS A SAMPLER ILLUSTRATING THE EXTRAordinary diversity of the Greek landscape: steep rocky cliffs in the east and south; pine forests in the north; and, in the central section, gentle meadows, cornfields, and deciduous trees. Until quite recently, the landscape of Achmet-Agha (now renamed Prokopian) brought to mind the Turks who succeeded the Venetians as rulers of Euboea. Turkish landowners developed Achmet-Agha and planted the land with their favorite flowers and trees: palms, cypresses, planes, tulips, roses, and lilies. An ingenious irrigation system even permitted them to have vast expanses of lawns.

Only the Lelantine Plain, between Chalcis and Eretria, is blessed with exceptionally fertile soil. Elsewhere, the high mountain ranges leave little room for agriculture.

In southern Euboea there is only one safe harbor, Karystos. Behind it stands the imposing Venetian fortress of Castel Rosso ("Red Castle") at the foot of Mount Ochi; it is from the upper part of this mountain that the famous green-veined marble is quarried.

At the southern tip of the island stands the cape known in antiquity as Caphareus ("the swallower"). Even today, sailors fear it because of its stormy sea here. It is called by its medieval name, Cavo d'Oro ("cape of gold"); it is believed that the waves washed ashore gold from nearby shipwrecks.

The Swiss archeologist P. Ducrey dug up a private residence of the Classical age, with magnificent mosaic floors made of red, black, yellow, and white pebbles depicting mythological themes and floral patterns. An extremely interesting building was discovered in Lefkandi in 1981. It dates from the tenth century B.C. and is 164 feet long and 32 feet wide. Scholars still do not know what its function was. Learning more about this structure is important because it represents a style of architecture not common in ancient Greece until some three centuries later. Inside the building, among other things, female skeletons with gold jewelry and even a piece of very ancient cloth were found.

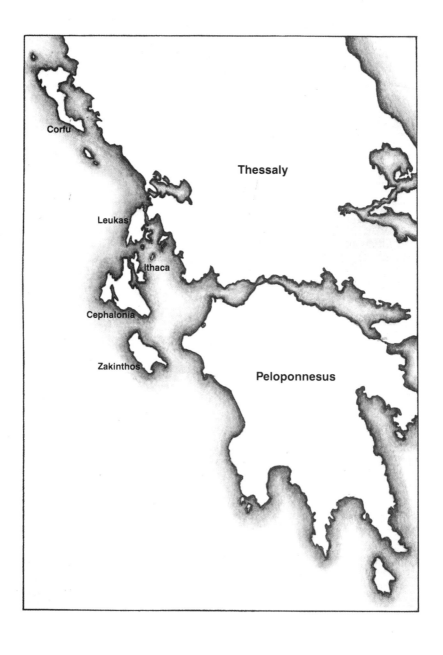

THE IONIAN ISLANDS

CORFU (KERKYRA)

THE LANDSCAPE OF CRESCENT-SHAPED CORFU (Kerkyra in Greek and Corcyra in Classical times) differs drastically from that of the mainland opposite. The northwest part of Greece, Epirus, rises like a steep wall from the Ionian Sea, and its few villages cling to the slopes for dear life; this heroic terrain has stamped the character of its people. Corfu, on the other hand, is a chain of softly rolling hills covered with thousands of olive trees and cypresses and broken by forested bays. Only the two bare peaks of Mount Pantokrator evoke even a remote resemblance to the Epirotic coast. Amid the forests of olive and cypress trees, countless wild plants, some of them quite rare, bloom throughout the year and transport the hiker into a state of euphoria. The Corfiot poet Mavilis wrote that the stranger who once drinks from the Kardaki spring will never return home.

The Corfiot speaks with a melodious voice, has an even temper, and has acquired a certain worldliness as the result of Western European influence. While the rest of Greece groaned beneath the Turkish yoke for centuries, Corfu and the other Ionian Islands were ruled by Westerners.

While the foreign occupation powers did not mingle with the local inhabitants, their influence is still evident everywhere even today. Their greatest services were to protect the Ionian Islands from Eastern conquerors and to provide gifted island children with the opportunity to study in Western Europe and apply the knowledge gained there in their homeland on their return.

Fortresses, palaces, and city and country villas have been built in a more or less Western European style. Ancient and medieval monuments are scarce on Corfu because it was repeatedly destroyed through the centuries.

For Homer, Corfu was a kind of paradise, the island of the Phaeacians blessed with all of the treasures of life, the Scheria of the *Odyssey*. Homer's description of the island has tempted archeologists to look for evidence of a Mycenaean empire on Corfu. But here, unlike at Troy and Mycenae, the archeologists' hopes were not fulfilled. They have sought the splendid palace of Alcinous in vain, and they will probably never find it.

Prehistoric settlements uncovered on

The island of Corfu.

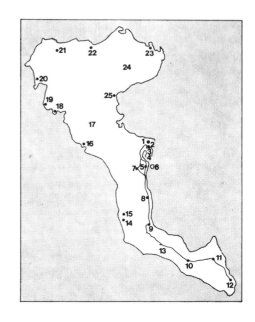

the west coast near Kephali, Aphiona, and Ermones lead us to presume that at that time the inhabitants lived in a closed agricultural society and maintained few contacts with the Mycenaean cultural centers of southern Greece. Instead, they traded with the people of Epirus, to whom they were related.

Almost nothing is known of Corfu's entry from mythical into historical times. A report from early history relates that the Eretrians first colonized Corfu, but archeological investigation has failed to substantiate this. The proofs of a somewhat later Corinthian settlement are much clearer. In 734 B.C., the Corinthians drove out the Eretrians and settled permanently. At that time, both the city and the island were called Corcyra. The Corinthians used the island as a base for their trading ships, which would set off across the Ionian Sea for Italy. Thanks to sea trade, Corcyra de-

veloped rapidly into a position of power, so it ultimately dared to break away from mighty Corinth. Thucydides reported that the first known sea battle took place in 664 B.C. between the fleets of the Corinthians and the Corcyrans. The latter emerged victorious and henceforth ruled the Adriatic

Sea. Common interests, nonetheless, so closely linked the island to Corinth that they later united in founding colonies on the Illyrian coast.

After Periander became the tyrant of Corinth in 620 B.C. and led his city-state to the pinnacle of political and economic power, the independence of Corcyra was a major irritant to him. He subjugated the island again and incorporated it temporarily into the Corinthian empire. The most important temples and public buildings on Corcyra were constructed during this phase of Corinthian rule. The death of Periander in 580 B.C. gave the Corcyrans the opportunity to shake off the Corinthian yoke, however, and now the island sought new partners—turning, among others, to Athens, which was then eager to break the trading monopoly of Corinth in the western Mediterranean.

During the Persian Wars, Corcyra dispatched its mighty fleet to aid the Greeks in 480 B.C., but it did not take part in the battle of Salamis. The other Greek city-states always condemned the isolation of the Corcyrans, and the Corinthians, who felt like abandoned protectors, made the most of this general censure. Ultimately, a quarrel over their common colony of Epidamnus led to open war between Corcyra and Corinth. The victory of the Corcyrans near Actium in 435 B.C. was a heavy blow for Corinth, which began to prepare to retaliate. This time, Corcyra asked Athens for help, but Corinth was victorious, primarily because of internal political disagreement among the Corcyrans. Their aristocratic party supported Corinth and the Peloponnesian League, but their democratic party preferred Athens. This party struggle was dramatically described by Thucydides.

Only in about 400 B.C. did Corcyra begin to recover from its bloody civil war. Then, as soon as it joined the Second Attic League in 375 B.C., it found itself involved in new warlike adventures. Once Macedonian rule began, the island lost its power for good, becoming only a naval base for whoever happened to command the western Mediterranean: it belonged to Agathocles, the king of Syracuse, then to the Macedonian king Demetrius, and later still to Pyrrhus of Epirus. Finally, in 229 B.C., it was plundered by Illyrian pirates. The Corcyrans then turned to Rome for help, and Rome took advantage of this to establish itself on the east coast of the Adriatic.

Distant view of Corfu from Christopher Wordsworth's Greece, *1844.*

Corcyra made no trouble for Rome as a province, and it enjoyed the Romans' protection until 31 B.C., when the island was entangled in the Roman civil war between Octavian (who later became Augustus) and Antony. Corcyra had the misfortune of aiding Antony. Before the great battle at Actium, Octavian's brother-in-law, Agrippa, sent troops to devastate the island. Most of the ancient buildings were leveled, and Corcyra required more than two centuries, until roughly 200 A.D., to recover. A second major city on Corcyra at that time was Cassiope, in the northeast.

Two pupils of the apostle Paul, Jason and Sosipater, brought Christianity to the island. Here, as everywhere in Greece, the first converts suffered persecution.

At the beginning of the fifth century A.D., the Byzantine emperor commanded that all the heathen cult shrines and the buildings of the ancient agora be torn down so that the stones could be used to build an imposing five-aisle basilica. The ruins of this church can be seen in what is now known as Palaiopolis; an epigram on the triumph of Christianity is legible on its entrance door. A century and a half later, this Early Christian center was sacked by the Goths. For centuries, the city had survived on the same site as in antiquity. But before the eleventh century, some of its inhabitants moved north, to the rocky peninsula that lies beyond the bay of Garitsa. On this natural fortress, protected by its cliffs, the people constructed a secure complex of bulwarks and took refuge against attacks by the Normans. In the later Middle Ages, the site was known as the Fortezza Vecchia; today, it is called Palaio Phrourio.

In 1203, the Crusaders' fleet dropped anchor in the waters below this fortress before sailing on to Constantinople. When the Latins conquered the Byzantine Empire in the following year, Corfu was first made dependent on the despot of Epirus (1210–1259), then on the Venetians (1259–1267), and then on the counts of Anjou (1267–1386). Then the Venetians regained control and kept a firm grip on Corfu from 1386 to 1797. Of all the foreigners who occupied the island, they had the most lasting influence. Twice, they protected Corfu from the Turks.

The Venetian Empire was dissolved by the Treaty of Campoformio, and Corfu came under French rule. The French stayed only a short time. Russians and Turks conquered the island in 1800 and formed the so-called state of the Seven Islands (Eptanissos Politeia), which was placed under Russian protection. This was the first modern Greek state with local self-government. (At this time, Count Kapodistrias was growing up on Corfu. He became a great Greek diplomat who played a prominent role in post-Napoleonic Europe, serving as foreign minister to the czar and, in 1827, the first governor of free Greece. The patrician house in which he was born was restored between 1977 and 1979. It now houses the College of Translation.) The Treaty of Tilsit (1807) once more awarded the Ionian Islands to France, but in the Treaty of Paris they were transferred to the British, who agreed that the Ionian state should have a legislature in its capital of Corfu. Lord Guilford, an English philhellene, founded a cultural center and university, the Ionian Academy, which people now are hoping to revive. Increasingly, the Corfiots pressed for union with Greece, and Queen Victoria granted their request in 1864, giving the Ionian Islands to the Greek nation. In World War II, Corfu was repeatedly bombarded. Though many of its buildings were destroyed, most of the old quarters of the capital survived.

The Palaio Phrourio: drawing by C. F. Sargent, 1844.

The two landmarks of the city of Kerkyra are the medieval Palaio Phrourio and the newer fortress above the harbor. The restoration of the former English barracks, from the nineteenth century, inside Palaio Phrourio was completed in the summer of 1982. These now house documents relating to the history of the island.

In 1979, thirteen icons by the priest-painter Emanuel Tsanes were discovered on the neglected choir screen of the church of St. George inside the old fortress.

This find caused quite a sensation. Tsanes fled Crete and the Turks in the seventeenth century, stopping on Corfu from 1646 to 1655 on his way to Western Europe. It was he who brought the Cretan icon style to the island. During his stay on Corfu, Tsanes painted icons for the choir screens of the churches of St. Spyridon and Sts. Jason and Sosipater. The ones from St. Spyridon's were moved to St. George's in the nineteenth century and then completely forgotten. These thirteen masterpieces were cleaned and restored in 1980. Against gold backgrounds, they depict among other things a stern Christ in a blood-red robe; Salome looking like an angel; angels who look like Tritons; a splendid baptism of Christ in the Jordan; and apostles with ancient Grecian features.

In front of Palaio Phrourio stretches the esplanade, a generous square. On the north side of this square stands the impressive palace built by the architect George Whitmore for Sir Thomas Maitland, the English Lord High Commissioner, in 1816. It boasts a Doric portico and two side wings in which are housed the museums of Byzantine and East Asian art. In the back galleries, there is also a fine array of Christian art: Early Christian mosaic floors, as well as frescos and icons typical of the Ionian Islands from the seventeenth to the nineteenth centuries. New acquisitions are constantly being added from various Corfiot churches, including icons by the Cretan painters Michael Damaskinos and Emanuel Tsanes.

To the west, the old town and its classical buildings stand, some of which are adorned with arcades on the ground floor. Proceeding farther into the old town, you pass through narrow alleys, lined with Italianate houses with wrought-iron balconies, to reach shady squares where you can listen to the Corfiots conversing in their melodious local dialect.

The patron saint of the island is the miracle-working Aghios Spyridon, whose relics were brought from Constantinople and placed in a silver shrine in Kerkyra. Four times a year, this shrine is carried through the city in a ceremonial procession. The relics of the Byzantine empress Theodora, who gave permission to put the icons back in their places after the Iconoclasts had demanded their removal, are preserved in the

noteworthy Metropolitan church. In countless smaller churches can be found lovely marble and wooden choir screens and icons. The Catholic cathedral, with its classical sixteenth-century façade, stands on the Town Hall square. The Town Hall, next to it, dates from the seventeenth century and is well worth visiting; it is a splendid Venetian building in which the Theater

San Giacomo was once housed. A bust of the Venetian general Morosini stands on its east wall surrounded by plump-cheeked angels. A few steps farther along, you come to the former palace of the Catholic archbishop from the eighteenth century. This edifice is now occupied by the Bank of Greece.

The old city flows imperceptibly into the new. The loveliest boulevard to stroll on here is the shoreline street of Garitsa, where high-rise buildings have unfortunately replaced many of the older classical ones. However, at the last moment before its collapse, the charming house of the scholar Thomas Flagginis, which stands on this promenade, was saved. Flagginis was born here in the seventeenth century. He

Corfu: drawing by W. Purser, c. 1844.

studied in Padua and then went to Venice, where he distinguished himself as a lawyer. In 1644, he founded a school where for centuries poor Greek children were taught in their mother tongue. Today the school is known as the Greek Institute of Venice for Byzantine and Post-Byzantine Scholarship.

In restoring the Flagginis house on Corfu, a project of the venerable literary society Anagnostiki Etaireia, drawings and paintings by the important Corfiot painters Yalinas and Ventouras were consulted. In 1982, a branch of the Goulandris Natural History Museum was opened in the house. Flora, fauna, and minerals from the Ionian Islands and the west coast of Greece are displayed here.

In the garden of the police station in Garitsa, you can visit the round grave of Menecrates, with an inscription from the sixth century B.C. The Archeological Museum is nearby. The monumental tomb lion in this museum (late seventh century B.C.) originally stood in an Archaic cemetery. It is distinguished by uncommon strength and presence. Also on display are terracottas, also from the seventh century B.C. These came from a temple that once stood in what is now the park of Mon Repos. The lions' heads from this temple were gargoyles, while slabs bearing the heads of women and gorgons adorned the eaves. A wealth of small art objects were votive gifts to the goddess worshipped here, probably Hera.

In the large hall of the museum is the famous west pediment from the temple of Artemis (early sixth century B.C.) near the Aghioi Theodoroi monastery. It is most impressive. Its gorgon, nearly 10 feet tall, is flanked by panthers, with mythological representations in the corners. This magnificent pediment is one of the best-preserved examples of Greek Archaic art, a testament to the talent of the early Greek

sculptors. Corfiot sculpture also produced masterpieces in Late Archaic times—for example, a pediment, discovered in 1974, that depicts Dionysus carousing with a youth.

As mentioned above, the ancient city of Corcyra lay to the south of the present-day one, covering the entire peninsula of Analypsis, from the end of Garitsa to Kanoni, whose name comes from the Russian cannon that still stands there. Here, you can see

Convent on Corfu: from Christopher Wordsworth's Greece, 1844.

ruins from Archaic until Roman times: a tower (Nerantzida) from the Classical period stands close to the Orthodox cemetery near the airport; an altar and sections of the temple of Artemis remain. Next to the monastery of Aghioi Theodoroi, in front of the entrance to Mon Repos, there are fragments of the basilica of Palaiopolis (early fifth century A.D.), erected by Bishop Jovianos. Portions of its mosaic floors are in the Municipal Palace Museum. This church was remodeled in the Middle Ages; it now has only one of its original five naves.

In the park of Mon Repos, part of which lies on the site of the ancient acropolis, two temples have been excavated. The larger of the two was probably dedicated to Hera; only scant remains were discovered *in situ.* The ruins of the second, on the eastern edge of the park, near the Kardaki spring (circa 500 B.C.), are still in relatively good condition; it is the best-preserved temple on Corfu.

The park of Mon Repos was laid out in the English style by the English Lord High Commissioner Sir Frederick Adam in the 1820s. Here, you can stroll through a wood where the variety of trees produces a symphony in green. The small classical palace was also built by Adam; it and the park belonged to the Greek royal family until the fall of the monarchy.

Walking northward from Mon Repos, you soon arrive at the lovely Byzantine church of Sts. Jason and Sosipater (eleventh century). It is composed for the most part of ancient building material and stands at the edge of the former harbor, now silted up, which bore the name of the mythical king Alcinous.

If you turn southward from Mon Repos, you come to the peninsula of Kanoni. Modern high-rise hotels have destroyed the charm of the idyllic area around Kanoni. Nevertheless, it is still pleasant to walk along the sea to visit the small Vlacherna monastery or to take a boat to the world-famous, cypress-covered islet of Pontikonisi, the "mouse island." A swampy area near the sea—in antiquity, this was one of Kerkyra's two harbors (Hyllaikos Limen)—has been partially drained and made into an airport.

Driving south along the east coast, you come to the Achilleion palace, which is today a casino. The palace was built for Empress Elisabeth II of Austria in 1890, after plans by the Italian Cavaliere Carito. It is in the depths of a charming park. The empress moved here after the tragedy of Mayerling, hoping to find solace following the death of her son. She named her refuge after the mythical hero Achilles and had a marble statue of this personage, fatally wounded before Troy, erected in the park. Kaiser Wilhelm II of Germany bought the

Odysseus: an ancient statue.

Achilleion from Elisabeth in 1908, and he donated an additional colossal Achilles statue in bronze.

On the west coast, nearly 14 miles west of the capital of Corfu, is the famous Palaiokastritsa, where, according to the French scholar Victor Bérard, we should expect to find the legendary land of the Phaeacians. Although archeological investigation has failed to confirm his suspicion, this enchanting landscape could easily convince the visitor that Homer's paradise was indeed here.

To become acquainted with the typical landscape of Corfu, it is best to go hiking in the center of the island. On these gently rolling hills is found a wealth of thriving plants that are quite rare elsewhere in Greece.

The broad plain known as Livadi tou Ropa is a dried-up lake. Again according to Bérard, the nearby bay of Ermones is the place where Odysseus landed after his return from Troy and met Nausicaa. The 2,985-foot peak of Mount Pantokrator, named after the monastery built in 1347 by the count of Anjou, dominates the northern part of the island. On the western slope of this massif, on a projecting cliff above the sea, stands the ruined monastery of Angelokastro. This foundation of the despot of Epirus was established on a spot naturally fortified by the surrounding cliffs. The north slope of the mountain descends more gradually to a number of bays with fine beaches. The bay of Roda was inhabited in antiquity; there are remains here of a temple from the fifth century B.C. Above the fishing village of Kassiopi lies a fortress of the same name that was rebuilt and expanded in the Middle Ages.

Unlike the north, the southern part of the island tends to be flat. There are not only sand beaches but even dunes around the lagoon of Korrisia. It is here that you come upon a fairly large village, Lefkimmi; its river is wide enough for sailboats.

In the west, near the source of the Mesonghi River, which is now only a swamp overgrown with reeds, stands the Byzantine fortress of Gardiki, partially constructed of ancient building materials. The Romans left architectural monuments everywhere along the west coast. There are surviving structures on the Kapsokavadi estate, for example, and in Moraitika there are remnants of a complex of baths.

Looking down on Corfu from an airplane, you get the impression of uninterrupted forest. In addition to the native Aleppo pines and beach pines, the ancients especially cultivated olives and grapes, boasting of an especially good local wine *(anthosmia)*. The Venetians encouraged the production of olives, and they paid 1,200 ducats for each hundred new plantings. As a result, the Corfiots neglected their vineyards and their pine forests. These olive trees are a feast for the eye, even though they no longer produce oil of competitive quality.

LEUKAS (LEFKADA)

LEUKAS IS LINKED BY LEGEND TO THE POETESS Sappho, who supposedly came here from Lesbos in the sixth century B.C. to fling herself into the sea for love. She plunged from the steep white cliffs of Levkadas, or as the natives call them today Kavos tis Kyras ("cliff of the Lady"), because her lover, Phaon, had left her. Leukas is associated with two other names in Greek literary history: it is the birthplace of the poets Valaoritis and Sikelianos.

Its landscape is a mixture of long sandy beaches, village squares shaded by plane trees, plains covered with olive and lemon orchards, steep mountains, and rugged cliffs. Architectural monuments preserve

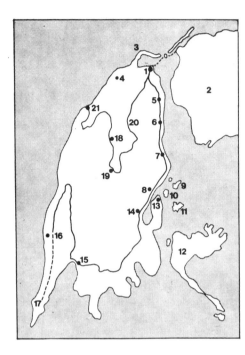

The island of Leukas.

1. Chora (Leukas)
2. Acarnania
3. Cape Giza
4. Phaneromeni monastery
5. Karyotes
6. Lyghia
7. Nikiana
8. Nydri
9. Island of Sparti
10. Island of Madouri
11. Island of Skorpios
12. Island of Meganissi
13. Cape Aghia Kyriaki
14. Vlychou
15. Vassiliki
16. Athani
17. Cape Leukadas
18. Karya
19. Englouvi
20. Sfakiotes
21. Aghios Nikitas

the memory of conquerors who fell on Leukas from all directions. Other ruined structures prevent the people from fully forgetting the devastation that earthquakes have caused here.

The first traces of human habitation on the island date from the early Neolithic period. Stone Age people lived in caves here. From the Mycenaean period, the finds are more extensive and more revealing. Leukas was colonized by Corinthians in the seventh century B.C. Strabo relates that Leukas was originally a mainland peninsula, but the Corinthians cut a canal through the isthmus, making the peninsula into an island. Thanks to this canal, the sea route to the harbors of Epirus and the Corinthian colonies was shortened considerably. Trade flourished, and the island's population rose to some 20,000. In the fifth centu-

ry B.C., Leukadians fought alongside the Greeks in their struggle against the Persians, and it sent ships to Salamis and troops to Plataeai. During the Peloponnesian War, it supported Corinth and Sparta. Philip II of Macedonia took over the island in the fourth century B.C., and after the death of Alexander the Great it passed from hand to hand. At the end of the period of the Diadochi, it was conquered by Pyrrhus of Epirus. In 197 B.C., it was taken by the Romans after a siege. After the sea battle at Actium, Leukas sank into obscurity.

Normans and Pisans later plundered the island, and, in 1293, the despot of Epirus, Nicephorus I, included it in his daughter's dowry when she wed Giovanni Orsini. Worst of all of the island's rulers were the counts of Anjou, who arrived at the beginning of the fourteenth century, stayed for sixty years, and cruelly oppressed the people. At last the Leukadians summoned the strength for a revolt, which is the subject of the epic poem *Photeinos* by Aristotelis Valaoritis.

In 1479, the Turks came; in 1684, the Venetians. The population shrank from 25,000 to only 9,000 as a result of plundering, confiscation, banishment, and mismanagement. The suffering of the people became virtually unendurable when epidemics of plague appeared along with earthquakes.

Under Venetian rule, Leukas was administered along with the six other Ionian Islands. At that time, the culture of the island split in two. On the one hand, there arose a kind of baroque city architecture and an urbane, almost Italian society; even the island's language and literature took on a Venetian color. On the other hand, the villages clung to their purely Greek life style, their linguistic and musical traditions. The small village churches did not alter their severe old icons and wall frescos, which derived from the traditions of Byzantium. Greeks can still hear the differences between the city and village dialects. In 1797 Leukas fell to the French, and finally, in 1815, to the British. The British stayed until 1864, when Leukas was united with the rest of Greece.

TO GET TO LEUKAS, YOU MUST DRIVE FROM ATHens via Corinth, Rion, Antirion, Agrinion, Amphilochia, and Vonitza (248 miles). You encounter the medieval aspect of the island immediately on arrival in Porthmeio, on the above-mentioned canal, where the fortress of Santa Maura looms. This structure was built by Giovanni Orsini in 1300 on a small island in a lagoon. It took its name from the church that the counts of Anjou had erected to St. Maura. The new town developed around the castle, extending closer to the sea. At that time, the main settlement and the entire island were renamed Santa Maura.

A ferry that can transport one bus and four small cars takes you across the narrow channel. Until only a few years ago, this ferry was drawn across by a pulley system; its crank was turned by a young woman. She has since grown into one of the island's characters, and she now operates an electrical mechanism that draws the ferry back and forth.

The town of Leukas dates from the Venetian period and lies on the strait opposite Acarnania, on the mainland. At first glance, it seems a melancholy place. The only true street leads past the churches of Aghios Spiridon and Aghios Minas to the main square and marketplace. The buildings are relatively unsturdy, especially their second stories of wood, occasionally covered with painted tin. Blocks of olive wood, cut from the virtually indestructible heart of the tree, strengthen the joints where two walls are fitted together. In the marketplace, it is possible to see the women in their lovely traditional costumes, which are here worn considerably more often in everyday life than in the rest of Greece. The young girls cover their deeply cut blouses with a triangular cloth. They wear finely pleated skirts of burgundy, forest green, or indigo blue, while the older women dress completely in black or brown cotton. The erect posture of all of these women, young and old, is noticeable; they carry jugs of water, wine, and oil on their heads and have had to adopt a rhythmic stride.

The most interesting of the town's buildings are the eighteenth-century churches, built during a period of religious freedom and economic and cultural prosperity on Leukas. Though they are influenced in style by the Italian baroque, neither the façades nor the interiors of these churches are overladen with ornament. They convey an overall impression of greater simplicity and severity than the Western baroque churches do. The churches of Leukas resemble those on Zakinthos; some of them were built by architects from Zakinthos, and the others by local builders who had studied the plans and ornamental motifs of structures on Zakinthos. The most interesting architectural element in each church is the iconostasis. In the villages, these are constructed of plain masonry, while in the city churches they are made of carved wood and painted gold. The sanctuary screen in the Aghios Minas church, from 1707, is executed in beautiful relief and is a masterpiece of Ionian carving. The icons are incorporated into the wall in such a way that they form a harmonious unity. On the central square of Leukas, there is another interesting church with a baroque iconostasis. It was dedicated to St. Spiridon in 1685 and remodeled in the late eighteenth century. Also worth seeing is the Pantokrator church on the main street; it boasts a richly decorated stone façade. In the small cemetery garden behind this church, you can see the graves of Aristotelis Valaoritis, his ancestors, and members of other patrician families. Strolling the alleyways of the town, you discover a number of other churches as well.

NORTH OF THE TOWN, AFTER WALKING ALONG A country road lined with olive groves, you come upon the small church of Ai-Ioannis-Antsouis, which was commissioned by the counts of Anjou in the fourteenth century. From here, the road leads down to the sea and one of the island's loveliest beaches, made up of tiny pebbles. In the background are ruined windmills, set against a cloud-less sky. It was here, in 1810, that Theodoros Kolokotronis and other Greeks who later distinguished themselves in the wars of liberation against the Turks fought for the English against the French, who then occupied the island. At the foot of the cliff called Ai-Ioannis, there are springs that bubble up below the surface of the sea and make the water temperature so cold that few like to swim here. The women from the nearby villages use the springs for washing, spreading their laundry on the gravel beach to dry.

Before Ai-Ioannis, a path leads from the road toward the Phaneromeni monastery. From this monastery, you have a splendid view of the island and the sea: extensive olive groves, the town, the lagoon, and the steep mountains of Epirus in the background. On the horizon to the west lie the islands of Paxoi and Corfu.

Another road leads southward from the main town into a serene and charming world. The sea lies to the left, and on the right you pass friendly villages with gardens full of flowers. Along this road you come to the lovely church of Panaghia Megalovrysiotissa, and shortly afterward you reach Kalligoni, where Nericus—capital of the island in prehistoric, Classical, and medieval times—lay on a flat-topped hill covered with olive trees. Among these trees you can see the ruins of the city. At the summit of the hill lay an acropolis whose Cyclopean walls are still partially visible. There are also cisterns, portions of an ancient aqueduct, stairs cut into the bedrock, and remains of later walls. A small Hellenistic theater is barely more than rubble.

Driving farther along the east coast road, you pass the villages of Karyotes and Lyghia, where fishermen draw their boats onto the beach—bright spots of color in the landscape. Off the coast of the lively harbor village of Nydri lie a whole row of islets that you can visit by motorboat: the round rock of Chelonaki, overgrown with wild olive trees; Madouri, which belonged to Valaoritis; Skorpios, the property of the famous Onassis family; and, farther into the open sea, Meganissi, known to the ancients as Taphos.

Across from Madouri, on the east coast of Leukas, lies Cape Aghia Kyriaki. A church of the same name leans against its cliffs. It is built on top of the ruins of an ancient temple of the Nymphs. From here, a path leads to the grave of the German archeologist Wilhelm Dörpfeld, who was convinced that Leukas—not Ithaca—was the home of the famous Odysseus.

In the Choirospilla ("pigs' cave"), near the village of Evgiros, Dörpfeld discovered traces from the Neolithic period, and on the plain of Nydri he uncovered tools, vessels, and small objects from Mycenaean times. But the results of Dörpfeld's excavation did not confirm his theory. Old people on Leukas still remember the German archeologist and his daily hikes, on which he investigated every last cranny of the island. They proudly recall his love for Leukas and its inhabitants. An obelisk, a monument to this scholar, has been erected on the summit of Aghia Kyriaki. All of the objects unearthed by Dörpfeld will eventually be

Santa Maura (Leukas): drawing from Christopher Wordsworth's Greece, *1844.*

displayed, along with some interesting Late Byzantine icons, in a museum to be built in Leukas.

A visit to the interior of the island and its sleepy mountain villages is worthwhile. Along the road leading from the capital to the largest of these villages, Karya, are the tiny villages called the Sfakiotes, whose inhabitants rebelled against Gratianos Ziorzos, the cruelest of the regents from the Anjou period, and also fought against the English in 1819. On the village square of Karya, you can drink ouzo in the shade of ancient plane trees; those who drive on to the village of Englouvi can feast on an excellent dish made of lentils.

Another outing takes you along the west coast from Athani to Cape Leukadas. This lonely landscape with its forested bays will soon be more accessible; a new road is being built. Votive gifts and especially coins reveal that the faithful came from all over Greece—even from Antioch, Smyrna, Cyzicus, and Colophon—to pay homage to the Leukadian Apollo. On the steep slope you can still make out the foundations of that temple, and shards lie between the stones. Climbing higher, you reach the famous cliff where Sappho plunged into the sea. In post-Classical centuries, incidentally, her example was frequently followed by unhappy lovers. The view from this cliff is breathtaking; the wall of the cliff falls nearly vertically into the dark blue sea.

In antiquity, those who had been condemned to death were thrown into the sea during festivals of Apollo. Of course, they could hope that they might survive with the god's help, especially because something resembling wings was probably tied around their shoulders to lessen the impact when they hit the surface of the water. It is also related that the inhabitants of the city of Leukas annually pushed a criminal off the cliffs. They would tie live birds to him to slow his fall; below, boats were waiting to retrieve him and take him away to another area.

Cape Leukadas (Kavos tis Kyras) embodies the hard and heroic character of Leukas, as opposed to the romantic charm of Madouri and the melancholy landscape of the lagoon. This is the Leukas of the poets who have sung of their homeland with such passion and the Leukas of the simple people who have stood up to fate so courageously. This is the Leukas of ancient myth, a symbol for the present-day islanders.

*I*THACA

WHEN YOUR SHIP ENTERS THE FJORDLIKE BAY OF Vathy, the capital of Ithaca, you cannot help thinking of heroic, adventurous, and tragic Homeric legends. Who could fail to be reminded here of the homesickness, the perseverance, and the cleverness of Odysseus, the patience and devotion of Penelope, or the gall of Penelope's suitors? A rich body of myth rests in the simple landscape of Ithaca, which is treeless in the south but covered by olive groves and vineyards in the north.

Ithaca, known in the local dialect as Thiaki, lies only 2 nautical miles east of the

Cephalonian peninsula of Erissos. The bay of Vathy gives Ithaca the form of a figure eight; a mountainous, slender isthmus called the Aëtos ("eagle") connects the southern and northern parts of the island. A small acropolis, which was excavated by the German archeologist Heinrich Schliemann, crowns one of the mountains and is referred to by the inhabitants as the Fortress of Odysseus (see map, p. 375).

An outing southward from Vathy to the ancient village of Perachori is recommended. Another paved road from Vathy leads north across the Aëtos. At one intersection, another road branches from it and snakes along the west coast past the picturesque villages of Ai Ioannis and Levki, while the main road continues inland along the foot of Mount Neritos (2,624 feet), past the village of Anoghi, and ends at Stavros. This route is interesting because you can make a short detour to the Panaghia monastery in Kathara, the most important religious center on the island. From Stavros, you pass lush olive groves on the way down to the sea at either the bay of Aphales in the north or the fishing villages of Frikes and Kioni in the east.

THE BRITISH, WHO GOVERNED ITHACA AND THE other Ionian Islands in the mid-nineteenth century, were the first excavators; more

The islands of Ithaca and Cephalonia.

1. *Vathy (Ithaca)*
2. *Isthmus of Aëtos*
3. *Anoghi*
4. *Stavros*
5. *Polio*
6. *Kathara monastery*
7. *Sami*
8. *Melissani*
9. *Aghia Ephimia*
10. *Drogharati*
11. *Tsarkassianos*
12. *Dighaleto*
13. *Poros*
14. *Palaiokastro*
15. *Aghios Ghiorghios*
16. *Kateliou*
17. *Mavrata*
18. *Arakli*
19. *Aghios Gherasimos*
20. *Mount Ainos (5,314 feet)*
21. *Aghios Andreas*
22. *Livathou*
23. *Kastro*
24. *Kokkolata*
25. *Krane*
26. *Minyas*
27. *Lakkithra*
28. *Metaxata*
29. *Kalligata*
30. *Arghostoli*
31. *Koutavos*
32. *Lixouri*
33. *Pale*
34. *Kipouria monastery*
35. *Kontojennada*
36. *Assos*
37. *Fiskardo*

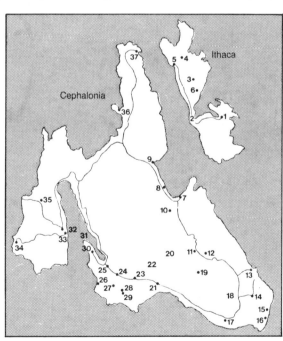

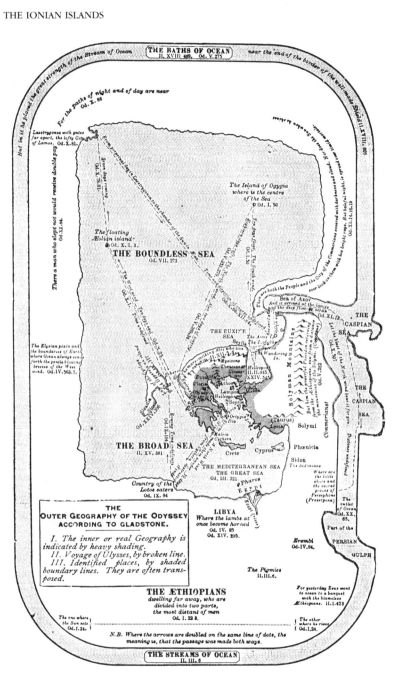

Route of Odysseus: map c. 1911.

precisely, they were treasure seekers. Splendid gold jewelry, silver vessels, and bronze objects from Ithaca now stand in the British Museum in London. These Classical and Hellenistic finds came from tombs below the acropolis.

Great interest in Homer's *Odyssey* led countless scholars to swarm across the island with the epic in hand, rather arbitrarily naming certain spots the stall of Eumaeus, palace of Odysseus, estate of Laertes, or the Arethusan spring. Other researchers, pointing to various obscurities in the *Odyssey*, explained that Ithaca could not have been Odysseus's homeland and raced off with their shovels to other islands. Among these were the German archeologist Wilhelm Dörpfeld who preferred Leukas, the Dutchman A.E.H. Goekoop who chose Cephalonia, and a Greek who insisted that Odysseus's home was on the small island of Paxos, near Corfu.

Only the British remained convinced that Ithaca was the island Homer had in mind. They systematically investigated it between 1930 and 1940. Each year, a major dig took place under the direction of the archeologists Heurtley and Sylvia Benton (see also "Zakinthos," pp. 384–392), at first around Stavros and then on the Aëtos. The finds from these excavations happily survived the catastrophic earthquake of 1953 and may be seen in Stavros (Archeological Collection) and Vathy (the local museum).

The English excavations make it possible to reconstruct the history of the island. It appears that Ithaca was first settled in the pre-Helladic epoch, toward the end of the third millennium B.C. The remains of a settlement in Pelikata, near Stavros, are proof of this. The same area was also inhabited during the Middle Helladic epoch (first half of the second millennium B.C.). The settlers of that period had connections with nearby

The Cyclops and Odysseus's men.

Leukas, which then boasted the important trading center of Nydri (see "Leukas," pp. 368–374).

From Mycenaean times (second half of the second millennium B.C.), more definite information exists. Settlements have been found near Tris Langhades, not far from Stavros, in Pelikata, in the bay of Pole, and on the Aëtos. These remains, especially the rather uninspiring ceramics, would seem to contradict the portrait of a wealthy Ithaca that Homer presents in the *Odyssey*.

However, it is possible to demonstrate that a period of prosperity did begin on Ithaca after 1000 B.C. A large number of Corinthian ceramics with geometric designs was discovered on the Aëtos, and splendid tripods came to light in the small cave near Pole that was held to be the home of the nymphs in the *Odyssey*. The exquisite votive gifts from this cave are reminiscent of the gifts given to Odysseus by the Phaeacians when they set him down on the beach of his home island. There is no reason to expect Homer to have been a flawless geographer. In the third century B.C., Eratosthenes, who was the director of the library in Alexandria, maintained that it would be just as impossible to discover the precise locations from the voyage of Odysseus as to find the shoemaker who stitched the leather hose for the winds of Aeolus.

Ithaca seems to have been an important trading station for Greece's maritime city-states, notably Corinth, which, as early as the tenth century B.C., expanded its influence over the coasts of Acarnania and the Ionian Islands and traded with Sicily and southern Italy. Ionian seafarers returning home would tell the islanders about their experiences in the Aegean Islands and about the cities of Asia Minor. These stories and the old Mycenaean sagas were both used by Homer.

Finds from the sanctuary on the Aëtos attest to Ithaca's connections to countless countries in the Geometric and Archaic periods: bronze votive gifts from Thessaly and Macedonia, ivory seals from the East, clay vessels from Rhodes, Ionia, and Corinth. At this time, local pottery workshops developed; they produced carefully painted vases and vessels.

During the Classical and Hellenistic periods, Ithaca had one important acropolis on the Aëtos and another near present-day

The Bay of Vathy: drawing from Christopher Wordsworth's Greece, *1844.*

Aghios Athanasios, north of Stavros. Major portions of these fortifications, whose names are unknown, managed to survive the 1953 earthquake. Little is known of the deities who were worshipped on Ithaca. An inscription from the sixth century B.C. relates that the goddesses Athena Polias and Hera Teleia were worshipped near Stavros. The deity worshipped in the small temple and sanctuary in modern Aghios Ghiorghios, on the Aëtos, is unknown. Relief slabs support the assumption that the nymphs and Pan dominated this cult during the Hellenistic period; these slabs were discovered in Stavros.

A female mask, which is rather well preserved, also dates from this time. It was found in the cave near Pole, and carries a votive inscription to Odysseus. This small ceramic find, of little artistic importance, proves that, during the Hellenistic period, the people of Ithaca had no doubt that their island had been the home of Odysseus. It is obvious that Odysseus's memory survived in this cave, where the splendid tripods that have been associated with him were discovered.

During the Roman period, Ithaca shared the fate of the Ionian Islands. Presumably, the city of Vathy was founded then, or so some recently discovered graves suggest. There are no architectural monuments surviving from the Byzantine period. In the eleventh century, though, Anna Comnenus, the emperor's daughter and an important author, noted that there was a city on Ithaca. The Crusaders who ruled the island similarly left no traces. Ithaca later came under Venetian rule, was devastated by the Turks, and, by the beginning of the sixteenth century, was virtually desolate. Only pirates used the bay of Vathy as a base of operations. A century later, the Cephalonians settled on Ithaca and began to cultivate the land, which was too poor to support them. They began to seek their fortunes as seafarers and make their living abroad—much as the islanders do today. After being ruled briefly by the French at the beginning of the nineteenth century, the island was administered by Britain for fifty years until 1864, when Ithaca was ceded to Greece, along with the other Ionian Islands.

CEPHALONIA

IN ANTIQUITY, LEUKAS, ITHACA, CEPHALONIA, and Zakinthos—the chain of islands in the Ionian Sea, beyond the entrance to the Gulf of Corinth—were stopovers that broke up the long sea journey to wealthy southern Italy and Sicily. The largest of these islands is Cephalonia (see map, p. 375).

This island is dominated by Mount Ainos, which is 5,314 feet high and covered with forests of Cephalonian firs. But Cephalonia's landscape presents dramatic contrasts: deeply cut bays, steep cliffs in the west, narrow inland gorges, and subterranean caves reveal its volcanic origins. Mount Ainos separates the landscape into an eastern part, which surrounds the wide, natural

Odysseus and the Sirens:
an ancient vase-painting.

bay of Sami and Aghia Ephimia, and a western one, with extensive forests and plantings near Livathou and Kranaia. The fertile plain of Arakli in the south provides food for most of the residents. The section between Pylaros and Fiskardo in the north is extremely mountainous. In the west, the Paliki peninsula is quite distinct from the rest of the island. Cephalonia is a conglomerate of small, independent, and highly diverse units. Its fertility is attributable to its abundant rainfall, something quite rare in Greece.

Today, when you sail into the harbor of Sami on a ship from the mainland, you are immediately reminded of the catastrophic earthquake of 1953, for the white concrete buildings seem all too new. Viewed from the sea, the walls of the ancient acropolis stand to the left. In the vale of Sami lie the caves of Drogharati and Melissani; the latter is distinguished by the brilliant colors of its subterranean lake. On a tiny island in the middle of this lake some interesting clay slabs from the Hellenistic period were discovered. On them, a circle of nymphs is dancing to the music of a flute-playing Pan. These finds prove that votive gifts were brought to Pan and the nymphs here, as well as in the cave near the village of Dighaleto. The ancients had to climb down into the cave of Melissani from above, which must have been hazardous. The cave is now more accessible, and you can explore it by boat.

From Melissani a curving road leads up Mount Ainos. On top of this peak lies the monastery named for the patron saint of the island, Aghios Gerasimos. The Peloponnesian monk Gerasimos Notaras fought for the survival of the Greek Orthodox faith on Cephalonia in the sixteenth century, when it was ruled by the Venetians. For this reason, he was declared a saint by the Greek Orthodox church. He was just one of the figures who helped to sustain the morale of the inhabitants during the centuries of subjugation under the Venetians, Turks, French, and British.

Driving down the western slope of Mount Ainos from the monastery, you can enjoy a panorama of bays that cut deeply into the land. The town of Arghostoli is separated from Lixouri by a large gulf. Their separation is more than geographical; their inhabitants are constantly feuding and insulting or snubbing each other.

In modern Arghostoli, one sees rather tasteless concrete buildings that attempt to reproduce the traditional buildings destroyed by the earthquake. Thanks to the cultural interest and creative drive of the islanders, Arghostoli boasts the Historical Museum of the Korgialeneios Library, where you can admire, among other things, the choir screens and icons from destroyed churches. It also accommodates extensive historical archives. The Archeological Museum houses testaments to the ancient heritage of Cephalonia from prehistoric until Roman times.

HEADING EAST FROM ARGHOSTOLI, ONE FIRST

passes the remains of the ancient city of Krane, then proceeds inland through friendly villages before coming to the medieval fortress and town of Aghios Andreas, built atop a steep cliff. This was the administrative center of Byzantine Cephalonia. The imposing complex of fortifications, still visible today, was laid out by Italian rulers—the Orsini family (twelfth to fourteenth centuries), the Tocci (fourteenth to fifteenth centuries), and the Venetians (fifteenth to eighteenth centuries). Its walls and gateways summon up images not only of lost battles and devastation but also of the enduring strength of humankind.

From here, the road leads farther south toward the sea, through a garden landscape. It is possible to interrupt this journey near the village of Kalligata and see a gold-painted wooden choir screen from the eighteenth century in the main church. Lord Byron lived in the next village, Metaxata, for a time before taking part in the Greeks' struggle for freedom from the Turks at Missolonghi (1824). In the south lie the fishing villages and inviting beaches of Kateliou, Skala, and Poros. Across the water lie Zakinthos and the Peloponnesus. In present-day Skala, you can still see a half-ruined villa with lovely mosaic floors from the third century A.D. right next to the shore. The mosaics were the work of a certain Krateros, and inscriptions explain that he was reproducing lost paintings of his time.

FROM ARGHOSTOLI IT IS ALSO POSSIBLE TO TAKE A small ferry across to Lixouri, on the Paliki peninsula. This is a region well worth exploring. On the western side of the peninsula, in Kipouria, facing the open sea, lies the monastery of the Panaghia, where the monks are quite hospitable. In the north, there is the village of Kontojennada, surrounded by vineyards, which has a splendid eighteenth-century iconostasis in its church of Aghios Ioannis.

The road to the north winds dramatically past steep cliffs. You ought to turn off this road to visit the imposing Venetian fortress of Assos, which lies across from a charming fishing village. In the seventeenth century, it was planned that the capital of the island would be built inside these walls, but the idea was never executed.

Fiskardo is a favorite spot for painters. It stands on the strait that separates Cephalonia from Ithaca, and it recalls the Normans and their leader Robert Guiscard, who died here in 1085 during one of his campaigns of conquest.

THE FIRST TRACES OF STONE AGE LIFE DEFINITELY date back to the Paleolithic, for characteristic stone tools of that period have been discovered here. Archeologists have also uncovered specific finds from the Neolithic, the last phase of the Stone Age (6000–2500 B.C.). It is hoped that more will one day be learned about the Early Bronze Age, which is not represented at all on Cephalonia, unlike on Leukas and Ithaca. Excavations in the village of Kokkolata, not far from Krane, reveal something of the cultural development of the island between 1600 and 1500 B.C. Boxlike individual graves and various vases found here reveal the existence of trade between Cephalonia and Leukas (where similar vessels have been discovered near Nydri). There also was trade with Ithaca (where ceramic finds in the same style were uncovered in the region of Pelikata) and for the western Peloponnesus. Though these vases have been uncovered only at this one site on Cephalonia, they prove the presence of a modest, permanent settlement of farmers who did not turn their pots on a wheel but formed

Greek priests in costume:
drawing by G. F. Sargent, c. 1844.

them by hand. Further investigation seems likely to confirm that during the Middle Bronze Age (2000–1500 B.C.), the links between the Aegean and the southern Ionian Islands were particularly close; presumably, seafarers from the Cyclades came here to get raw materials—for example, wood for building. Excavations on Cythera and Leukas suggest that the eruption of the volcano on Thira abruptly broke off this traffic. It is also highly probable that this event led to the otherwise unexplained interruption in relations between Cephalonia and the Greek mainland, especially the Peloponnesus; for two centuries, Cephalonia remained isolated from the Mycenaean cultural centers flourishing on the Peloponnesus; nothing at all is known about the island during this period.

It has been determined that shortly after 1300 B.C., a sudden economic flowering took place on Cephalonia, Ithaca, and Zakinthos but not on Leukas and Corfu. Presumably, the more southerly islands profited from the fact that they lay on the route from the west coast of the Peloponnesus—from Pylos, for example—to southern Italy and Sicily. At this time, mainland Greeks appear to have come to settle on Cephalonia. These new residents, Homer's *megathymoi Kephallenes* ("great-hearted Cephalonians") gave the island its later name. Cephalonia doubtless offered a haven to refugees from Achaea and Messenia during the decades of unrest that preceded the collapse of the Mycenaean world. One proof of this are the funerary gifts—bronze weapons, jewelry, seals, and gold coins—that came from Italy and Achaea and were discovered in Lakkithra.

The acropolis of Krane was probably first fortified in Mycenaean times. In the village of Aghioi Theodoroi, near Same, a Mycenaean house was found, and it is hoped that further interesting discoveries will turn up here.

It is likely that between 1300 and 1050 B.C., the island was uninhabited. This is apparent primarily from the sudden disuse of the Mycenaean cemeteries excavated in Kokkolata, Diakata, Masarakata, Parisata, Kontojennada, Lakkithra, and Metaxata. The barrow graves discovered in the cliffs were intended for whole families and were used for centuries. There is also a Mycenaean barrow grave in Mavrata, in the south of the island.

Almost nothing is known about the island between the eleventh and seventh centuries B.C., when Dorians emigrated to Cephalonia. Not until the seventh century B.C. does interesting evidence again appear: in the old Mycenaean barrow graves, there developed a cult of heroes and ancestors. Perhaps Cephalonia emerged from its isolation once the trading activity of the Euboeans and Corinthians had resumed in the Ionian Sea, at a time when they colonized Corcyra (Corfu) and Leukas. Once more there was lively trade with southern regions of Italy and Sicily.

The ruins of a temple in Minies, near Livathou, betray Corinthian influence in the architectural elements made of clay. Beautifully worked capitals from a Doric temple near the Aghios Ghiorghios church in Skala reveal that the sixth century B.C. was one in which there was considerable building activity. The object of the most important cult on Cephalonia was Zeus Ainesios, to whom an open-air altar on Mount Ainos was consecrated. This Zeus is mentioned in a fragment attributed to Hesiod.

IN MYCENAEAN TIMES, THERE WERE PROBABLY four kings who divided the island into four administrative realms; these were later supplanted by four city-states. Thucydides was still able to characterize Cephalonia in his history of the Peloponnesian War as a *tetrapolis*, or four-city island.

Krane, which lies at the southern end of the gulf known as Koutavos, was the most important of the four city-states in the fifth century B.C. The massive fortifications of its acropolis surrounded the hilltop. On the summit stood a small Doric temple consecrated to Athena. Gateways at strategic spots served to regulate traffic. Whenever danger threatened, the inhabitants of the neighboring villages sought refuge behind the acropolis. In the southwest, near the harbor, lay the center of the city, or agora; behind it, on the slope of the hill, was the residential area. The main street led up to the south gate of the acropolis. A spring to the north provided the city with an abundant supply of water. Near it, an inscription from the base of a votive statue has been deciphered. It says that there was once a temple here dedicated to Demeter and Persephone. In the forested region of Livathou, there were numerous settlements and villages, as countless cemeteries and

grave steles attest. Some of these steles are simple, unornamented rectangular stones. Nothing is carved on them but the name of the deceased.

The second city-state, Pale (present-day Palaiokastro), lies near Lixouri. Only traces of its acropolis are preserved. In the neighboring village of Soulari, a lovely Doric capital was found (now in the Arghostoli Museum), suggesting that an important temple existed in the mid-fifth century B.C.

More is known about the third city-state, Pronnoi. The extensive fortification walls of this city (near modern Dakori) were, as Polybius said, "difficult to storm." Here, a cemetery from the sixth century B.C. and a number of interesting grave steles ornamented with reliefs have been excavated. A temple whose altar was carved into the cliff crowned the acropolis. Additional important fortified sites in the eastern and northern portions of the plain reveal that Pronnoi had to defend itself against its powerful neighbors, Same and Krane.

Same (Sami), whose acropolis extended across two summits, was the fourth city-state. Some painted grave steles found in the cemeteries on the western slope of Aghios Phanentes hill, and now displayed in the Arghostoli Museum, are of particular interest. Same was noted for its terraces with retaining walls. Houses stood on these, under the protection of the acropolis.

Despite their small size, the city-states of Cephalonia obviously had a strong tendency toward autonomy, which explains their numerous walls and extensive fortifications. Each of them minted its own coinage, and in wartime, each went its own way, both against outside enemies, as in the Persian Wars, and in intra-Greek conflicts such as the Peloponnesian War. Pale sided with the Greeks against the Persians at the battle of Plataea in 479 B.C. Krane support-ed Athens during the Peloponnesian War (while the other Cephalonian city-states backed Sparta) and sheltered the Athe-nians' Messenian allies in 421 B.C. Twenty years later, Sparta forced these Messenians to leave Cephalonia and emigrate to Sicily. During that time, the Athenian influence in the Ionian Sea was uncommonly strong. Probably as a result, a mythical tale arose that an Attic hero named Cephalus had once freed the island of pirates and given it his name.

Same was the only Cephalonian city-state that held out for months against the Romans, finally capitulating in 187 B.C. The Romans then ruled Cephalonia until the fifth century A.D., eliminating any sort of in-dependence of the individual city-states. The Cephalonians lived relatively peaceful-ly under Roman rule, rebuilt their ruined buildings, and cultivated the land. In the north, a new city called Panormus (pres-ent-day Fiskardo) was laid out, and many wealthy Romans built splendid villas here; remains of these may still be seen. In the so-called Rakospito of Same, a complex of baths with mosaic floors can be admired *in situ*, and an interesting bronze head from the third century B.C. is displayed in the Arghostoli Museum. Another half-ruined Roman villa can be seen near the harbor of the neighboring village of Aghia Euphimia. In a Roman villa in Vatsa (Paliki), there is a mosaic floor representing a trident and dolphins.

It can be assumed that the Cephalonians were not Christianized until the second century A.D. When the Roman Empire was divided in 395 A.D., they fell to Byzantium, and therewith ends the ancient history of Cephalonia.

ZAKINTHOS (ZANTE)

ZAKINTHOS IS A GARDEN, BORDERED ON THE west by a high wall of mountains and open to the sea on the south and east. Its rolling hills and valleys are overgrown with grapes, olive trees, and fruit trees, inter-rupted only by rows of cypresses, beds of roses and violets, and the wild hyacinths that gave the island its name. Homer praised it as "woodland Zacynthus," and Vergil wrote, "Already Zacynthus appears to be awash in its leafing groves," and the Venetians called the island Fior de Levante (Flower of the East).

Nineteenth-century travelers and con-temporary poets have repeatedly ex-pressed delight at the island's beauty and rich vegetation. Even the mountain ranges formed by the two capes of Skopos in the south and Skinari in the north does not de-tract at all from the overall impression of abundance and serenity.

Zakinthos lies only 10 miles off the coast of the Peloponnesus. One of its geological points of interest is the tar pits near the vil-lage of Keri, near the bay of Lagana in the south; these were mentioned by Herodo-tus but have been inactive for years. In the same vicinity, a cliff that falls vertically into the sea boasts startling bands of gypsum. Not far away is the spot where the oldest traces of Neolithic life on Zakinthos were found. Even on the beaches, you may occasionally encounter petrified bones from the Paleolithic period, as you can on the nearby Peloponnesian coast.

The island's Classical Greek name, Zacynthus, was supposedly derived from a hero of that name, a son of King Dardanus of Troy and a descendant of Apollo. According to legend, Zacynthus, with his followers, came from Arcadia and founded the city on the island's east coast. He gave the acropolis the name of his hometown, Psophis. This city was the only one on the island in antiquity, and the modern town lies upon the ruins of the old one. The settlements on the slopes of the mountains and on the plains have never been more than villages.

The island's importance as a stopover for ships doubtless contributed to its economic and cultural development; it lies on the shipping lanes leading from east to west and from Venice to Crete and Africa. Since antiquity, the Zakinthians were expert seafarers; they sailed as far as Spain to found the colony of Saguntum.

The island shared the general history of the rest of Greece. It changed its allegiance various times during antiquity, occasionally taking the Athenians' side and at other times the Spartans'. Athenaeus wrote that the Zakinthians were not particularly warlike and that they loved "to live in easy abundance."

Christianity spread to the island in the third century A.D. In 466, the Vandal king Gaiseric devastated the island, and attacks by pirates followed for centuries; the obvious conclusion is that there was rich booty to be taken here. During the heyday of the Byzantine Empire, Zakinthos belonged to the administrative region of Cephalonia and Illyria. In the twelfth century, when the Franks arrived, Zakinthos was ruled, along with Cephalonia, by the Orsini family. These Italian counts created the environment for a way of life that distinguishes the Ionian Islands from the rest of Greece.

After the Crusaders conquered Byzantium, the small island state of Zakinthos and Cephalonia remained in existence. In the fourteenth century, under the rule of the De Tocco family, it expanded to include Epirus and Acarnania. Its population rose to 25,000, and the economic condi-

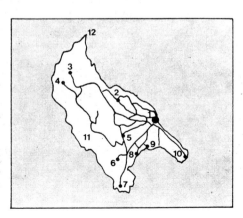

The island of Zakinthos.

1. *Zakinthos*
2. *Kalipadosi*
3. *Volimai*
4. *Anaphonitria monastery*
5. *Machairadosi*
6. *Pantokrator*
7. *Keri*
8. *Lagana*
9. *Kalamaki*
10. *Vasiliko*
11. *Mount Vrachionas*
12. *Cape Skoinari*

tions on the island were excellent. The medieval town of Zakinthos stood on the site of the ancient acropolis. At that time, there were few houses along the coast.

The Venetians conquered Zakinthos in 1485 and altered its administration. The inhabitants were permitted to practice their Greek Orthodox faith once again; they had been forbidden to do so under the De Toccos. The social order developed under the Venetians persisted until the beginning of the twentieth century. There were the *nobili* (Greeks elevated to the nobility by the Venetians), the *civili* (well-to-do merchants), and the *popolari* (artisans and poorer townsfolk). The peasants lived

Zakinthos: drawing by S. Pomardi, 1819.

completely on their own and took no part in the political and social life of the town. Schools were founded in the capital and the sons of the wealthy studied abroad.

When Venice lost its Greek bases—Naupactus, Methoni, Koroni, Monemvasia, Nauplia, Crete—to the Turks and Turkish rule became more severe, more and more Greeks sought refuge on Zakinthos. The arrival of Cretan painters and poets had a broad and lasting effect on the island's art and literature and led to a cultural renaissance. The fame of the Zakinthian poets Ugo Foscolo, Dionysios Solomos, and Andres Kalvos and the painters Doxaras, Koutousis, and Kantounis spread far beyond Zakinthos

in the eighteenth and nineteenth centuries.

Venetian rule and the influx of Cretan settlers left their stamp on the island's culture. For example, the Baroque style became predominant, especially in church architecture. The artisans organized themselves in guilds to which they paid dues, and soon these craft guilds became so wealthy that they could build their own churches. In doing so, they tried to compete with the nobility. The tailors built the church of Aghios Athanasios, the stonemasons Aghios Basileios, and the gardeners and fruit merchants Aghios Gerasimos.

Though the Venetians encouraged agriculture to the point that everyone received a premium for planting a new olive tree, the peasants had no active political role. The political influence of the guilds, on the other hand, was decisive. In 1797 the *popolari* rebelled, drove out the Venetians, and assumed power. This revolt was triggered by the ideas of the French Revolution. A kind of St. Bartholomew's Night took place: French soldiers who had conquered Italy landed on Zakinthos and burned the Libro d' Oro (the "golden book" in which the register of the nobility was kept) and planted the "freedom tree." For two years, there was a kind of Jacobin rulership set up by the Zakinthians with the help of the French.

After bloody battles, the Russians and Turks arrived in 1799, and they ruled the island jointly for ten years. Then, in 1809, the British came. Zakinthos was returned to Greece along with the rest of the Ionian Islands in 1864.

The British were not at all oppressive to the Zakinthians. Rather, they contributed to the general prosperity by initiating public works like the building of streets and bridges. English travelers from that period reported how pleasant it was to stay on Zakinthos. Though the landscape itself reminded them of Devonshire, they found the overall character of the island to be Greek and Venetian.

City life on Zakinthos was varied. There were theaters and concerts, masked balls and receptions. In addition to enjoying these diversions, the members of the social elite formed a cell of the secret organization (Philiki Etaireia) that was preparing for the revolt against the Turks; they also created the Ionian Academy, a school of fine arts that was later moved to Corfu and then, in 1835, to Athens. There were two especially active private societies comparable to English clubs. One was made up chiefly of conservatives, the other of so-called progressives.

The islanders owed their prosperity to the production of textiles, which were sought after in Western Europe, ceramics, soap, and naphthalene. Other export articles were *mandolata* (a sweet almond cake), sausages, and wine. The island sent licorice root to Constantinople and Smyrna and even to England and Germany. The sap extracted from this root was added to cough syrups and chewing tobacco. Agricultural products such as olive oil, grapes, and beeswax were shipped to Russia.

ARCHITECTURAL MONUMENTS REPRESENTATIVE of the island's long history are few, for natural catastrophes, far more than battles, have devastated the island. One of the most severe earthquakes took place in 1514–1515, when the fortress, it is said, split asunder and the greater part of the old city was destroyed. In 1822, the church of Aghios Sosti sank into the sea. In the 1953 earthquake, more than 90 percent of the buildings on Zakinthos—including beautiful churches, patrician houses, and art galleries—were leveled. What could be

A church in Zakinthos, from Annie Brassey's Sunshine and Storm in the East, *1890.*

salvaged, with great difficulty, is now displayed in the Byzantine Museum on Solomos Square. This museum, like most of the town's buildings, has been rebuilt in the classical style. Under the direction of the Byzantine scholar Manolis Chadzidakis, a number of frescos, mostly from Late Byzantine churches, were preserved and moved here. In addition, the museum houses Hellenistic sculptures and splendid gilt wooden choir screens.

After the earthquake of 1953, the city was rebuilt so quickly that there was no time to study the ancient remains that lie beneath it. Archeologists thus concentrate on the soil outside the city. By accident, they discovered a Mycenaean tomb at the southwestern end of the island near the village of Keri, and, in 1971, a whole Mycenaean cemetery near the village of Kambi on the steep west coast. A Hellenistic grave from the third or second century B.C. was found on the slope of Kastro hill. The English archeologist Sylvia Benton discovered Mycenaean and Roman graves, as well as clay shards from the sixth and fifth centuries B.C. on the acropolis hill near Vasiliko, in the southeast corner of the island.

The most important private collection on Zakinthos belongs to the Romas family (it was formerly the collection of Count Cesare Roma). Only three of its inscriptions survived the earthquake of 1953. One of them indicates that the patron goddess of the island was Artemis Opitais.

From the capital, you can hike to noteworthy churches (for example, Anaphonitria and Aghios Ghiorghios ton Krimnon) and monasteries (such as Skopiotissa) with wrought-iron grills over their windows and tall, slender bell towers that are especially pleasing because they are not overly ornamented.

In the countryside, you can also see

splendid Italianate villas that seem more charming than ever in their half-ruined state. These villas and their grounds were the pride of the *nobili* and the *civili*. One of them, called Sarakina, belonged to the Lutzi family and is Venetian red, with dark green shutters and white columns at the entrance. Most of these villas are surrounded by gardens and stand in parks where peacocks strut and display their fans. The Villa Carrer, near Paliokantouno, was designed by the German architect Ziller, and other famous architects have also built on Zakinthos.

IN SPITE OF THE DEVASTATIONS OF NUMEROUS earthquakes, Zakinthians have been able to salvage the age-old traditions of more idyllic times. On summer evenings, the young men stroll beneath the windows of the young women and sing love songs. The Christmas and Easter celebrations and the folk festivals in honor of St. Dionysios, in August and December, are unique. On August 24, the feast of St. Dionysios, pilgrims come from all over Greece to take part in the spectacular celebration filled with music. At Carnival, one of the citizens is dressed as the holiday, and is symbolically led to his grave on the last Sunday before Lent. During the three-week-long festival, there are improvised speeches to which the town and country residents listen with delight.

CYTHERA (CERIGO)

CYTHERA IS ONE OF THE "SEVEN ISLANDS" *(Heptanisi)* in the Ionian Sea. It is now part of the administrative district of Piraeus, from which it can be reached in about fifteen hours by boat. When the wind blows from the north, the ship docks in the harbor of the capital, Kapsali, but when there is a south wind, the boat drops anchor in the bay of Aghia Pelaghia. The shortest passage is from the Peloponnesian coast, but even those who choose this crossing are at the mercy of rough winds.

The actual landscape of the island is completely different from the one painted by Watteau between 1717 and 1719 in his dreamy *Pilgrimage to Cythera*. On this grim island, it is virtually impossible to imagine Watteau's women in their silken dresses, the plump, rosy-cheeked cupids, the tall leafy trees, and the green lawns that slope down to the sea. But Watteau was not the only artist to portray Cythera so idealistically; French poets from the eighteenth and nineteenth centuries continually did so, for in mythology Cythera was Aphrodite's birthplace. Artists have pictured it as the goal of all yearning, an ideal setting for lovers, and the site of all manner of frivolous adventures.

In Greek mythology, when the goddess was born from sea foam, she was carried to Cythera in a shell by the gentle breath of Zephyrus. She tried to cover herself, and the first thing she saw was a dense thicket of myrtle, behind which she hid to protect herself from the gaze of the satyrs. Hence

The island of Cythera.

1. Kapsali (Chora)
2. Drymon
3. Phratsia
4. Metata
5. Mylopotamos
6. Diakophti
7. Avlemonas
8. Potamos
9. Aghia Pelaghia
10. Karavas

the name Myrtoëssa. Aphrodite next went to Cyprus, where she was clothed in exquisitely scented garments and led to the Olympian gods. She then planted the first myrtle tree in her shrine at Paphos in memory of the shrubbery on Cythera, and henceforth she wore a crown woven of its blossoming branches; the Muses also made her a myrtle wreath of victory after the Judgment of Paris. "Because Cythera is really not an inviting island and on the whole rather cheerless," one German traveler wrote, "Aphrodite doubtless decided not to stay there, and the father of the winds, Aeolus, blew her on to Cyprus."

After Paris kidnapped the lovely Helen in Sparta, they supposedly stopped at this sanctuary on their way to Troy. Goethe uses this tradition in his *Faust II,* in which Helen says:

For since I left this threshold without care,
Seeking out Cythera's temple in accord with ancient rite,
But was captured there by a robber, the Phrygian one,
Much indeed has happened....

AT THE BEGINNING OF THE NINETEENTH CENTURY a French architect, A.L. Castellan, saw the columns of this temple half sunk in the sea and sketched them; oddly enough, the islanders at that time referred to the ruins as the palace of Menelaus. Today, they relate that when Aphrodite saw the beauty of the mortal Helen entering her temple on Cythera, the goddess suffered an attack of jealousy and broke out of her statue. Aphrodite then did all she could to speed Helen on to Troy. After the close of the ten-year Trojan War, which Helen's flight had caused, the few returning Greek survivors cursed both Aphrodite and Cythera.

SINCE THE ANCIENTS HAD NO IDEA WHERE THE Greek name of the island, Cythera, actually came from, it was associated, as in similar cases, with a hero of that name—a certain Cytherus, who supposedly founded the first settlement on the island. Another ancient name for the island was Porphyrousa, which is derived from *porphyra* ("purple"); some of the chief Greek hunting grounds for the purple mollusk were the coasts of Cythera, Laconia, and the Gulf of Corinth. Its fluid is originally white; when exposed to sunlight, it darkens progressively from lemon yellow to greenish yellow, then green, violet, and deep violet. Since this process could be interrupted at any stage, the Greeks were able to use this mollusk to produce dyes of the most varied shades of color.

Ceramic finds suggest that Minoan ships docked at Cythera as early as the second millennium B.C. At Avlemona on the east coast, traces of a Minoan settlement (circa 1600 B.C.), abandoned in Mycenaean times, have been discovered.

Cythera played a strategic role in the age-long struggles of Sparta; it was the gateway for anyone who hoped to conquer Lacedaemon by sea. Herodotus relates that after the battle of Thermopylae, Xerxes asked Demaratus, a former king of Sparta who had defected and obtained the trust of the Persian king, just how he could conquer Lacedaemon most easily; Demaratus gave him the following advice: "You should, then, dispatch 300 ships of your naval force to the Laconian coast. Off that coast there lies an island called Cythera, which Chilon, the wisest man amongst us, said would be more advantageous to the Spartans if sunk to the bottom of the sea, than if it remained above water."

In 424 B.C., during the Peloponnesian War, the Athenian general Nicias occupied Cythera. In so doing he completed the blockade of the Peloponnesus with which

Cythera: engraving from The Mediterranean Illustrated, *1877.*

Athens hoped to force Sparta to its knees. After the death of Cleon, one of the Spartans' demands was that Athens should return the island of Cythera to them.

The ancient inhabitants lived a frugal, Spartan way of life. One of Aristotle's pupils, Heraclides of Pontus, reports that they were industrious, studious, and thrifty. They ate almost nothing but goat's cheese and figs.

Cythera continued to be of importance to the Lacedaemonians until Roman times. The Spartan tyrant Gaius Julius Eurycles was one of the very few to fight on the side of Octavian against Antony; as a reward, Octavian, who had become Emperor Augustus, presented him with the island of Cythera as his personal fiefdom.

The Venetians first came to the island in 1207 and named it Cerigo. Their leader, Marco Venieri, called himself a direct descendant of Aphrodite and "count of Cerigo." A century-long feud between the Venieri and the local ruling family, the Eudomonojanni, was temporarily resolved when a Greek bride received the island as a wedding present.

In the eighteenth and nineteenth centu-

ries, Cythera basically shared the fate of the other Ionian Islands; it was ruled successively by the French, the Russians, and the British; and was finally incorporated into the recently founded Greek state in 1864. Off the cliffs of Cythera, as dangerous in antiquity as they are today, the ship *Mentor* was sunk at the beginning of the nineteenth century. It was one of the thirty-three ships that was carrying the ancient art treasures that Lord Elgin had stolen from Greece to bring to England. With the help of divers from Kalymnos, Spetsai, and Malta, he was able to recover some statues from the sea. The islanders still speak of sunken treasures thought to be lying in the bay of Avlemona, in the east, where the *Mentor* went down. In our own day, Cythera again became associated with bitter memories; in 1970, the military dictatorship exiled twenty-four of its political opponents to Aghia Pelaghia.

IN AGHIA PELAGHIA, THERE ARE ONLY OLD PEOPLE and children; young adults tend to emigrate. The rocky soil is poor and supports only a few olive trees, vegetables, sheep, and goats. The local thyme continues to provide adequate nourishment for bees, however, and Cytherian honey is highly prized. The 5,000 inhabitants live mainly on money sent by relatives who have emigrated to Australia.

Can one recommend Cythera to the traveler who is tired of civilization and eager to find an unspoilt summer vacation spot? Yes and no. All that can be said is that visitors who prefer the simple life and are content with village hotels and modest taverns will certainly enjoy themselves. There are no impressive ancient ruins, but a number of interesting Byzantine and post-Byzantine churches are well worth visiting.

Inside the high Venetian fortress above

Boreas, the North Wind, carrying off the maiden Orithyia: an ancient vase painting.

the main town, Chora, there are four churches. Somewhat farther downhill, in the medieval part of Chora, the so-called Mesa Vourgho, there are another fifteen churches. The following are of particular interest for lovers of Byzantine art: a double church, consecrated to Aghios Ioannis Chrysostomos, Aghios Philippos, with frescos from the fifteenth to the eighteenth centuries; and one consecrated to Aghios Athanasios, with wall paintings in which the saints are portrayed in seventeenth-century Western European clothing.

Outside Chora, there are two churches consecrated to Aghios Demetrios worth seeing, in Kambanika and in Pourko. The latter church consists of four separate chapels with particularly fine frescos from the twelfth century. On a fresco in the church in Kambanika, St. Demetrios is shown killing a warrior in Crusaders' armor. This twelfth-century painting came to light only when painting of a later date began to flake off. Portions of the walls carry as many as four separate layers of painting.

Energetic hikers may visit Palaiochora, a destroyed medieval city on the east coast, which stands on a steep outcropping of rock. At Mylopotamos, on the west coast, the ruins are somewhat more extensive. A stone lion of St. Mark can be seen at the entry gate.

At about an hour's walk, there is a magnificent cave with stalagmites and stalactites. In the various chambers of this cave, the fossilized remains of ancient sea creatures can be discerned. Monks built a modest chapel at the entrance to this cave; in the eleventh and twelfth centuries, it was decorated with pictures of the saints done by local artists.

The shrine of the miracle-working Panaghia Myrtidiotissa is a place of pilgrimage for the people of Cythera. The icon of the Virgin is said to have healed numerous sick people and performed astonishing miracles. For example, she is said to have changed a number of pirate ships into tiny islands that can be seen from this spot. According to legend, a shepherd was watching his sheep here when he heard a voice that seemed to come from a myrtle bush. He followed the voice and discovered in the bush the icon of the Virgin with a black face. In Byzantine art, this type of black image is called Myrtidiotissa, which is actually one of the ancient names of Aphrodite, "the goddess of myrtle."

BIOGRAPHIES

Maria Anagnostopoulou

was born in Athens, she received her diploma in classical archeology at the University of Athens. From 1951 to 1960 she worked at the Athens Ecole Française d'Archéologie. At the same time she was involved in setting up the Heraklion Museum and the Acropolis Museum in Athens. Between 1960 and 1967 she devoted herself to the museum and the archeological precinct at Eleusis, and with the Greek Department of Antiquities she took part in the excavations in Voula and Eleusis. In 1969 and 1970 she organized the archeological collections of the Musée d'Art et d'Histoire in Geneva. In addition, from 1957 to 1964 she edited the art history section of the publication *Eleutheria*, and she is a member of the International Society of Art Critics.

Maria Brouskari

was born in Cairo in 1929, and between 1947 and 1952 she studied archeology and classical philology at the University of Athens. Since 1953 she has worked in the Acropolis Museum, devoting herself primarily to the structures and their preservation. In addition, she has worked on the cataloguing of finds. Since 1973, she has been helping to set up the Kanellopoulos Museum in the old part of Athens. She has published books about the Acropolis Museum and the monuments of the Acropolis. Among her articles in German are "Parthenon Fragments," "The Sixth Caryatid," and "On the Western Pediment of the Parthenon."

Angeliki Charitonidou

was born in Thessalonike. At Thessalonike University she studied literature and archeology. While a high school teacher, she married the archeologist Serafin Charitonides, and worked with him in various excavations in the region of the Argolis and elsewhere.

Chrysanthe Cleridi

was born on Cyprus and educated in England, where she worked for the BBC. Since 1957 she has worked as a journalist in Greece, from 1957 to 1967 as a dance critic. She is the editor of the journal *Vima* and a contributor to periodicals in Greece and abroad.

Georg S. Dontas

studied classical archeology in Athens and Munich. Between 1948 and 1954 he worked as a curator, and from 1954 to 1962 as curator on the Acropolis. From 1962 to 1966 he served as ephor of the Ionian islands on Corfu. In 1967 he was director of the National Museum in Athens; since then he has been the director of the Acropolis Museum.

Vanna Hadjimihali-Svoronou

earned a liberal arts degree from the German Preparatory School in Athens. She took her qualifying examination at the Sorbonne, and received an equivalent degree at the Institute of Art and Archeology in Paris. At the Ecole Pratique des Hautes Etudes in Paris she earned still another diploma. Between 1953 and 1956 she was an assistant at the famed Centre National de la Recherche Scientifique in Paris, where she concentrated on dwelling construction in ancient Greece. At the same time, she was a contributor in archeology to the French journal *Cahiers d'Art*. Since 1958 she has been a scholar at the French Archeological Institute in Athens. In 1966 she compiled a catalogue dealing with secular architecture on Cyprus and elsewhere and became a professor of the history of ancient art at the Knubly School in Athens. Since 1967 she has been a member of the French excavation team in Lato, on Crete.

Petros Kalligas

was born in Athens in 1934. He studied philology and archeology at the University of Athens and at Oxford. He is a member of the Greek Archeological Society and the British School of Archaeology at Athens. Since 1963 he has worked as a curator at the Acropolis Museum, on the Ionian islands, and in Epiros. He has conducted excavations on Cephalonia and Corfu, and helped to set up the museums on Corfu, Cephalonia, and Ithaca. Since 1973 he has worked in the division of bronze finds at the National Museum in Athens. He has published countless articles in archeological journals.

Athina Kalogheropoulou

is a philologist and archeologist, and the editor-in-chief of the Greek Archeological Office (Archaeologikon Deltion) and of the Athens Archeological Annals. From 1957 to 1967 she was archeological editor for the newspaper *Eleutheria* in Athens, and since 1974 the archeology editor of the journal *Kathimerimi*. She teaches archeological topography at the College of Greek Tourism.

Eleni Karapanajoti-Valaoriti

was born in Athens in 1940, and studied classical philology in Geneva. Since 1964 she has regularly reported the latest results of archeological investigations in, among other journals, the periodical *Vima* (Athens).

Ilias Kolias

was born in Piraeus in 1936, and studied archeology at the University of Athens. He specialized in Byzantine art, and worked under Manolis Chatzidakis at the Byzantine Museum. In 1965 he became a curator, assigned by the Archeological Office to oversee and restore the Byzantine art monuments in the Dodecanese. He has led archeological digs on Rhodes and Karpathos, and has published studies on Byzantine art and the art monuments of the Knights of St. John in the Dodecanese, as well as on more recent artistic epochs. He is a member of the Greek Archeological Society and teaches at the school for tourist guides on Rhodes.

Michalis Komninos

was born in 1925, studied law at the University of Athens, and at the London School of Economics specialized in admiralty law and comparative maritime law. In addition to his legal work he has lectured and published articles dealing primarily with questions of the law of the sea. In 1966 he set up the museum on Kastellorizon. He has published the books *The Dialect of Kastellorizon* (1962) and *Funeral Songs of Kastellorizon* (1970).

Aris Konstantinidis

was born in Athens in 1913. Between 1931 and 1936 he studied architecture at the Technical College in Munich. From 1942 to 1950 he served as an architect in the Ministry of Transport in Athens. Since 1946 he has had his own office in Athens. From 1955 to 1957 he was the director of the design division of the Organization for Workers' Housing, and from 1957 to 1967 director of the design department in the Center for Tourism, both in Athens. Between October 1967 and July 1970 he taught as a guest professor at the Technische Hochschule in Zurich. On April 19, 1978, he was awarded an honorary doctorate from the University of Thessalonike.

Konstantinidis is a noted lecturer on Greek architecture and has published numerous articles in Greek and foreign technical journals and reference works. Two of his books about the island of Mykonos were published in Athens in 1947 and 1953.

Grigoris Konstantinopoulos

was born in Tripolis in Arkhadhia. He studied philology, archeology, ancient history, and art history, and has a doctorate from the University of Athens and an honorary doctorate from the University of Würzburg. He is a member of the Greek Archeological Society and the German Archeological Institute. Since 1964 he has led excavations on Rhodes and Kos.

Marina Lada-Sulzberger

was born and raised in Athens, and married noted *New York Times* journalist Cyrus Sulzberger in Jerusalem in 1942. The couple has made many trips around the world, including visits to numerous crisis areas and war zones. Since the end of the Second World War she has made her home in Paris, but every summer she has brought her children and grandchildren to her family's residence on Spetsai for the summer holidays.

Demetrios I. Lazarides

was born in Kavalla in 1917. He studied at the University of Thessalonike and with a scholarship from the French government in Paris at the Sorbonne, the Collège de France, the Ecole des Hautes Etudes, and the Ecole du Louvre. He has been a member of the Antiquities Administration since 1968. From 1942 to 1945 he was curator of antiquities in Thessalonike. From 1945 to 1965 he served as epimelet and then ephor for eastern Macedonia and Thrace in Kavalla, from 1965 to 1966 as ephor of Athens and Megara, and from 1966 until February 1968 as ephor of Attica and Euboea. He has since retired, and is working as a scholar at the Centre Ecestique in Athens (in the field of ancient Greek cities). He has lectured at various international congresses.

Lazarides earned his doctorate in Thessalonike in 1960, and in 1971 he was awarded an honorary doctorate at the University of Besançon. He organized the rebuilding of the museums of Kavalla, Philippi, Skyros, Salamis, and, in part, Thasos. Between 1940 and 1972 he led important excavations in Abdera, Amphipolis, Philippi, Neapolis (Kavalla, sanctuary of the Parthenos), and on Mount Pagghaion (the tumulus grave of Nikesiane). In 1975 he became director of the Archeological Service.

Articles and reports about his excavations have been included in various encyclopedias and journals.

Lila Marangou

was born in Athens in 1939. In 1961 she earned degrees in history and archeology at the University of Athens. Between 1959 and 1963 she worked as a research assistant at the National Museum in Athens under the direction of Professor Christos Karousos. In 1963 she was awarded a state scholarship for further study abroad. From 1963 to 1965 she studied archeology, classical philology, and art history at the universities of

Tübingen and Bonn. Between 1965 and 1968 she held a research scholarship from the Alexander von Humboldt Foundation, and in 1967 she received her doctorate from the University of Tübingen for her dissertation for Professor Ulrich Hausmann, "Lakonian Carving in Ivory and Bone." Since 1969 she has been at the Benaki Museum in Athens, preparing a publication on Roman and late antique bone carvings.

Evi Melas

was born in Athens, where she lives permanently. She studied law at the University of Athens. She has translated works into Greek, adapted pieces for theater and radio, and written short radio plays of her own. Collections of her stories have been published by the Swiss Atlantis-Verlag and the Kurt Desch-Verlag in Germany. Since 1959, she has been a correspondent for the *Münchner Merkur, Die Welt*, and the *Stuttgarter Zeitung*. She has also contributed occasionally to the Austrian Radio, the journal *Christ und Welt*, and other publications. She worked on the Merian volumes *Macedonia, Athens, Lesbos*, and *Crete*, and the Piper books *Two More Days in...* and *Two Weeks on....* For DuMont, she has written the German Art and Travel Guides *Athens* (1975) and *Rumania* (1977) and, for the Richtig Reisen series, the volume *Greece: Delphi, Athens, Peloponnesus, and Islands* (1980). In addition, she edited the German *Temples and Shrines of the Gods in Greece* (1970), *Ancient Churches and Monasteries of Greece* (1972), and *The Greek Islands* (1973). Evi Melas is a member of the International Press Institute (IPI).

His Royal Highness Prince Michael of Greece

was born in Rome on January 7, 1939, the son of Prince Christophoros of Greece and Princess Françoise of France. He attended preparatory school in Spain and France and earned a degree in political science at the Institut d'Etudes Politiques of the University of Paris. He served for four years in the Greek army, is married, and has two children. He lives in Athens and Paris.

He has published the novel *Sur le sable d'un été* under a pseudonym (Paris, 1969) and under his own name a volume of reminiscences and reflections, *Ma sœur l'Histoire ne vois-tu rien venir?* (Paris, 1970), which was awarded the Cazes Prize. He has also written an historical study on the Minoan epoch of the island of Crete, *La Crète, épave de l'Atlantide* (Paris, 1971).

Kostas Pharmakides

was born on Syme in 1929. He studied dentistry at the University of Athens, where he earned his diploma. He lives and works on Syme. As an amateur painter, he has exhibited in various international shows, including one in Cologne in 1962. His special fields of knowledge include Greek folklore and archeology.

Kostas Ptinis

comes from Samos, and has spent most of his life on his native island. He studied law at the University of Athens, but became a journalist and edits the newspaper *Ellas* on Samos. Ptinis has published various historical studies in Greek, including *Life on Samos in Antiquity; The Island and the War of Liberation Against the Turks in 1821; Prominent Greek Orthodox Priests on Samos; The History of Samos Between 1834 and 1912;* and *Samos in the Second World War.*

Kurt Schreiner

studied practical design at the College of

Art and Design in Cologne as well as German and art history at the University of Cologne. He is now a schoolteacher and a regular visitor to the Greek Islands.

Petros G. Themelis

was born in Thessalonike in 1936 and studied classical philology and archeology at the university there, earning his degree in 1959.

Between 1954 and 1962 he participated as an assistant at the Thessalonike Museum on excavations in Macedonia, chiefly in Palla. Beginning in 1963 he served as epimelet of classical antiquities in the Greek Archeological Service, first in Elis and Messenia (1963–1968), then on Euboea and in Attica (1968–1975). In 1972 he earned his doctorate at the University of Munich for his work on early Greek tomb structures.

Nikos Zapheiropoulos

was born in 1912 in Papsani (Thessaly). He studied archeology in Athens, Munich, and Tübingen. Between 1942 and 1972 he was epimelet and then ephor in Attica, Patras, Olympia, and the Cyclades.

He has participated in excavations in Pharas Achaia (Mycenaean and Geometric tombs); in Arta (a cemetery from the Classical period); on Naxos (a Mycenaean necropolis); and on Thira (Archaic and classical necropolis).

Photeini Zapheiropoulou

was born in Athens in 1931. She studied history and archeology at the University of Athens, the Athens Archeological Institute, and the Sorbonne, where she earned the Licence des Lettres. Between 1957 and 1959 she worked for the government as an archeological assistant in the museums of Nauplia, participating in excavations in Diolkos and of the Archaic temple in Galataki near Corinth, and the Cyclades, doing excavation on Tenos, Naxos, and Andros. Since 1960 she has worked as a government official in the Archeological Service, on the Acropolis in 1960, in Thessalonike from 1961 to 1963, and from 1964 to the present in the Cyclades. She has published articles about the excavations in the Odeion and the Palace of Galerius in Thessalonike as well as about her work in the Cyclades.

Eos Zervoudaki

was born in Athens in 1934. She studied archeology and history at the University of Athens from 1952 to 1957. In 1958 she continued her study of classical archeology at the University of Bonn, where under Professor E. Langlotz she earned a doctorate for her work on Attic polychrome relief pottery from the late fifth and fourth centuries B.C. Between 1961 and 1965 she worked as an assistant in the National Museum in Athens. Since 1965 she has been a curator for classical archeology in the Dodecanese.

PRACTICAL TRAVEL SUGGESTIONS

USEFUL ADDRESSES

Tourist Board

To request information about specific islands, accommodations, travel, or customs in Greece, write or phone a branch of the Greek National Tourist Organization (G.N.T.O., or E.O.T., as it is known in Greece) in North America, the United Kingdom, or Greece.

Locations in North America *New York* (Main Office): Olympic Tower, Fifth Floor, 645 Fifth Avenue, New York, NY 10022 (212-421-5777). *Chicago:* 168 North Michigan Avenue, Chicago, IL 60601 (312-782-1084). *Boston:* National Bank of Greece Building, 31 State Street, Boston, MA 02109 (617-227-7366). *Los Angeles:* Suite 1998, 611 West Sixth Street, Los Angeles, CA 90017 (213-626-6696). *Canada:* 1233 De La Montagne, Montreal, Quebec H3G IZ2, Canada (514-871-1535), and Suite 1403, 80 Bloor Street, Toronto, Ontario M5S 2V1, Canada (416-968-2220).

Location in the United Kingdom and Ireland 195-197 Regent Street, London WIR 8DR (734-5997).

Locations in Greece *Athens* (Main Office): 2 Amerikis Street (01-322-3111/2/3/4/5/6/7/8/9). *Piraeus:* Directorate of Tourism of Eastern Mainland and the Islands, Marina Zea (01-413-5716/4709/5730). *Cephalonia:* Town Hall, Arghostoli (0671-22847). *Corfu:* The Governor's House, Kerkyra (0661-30298/22227/30360). *Kos:* Information Desk, Akti Kountourioti (0242-28724). *Rhodes:* 5 Archbishop Makariou and Papagou Streets (0241-23655/23255).

Embassies and consulates

United States United States Embassy, 91 Vass. Sophias Avenue, 115-21, Athens (721-2951).

Canada Canadian Embassy, No. 4 I. Gennadiou Street, 115-21, Athens (723-9511).

United Kingdom British Embassy, No. 1 Ploutarchou Street, 106-75 Athens (723-6211).

PAPERS AND DOCUMENTS

Visas and passports

Citizens of the United States, Canada, and the United Kingdom do not need visas to enter Greece if they plan to stay less than three months. Only a valid passport is required. Travelers who plan to stay longer than three months must request permission by applying in person to the Aliens Bureau. This request must be made at least twenty days before the end of the first three months in Greece. To follow this procedure, get in touch with the Aliens Bureau, 9 Halkokondyli Street, Athens (362-8301), or the Aliens Center, 37 Vass. Constantinou, Piraeus (417-4023).

Immunizations

United States, Canadian, and British citizens traveling to Greece directly from their countries do not need any immunization vaccines. However, tourists entering Greece from another country may need vaccinations. For information, Americans should consult the local Board of Health or the Center for Disease Control in Atlanta. Canadians should consult the local municipal or provincial Department of Health, or the medical services branch of Health and Welfare Canada, Jeanne Mance de l'Eglantine Street, Ottawa, Ontario K1A OL3. In the United Kingdom, check with the London Office of the G.N.T.O. (see p. 401 for address and phone number).

TRANSPORTATION TO GREECE

Greece is easily reached from the United States, Canada, and the United Kingdom. Whether you are traveling directly from North America or from another country, there are several schedules and means of transportation to choose from.

By plane

Flights from the United States Olympic Airways provides one nonstop flight every day, departing from New York's J.F.K. Airport, to and from the West Air Terminal in Athens. Also from J.F.K. Airport, TWA offers one nonstop flight every day to and from the East Air Terminal in Athens. Most European airlines provide connections from North America to Greece via major cities in Europe.

Flights from Canada All European carriers schedule connecting flights.

Flights from the United Kingdom British Airways offers one nonstop flight daily, originating from London's Heathrow Airport, to and from the East Air Terminal in Athens. Additional flights throughout the week are sometimes available.

Charter Flights A number of tour companies provide charter flights to Greece from North America and the British Isles. For more information, write or phone a branch of the Greek National Tourist Office (G.N.T.O.) in the United States, Canada, or the United Kingdom.

By ship

Sailing from Egypt To sail between Alexandria and Piraeus, book passage with Adriatica Lines. This once-a-week crossing takes about 28 hours. Agents in the United States: Extra Value Travel, Inc., 437 Madison Avenue, New York, NY 10022 (212-750-8800).

Sailing from Italy To sail between Venice and Piraeus, book passage with Adriatica Lines. This once-a-week crossing takes about 42 hours. Agents in the United States: Extra Value Travel, Inc., 437 Madison Avenue, New York, NY 10022 (212-750-8800). Vacationers who have more time can sail between Ancona and Patras. The twice-weekly crossings, on the Strintzis Line, take about 36 hours. Agents in the United States: Time and Tide, Inc., 1416 Second Avenue, New York, NY 10021 (212-861-2500).

The voyage between Brindisi and Patras, via Corfu, is not quite so long. From Brindisi to Corfu the voyage is 10 hours; from Corfu on to Patras the trip takes 8 hours. From March through October there are between one and four crossings daily. From November through February ferries travel the route only three to four times a week. Passage on this trip can be booked with: (1) Hellenic Mediterranean Lines, 200 Park Avenue, New York, NY 10166 (212-697-4220) represented by Extra Value Travel, Inc., agents for the Venice-Piraeus trip; (2) Fragline, represented by Time and Tide, Inc., agents handling the Ancona-Patras route; or (3) Strintzis Line, also represented by Time and Tide, Inc.

By private means

By Plane The first landing and final departure of a private plane must take place at one of the international airports—in Athens, Thessalonike, Rhodes, Heraklion in Crete, or Corfu. For further information about procedures, write or phone the Greek Civil Aviation Authority (Y.P.A.) of the Ministry of Communication, P.O. Box Y.P.A., Athens Airport Post Office (894-7121).

By Yacht Private yachts must enter and leave Greece through one of these major ports: Aghios Nikolaos (Crete), Alexandroupolis, Arghostoli (Cephalonia), Chios, Chania (Crete), Hermoupolis (Syros), Heraklion (Crete), Itea, Kalamata, Katakolo, Kavalla, Kos, Lavrio (Attica), Myrina (Lemnos), Lesbos, Nauplia, Patras, Preveza, Pythagoreion (Samos), Pilos, Rhodes, Thessalonike, Volos, Vouliagmeni (Attica), Zakinthos, and Zea (Piraeus).

By Car Travelers driving to Greece must either ferry their cars to one of the country's major ports or enter the country overland. There are five border stations, which are open 24 hours a day: Yugoslavia—Evzoni, 330 miles from Athens; Yugoslavia—Niki, 380 miles from Athens; Bulgaria—Promahonas, 442 miles from Athens; Turkey—Kastania, 591 miles from Athens; Turkey—Kipi, 535 miles from Athens.

TRANSPORTATION INSIDE GREECE

Various means of transportation are available to vacationers who want to visit the islands.

By plane

Olympic Airways flies from Athens to many of the islands, including Corfu, Cephalonia, Zakinthos, Cythera, Lemnos, Lesbos, Chios, Samos, Kos, Rhodes, Mykonos, and Thira. There are also a few connecting flights between certain islands. Make reservations by calling Olympic's toll-free number, 800-223-1226, or by contacting the following offices of this airline: *Boston*: 716 Statler Office Building, 20 Park Plaza, Boston, MA 02116 (617-542-5810). *Chicago*: 7th floor, 168 North Michigan Avenue, Chicago, IL 60601 (312-329-0400). *Houston*: Suite 150, 263 North Belt East, Houston, TX 77060 (713-445-3080). *Los Angeles*: 530 West Sixth Street, Los Angeles, CA 90014 (213-624-6441). *New York*: 647-649 Fifth Avenue, New York, NY 10022 (reservations 212-838-3600, ticket office 212-750-7933). *Washington*: 1000 Connecticut Avenue N.W., Washington, DC 20036 (202-659-2511).

Or make reservations by calling Olympic Airways representatives in the United States. *Atlanta*: 404-393-0282. *Cleveland*: 216-235-1440. *Dallas*: 214-630-1342. *Detroit*: 313-961-7257. *Hartford*: 203-525-2187. *Miami*: 305-940-9970. *Minneapolis*: 612-545-3483. *Philadelphia*: 215-643-4768. *San Francisco*: 415-897-8480. *Tampa*: 305-940-9970.

In Canada, make reservations through these Olympic representatives. *Montreal*: 1200 McGill College Avenue, Montreal, Quebec H3B 4G7 (514-878-3891, reservations 514-878-9691). *Toronto*: Suite 1403, 80 Bloor Street West, Toronto, Ontario M5S 2V1 (416-925-2272).

In the United Kingdom, write or call Olympic Airways office at 141 Bond Street, London W1Y 0BB (493-7262, reservations 493-1233).

By Bus to the Airport Keep in mind that all Olympic Airways flights operate from the West Airport Terminal. The airline provides bus transportation between its Athens offices and this terminal. Public buses to the airport are also available. Rather inconveniently, public buses cannot enter the airport proper, so be sure to get out at the airport stop. The bus follows the coastal route and can be boarded en route. From Piraeus, take bus #122, Ano Voula, which departs from Theotoki Street; the ride takes about 45 minutes.

By boat

When sailing from one Greek island to another across the sparkling Ionian or Aegean seas, plan your trip by picking from an extraordinary number of passenger and car ferries. Please note that reservations and tickets are available only in Greece and that schedules often change. Here are some of the most traveled sea routes:

1. Piraeus to Syros to Tenos to Mykonos
2. Piraeus to Paros to Naxos to Ios to Thira
3. Piraeus to Kythnos to Seriphos to Siphnos to Melos
4. Piraeus to Patmos to Leros to Kalymnos to Kos to Rhodes
5. Piraeus to Icaria to Samos
6. Piraeus to Chios to Lesbos
7. Igoumenitsa to Corfu
8. Patras to Cephalonia to Ithaca

These routes operate all year round. Routes 4 and 6 leave Piraeus in the evening for an overnight trip. Routes 1, 2, and 3 leave Piraeus early in the morning and return to Piraeus the same day via the same ports. Keep in mind that boats leaving from Piraeus are usually larger and faster than those which first depart from a specific island. Furthermore, tickets are usually sold on a point-to-point basis. The ferries on these popular routes provide cabins (by reservation only) and dining facilities. The duration of your crossing will vary with the particular vessel and the number of intermediate ports.

For information about specific schedules, call the G.N.T.O. or the Tourist Police at 171. Other sources are the Piraeus Port Authority (451-1411) and any travel agency. Remember to reconfirm schedules before you depart, as time of sailing can vary according to the season.

By hydrofoil

If traveling to an island by ferry is too slow for you, consider taking the hydrofoil. Ceres Company will speed you across the water in its Flying Dolphins. These operate from Zea port in Piraeus to the Saronic Islands and to ports along the eastern coast of the Peloponnesus. Cars are not carried on the Flying Dolphins. For reservations, write or call Ceres Company, 8 Themistouleous Street, Piraeus (452-7107).

By cruise ship

Cruising from one Greek island to another is a magical experience, dazzling in the piercingly bright colors of the Mediterranean. There are schedules to fit nearly any itinerary, from luxurious week-long cruises to day-long outings that call at three islands—Hydra, Paros, and Aegina—departing from the marina at Flisvos. No matter what time of year, a cruise ship in Greece is ready to set sail.

Cruise Operators or Representatives in the United States Chandris Cruises, Inc., 666 Fifth Avenue, New York, NY 10019 (212-586-8370); Costa Line, Inc., 1 Biscayne Tower, Miami, FL 33131 (305-358-7325); Cycladic Cruises, 331 Madison Avenue, New York, NY 10017 (212-697-5647); Epirotiki Lines, Suite 1900, 551 Fifth Avenue, New York, NY 10017 (212-599-1750); Hellenic Mediterranean Lines, 200 Park Avenue, New York, NY 10017 (212-697-4220); Heritage Cruises, 132 East 70th Street, New York, NY 10021 (212-582-8815); K Lines-Hellenic Cruises, Fifth Floor, 645 Fifth Avenue, New York, NY 10022 (212-751-2435); Med Sun Lines, c/o Vantage Tours, Inc., Courtyard Suite 106, 900 North Federal Highway, Pompano Beach, FL 33062

(303-785-2801), or c/o Sea Connection Center, Suite 808, 6399 Wilshire Boulevard, Los Angeles, CA 90049 (213-655-4221); Sea Goddess Cruises, 5805 Blue Lagoon Drive, Miami, FL 33126; Norwegian American Line, 29 Broadway, New York, NY 10006 (212-422-3905); Intercruise Ltd., c/o Limex European Tours, 131 North State Street, Lake Oswego, OR 97034 (503-636-5668); Royal Cruise Line, One Maritime Plaza, San Francisco, CA 94111 (415-788-0610 or 800-227-4534); Saronic Cruises, c/o Travelforce, Inc., Suite 3111, 350 Fifth Avenue, New York, NY 10118 (212-563-9292); Sun Line Cruises, One Rockefeller Plaza, New York, NY 10020 (212-397-6400); Swans Hellenic Cruises, c/o Exprinter, 500 Fifth Avenue, New York, NY 10110 (212-719-1200); Viking Tours of Greece, 230 Spruce Street, Southport, CT 06490 (203-259-6030 or 212-221-6788).

Cruise Operators or Representatives in Canada Cycladic Cruises, Aviatours, Suite 506, 1470 Peel, Montreal, Quebec, H3A 1T1; Epirotiki Lines-Traveline Canada, 80 Bloor Street West, Toronto, Ontario M5S 2V1; K Lines-Hellenic Cruises, Nordic Tours, No. 1, 10715–135A Street, Surrey, British Columbia V3T 4E3; Intercruise Ltd., Victours, Suite 209, 3710 Chesswood Drive, Downsview, Ontario M3J 2W4; Sun Line Cruises, Margaret Deroo, 2677 Lakeshore Boulevard West, Toronto, Ontario M8V 1G6; Swan Hellenic Cruises, Private Label Arrangements Ltd., 42 Mercer Street, Toronto, Ontario M5V 1H3; Med Sun Lines Ltd., Touram, Suite 800, 1440 St. Catherine Street West, Montreal, Quebec H3G 1R8.

Cruise Operators in the United Kingdom Ocean Cruise Lines, Travelers, 6–10 Frederick Close, Stanhope Place, London, W2 2HD (01-402-8302).

Yachting

A sail among the Greek Islands is pleasurable and fascinating. In fact, no fewer than 2,000 islands of unsurpassed beauty and historical importance are scattered across the Aegean and Ionian seas.

Compelling reasons for taking the helm (or for letting a hired crew do it) are that traveling in a sailboat can be less costly than staying in hotels night after night. Moreover, yachts can dock at islands that the crowded ferries pass by, allowing adventurous sailors to enjoy the hospitable and friendly charms of a less commercial Greece.

Phone Numbers of Major Ports Cephalonia (Arghostoli), 0671-22224; Chios, 0271-22837; Corfu, 0661-30481; Kos, 0242-28507; Lemnos (Myrina), 0276-22200; Lesbos (Mytiline), 0251-28827; Rhodes, 0241-27690; Samos 0821-89240; Syros (Hermoupolis), 0281-22690; Zakinthos, 0695-22224; Piraeus (Zea), 452-5315. In addition to their port authorities, these marinas have agencies dealing with customs, health, passport control, and currency. Many also offer anchorages, food stores, and bunks.

Chartering a Yacht More than 1,000 yachts are available for charter in Greece. Choose a vessel that suits your needs and experience, either with or without a crew. All yachts are registered with the government and are inspected annually by the Ministry of Merchant Marine. All crews are licensed. For more information about chartering a yacht, contact yacht brokers in North America or the United Kingdom.

To find out more about the regulations for chartered yachts, write or call the Greek Yacht Brokers and Consultants Association, 56 Vass. Pavlou Street, Kastella-Piraeus or the Hellenic Professional Yacht Owners Association, A7 Marina Zea, Piraeus.

Renting a car

Rental cars are available from several agencies. As in most countries, prices vary according to the type of car, season, and length of rental. The rates include insurance, oil, and road maps. Bear in mind that prices do not include local taxes and duty stamps, which run about 19 percent of the total fee. You can also purchase full collision insurance for $5 to $6 a day.

Renting a car by the day will cost anywhere

from $10 to $50, depending on the model, plus 14¢ per kilometer. Weekly rentals, with unlimited mileage, start at $150. To make reservations, write or call the Association of Car Rental Enterprises, 314 Syngrou Avenue, Kallithea, Athens (951-01).

Driver's License   Visitors who plan to drive in Greece should possess an International Driver's License. The A.A.A. in the United States, the C.A.A. in Canada, and A.A. in the United Kingdom, or the Greek Automobile Touring Club (E.L.P.A.) will issue such a license. E.L.P.A. headquarters is in Athens: 2-4 Messogion Street (779-1615) or 6 Amerikis Street (363-8632).

Rules of the Road   As elsewhere in Europe, motorists in Greece drive on the right side of the road. Passing on the right is strictly forbidden. Other traffic rules are the same as those in the rest of Europe. Road signs are written in Greek and repeated phonetically in the Roman alphabet.

Taxis

There is a flat charge of Drs 20 after you've flagged a taxi; riders are also charged Drs 14.50 for each kilometer outside the city zone (almost $9 dollars), including return. Extra fees include Drs 20 for boarding a taxi at airports and seaports, Drs 10 for every piece of luggage over 22 lbs., Drs 200 for every hour kept waiting, and a surcharge during the Christmas and Easter holidays. There is also a minimum total fare of Drs 50. All these rates may change without notice.

CURRENCY

Greece permits the free and unlimited importation of foreign currency, gold, and coins. A declaration of foreign currency, however, *must* be made at the time of entry, when the traveler will receive a corresponding voucher. Tourists are permitted to import and export Greek currency, the Drachma, up to Drs 3,000 per person. These Drachmas must be in the form of bank notes. Sums exceeding $500 (U.S.) can be taken out of the country, *if* they are declared at the time of entry.

Exchanging money

All banks and most hotels will buy foreign currency at the official rate of exchange fixed by the Bank of Greece. For information about banking hours, see the next section.

BASIC INFORMATION

Banks

Banks are open for business from 8 A.M. to 2 P.M. daily, except on Saturday, Sunday, and official public holidays. However, to make it easier for tourists to exchange currency, many banks keep their doors open throughout the afternoon and on Saturday. Some even remain open on Sunday. The G.N.T.O. makes available the addresses of banks operating after regular hours. Obtain such information by calling or writing the local branch of this agency (see addresses on p. 401). Note that all banks are authorized to buy foreign currency at the official rate of exchange fixed by the Greek government.

Post Office

Post offices are open Monday through Saturday from 7:30 A.M. to 7:30 P.M.

Legal holidays

New Year's Day (January 1)
Epiphany (January 6)
Shrove Monday
Feast of the Annunciation and Independence Day (March 25)
Good Friday
Orthodox Easter
Labor Day and Flower Festival (May 1)
Assumption of the Holy Virgin (August 15)
National Holiday (October 28)
Christmas (December 25)
Boxing Day (December 26)

Electric current

Throughout Greece the standard household electric current is 220 AC. In a few places, however, 110 DC voltage is available.

Shopping

Visitors to the Greek Islands have no trouble filling their shopping bags with traditional handicrafts, jewelry, flokati rugs, pottery, onyx, marble, and alabaster. Bargain hunters will want to pay special attention to shoes, handbags, and furs. While exploring the islands, keep an eye out for specialties of particular regions. For example, some of the finest embroidery in Greece can be found on Skyros, Leukas, and Rhodes. Markets in Siphnos and Skopelos have won special favor with vacationers for their displays of ceramics. Rhodes boasts a duty-free port and good buys in furs, jewelry, and leather items.

Be sure to plan a stop in Piraeus to venture among the many lively shops there. These sell almost any item one could dream of, and at very reasonable prices. A real treat is to explore the local flea market, which is a treasure trove of everything from brass beds to earthenware to antique lace.

If you've developed a liking for traditional Greek handicrafts, set aside time to browse among the displays inside branches of the National Organization of Greek Handicrafts. Although only carpets are sold in these showrooms, indulge your curiosity and then look for favorite articles in local shops. *Corfu*: 32B Xenofontos Stratigou Street (0661-32167). *Rhodes*: 33 Ipoton Street (0241-20050). *Leukas*: 103 Stratigou Mela Street (0645-23522).

Shopping Hours

Shopping hours for stores most popular with tourists are as follows:

General Trade Stores
Monday, Wednesday, and Saturday: 8 A.M. to 2:30 P.M.
Tuesday, Thursday, and Friday: 8 A.M. to 1:30 P.M. and 5 to 8 P.M.

Food Stores
Monday, Wednesday, and Saturday: 8 A.M. to 3 P.M.
Tuesday, Thursday, and Friday: 8 A.M. to 2 P.M. and 5:30 to 8:30 P.M.

Butchers and Fish Markets
Monday, Wednesday, and Saturday: 7:30 A.M. to 2 P.M.
Tuesday, Thursday, and Friday: 7:30 A.M. to 2:30 P.M. and 5:30 to 8:30 P.M.

Barbers and Hairdressers
Monday and Wednesday: 8:15 A.M. to 2 P.M.
Tuesday, Thursday, and Friday: 8:15 A.M. to 1:30 P.M. and 4:30 to 8:30 P.M.
Saturday: 8:15 A.M. to 5 P.M.

Pharmacies
Monday and Wednesday: 8 A.M. to 4 P.M.
Tuesday, Thursday, and Friday: 8 A.M. to 2 P.M. and 5 to 8 P.M.

Florists
Daily except Sunday: 8 A.M. to 9 P.M.

Dry Cleaners
Monday and Wednesday: 8 A.M. to 4 P.M.
Tuesday, Thursday, and Friday: 8 A.M. to 2 P.M. and 5 to 8:30 P.M.

Credit cards

Many hotels, restaurants, and cosmopolitan shops accept major credit cards. Keep in mind, however, that credit cards are still not used as frequently in Greece as in the United States, Canada, and the United Kingdom. Traveler's checks, however, are more widely accepted in the islands and on the mainland. Vacationers will generally find this form of payment easier to deal with.

Language

Many Greeks speak English, as it is taught in the schools as a second language. Moreover, English is spoken in most restaurants and department stores, and by the Tourist Police, who wear badges on their lapels depicting the British or American flag.

Climate

The Greek Islands are a haven for sun worshippers. Greece has, in fact, logged nearly 3,000 hours of sunlight per year. Its southern location ensures mild winters and warm summers, cooled by the refreshing seasonal breezes known as *meltemia.*

Clothing

Whatever the season, plan to wear lightweight hiking shoes, rather than sandals, when walking around the islands. Footpaths are often studded with loose rocks and prickly vegetation: in some places, poisonous snakes will slither across the trail. Going barefoot is not recommended. Some sort of head covering, such as a scarf or wide-brimmed hat, will provide much-needed protection from the blazing midday sun and the strong wind. And, of course, sunglasses help vacationers avoid grimacing in a perpetual squint.

In the summer months, casual clothing made of lightweight fabrics will keep you comfortable. For the cooler breezes at night, a shawl, sweater, or jacket may be necessary. If you are traveling in the fall, winter, or spring, pack interchangeable coordinates, preferably made of man-made fibers and/or wool. Such clothing is well suited to the varying temperatures. A rain coat with a zip-out lining will complete your wardrobe.

Other clothing tips: Most restaurants welcome an informally dressed clientele, although a few posh establishments require a jacket and tie for men. If a spirit of adventure lures you to the casinos, remember that women are expected to wear a cocktail dress or pantsuit and that men should place their bets in a jacket and tie. And even though the Greek islands are sunny and casual, swimsuits are not proper attire for visiting archeological sites. Vacationers who tour monasteries and churches must also observe rules about dress: Women should wear a sleeved dress of an appropriate length and men should don slacks and a shirt. Those who visit the islands on board a cruise ship will want to pack bright, casual clothes for the day and more formal wear, such as a cocktail dress or a jacket and tie, for evening festivities.

Time zone

Greek time is 2 hours ahead of Greenwich Mean Time and 7 hours ahead of Eastern Standard Time; that is, when it is 12 noon in Greenwich, it's 2 P.M. in Greece.

TRAVELING WITH PETS

Take your pet with you to Greece only if you are prepared to observe certain regulations. You must be able to show officials a health certificate from your country verifying that:

1. Dogs have received an anti-rabies injection within 1 year of the time of entry.
2. Cats are healthy and free of any contagious diseases.
3. Singing birds have come from areas in which no parrot fever has been detected in the last 6 months.

BUYING ART AND ANTIQUITIES

Antiquities

The Greek government has strict rules forbidding anyone to export antiquities and works of art found in Greece. But if you covet a particular vase or would like to add a potsherd to your collection back home, it's sometimes possible to overcome these restrictions. To take certain objects out of the country, you must receive permission from the Ministry of Culture and Sciences. This arm of the government will most likely levy an export fee, collected on behalf of the Archeological Revenue and Expropriations Fund (T.A.P.A.). The Antique Dealers and Private Collections Agency at the Archeological Service, 13 Polignotou Street, Athens, will also grant—or deny—permission to export antiquities.

Before buying any antique items in Greece, check with these agencies to find out whether your purchase could be taken out of Greece. If customs officials discover that you are carrying antiquities in your luggage without an export permit, the articles will be confiscated and you may be prosecuted.

Copies of art works

Visitors are free to take any castings and copies of works of art with them when leaving Greece. On sale in the National Archeological Museum of Athens, 1 Tossitsa Street, are castings of all the exhibits in the museums throughout Greece as well as copies of paintings and frescos.

ACCOMMODATIONS

Throughout the Greek Islands vacationers will encounter a wide range of accommodations—all the way from a modestly appointed hotel room to a fully furnished guest house, imbued with the civilized charm of a restored cloister.

Rating system

To offer guidance in the search for lodgings that will suit your personal taste and budget, the G.N.T.O. has put together a system that rates all Greek hotels. The rating a hotel receives is based on the size of its rooms and public areas, as well as on the quality of its furnishings and services.

Deluxe (L) Large, attractive public areas and rooms. Restaurant. Daily rates are based on the European plan (continental breakfast only) or the half-board plan (continental breakfast and lunch or dinner).

First Class (A) Slightly smaller, with attractive public areas and rooms. Restaurant. Daily rates, like those of the deluxe hotels, are keyed to the European or half-board plan.

Second Class (B) Superior tourist hotels offering comfortably furnished rooms and public areas.

Third Class (C) Modest furnishings with adequate sleeping accommodations.

Fourth Class (D) and Fifth Class (E) These hotels usually predate World War II and offer minimal comforts.

Approximate Rates (in Drachmas)				
Class	Single with Bath (Min.–Max.)	Double with Bath (Min.–Max.)	Breakfast (Min.–Max.)	Lunch or Dinner (Min.–Max.)
L	4,500–11,900	4,000–10,500	250–515	850–1,500
A	3,500–4,500	2,500–3,500	200–300	650–900
B	1,950–2,500	1,500–1,800	150–200	500–850
C	1,075–2,500	600–1,500	—	—
D	850–1,500	600–950	—	—

These rates do not reflect several other items, including a service charge of 15 percent of the bill. Moreover, vacationers often find further costs tacked onto their bill if their rooms come with hot water, heating, or air conditioning. Such charges usually run between Drs 150 and 200. The total bill will also include an 8 percent government tax. In some cases, hotel keepers add a surcharge of 10 percent for short stays of only one or two nights. Still other items reflect seasonal increases. The regular tax in a hotel bill is often increased to 20 percent if you stay at Class B, C, D, and E hotels any time from July 1 to September 15; in the peak season, L, A, and B hotels sometimes require that you pay for the half-board plan.

Reservations

To make reservations before you arrive, contact hotel representatives in the United States and Canada. Or make reservations by writing or calling the Hellenic Chamber of Hotels, 6 Aristoudou Street, Athens (011-301-323-6962). Another option is to stop by the branch office of the Hellenic Chamber of Hotels, National Bank of Greece Building, 2 Kar. Servias Street, Athens (from 8:30 A.M. to 8 P.M. Monday through Saturday; from 11 A.M. to 5 P.M. on Sunday).

Xenia Hotels

Xenia Hotels are built and run by the G.N.T.O.; they offer simply furnished rooms, generally in hotels rated B or C. To find out the location of these hotels, call or write the G.N.T.O. at any of the offices listed on page 401.

Guest houses

Throughout the islands are newly restored villages that evoke the picturesque charm of a small town in Greece. Revamped by the G.N.T.O., these villages present a range of unique, modernized accommodations. Once you've said good-bye to the hectic, urban pleasures of Athens, treat yourself to the quiet virtues of an island village.

Oia, Thira   Overlooking the northern coast, this village features 26 guest houses that sleep anywhere from two to seven people. Each sunny, white-washed guest house is decorated with embroidered tablecloths and curtains, hand-carved furniture, and brilliantly colored rugs. In addition to these traditional touches, guests have at their disposal a kitchen, bath, veranda, and small garden. For reservations, contact Paradosiakos Ikismos Oias, Oia, Thira (0286-71234).

Mesta, Chios   Mesta, a fourteenth-century village, reflects the architectural style common to the Genoese, trading partners with the Greeks. Its houses are arranged in a circle, surrounded by a protective wall. Bright and attractive, every guest house opens onto a courtyard and is decorated with local handicrafts. Each house sleeps five people, with rates around $35 a night. Reservations can be made by getting in touch with Paradosiakis Ikismos, Mesta, Chios, or Mrs. Dimitra Kaplaneli, Mytiline, Lesbos (0215-27908).

Psara A mere dot of an island, Psara is northwest of Chios. Here the adventurous tourist will find a restored church cloister now open as a guest house, offering bed and breakfast (with shower) for around $15 a night. Reservations are available through any branch of the G.N.T.O. (see addresses on p. 401).

Fiskardo, Cephalonia On the northern coast, Fiskardo is a small port whose streets are lined with quaint houses built in the last half of the nineteenth century by wealthy seafarers. Guest houses here can sleep from six to eighteen people. For a double room with shower you'll pay around $15. Reservations can be made through Paradosiakos Ikismos Fiskardou, Fiskardo, Cephalonia (0286-51397/51398).

FOOD AND DRINK

Dining out in the islands is usually an informal, friendly affair, enriched by the savory spices of Greek cuisine and by the warm, generous nature of the people. Dinner is served after 8 P.M., often at open-air tables.

Greek specialties

Restaurant menus offer an appetizing selection of *mezedes*, or hors d'oeuvres; salad; a main dish of a casserole, grilled meat, or fish; cheeses; and dessert. When selecting hors d'oeuvres, be sure to try such specialties as *dolmadakia* (meat or rice rolled in grape leaves) and *kolokithakia* (deep-fried zucchini), which is usually served with *tsatsiki* (cucumber, yogurt, and garlic spread). Other favorites are *kalamarakia* (deep-fried squid), *tyropitakia* (cheese wrapped in thin layers of pastry), not to mention the meatballs, stuffed peppers, and pickled octopus. These almost infinitely various hors d'oeuvres are served on small plates placed in the middle of the table family-style.

While deliberating over the entrées, don't miss a chance to sample the famous *souvlaki*, charcoal-grilled lamb or pork. Another frequently served dish is moussaka, a bubbling casserole layered with ground meat, eggplant or potatoes, and eggs. Freshly caught shellfish and fish are also tasty fare throughout the islands. Menus often feature *psari plaki*, baked red snapper basted in fragrant olive oil. Your portion will be garnished with sliced tomatoes, lemon wedges, and a sizzling topping of scallions, crushed garlic, and bread crumbs. For a variation on these Mediterranean flavors, try *psari savori*, crisp white fish fillets fried in olive oil and covered with a thick tomato sauce generously seasoned with garlic, bay leaf, and red wine. A memorable shellfish entrée is *garides me saltsa*, delicate pink shrimp in a tomato and feta cheese sauce laced with white wine.

With the entrée you'll most likely be served a salad; *horiatiki*, the usual Greek salad, is a delectably fresh combination of sliced cucumber, tomato, feta cheese (white, semi-soft, unsalted cheese), and olives with a vinaigrette dressing.

For dessert, leave room to sample the heady pleasures of baklava (fine layers of pastry laced with honey and chopped walnuts or pistachio nuts) or *kataifi* (chopped nuts wrapped in shredded wheat with a honey sauce). In the summer, dessert selections include an enticing array of such fresh fruits as peaches, melons, and pears. Finally, it's customary to polish off a Grecian feast with a cup of strong Greek coffee, very similar to Turkish coffee.

Restaurants

Several types of restaurants are common throughout Greece. They include:

1. *Estiatorion:* A conventional, expensive restaurant.
2. *Taverna:* Like a traditional, rural inn, the taverna boasts a full, varied selection of hors d'oeuvres, usually prepared and served by the family that owns the establishment. It is usually less expensive than the estiatorion.
3. *Psistaria:* On entering this barbecue-style restaurant, you'll see hunks of lamb, chicken, and pork roasting on a large spit. The meal also includes salad, french fries, and cheese.
4. *Psarotaverna* (fish tavern): Usually located near the port, these eating places feature the owner's catch of the day.

Tipping

Most restaurants add a 15 percent service charge to the bill, so don't make the mistake of leaving a double tip. When the service has been exemplary, the Greek custom is to leave some loose change on a plate for the waiter, with an equal amount on the table for the busboy, who works for tips alone. Occasionally, a service charge is not included. In that case, waiters expect from 12 percent at most restaurants to 20 percent at the more expensive places. To prevent confusion, most menus list prices for food and drink alone and then list the prices with service and tax added.

Drinking customs

A local custom popular with many visitors to the islands is sipping ouzo. Ouzo is a clear apéritif, flavored with anise. It is usually mixed with a little water, which swirls in the drink to turn it cloudy. Your tall, thin glass of ouzo will often be accompanied by a *mesé*, a small plate of olives, tomato slices, and cubes of cheese, tasty snacks speared with toothpicks.

Coffee is most often drunk in a *kapheneia*, a Greek coffee house. It's served in demitasse cups and resembles Turkish coffee: finely ground, with the dark, bitter grounds permitted to settle at the bottom of the cup. Don't forget to specify your preference when ordering this exceptionally strong coffee—*pikro* means bitter; *metrio*, semisweet; and *gliko*, sweet.

No matter what you've ordered, your waiter will always bring a fresh glass of ice water to the table. In the country it is usually spring water, so drink it without worry.

Before your meal, you may want to consult a wine list. Retsina, the common table wine, has a slight, acidic flavor of resin, which startles some people at first. Restaurants also keep on hand a variety of red and white wines that lack this resinous taste. Among Greeks and tourists alike, the most popular red wine is Demestika, a simple table wine.

MEDICAL INFORMATION

It is recommended that vacationers, to be on the safe side, bring to Greece their preferred medications for intestinal and stomach disorders, seasickness, insect bites, and sunburn. However, travelers do not need to worry about catching serious diseases, and citizens from the United States, Canada, and the United Kingdom do not need any immunizations before entering Greece.

Emergencies

Urgent cases requiring immediate hospital treatment are handled by several hospitals on a 24-hour basis. Call 166.

Tourist Police Stations

The Metropolitan Police operates Tourist Police Stations in Athens, Piraeus, and Corfu. The Gendarmerie maintains similar stations throughout the mainland and islands to help tourists. *Athens:* Metropolitan Tourist Police Headquarters, 7 Syngrou Avenue (9214-392). *Piraeus:* Piraeus Tourist Police Station, Akti Miaouli (452-3670). *Corfu:* Corfu Tourist Police Station, Arseniou Street (0661-39503).

ACCESS

Greece extends a cordial welcome to all disabled visitors. Many cruise ships that call on ports throughout the Greek Islands are specially designed to meet the needs of the disabled. Flights on Olympic Airways are also available to many of the larger islands. It is difficult, however, for the disabled to reach some of the archeological sites in Greece.

Several tours provide services for disabled travelers: Evergreen Travel Service, Inc., 19429 44th Avenue, West Lynwood, WA 98036; Flying Wheel Tours, 148 West Bridge Street, Owatonna, MN 55060; Rambling Tours, P.O. Box 1304, Hallandale, FL 33009.

Helpful resources include Lois Reamy's *Travelability* (Macmillan) and Louis Weiss's *Access to the World* (Facts on File).

STUDENT TRAVEL

To trim their expenses, student travelers to Greece should carry the International Student Identification Card. This card permits the holder to receive discounts on transportation fares and admission fees to museums and archeological sites. The I.S.I. card is issued by most colleges and universities in the United States as well as by the Council on International Educational Exchange (C.I.E.).

Students in the United States can also apply for the card by writing to the C.I.E., 205 East 42nd Street, New York, NY 10017 or by stopping by the office on 356 West 34th Street (212-661-1414).

In Canada, students can write or phone Tourbec, 1440 rue St. Denis, Montreal, Quebec H2X 3J8 (514-288-4455), or A.O.S.C., 44 St. George Street, Toronto, Ontario M5G 2E4 (416-979-2604).

In the United Kingdom, students can obtain the I.S.I. card by applying directly to the appropriate agency at their college or university.

SPORTS AND RECREATION

The Greek Islands offer the sports lover many chances to have fun and stay in top form. Whether your favorite pastime ranges from swimming to golfing or from mountain climbing to fishing, you will never run out of ways to make your visit memorable.

Swimming and beaches

Treat yourself to a dip in the enchantingly blue seas and then swim back to shore to soak up the sun on one of the G.N.T.O. beaches. These well-equipped beaches provide dressing rooms, piers, playing fields, tennis courts, volleyball and basketball courts, children's playgrounds, snack bars, restaurants, and discos. Canoes and paddleboats are for rent. Most beaches are open from May 15 to October 31 and charge a nominal admission fee.

Two major beaches are *Zakinthos*: Zakinthos Beach (0695-28077), and *Mytilene on Lesbos*: Tzamakia Beach, about half a mile out of town (0251-27908).

Water skiing

The islands make water skiing easy and accessible for expert and novice alike. Various clubs and schools provide equipment to rent; they also hold classes in water skiing.

Water Skiing Club and School   *Corfu*: Kassidokosta School, Palace Hotel, Komeno Bay (0661-91481), open May 1 to October 15: private instructors also teach courses at various hotels on the island, around Messongi, Nissaki, Kanoni, Roda, Dassia, Pirgi, Gouvia, Aghios Ioannis Peristeron, Akti Barmati, Moraitika, Benitses, Sidari, Alikies, Kondokali, Ipsos, and Perama. *Cythera*: Cythera Island Naval Club (0733-31208/31209). *Lesbos*: Naval Club, Mytilene, Makri Gialos Terminal (0277-28582). *Paros*: Zannou School (0298-23635). *Rhodes*: Rhodes Naval Club, 9 Platia Koundouriotou (0241-23287). *Skiathos*: Kassidokosta School, 37 Papadiamanti Street (0424-42667/42814). *Chios*: Chios Naval Club, Belavista Street (0271-23448).

For further information about water-skiing instruction and rentals, get in touch with the Water Skiing Federation, 32 Stournara Street, Athens (523-1875).

Sailing

Sailing enthusiasts will want to try their hand at the helm while exploring island coastlines and the open waters of the Aegean or Ionian Sea. Constant breezes and clear skies will delight both the novice and the seasoned sailor. For specific information about weather conditions and facilities, write or call the Sailing Federation, 15/A Xeno-fondos Street, Athens (323-5560/6813). Again, several clubs provide instruction in sailing.

Sailing Clubs and Schools   *Corfu*: Naval Club (0661-39805/30471). *Syros*: Naval Club (0281-28666/22336).

Regattas   Whether as spectator or participant, sailors should inquire about the various regattas organized each year by several sailing clubs, including the Piraeus Sailing Club, Mikrolimano, Piraeus (417-7636). Avid sailing buffs will not want to miss the premier regatta held in July during International Aegean Sailing Week. For more details about this event, write or call the secretary of the Hellenic Offshore Racing Club, 4 Papadiamanti Street, Mikrolimano, Piraeus (412-3357/2352).

Wind surfing

Wind-surfing boards can be rented at all G.N.T.O. beaches and at some schools that teach water skiing. It is much easier to rent than to bring your own equipment. If you do bring your own board to Greece, regulations require that a Greek national guarantee that you will leave with the board and not try to sell it in Greece. To obtain more information about rentals and surfing conditions, write or call the Hellenic Wind-Surfing Association, 7 Filelinon Street, Athens (323-0068/ 0330). This organization also sponsors group excursions and contests.

Fishing

Greek waters offer the angler many fertile and scenic fishing spots, especially during the summer and fall. A day's catch might include red snapper, mackerel, or porgy. In the villages of most islands you will find that boats and fishing tackle are for hire. At Piraeus, on Moutsopoulou Quay, small craft and boats can be rented from individuals licensed by the Port Authority.

One good fishing trip begins by setting sail for Leros and Rhodes in the Dodecanese cluster of islands. In Leros, ask a local skipper to show you around or rent a boat and explore these coastal fishing spots: Aghia Marina, Koukouli, Kithoni, Panagres, Blefouti, Gourna, Lepida, and Temenia. On Rhodes, likely places for casting a line are Lindus, Camirus, and Genadi.

Two agencies in Greece will be happy to answer your questions about fishing: the Amateur Anglers and Maritime Sports Club, Akti Moutsopoulou in Piraeus (451-5731), and the Piraeus Central Harbormaster's Office (451-1311).

Underwater diving

Scuba enthusiasts should probably look for other diversions while touring the Greek Islands. The Greek government enforces stringent rules forbidding underwater diving and fishing in all but a few locations. No night dives are allowed. These rules are designed to protect the nation's cultural heritage. In particular, the government wants to protect any submerged antiquities that may be undiscovered. Diving lessons are available, however, at Piraeus, through the P. Lami School, Akti Moutsopoulou, Pasalimani (413-8026).

Exploring caves

Spelunkers will be kept busy in the Greek Islands. The Hellenic Speleological Association has recorded some 7,000 limestone formations, including caves and abysses (nearly 3,400 of which are located on Crete). Many are unguarded, but permission to explore them is necessary. To request permission and to find out precise locations, stop by the local Tourist Police Office. Several caves have been made more accessible to tourists:

Cephalonia, "Drongorati"   Near the village of Haliotata, this cave is 314 feet long, 149 feet broad at its widest point, and 69 feet deep.

Cephalonia "Melissani" (Deep Lake-Cave) Belonging to the village of Karavomilos, this cave has a length of 528 feet, with a width of 132 and a height of 119 feet. Visitors gaze down at the cave's lake from a dizzying height, watching a brilliant play of sunlight on the water.

Cyclades Islands, "Antiparos" (an Abyss Cave)   To reach this formation, rent a motor-boat from nearby Paros. Tourists then ride pack animals from the beach up to the cave. Its maximum width is 231 feet.

Playing tennis

Practice your backhand swing or polish other strategies on the tennis court while touring Greece. There are several courts throughout the islands. *Corfu*: Corfu Tennis Club, 4 Romanou Street, Corfu Town (0661-37021, 39542). *Rhodes*: Rhodes Tennis Club (0241-2230).

Mountain climbing

Most of Greece's mountains are on the mainland, but rugged climbs, with breathtaking views, are to be had on some of the islands. To make hikes easier on the body and spirit, the Greek Skiing and Alpine Federation has set up refuge huts on several peaks.

For information on the facilities at these huts, write or call the Greek Skiing and Alpine Federation, 7 Karageorgi Servias Street, Athens (323-4555). Avid climbers may want to take part in an excursion to the peak of such a mountain. In that case, get in touch with the Greek Touring Club, 12 Politehniou Street, Athens (524-8601), or with the Federation of Excursion Clubs of Greece, 4 Dragatsaniou Street, Athens (323-4107).

Golfing

In Rhodes, sign up for a round of golf at the Afandou Golf Club, 11 miles from the town of Rhodes (0241-51225/6). The club features an 18-hole course, 5,540 feet long for the men's links and 5,090 feet long for the women's links. Par is 70. At the club are changing rooms, a restaurant, and lounges, as well as a pro shop. If you feel like sinking a few putts on Corfu, stop by the Corfu Golf Club (0661-944220/1). It's located in the Ropa Valley, 10 miles from the town of Kerkyra and offers an 18-hole course, with a par of 72. Amenities include a practice range, changing rooms, lockers, restaurant and lounges, and a pro shop.

FESTIVALS

Throughout the Greek Islands, ancient customs and traditions are kept alive every year through lively festivals. Many are religious celebrations, linked to colorful rituals of the Greek Orthodox Church.

Epiphany—January 6

On this day, all over Greece, the waters are blessed. Crucifixes are immersed in seas, lakes, and rivers. At the port of Piraeus a special ceremony is held.

Carnival Season—three weeks before Ash Wednesday

The Greeks celebrate Carnival with exuberance. During this time you'll see festivities marked by fancy-dress balls, masquerade parties, practical jokes, and parades of carnival chariots. In various parts of Greece the revels are associated with local customs. Especially showy and memorable is the carnival merry-making on Zakinthos, Chios (Mesta and Olimbi), Skyros, Cephalonia, Lesbos (Aghiasos), Karpathos, and Euboea (Aghia Anna).

Independence Day—March 25

On this national holiday army units parade through major towns and cities.

Good Friday

In towns and villages, worshippers carry lighted candles and follow the procession of the Epitaphios. It is a moving, time-honored spectacle.

Holy Saturday

On the Saturday before Easter Sunday, church bells ring to celebrate the resurrection of Christ. After a religious ceremony congregations return home to dine on the traditional feast of red-dyed, hardboiled eggs and Magritsa soup.

Easter Sunday

This is the most important public and religious holiday in Greece. It is celebrated with a banquet of red-dyed eggs and spit-roasted lamb, followed by dancing in regional costumes.

Feast of St. George—April 23

On the island of Lemnos in the village of Kaliopi horse races are held to mark this event. In the village of Pyli on Kos, tourists join the crowds to watch horse races, as well as local singing and dancing.

Labor Day—May 1

Also known as the Flower Festival, this holiday is marked by a general exodus to the country for picnics, with celebrations throughout the mainland and the islands.

Navy Week—end of June through July 1

Acknowledging its ancient ties to the sea, Greece celebrates Navy Week with entertainment and pageantry in various coastal towns. Fishermen put on a special show at the village of Plomari on Lesbos.

Music Festival—end of July

The island of Ithaca sponsors a music festival.

Prose and Art Festival—August

On Leukas there is a summer panoply of theatrical performances, concerts, lectures, and folk dancing.

Hippokrateia Festival—August

If a summer excursion takes you to Kos, hold a spot in your itinerary for the performances of ancient drama, displays of popular art, flower shows, and the reenactment of the Hippocratic Oath.

Assumption of the Virgin Mary—August 15

On Tenos, observe the rituals of this major holiday, which is celebrated here with more pomp than in any other part of Greece.

Pirates' Raid—August 23

In Naousa, on Paros, villagers take part in pageantry marking a pirates' raid.

Cricket—September

Watch a week, or just an afternoon, of cricket matches on Corfu. Visiting foreign teams battle for victory.

New Year's Eve—December 31

If you plan to ring in the new year on Chios, don't miss the parade of local seamen carrying impressive model ships around the town, singing carols unique to the island. The procession winds up in the central square, where prizes are awarded for the best model ships.

SPECIAL EVENTS

These annual functions are sponsored by the G.N.T.O.

Thasos Festival—July and August

On this island performances of classical Greek drama are presented.

Sound and light shows—early April through late October

Held on Rhodes, in several languages, are sound and light shows that throw into brilliant relief the island's stunning ruins from ancient times. Similar shows are given on Corfu, from the middle of May to late September.

MUSEUMS AND ARCHEOLOGICAL SITES

Hours and admission fees

Admission to museums and archeological sites is free on Sunday and on these holidays: January 6, Shrove Monday, Holy Saturday, Easter Monday, May 1, Whitsunday, August 15, October 28, and December 26.

Entrance fees vary from Drs 35 to Drs 70 per person. Those who qualify for reduced fees include foreign students who present a student identification card, Greek citizens under the age of 18 who present their police identity card, and school pupils accompanied by teachers.

Archeological sites and museums are closed on these holidays: New Year's Day, March 25, Good Friday afternoon, Easter Sunday, and Christmas Day. Generally, they are open from 8 A.M. to 12:30 P.M. on these half-holidays: Christmas Eve, New Year's Eve, January 2, the first Saturday of Carnival, Holy Thursday, and Easter Tuesday.

Piraeus

Maritime Museum of Piraeus, Akti Themistokleous, Freatida quarter of the port of Piraeus (451-6822), open 9 A.M. to 12:30 P.M. on weekdays and 10 A.M. to 1 P.M. on Sunday and holidays, closed on Monday. On view are models of ships from ancient to modern times, as well as busts, uniforms, and paintings of the 1821 War of Independence. *Piraeus Archeological Museum*, No. 31 Harilaou Trikoupi (452-1598 or 451-8388), open 9 A.M. to 3 P.M. on weekdays and 9 A.M. to 2 P.M. on Sunday and holidays. Exhibits include relics from the Classical, Hellenistic, and Roman periods. Of special note are the statues of Hermes of Kifissia, Athena, and Artemis.

Aegina

Museum (0297-22637), open 9 A.M. to 3:30 P.M. on weekdays and 10 A.M. to 3 P.M. on Sunday and holidays, closed on Tuesday. Among the displays are architectural fragments from the temple of Aphaea, stele from tombs in the Attic style, and a sphinx believed to be Attican. Temple of Aphaea (0297-32398), open 9 A.M. to 3:30 P.M. on weekdays and 10 A.M. to 3 P.M. on Sunday and holidays. Poised on a cliff overlooking Aghia Marina Bay, this temple was dedicated to the Aphaean goddess. It is built in the Doric style and is considered to be an outstanding example of early classical architecture. Pediments on the temple portray Greek campaigns against Troy, in which heroes from Aegina, including Ajax, earned acclaim.

Thira

Museum (0286-22217), open 9:30 A.M. to 4 P.M. on weekdays and 10 A.M. to 3 P.M. on Sunday and holidays, closed on Tuesday. On exhibit are prehistoric pottery and other artifacts, an extensive collection of Thiraic vases of the seventh and sixth centuries B.C., Archaic and classical sculpture, and Hellenistic and Roman statues. *Archeological site of ancient Thira,* open 9:30 A.M. to 4 P.M. on weekdays and 10 A.M. to 3 P.M. on Sunday and holidays. This ancient Doric town was a thriving community during the third and second centuries B.C., when the island functioned as a naval base for the Egyptians. Among the clusters of houses are marketplaces, baths, theaters, and temples. *Thira Akrotirion Archeological Site* (0286-3128), open 9:30 A.M. to 4 P.M. on weekdays and 10 A.M. to 3 P.M. on Sunday and holidays. This Minoan city was destroyed around 1500 B.C., when the volcano on Thira erupted. Just like

Pompeii, houses of two and three stories, plazas, and shops were buried under lava. During the excavation, archeologists unearthed splendid frescos—now displayed in the National Archeological Museum in Athens—as well as vases and utensils.

Rhodes

Museum (0241-27674), open 9:30 A.M. to 4 P.M. on weekdays and 10 A.M. to 3 P.M. on Sunday and holidays, closed on Tuesday. Housed in the Hospital of the Knights, this museum displays ancient coins, pottery, and sculpture, including the Kneeling Venus (first century B.C.) and stele from the tomb of Timarista and Krito (fifth century B.C.). Take time to stroll through the Decorative Arts Collection (open only 9 A.M. to 1 P.M. on Monday, Wednesday, and Friday). *The City Walls,* open 3 P.M. to 5 P.M. Monday and Saturday. Protecting the city are massive fortifications, studded with bastions, battlements, and gates. A moat makes this fortress complete. Together these structures are fine examples of the art of fortification in the fifteenth and sixteenth centuries A.D. *Palace of the Grand Masters of St. John* (or Palace of the Knights), open 9:30 A.M. to 4 P.M. on weekdays and 10 A.M. to 3 P.M. on Sunday and holidays, closed on Tuesday. Fully restored, this medieval castle features exceptional wooden ceilings, marble floors, ancient mosaics imported from Kos, and alabaster windows. Inside is a collection of furniture of exemplary European craftsmanship from the sixteenth and seventeenth centuries. *Acropolis of Ialysus,* open 9 A.M. to 3:30 P.M. on weekdays and 10 A.M. to 3 P.M. on Sunday and holidays. Foundations of the temple here date back to the third century B.C. and are visible as a result of recent excavation. On this site is also a monastery of Panaghia of Philerimos, built by the Order of St. John. *Acropolis of Lindus,* open 9:30 A.M. to 4 P.M. weekdays and 10 A.M. to 3 P.M. on Sunday and holidays. A majestic staircase, beginning with a colonnade, leads to a terrace on which stand the ruins of fifth-century B.C. propylaea. Farther on is a fourth-century B.C. temple of the Lindian Athena, high on a cliff. *Camirus* open 9:30 A.M. to 4 P.M. on weekdays and 10 A.M. to 3 P.M. on Sunday and holidays. Meander through the excavations of this ancient city, known as the "Pompeii of Rhodes." It includes a third-century B.C. sanctuary with the ruins of a Doric temple. Excavations have also brought to light various dwellings, an agora, and a temple of Athena.

Delos

Archeological site (0289-22259), open 9:30 A.M. to 4 P.M. on weekdays and 10 A.M. to 3 P.M. on Sunday and holidays. Vacationers fascinated by ancient history will want to visit this island, which is, in fact, one large archeological dig. Its monuments date back to various periods, but most are dedicated to the Ionic worship of Apollo. For a thousand years, Delos figured as the political and religious center of the Aegean, sponsoring many religious festivals in honor of Apollo. Among the structures you'll find four temples built between the seventh and fourth centuries B.C., as well as the sanctuary of the bulls, a stadium, gymnasium, and palestra.

Also of interest

Andros

Archeological Museum (0282-23664), open 9 A.M. to 3:30 P.M. on weekdays and 10 A.M. to 3 P.M. on Sunday and holidays, closed on Tuesday. *Museum Basil and Elisa Goulandris* (0282-22650), open 10 A.M. to 2 P.M. every day. Features modern art.

Corfu

Archeological Museum (0661-30680), open 9 A.M. to 3:30 P.M. on weekdays and 10 A.M. to 3 P.M. on Sunday and holidays, closed on Tuesday. *Museum of Asiatic Art* (0661-23124), open 9 A.M. to 3:30 P.M. on weekdays and 10 A.M. to 3 P.M. on Sunday and holidays, closed on Tuesday.

Kos

For information about buildings and sites, phone 0242-28326. *Museum*, open 9:30 A.M. to 4 P.M. on weekdays and 10 A.M. to 3 P.M. on Sunday and holidays, closed on Tuesday. *Castle*, open 9 A.M. to 3:30 P.M. on weekdays and 10 A.M. to 3 P.M. on Sunday and holidays, closed on Tuesday. *Restored ancient dwellings*, open 9 A.M. to 3:30 P.M. on weekdays and 10 A.M. to 3 P.M. on Sunday and holidays. *Asclepieion* (0242-28763), open 9:30 A.M. to 4 P.M. on weekdays and 10 A.M. to 3 P.M. on Sunday and holidays.

Lesbos (Mytilene)

Archeological Museum (0251-22087), open 9 A.M. to 3:30 P.M. on weekdays and 10 A.M. to 3 P.M. on Sunday and holidays.

Melos

For information on all buildings and sites, phone 0287-21620. *Archeological site*, open 9 A.M. to 3:30 P.M. on weekdays and 10 A.M. to 3 P.M. on Sunday and holidays. *Archeological Museum*, open 9 A.M. to 3:30 P.M. on weekdays and 10 A.M. to 3 P.M. on Sunday and holidays, closed on Tuesday. *Catacombs* are temporarily closed.

Mykonos

Archeological Museum (0289-22325), open 9 A.M. to 3:30 P.M. on weekdays and 10 A.M. to 3 P.M. on Sunday and holidays.

OVERVIEW

To make your choice of a destination or route somewhat simpler, important information about each of the islands covered in this book is summarized in the following tables.

This information has been gathered from the following sources: queries to town officials on the various islands; the brochure "General Information," issued by the Greek National Tourist Office; and travel schedules. Where no information was available—in most cases, dealing with less-visited islands—we have inserted an asterisk.

Islands and island groups

The number beneath the name of the island helps you to find the island on the map inside the front cover. The page number following in parentheses indicates the first page of the chapter dealing with that island. (In the table, Euboea is included with the Cyclades.)

Accommodation

In addition to the facilities listed, it is possible to stay overnight in monasteries on some of the islands. Information may be obtained from the local tourist officials.

Getting there

The details regarding transportation connections

are intended to provide only a general idea of frequency and routes; they are often changed to adapt to demand. In addition, in many cases there are small local shipping lines. If two figures appear in the "Duration" column, it means that the ship docks at additional ports in between.

Specialties

Only items that are unusual or of high quality are listed.

Folk festivals

Easter is the most important religious holiday in Greece, and it is celebrated throughout the country. Assumption (August 15) is also universally celebrated. If this fesitval has been listed, it indicates that its celebration on the particular island is especially extravagant. The folk festivals included in the table are only those that occur during the main tourist season, May to September.

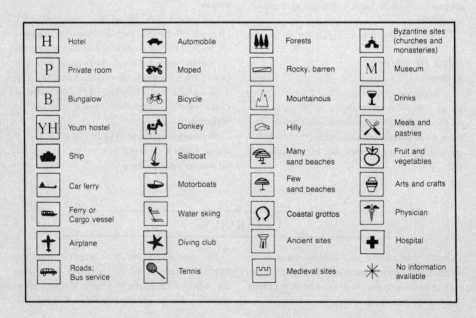

Symbol	Meaning	Symbol	Meaning	Symbol	Meaning	Symbol	Meaning
H	Hotel		Automobile		Forests		Byzantine sites (churches and monasteries)
P	Private room		Moped		Rocky, barren	M	Museum
B	Bungalow		Bicycle		Mountainous		Drinks
YH	Youth hostel		Donkey		Hilly		Meals and pastries
	Ship		Sailboat		Many sand beaches		Fruit and vegetables
	Car ferry		Motorboats		Few sand beaches		Arts and crafts
	Ferry or Cargo vessel		Water skiing		Coastal grottos		Physician
	Airplane		Diving club		Ancient sites		Hospital
	Roads; Bus service		Tennis		Medieval sites		No information available

	Saronic Gulf — Aegina 3 (p. 26)	Hydra 5 (p. 41)	Poros 4 (p. 37)	Salamis 2 (p. 23)	Spetsai 6 (p. 45)	Cyclades — Amorgos 23 (p. 163)
Medical Facilities	(present)	(present)	(present)	(present)		(present)
Folk Festivals		June: Miaoulia (navy); August 15: Assumption (Songs and folk dancing)			Naval Festival from August 15; August 28: Feast of the Appearance of the Holy Virgin	
Typical Specialties	Pistachios; Pottery	Almond cakes; Baklava; Silver jewelry; Embroidery; Ceramics	Eggplants Moussaka; Lemons Preserves; Seville oranges	Octopus (grilled); Fish	Fish; Octopus; Ceramics; Sandals; Grapes; Figs; Fabrics	
Points of Interest	(icons)	(icons)	(icons)	(icons)	(icons)	(icons)
Landscape Features	(icons)	(icons)	(icons)	(icons)	(icons)	(icons)
Rental Items & Facilities	(icons)	(icons)	(icons)	(icons)	(icons)	
Duration (in hours)	1/4; 1/2; 1/4	1½–4; 1	3; 3/4; 2–3	3/4; 1/4	4–5; 1½	10–20
Starting Point	Piraeus; Piraeus (also direct to Aghia Marina); Piraeus	Piraeus; Piraeus (cargo vessel)	Piraeus; Piraeus (cargo vessel); Galatas (small boats)	Piraeus; Perama	Piraeus; Piraeus (cargo vessel)	Piraeus
Frequency (per week)	11; daily; 3	3x daily; 2x daily	daily; 4 daily; 40–50	every 1/2 hour; every 1/4 hour	3x daily; 2x daily	2
Boat Service	(icons)	(icons)	(icons)	(icons)	(icons)	(icons)
Accommodation	H; P; B	H; P	H; P	H	H; P	H; P
Roads	(present)		(present)	(present)		
Population (in thousands)	10	2.5	4.3	27	3.5	1.8
Size (in square miles)	33	21	12	36	8.5	45

	Andros 8 (p. 72)	Cimolus 18 (p. 145)	Delos 13 (p. 97)	Euboea 47 (p. 343)	Ios 22 (p. 160)	Keos (Tzia) 7 (p. 65)	Kythnos 9 (p. 77)
Medical Facilities	✈		✳		✈ ✚	✳	✴	✳
Folk Festivals	July 22: Balo Festival in Batsi (dance) August 15: Assumption End of August: International Sailing Competition				July 26: Aghia Paraskevi	September 29: Local festival	
Typical Specialties	Froutalia (soufflé) Fish Honey Macaroons	Pyrite			Native wines Seafood specialties Cherries Melons	Fish	
Points of Interest	M	M	M	M			
Landscape Features							
Rental Items & Facilities							
Duration (in hours)	3	8	1	1 / 1 / 1 / 2	7–10 / 7–10	3 / 2	4
Starting Point	Rafina (bus from Athens)	Piraeus	Mykonos	Arkitsa / Rafina (bus and train from Athens, drawbridge from the mainland to Chalcis) / Oropou / Rafina-Karystos	Piraeus / Piraeus / Thessalonike	Piraeus / Rafina / Laurium	Piraeus
Frequency (per week)	2–5x daily	3	daily	daily / daily / daily / daily	9 / 3 / 2	2 / 8	3
Boat Service							
Accommodation	H P	P		H P B	H YH	H P	H P
Roads							
Population (in thousands)	10.5	1.4		174	1.3	1.7	1.5
Size (in square miles)	156	12	2	1,382	41	40	33

Category	Melos 19 (p. 147)	Mykonos 12 (p. 94)	Naxos 17 (p. 120)	Paros 16 (p. 111)	Pholegandros 20 (p. 155)	Seriphos 14 (p. 102)
Medical Facilities	✳	✳	(symbol)	(symbol)	(symbol)	(symbol)
Folk Festivals	August 12: Adamandia (in Adamas)		July 16–18: Naxos Festival	July 29: Wine Festival; August 15: Assumption	July 27, August 6, August 15: Folk festivals	August 15–17: Assumption
Typical Specialties	Obsidian	Fish; Hand-woven fabrics; Rugs; Jewelry	Fruit	Native wines; Cheese	Native wines (dark); Fish; Hand-woven rugs	Native wines
Points of Interest	(symbols)	(symbols)	(symbols)	(symbols)	(symbols)	(symbols)
Landscape Features	(symbols)	(symbols)	(symbols)	(symbols)	(symbols)	(symbols)
Rental Items & Facilities	✳	✳	✳	(symbols)	(symbols)	(symbols)
Duration (in hours)	7–9½ / ¾	5–6½ / 3¾	7–8	5½–7 / 5½–7	12	5–6 / 4–5
Starting Point	Piraeus / Athens	Piraeus / Thessalonike / Athens	Piraeus / Thessalonike	Piraeus / Piraeus	Piraeus	Piraeus / Piraeus
Frequency (per week)	5–8 / 3	18 / 2 / 21	18 / 2	20 / 12	4	8 / 8
Boat Service	(symbols)	(symbols)	(symbols)	(symbols)	(symbol)	(symbols)
Accommodation	H / P	H / P / YH	H / P / YH	H / P	H / B / P	H / P
Roads	(symbol)	(symbol)	(symbol)	(symbol)		(symbol)
Population (in thousands)	4.5	3.9	14.2	6.8	1	1
Size (in square miles)	58	34	173	72	14	28

	Sikinos 21 (p. 158)	Siphnos 15 (p. 105)	Syros 10 (p. 80)	Tenos 11 (p. 84)	Thira (Santorin) 24 (p. 169)	Sporades — Skiathos 44 (p. 313)	Skopelos 45 (p. 316)
Medical Facilities	(icon)	(icon)	(icon) + (icon)	(icon)	(icon) + (icon)	(icon)	(icon)
Folk Festivals		(icon)			August 15: Assumption; July 23: Aghios Palaghias		
Typical Specialties	Native wines	Honey; Ceramics, Weaving	Lukumia (Turkish honey), Mandolata (nougat)	Native wines	Native wines (sweet)	(icon)	Sweet almond cakes; Plums; Almonds; Textiles
Points of Interest	(icons)	(icons) M	(icons) M	(icons) M	(icons) M	(icons) M	(icons)
Landscape Features	(icons)	(icons)	(icons)	(icons)	(icons)	(icons)	(icons)
Rental Items & Facilities	(icons)	(icons)	(icons)	(icons)	(icons)	(icons)	(icons)
Duration (in hours)	12	5–6	5; 5; 5	4–5; 4; 4–5	8–12; 8–12	3; 3; 5; 3/4	4; 5; 3/4
Starting Point	Piraeus	Piraeus	Piraeus; Porto-Rafti, Rafina; Piraeus	Piraeus; Rafina; Rafina	Piraeus; Piraeus	Aghios Konstantinos (bus from Athens); Volos; Kymi; Athens	Aghios Konstantinos; Volos; Kymi
Frequency (per week)	3	8	7 daily; 3x daily	15; 4; daily	10; 2	11; 19; 3; 7–10	8; 16; 4
Boat Service	(icon)	(icon)	(icon)	(icon)	(icon)	(icon) + (air)	(icon)
Accommodation	H; P	H; P	H; P	H; P	H; P; YH	H; P; B	H; P
Roads			(icon)	(icon)	(icon)	(icon)	(icon)
Population (in thousands)	0.5	2	18.6	8.2	6.4	3.9	4.5
Size (in square miles)	16	28	32	75	29	24	37

	Skyros 46 (p. 337)	Cephalonia 51 (p. 379)	Corfu (Kerkyra) 48 (p. 359)	Cythera (Cerigo) 53 (p. 390)	Ithaca 50 (p. 374)
Medical Facilities	✚	✚	✚		✚
Folk Festivals		August 16; October 20: Aghios Gerasimos; August 15 in Markopoulo; August 23 in Lixouri	August 1: Aghios Spiridon; August 15 in Kassiopi; August 15: Pilgrimage to Pantokrator; August 23: Church festivals in Gastouri and Pelekas		September 1–15: Theater Festival (Odysse)
Typical Specialties	Fish; Lobster; Figs; Furniture; Embroidery; Weaving; Ceramic and copper pots	Rombola (sweet wine); Meat patés; Fish patés; Bakaliaropitta (spiced meat); Grapes	Native wines; Liqueur (kumquat); Pasticciada (spiced veal); Sweets; Mandolato (nougat); Hand-woven fabrics; Embroidery; Silver Jewelry	Lamb casseroles	Ravani (cake)
Duration (in hours)	11½; 2¼ (6½); 2	4; 1	17–24; 36; 16; 2; 11; 1; ½	12; 11–14; 6	4–5; 1 (3)
Starting Point	Volos; Kymi (Euboea) (bus from Athens, ferry to Kymi); Kymi	Patras; Athens	Piraeus; Ancona, Italy; Brindisi, Italy; Igoumenitsa; Patras; Athens; Ioannina	Githion; Piraeus; Kastelli	Patras (via Sami); Athens to Cephalonia (then on by bus and boat)
Frequency (per week)	4; daily; 4	18; 7–10	✳; 9x; daily; 8–23; 2	1; 2; 1	4–8; 7–10
Accommodation	H; P	H; P	H; P; B; YH	P	H; P
Population (in thousands)	2.5	37	90	5	5
Size (in square miles)	80	287	236	110	36
Island Group/Island	Skyros 46 (p. 337)	Ionian Islands — Cephalonia 51 (p. 379)	Corfu (Kerkyra) 48 (p. 359)	Cythera (Cerigo) 53 (p. 390)	Ithaca 50 (p. 374)

Category	Leukas (Lefkada) 49 (p. 369)		Zakinthos (Zante) 52 (p. 384)			Dodecanese — Astypalaia 25 (p. 185)		Kalymnos 33 (p. 241)		Karpathos 28 (p. 193)		Kastellorizon (Megiste) 29 (p. 196)	Kos 32 (p. 219)		
Medical Facilities	✳		✳			✈	✚	✳		✈		✈	✚		
Folk Festivals	August 11: Festival in Karya (folk costumes) August: International Folk Dance Festival		August 24: Aghios Dionysios					August 15: Assumption		June: Feast of Aghioi Apostoli			August 15: Assumption in Antimadsia September 8 in Kardamena		
Typical Specialties	Fish	Embroidery and lace	*Pasteli* (made of sesame seed and honey) *Mandolato* (nougat)					Dolmades		Oranges	Silver jewelry	Native wines / Fish	Native wines	Inexpensive fabrics (duty-free)	
Points of Interest	(icons)		(icons)		(icons)	(icons)		(icons)		(icons)		(icons)	(icons)		
Landscape Features	(icons)		(icons)			(icons)		(icons)		(icons)		(icons)	(icons)		
Rental Items & Facilities	✳		✳			(icons)		✳		(icons)		(icons)	(icons)	(icons)	
Duration (in hours)	✳	1¼	1½	1		14 ✳		13 1		24	¾	5–6	14–18	18	1
Starting Point	Piraeus (joined to mainland by bridge)	Athens	Kylini	Athens		Piraeus / Rhodes		Piraeus Kos		Piraeus	Rhodes	Rhodes	Piraeus	Piraeus	Athens
Frequency (per week)	3	4–7	3x daily	3–4		1 2		4–5 4–5		1	4	2	7	3	7
Boat Service	(icon)	(icon)	(icon)	(icon)		(icon)		(icon)		(icon) (icon)		(icon)	(icon)	(icon)	(icon)
Accommodation	H	P	H	P	YH	H		H	P	H	P	H	H	P	B
Roads	(icon)		(icon)			(icon)		(icon)		(icon)		(icon)			
Population (in thousands)	28		45			14		13		6		0.3	20		
Size (in square miles)	115		155			38		42		116		3.5	114		

	Leros 34 (p. 249)	Nisyros 26 (p. 187)	Patmos 35 (p. 251)	Rhodes 30 (p. 199)			Syme 31 (p. 215)	Telos 27 (p. 190)	Chios 38 (p. 273)		Icaria 36 (p. 261)
Medical Facilities	✚	✳	✚	✚ ✚			✳	✚ ✚	✚		✳
Folk Festivals	August 15 in Kastro		May 1 in Mandraki; *koupa* dancing	May 8: Aghios Theologos; August 6: Feast of the Savior	June 28 in Lindus; July 29 at Aghios Soulas; August 14–22 in Kremasti; July 15–September 30: Wine Festival in Rodini Park						
Typical Specialties	Dark wines; Honey; Hand-woven rugs; Knitted items		Native wines		Ceramics; Silver jewelry				Fruit; Preserved fruit; Masticha liqueur		
Points of Interest											
Landscape Features											
Rental Items & Facilities											
Duration (in hours)	10–12 / 8		18	10	17½ / 17½ / 1			24½	22	10 / 1	8–12
Starting Point	Piraeus / Rhodes		Piraeus	Piraeus / Rhodes	Piraeus / Piraeus / Athens			Piraeus	Piraeus	Piraeus / Athens	Piraeus
Frequency (per week)	4–8 / 5		1	daily	12 / 8 / 34			1	1	7 / 10	4
Boat Service											
Accommodation	H / P		P	H / P	H / P / B			H / P	P	H / P	H / P
Roads											
Population (in thousands)	8.5	✳	1	63			✳	✳	62		9.5
Size (in square miles)	21	✳	19	542			✳	✳	136		100
Island Group / Island (Number refers to location on map inside front cover; page number to location in text)	Leros 34 (p. 249)	Nisyros 26 (p. 187)	Patmos 35 (p. 251)	Rhodes 30 (p. 199)			Syme 31 (p. 215)	Telos 27 (p. 190)	**Eastern and Northern Aegean** — Chios 38 (p. 273)		Icaria 36 (p. 261)

Category	Lemnos 41 (p. 291)	Lesbos 40 (p. 282)	Psara 39 (p. 281)	Samos 37 (p. 267)	Samothrace 42 (p. 298)	Thasos 43 (p. 303)
Medical Facilities	(icons)	(icon)		(icon)	(icons)	(icon)	(icon)
Folk Festivals	August 15 in Panaghi; August 23: Aghios Charalambos (in Plaka)	May: Feast of the Bull (in Aghia Paraskevi)		June 22: National Festival	August 6: Church Festival with *samiotiko* dances	
Typical Specialties	Native wines (muscatels); Fish; Honey; Cheese; Peaches; Plums	Ouzo; Fish; Black olives; Fruit	Fish	Fish (Prawns)	Native wines (muscatels)	Honey
Points of Interest	(icons)	(icons)		(icons)	(icons)	(icons)
Landscape Features	(icons)	(icons)	(icon)	(icons)	(icons)	(icons)
Rental Items & Facilities	(icons)	(icon)		(icons)	(icon)	(icon)
Duration (in hours)	4 days; 3/4; 1/2	14; 14; 1	2–4	12–14; 12–14; 1	18¾; 2	1¼; 3/4
Starting Point	Circle: Kymi-Kavalla-Lesbos; Athens; Thessalonike	Piraeus; Piraeus; Athens	Chios	Piraeus; Thessalonike; Piraeus; Athens	Piraeus; Alexandroupolis (passengers only)	Kavalla; Keramoti
Frequency (per week)	4; 7; 2	10; 7; 21	4	4–7; 2; 4–5; 20	1; 7	4x daily; 6x daily
Boat Service	(icons)	(icons)	(icon)	(icons)	(icons)	(icons)
Accommodation	H; P; B	H; P	H; P	H; P; YH	H; P	H; P
Roads	(icon)	(icon)		(icon)	(icon)	(icon)
Population (in thousands)	18	120	0.5	40	38	16
Size (in square miles)	173	629	17	182	68	154

I N D E X

Index of People

Index of Places

Entries and numbers in boldface indicate the main points of interest and main discussions of the place cited. References to color plates are in italics and noted in parentheses.

C R E D I T S

Black-and-white photographs

Anthony-Verlag, Starnberg, p. 42
Benaki Museum, Athens, pp. 159, 340

Ecole Française d'Athènes, Athens, p. 97
Nicos Kontos, Athens, pp. 14 (top), 314, 344

Drawings and plans

Sally Benson, *Stories of the Gods and Heroes*, illustrations by Steele Savage, New York, 1940, figs. pp. 99, 263, 285, 295, 377

British Naval Intelligence Division, *Dodecanese*, London, 1941, 1943, fig. pp. 246–247

Buchholz and Karageorghis, *Prehistoric Greece and Cyprus*, New York, 1973, fig. p. 35

William Stearns Davis, *A Day in Old Athens*, New York, 1914, figs. pp. 43, 44, 46, 47, 75, 153, 157, 280, 306, 319

Charles Mills Gayley, *The Classic Myths in English Literature and in Art*, New York 1893, 1911, 1939, figs. pp. 71, 76, 90, 103 (top and bottom), 104, 11‾ 152, 165, 189, 198, 214, 21⸲ 264–265, 287, 292–293, 29⸲ ⸲⸲, 339, 352, 368, 376, 380, 394

Lois Knidlberger, *Santorin: Insel Zwichen Traum und Tag*, Munich, 1965, figs. pp. 177, 179, 182 (top and bottom)

Text Credit

Page 282: Excerpt from "The Destruction of Psara" by Dionysios Solomos, translated by Rae Dalven, from *Modern Gr Poetry*, New York, 1949, 1971

The text was set in ITC Garamond by TGA Communications, Inc.
New York.
The book was printed and bound by Novagraph, S.A.
Madrid.

The Publisher has made every effort to verify
that the information in this book is accurate and
up to date. Readers are invited to write with more
recent information.